A NEW, INTERPRETIVE TRANSLATION
OF ST. ANSELM'S
MONOLOGION AND PROSLOGION

A NEW, INTERPRETIVE TRANSLATION OF ST. ANSELM'S MONOLOGION AND PROSLOGION

BY JASPER HOPKINS

THE ARTHUR J. BANNING PRESS
MINNEAPOLIS

Library of Congress Catalog Card Number 86-70086

ISBN 0-938060-33-3 (cloth edition)
      0-938060-34-1 (paperback edition)

Printed in the United States of America

Denique rationali naturae non est aliud esse rationalem quam posse discernere iustum a non-iusto, verum a non-vero, bonum a non-bono, magis bonum a minus bono.

Monologion 68

Distribution of the present book was delayed until September 1987 because G. E. M. Anscombe's article—an article cited extensively in the present Introduction—was rescheduled (by the editors of *The Thoreau Quarterly*) from Volume 16 to Volume 17, Numbers 1 & 2 (Winter/Spring 1985). This double issue actually appeared during the summer of 1987. Anscombe's article, as it was actually published, has *two* footnotes--the second of which was not contained in the final manuscript made available to Professor Hopkins prior to rescheduling

PREFACE

In the history of Western Medieval Philosophy no two short works are more important than St. Anselm's *Monologion* and *Proslogion.* The former, whose title means "a soliloquy," was composed during the second half of 1076; the latter, whose title signifies "an address," of the soul to God, was written between 1077 and 1078. Both treatises represent bold philosophical ventures. For both set forth putatively compelling considerations (*rationes necessariae*) that purport to establish the existence, unicity, and trinity of the Divine Being. The content of the *Monologion* is largely motivated by St. Augustine's *De Trinitate*; the style of the *Proslogion* is generally reminiscent of the *Confessions.* From *De Trinitate* Anselm draws the very terminology whereby, in the *Monologion*, God is said to be *tres substantiae vel tres personae*; and from the *Confessions* he borrows, for his *Proslogion*, not only the tone of prayerful invocation but also the description of God as *aliquid quo melius cogitari non potest.* Anselm wrote these two works in Normandy, while he was prior of the Benedictine monastery at Bec-Hellouin. When the second of them was attacked, presumably within a year and a half of its completion, Anselm requested that both the attack and his own response be appended to all future transcriptions thereof. Neither Anselm nor his biographer, Eadmer, seems to know anything about the attacker—not even his name or his whereabouts. We ourselves learn—not from Anselm but from manuscript copyists[1]—that the critic of Anselm was Gaunilo by name, monk of the Benedictine abbey at Marmoutier, on the outskirts of Tours, France. Of Gaunilo little else is known, except that before entering the monastery he was treasurer and provost of the basilica of St. Martin of Tours. His decision not to attach his name to his critique was not the result of any hesitancy to contend with Anselm, who by now was abbot of the monastic community at Bec—a community made famous through the reputation of Anselm's teacher and predecessor as abbot, Lanfranc of Pavia. Rather, Gaunilo, in leaving aside his name, was motivated by the same considerations of modesty that led Anselm, initially, to omit his own name from the *Monologion* and the *Proslogion,* which were first circulated under the respective titles "*An*

Example of Meditating about the Rational Basis of Faith" and *"Faith Seeking Understanding."*

In our own day Anselm's *Proslogion* argument still has its Gaunilo-like detractors. But already it likewise has had, and no doubt will continue to have, its share of eminent defenders such as Charles Hartshorne and Norman Malcolm, who reinterpret it in new ways. Since a judicious appreciation of the *Proslogion* is possible only in the light of the *Monologion's* fuller disclosure of Anselm's metaphysics, both works should be read together; and both are here presented together in English translation. Like all translations, the present one is interpretive. But unlike other translations of the *Monologion* and the *Proslogion*,[2] the present one is more self-consciously interpretive in three ways. (1) First of all, the accompanying introduction and notes explicitly call attention to a multitude of interpretive considerations that bear in an intrinsic way upon the translation qua translation. Thus, there is an explanation given for rendering the second sentence of *Proslogion* 3 as "For there can be thought to exist something which cannot be thought not to exist . . . " rather than as "For it can be thought to be something which cannot be thought not to exist . . . "—either of which translations is necessarily interpretive. Similarly, there is a discussion of why, vis-à-vis the *Monologion*, *"essentia"* is sometimes rendered by "being" and sometimes by "essence"—why, given Anselm's usage, this switch is unavoidable. (2) Moreover, through the use of brackets [i.e., strokes] Anselm's tacit meanings are filled out, so that his thoughts may become more readily intelligible to the English-speaking reader. Most of these expansions are uncontroversial; some, however, are more significantly interpretive. In *Proslogion* 2 the sole occurrence of " . . . *quod maius est"* is construed by the words " . . . something which is greater |than existing only in the understanding|"; and in *Monologion* 32 the sentence *"Nempe omne verbum, alicuius rei verbum est"* is taken to mean "Without doubt, every word |or image| is a word |or an image| of some thing." In the case of both these translations an effort is made to indicate—whether in the introduction or in the notes or through the references—why the expansions are deemed to be correct. (3) Finally, here and now, in the Preface, I expressly reject—and this rejection is itself interpretive—the assumption made by F. S. Schmitt to the effect that Anselm, in writing the *Proslogion*, weighed each word exactly.[3] Presumably, Schmitt regarded this judgment not as an assumption but as a *conclusion*—i.e., as an inductive inference from the texts of

the *Proslogion* and the *Reply to Gaunilo*. As a basis for his "inference" he may have had in mind phenomena such as Anselm's dismissal of Gaunilo's suggestion to substitute "to be understood" (*"intelligi"*) for "to be thought" (*"cogitari"*) in the sentence *"summa res ista non esse nequit cogitari"*—regarding which sentence Anselm writes: "it was necessary to say 'cannot be thought.' " But such a passage, by itself, will not sustain Schmitt's claim. Indeed, even a fuller, more patient, inductive examination of Anselm's texts will not corroborate the view that Anselm weighed each word—weighed it exactly—in the course of writing the *Proslogion*. In fact, much of the confusion over just how to specify the structure of Anselm's line of reasoning in *Proslogion* 2-3 results from Anselm's not having weighed his words exactly, so as to eliminate thought-impeding ambiguities. In the end, then, Schmitt's judgment, far from being a textually justified inference, is nothing more than an *a priori* verdict which he somehow felt would be useful in supporting his antecedent decision to prepare a translation that was quite literal.

Other such pseudo-inductive conclusions are equally objectionable from the viewpoint of a critical study of the Anselmian texts—"conclusions" such as the following: (1) that Anselm "is never loose in his language";[4] (2) that he "had a propensity for developing technical terminology";[5] (3) that his thought is "easy to understand";[6] (4) that his "primary mode of thought is grammar";[7] (5) that his "ideas and language are clear and simple; the difficulty lies in comprehending the ideas expressed."[8] Though these five claims should be spurned as baseless, the denials of these claims must not themselves be supposed to constitute an *a priori* interpretive grid that is to be *imposed* upon the texts. For the denials emerge from an examination of the relevant passages "on their own merits," so to speak. At the very outset, then, an interpreter has the task of determining whether or not some particular thought of Anselm's is imprecisely expressed, whether or not a given idea or expression of his is clear and simple, whether or not his terminology tends to be technical, etc. Once the conclusions begin to emerge, in the light of many passages, they may be worked into an interpretive scheme which can then be brought to bear upon dubious or borderline cases. Once having recognized, for example, that at times Anselm *is* loose in his language, and even loose in his thinking, an interpreter need not strain so hard in insisting that the expression *"aliquid quo maius nihil cogitari potest"* must be an indefinite description, which Anselm is systematically distin-

guishing from *"id quo maius nihil cogitari potest."* For the interchanging of the two expressions may be an instance of Anselm's expressing himself loosely. Whether or not, all things considered, the interchanging *is* deemed to be such an instance, the phrasing of the translation will not be affected: *"aliquid"* will still be translated as "something," and *"id quo"* as "that than which." Yet, at other times a given interpretive judgment *will* affect the manner of translating: if Anselm is sometimes loose in his thinking and articulating, then there is reason to judge the neuter demonstrative pronoun *"illud,"* in *Reply to Gaunilo* 7:11, to be a reference to *deus* rather than to *id quo maius cogitari nequit*; and the translation will have to reflect this judgment.

Though, indeed, the present translation is necessarily interpretive, it is, nonetheless, conservatively so. For it is a reliably close translation. As F. S. Schmitt, M. J. Charlesworth, and A. C. Pegis rightly recognize, only a literal translation can avoid the pitfalls that inevitably accompany the "free translation" of philosophical texts. Of course, there would be little value in a translation so literal that, in effect, it rendered Anselm's thoughts into Pidgin English.[9] The present version, then, aims to be both reliable and literate. Whatever its merits and demerits, it is superior to the version which was prepared by me twelve years ago[10] and whose use should now be discontinued.

The first two sections of the immediately succeeding Introduction are revisions of two articles that originally appeared in *The New Scholasticism* and *The Southern Journal of Philosophy* respectively.[11] I thank the respective editors, Ralph McInerny and Nancy D. Simco, for allowing the republication of these in their new form. A grant from the McMillan Fund of the College of Liberal Arts at the University of Minnesota made possible my trip to Oxford University to examine Manuscripts Bodley 271 and Rawlinson A.392. The Department of Western Manuscripts at the Bodleian Library kindly granted permission for the publication of the present transcription of the Latin texts from Bodley 271; and Dr. Albinia de la Mare was generous in answering manuscript questions which I posed to her prior to my actual visit to the Bodleian. Also helpful, in other necessary ways, was the staff of the Wilson Library at the University of Minnesota, as well as Dr. Julian Plante and his staff at the Hill Monastic Library, St. John's University, Collegeville, Minnesota. Finally, Joel Wilcox, my graduate teaching assistant and doctoral dissertation

advisee, performed the invaluable service of proofreading with me the final typeset pages of the entire book.

The bibliography is intended to supplement, rather than to overlap with, the two other lists that appeared in previous of my works.[12] The Introduction was written exclusively for scholars in the field of Anselm Studies, with the result that other readers may well prefer to proceed directly to the translations. The Introduction does not aim to provide a balanced overview of the main conceptual and textual problems that arise from the *Monologion* and the *Proslogion*, for not even a separate book could succeed in doing that. Rather, it focuses intensively upon three recent interpretations of the *Proslogion* proof. And by exhibiting the shortcomings of these three accounts, it illustrates how the conceptual and the translational are inseparably interlaced in any interpretation of a medieval Latin philosophical text.

Jasper Hopkins
Professor of Philosophy
University of Minnesota

CONTENTS

A NEW, INTERPRETIVE TRANSLATION OF ST. ANSELM'S MONOLOGION AND PROSLOGION

INTRODUCTION

I. On Understanding and Preunderstanding St. Anselm.

Among the more recent publications on St. Anselm's ontological argument Richard Campbell's *From Belief to Understanding: A Study of Anselm's Proslogion Argument on the Existence of God*[1] is perhaps the most noteworthy. For it presents an interpretation of *Proslogion* 2-4 which attempts to be exegetically sensitive as well as philosophically penetrating. Indeed, Campbell hints that he has understood the structure and the relevance of Anselm's argument better than anyone else between Thomas Aquinas and Max Charlesworth (pp. 4-5).

I

Beginning with his own literal translation of *Proslogion* 2-4, Campbell proceeds to ' intain that Anselm's *unum argumentum* is in reality *a single form la* that generates *a single chain of reasoning*, the crux of which has three different stages.[2] Stage One begins in *Proslogion* 2 and aims at establishing the existence of something than which a greater cannot be thought. Stage Two is initiated at the start of *Proslogion* 3 and sets out to show that "something-than-which-a-greater-cannot-be-thought so truly is that it cannot even be thought not to be." But although "Anselm has shown that something-than-which-a-greater-cannot-be-thought exists in reality and cannot be thought not to be, he has still to establish that God is the only such thing" (p. 19). Accordingly, the argument is completed by a third stage, which commences with Anselm's words *"Et hoc es tu, domine deus noster"* in the middle of *Proslogion* 3 and continues through *"Solus igitur verissime omnium, et ideo maxime omnium, habes esse—quia quidquid aliud est, non sic vere, et idcirco minus, habet esse"*—the remaining material, down to the end of *Proslogion* 4, serving as a kind of appendix.

In successive chapters Campbell examines the intricacies of these stages, carefully working out the steps contained in each of them. Following the lead of Richard La Croix (*Proslogion II and III: A Third Interpretation of Anselm's Argument*), he disagrees with Hartshorne and Malcolm that *Proslogion* 3 by itself contains an independent argument

3

for God's *existence*. But he also disagrees with La Croix himself, who regards Anselm as requiring the entire *Proslogion* in order to prove *God's* existence. By contrast, Campbell contends that Anselm believed he had demonstrated the existence of God within *Proslogion* 2-3 (pp. 11, 177).

After presenting a logical formalization of the entire chain of reasoning, Campbell devotes two chapters to discussing "the force of the Argument" and "the relevance of the Argument" respectively. Here he expands upon his earlier denial that Anselm is "engaged in an *analysis* of the *concept* of God, from which it is supposed to follow that God exists" (p. 3). Indeed, he views Anselm as a proto-Wittgensteinian who begins his line of argumentation with the speech-act of uttering the words "something than which nothing greater can be thought."[3] The Fool, too, in making his denial, uses these words, which he understands. And Anselm shows him that, strictly speaking, his denial that such a being exists is unintelligible. What is at stake here, remarks Campbell, is something parallel to Wittgenstein's claim, in the *Philosophical Investigations*, that we cannot use our natural language to deny the existence of the external world (pp. 197, 213). Similarly, within the framework of Anselm's religious language there is no intelligible way to deny God's existence, once we understand what God is. Accordingly, Anselm's argument does constitute a proof in the sense of showing that *if* anyone understands and uses the description "something than which a greater cannot be thought," then he is rationally required to affirm the existence of such a being (pp. 193, 220). But it is *not* a proof in the further sense of showing that anyone *is* required either to use the description or to call the described-being God.

Thus, Anselm's argument is *a posteriori*: "Insofar as this derivation sets out from Anselm's speech-act in using the words 'something-than-which-nothing-greater-can-be-thought,' which is an *empirical event*, he cannot be taken to be presenting an *a priori* argument" (p. 199). Ironically, but insightfully, Campbell calls in Kant as the principal witness for the defense of Anselm, since for Anselm the proposition "God exists" *could not be analytic* (pp. 57-58). Elsewhere Campbell tackles nearly every major philosophical issue bearing upon the interpretation of the ontological argument. For instance, he deals with the semantics of possible worlds, rejecting David Lewis' account of Anselm and actuality. And he also asserts that the phrase "*id quo maius cogitari nequit*" is not, in

Proslogion 2-3, a definite description, although the phrase *"aliquid quo maius nihil cogitari potest"* is an indefinite description (pp. 88, 32-34).

II

Although, in many respects, I find Campbell's interpretation impressive, I would like to register the fundamental reservations which follow. My procedure will be to start with some points which appear trifling and then to use them to make headway with some other points that are not so trifling.

To begin with, then, Campbell has trouble with Anselm's two words *"sic"* and *"sicut."* For example, consider the following passage in *Proslogion* 4:

> *Deus enim est id quo maius cogitari non potest. Quod qui bene intelligit, utique intelligit id ipsum sic esse, ut nec cogitatione queat non esse. Qui ergo intelligit sic esse deum, nequit eum non esse cogitare.*[4]

Campbell renders this passage as:

> For God is that-than-which-a-greater-cannot-be-thought. Whoever properly understands this understands thereby that this same thing so is that not even for thought can it not be. Therefore, whoever understands that God is in such a way cannot think that he is not.

Thereby, he shows his failure to recognize that although *"sic"* is being used adverbially in the sentence which correlates it with *"ut,"* it is being used adjectivally in the very next sentence, where it is not correlated with an *"ut."* Indeed, the passage should be translated as (something like):

> For God is that than which a greater cannot be thought. Anyone who rightly understands this |i.e., rightly understands what is signified by "that than which a greater cannot be thought"|, surely understands that that |than which a greater cannot be thought| exists in such way that it cannot even conceivably not exist. Therefore, anyone who understands that God is such |a being| cannot think that He does not exist.[5]

Or again, let us consider Anselm's statement in *Reply to Gaunilo* 2:

> *Sicut enim quod cogitatur, cogitatione cogitatur, et quod cogitatione cogitatur, sicut cogitatur sic est in cogitatione: ita quod intelligitur intellectu intelligitur, et quod intellectu intelligitur, sicut intelligitur ita est in intellectu.*

Campbell translates this as:

> Just as what is thought is thought *by* thought, and what is thought by thought is

thus, as thought, *in* thought, so also what is understood is understood *by* the understanding, and what is understood by the understanding is thus, as understood, *in* the understanding (p. 42).

Campbell then intimates that Anselm's statement is not as clear as is desirable. But, indeed, the problem is not with Anselm's statement but with Campbell's translation. A more accurate translation would be (something like):

> For what is thought is thought by thinking; and with regard to what is thought by thinking: even as it is thought, so it is in |our| thinking. Similarly, what is understood is understood by the understanding; and with regard to what is understood by the understanding: even as it is understood, so it is in the understanding.

In this passage Anselm uses "*sicut . . . sic*" and "*sicut . . . ita*" interchangeably. He is *not* making a point about the *manner* in which something is in our understanding (i.e., he is not saying that a thing is in the understanding in the manner in which it is understood).[6] Rather, he is making the point that if something is understood, then what is understood is in the understanding. (Thus, if "something than which a greater cannot be thought" is understood, then something than which a greater cannot be thought is in the understanding.) This is why in the sentence immediately preceding the one in question he writes: "*Vide quia consequitur esse in intellectu, ex eo quia intelligitur.*"

Campbell's problem with "*sic*" and "*sicut*" becomes more acute in *Proslogion* 2, where he translates

> *Ergo, domine, qui das fidei intellectum, da mihi, ut quantum scis expedire intelligam, quia es sicut credimus, et hoc es quod credimus.*

as

> Well then, O Lord, you who give understanding to faith [,] give me, so far as you know it to be beneficial, to understand that you are just as we believe, and that you are what we believe (p. 6).

Now, this translation is not in very clear English.[7] For what in the world is meant by "that you are just as we believe"? Campbell tells us that it is a statement about the *manner* in which God exists. Well, maybe that's what *he* means by his English words; but do these English words accurately translate the Latin clause "*quia es sicut credimus*"? Or is Campbell wrong in taking "*sicut*" here to be a word indicating *manner*, even as he was wrong about "*sic*" in *Proslogion* 4 and in *Reply to Gaunilo* 2?

Campbell thinks that this first half of Anselm's prayer is answered in the second part of *Proslogion* 3, where Anselm comes to *understand* (as contrasted with merely holding a religious *belief* about) the manner of God's existence: viz., that God exists in such way that He cannot be thought not to exist.[8] In fact, Campbell's insistence that the opening prayer in *Proslogion* 2 displays Anselm's intent to establish a truth about the manner of God's existence leads him to side, in part, with A. Stolz's interpretation. Thus, he agrees with Stolz that *"vere esse"* does not mean real existence in the sense that things other than God have real existence (p. 173). Nor does it mean real existence in contrast to the unreality of illusions or fictions (p. 175).

Yet, Campbell ought not to agree with Stolz even to the limited extent that he does. For in the context of *Proslogion* 2 and 3, Anselm *does* mean by *"vere esse"* real existence in the sense that things other than God have real existence and in the sense that illusions and fictions do not have it. Indeed, for Anselm, whatever exists *in re* exists *vere*. This is why he uses the word *"vera"* of things which exist *in re* (*Reply to Gaunilo* 6:6 = *S* I, 136:8).[9] Moreover, this is why in *Proslogion* 3 he claims not merely that God truly exists but that God exists most truly of all (*verissime omnium . . . habes esse*), thereby implying that there are things other than God which also truly exist. So, then, *Proslogion* 2 "proves" that something than which a greater cannot be thought exists truly; and *Proslogion* 3 shows that it exists *so* truly that it cannot even be thought not to exist. [Once again, the word *"sic"* (in *"Sic ergo vere est... ut... "*) is so very important.] In *Proslogion* 3 Anselm does not deny that things other than God exist truly. Rather, he denies that they exist as truly as does God: *quidquid aliud est non sic vere, et idcirco minus habet esse*. So *"vere esse"* is not an expression which Anselm is reserving exclusively for discourse about God.[10]

To return to the opening prayer of *Proslogion* 2: In asking to understand *quia es sicut credimus*, Anselm is not asking to understand something about the unique *manner* in which God exists. Rather, he is asking to understand *that* God exists. This fact is confirmed by both the *Proslogion* preface and *Reply to Gaunilo* 10. In the former, Anselm indicates that he is seeking to prove (1) that God truly (really) exists and (2) that He is the Supreme Good and whatever else we believe about the Divine Substance. Now, the opening prayer in *Proslogion* 2 is rightly viewed only in the context of what, in the *Proslogion* preface, Anselm explicitly

claims to be aiming to do and, in the *Reply*, explicitly claims to have succeeded in doing. In the preface his words are *"quia deus vere est"* and in the *Reply "revera probetur existere."* The latter clause is used in place of *"probasse . . . re ipsa existere,"* which occurs a few lines earlier; and the former has reference not to *Proslogion* 3 but to *Proslogion* 2, where Anselm uses the chapter-title *"Quod vere sit deus."* (Since he *believes* that God is something than which a greater cannot be thought, it is easy for him to use the word *"deus"* in the chapter-title, even though in Chapter 2 itself his argument has not yet reached the point of *understanding* that God is something than which a greater cannot be thought.) Since (as we have seen) Anselm is here taking whatever exists *in re* to be a *truly* existing thing, and vice versa, his preface tells us that he is aiming to prove that God exists in reality. And—with the proviso about justifying the identification of something than which a greater cannot be thought with God—he does "prove" this point in *Proslogion* 2. Neither in the above-mentioned passage of his preface nor in the corresponding passage of *Reply* 10 does Anselm mean—when he speaks of proving *quia deus vere est* and *revera existit*—proving that God exists *so* truly that He cannot be thought not to exist (although he does aim, in *Proslogion* 3, to prove this last point too).

Accordingly, an appropriate translation of the opening prayer will be:

> Therefore, O Lord, You who give understanding to faith, grant me to understand—
> to the degree You know to be advantageous—that You exist, as we believe, . . .

Unfortunately, Campbell scorns this translation, not understanding the role of *"sicut."* Similarly, he misses the significance of the second half of the prayer, which adds the expression: " . . . and that You are what we believe |You to be|." Both in his preface and in *Reply* 10 Anselm has made clear what he means by this expression. What he wants to understand is that God is whatever we do believe, and ought to believe, about the Divine Substance. Because immediately following the prayer there occur the words "Indeed, we believe You to be something than which nothing greater can be thought," Campbell thinks that Anselm is asking to understand that God is something than which nothing greater can be thought. Thereby he fails to realize that Anselm introduces this formula as a starting point for understanding *both* that God exists *and* that He is whatever we believe about the Divine Substance. And, according to *Reply* 10, the Divine Substance is believed to be whatever we think of as

being better for it to be than not to be. Now, in the *Proslogion* Anselm's reasoning does not reach this point until Chapters 5 ff.[11] So Anselm's prayer is not fully answered by the end of *Proslogion* 3. For by the end of *Proslogion* 3 Anselm has not yet concluded that that than which a greater cannot be thought is all the many things—omnipotent, merciful, impassible, eternal, supremely good, etc.—which we believe about the Divine Substance.[12]

Anselm proves that God is something than which a greater cannot be thought by proving that something than which a greater cannot be thought is God—i.e., that it has all the attributes which are ascribed by the Christian religion to God. Richard La Croix rightly recognizes that, *strictly speaking*, this proof is the product of the *entire Proslogion* (or at least through *Proslogion* 23). By contrast, Campbell contends that *Proslogion* 3 contains an "argument" for the claim that God is the one and only being than which nothing greater can be thought (p. 128). For it contains the premise "If any mind could think of something better than You, the creature would rise above the Creator and would sit in judgment over the Creator—something which is utterly absurd." And from this premise there follows immediately that God is the only being than which nothing greater can be thought. But, of course, this "argument" is question-begging. For it virtually assumes that there is one and only one Creator. Campbell concedes that this reasoning will not "carry any force with someone who does not believe that God is the creator of everything else there is" (p. 135). Furthermore, he maintains, this belief is not argued for in the *Proslogion*. "Anselm simply appeals to it as an article of faith . . . . Just because this development of the Argument does involve an appeal to religious doctrine, it will impress an atheist not one whit. But then Anselm shows no sign of wanting to impress the atheist; he simply seeks understanding of his own belief . . . . Anselm has convinced himself that he can affirm that there does exist such a nature as something-than-which-nothing-greater-can-be-thought, and he now has found reason elsewhere in his belief-system for identifying that nature as God" (pp. 135-136).

Let us be clear about Campbell's position. He views the "linch-pin" (p. 11) of Anselm's *unum argumentum* as being contained completely in *Proslogion* 2-3 (implying that *Proslogion* 4 is a kind of addendum). And he views Anselm's reasoning in this section as culminating with the identification of God as the one and only being than which none greater can

be thought. Moreover, he sees that unless this identification can be successfully argued, Anselm will not have established that *God* exists. But he regards the culmination of Anselm's argument as question-begging and as evidence for the conclusion that Anselm was not really trying to impress the atheist. He views Anselm's argument as, in last analysis, carrying no weight against the Fool because the Fool has been given no reason for accepting the Christian doctrine of creation.

Now, this interpretation of Campbell's seems to me to be wrong. Campbell is saddled with the interpretation because of the way he construes the opening prayer of *Proslogion* 2—because of the way he has read "*quia es sicut credimus, et hoc es quod credimus.*" For my part, I take the prayer in a different way and do not see Anselm's argument as culminating in Chapter 3 with a question-begging appeal to an article of religious faith. In Chapter 3 Anselm does *affirm* that God is something than which a greater cannot be thought. And he does *believe* that there is only *one* thing than which a greater cannot be thought; for he *asserts* that God alone cannot be thought not to exist. But in Chapter 3 he does not *produce* any rational support for this assertion.[13] Therefore, his argument is not complete by the end of Chapter 3. In fact, he uses Chapter 5 to show that there is only one being than which a greater cannot be thought; and he uses the rest of the *Proslogion* to show that this one being has all the attributes which the Christian religion ascribes to God.

Assuredly, Chapter 5 *does* present a philosophical consideration to support the belief that there is only one thing than which nothing greater can be thought. For Anselm *there* maintains that whatever *alone* exists *per se* and creates *all else* from nothing is greater than what does not alone exist *per se* and create all else from nothing.[14] (For it does not share its prerogatives with any other being.) This consideration has the same status as (1) the presupposition that existing both in the understanding and in reality is greater than existing in the understanding alone or (2) the presupposition that being unable to be thought not to exist is greater than being able to be thought not to exist. And however one finally appraises the reasonableness of these metaphysical presuppositions, they are certainly not articles of religious faith.

But at this point Campbell regards Anselm as opening up in Stage Three (i.e., in the second half of *Proslogion* 3) a second, and independent, "leg of reasoning" whereby from a new premise (viz., the premise

"except for You alone, whatever else exists can be thought not to exist"), in conjunction with Stages One and Two, two conclusions are validly derivable: (*a*) that God exists and cannot be thought not to exist, and (*b*) that God is that than which a greater cannot be thought.[15] Now, on one construal of the new premise "except for You alone, whatever else exists can be thought not to exist" this entire second leg of reasoning is question-begging, as Campbell observes. For on one construal Anselm will be seen to assume the very thing he is supposed to be proving: to wit, that one and only one thing—viz., God—cannot be thought not to exist, since one and only one thing is something than which a greater cannot be thought. But even if we follow Campbell (p. 146) in repudiating the foregoing construal and construing the new premise in the minimal sense of "anything which is not God can be thought not to exist," Anselm's argument still will be question-begging—if, as Campbell asserts, Anselm's argument is to be regarded as complete by the end of *Proslogion* 3. For Anselm needs to establish not simply that "anything which is not God can be thought not to exist." He needs to establish that "because God *alone* is something than which a greater cannot be thought, anything which is not God can be thought not to exist." For if more than one thing is such that it is something than which a greater cannot be thought, or if God is not something than which a greater cannot be thought, then it is not the case that God alone cannot be thought not to exist. But nowhere in *Proslogion* 3—not even in this alleged second leg of reasoning—does Anselm, in a noncircular or non-question-begging way, *establish* (as opposed to assume) either that only one thing is something than which a greater cannot be thought or that God Himself is something than which a greater cannot be thought. In *Proslogion* 3 it is the case that Anselm's reason for *believing* that God alone cannot be thought not to exist is his belief that God alone is something than which a greater cannot be thought; it is *not* the case that his reason for believing that God alone is something than which a greater cannot be thought is his belief that God alone cannot be thought not to exist.[16] In *Proslogion* 3 Anselm's argument is not complete. Not until *Proslogion* 5 does he contend that there is only one thing that exists *per se* and creates all else from nothing. Once this single Being, believed by Anselm to be God, will have been shown to possess the attributes which the Christian faith believes to be essential to the Divine Being, it will have been shown to be the God whom Anselm is addressing. (A creator who is, for example,

either not just or not merciful would not be the God Anselm is seeking and petitioning.)

So in *Proslogion* 2-4 Anselm *believes* that God is the one and only being than which nothing greater can be thought, even though he only subsequently offers the *ratio* for his *fides*. Nonetheless, it is because he *anticipates* this *ratio* that he uses the word "God" in the title of Chapter 2 and introduces in Chapter 3 the consideration about the Creator. Because of this same anticipation, he uses in *Proslogion* 4 (what *we* would call) a definite description (*"Deus enim est id quo maius cogitari non potest"*) before having justified his belief that there is only one *aliquid quo maius cogitari non potest*. To be sure, Anselm does not have a theory of descriptions—whether definite or indefinite. Nevertheless, nothing prevents our seeking to determine whether or not his formula, as employed, has the same role as does a definite description. And in *Proslogion* 4 it clearly does. Campbell thinks that Anselm was intuitively aware of the distinction between definite and indefinite descriptions and that he systematically invoked this distinction in *Proslogion* 2-4. I do not deny that Anselm may have been intuitively aware of some such distinction; but I do deny that he made systematic use of it in *Proslogion* 2-4.[17] [Analogously, he is aware of certain distinctions between *cogitare* and *intelligere*; but he is not insisting upon these distinctions when he switches from using the word *"intelligi"* to using the word *"cogitari"* in *Proslogion* 9:43-44 (= *S* I, 108:12-13). Or again, he is aware of various distinctions between *melius* and *maius*; but he is not insisting upon these distinctions when he switches from saying *"quo nihil maius cogitari potest"* to saying *"quo nihil melius cogitari potest"* in *Proslogion* 14:4 (= *S* I, 111:9) and in *Proslogion* 18:26-27 (= *S* I, 114:21-22).] I claim that Anselm was assuming, even in *Proslogion* 2 and 3, that there is only one being than which a greater cannot be thought, and that this being is God.[18] Even while making this assumption he was in the process of justifying[19] it—in the way I have indicated—in *Proslogion* 2-5 together with the remainder of the *Proslogion*. Thus, in *Proslogion* 4 he used a definite description even though his justification for doing so requires at least *Proslogion* 5.

We are now in a position to detect the major[20] weakness of Campbell's interpretation of Anselm's argument: viz., that Campbell is overly charitable to Anselm. Indeed, he views him not only as operating clearly with definite and indefinite descriptions but also as never confusing *use*

and *mention*, as setting forth a theory of intentionality which anticipates Brentano's, as convicting Gaunilo of having contradicted himself, as arguing à la Wittgenstein,[21] etc.—all in the name of the maxim that Anselm is too keen a thinker to have missed such points. Correspondingly, Campbell is overly *un*charitable to Gaunilo. For instance, he does not recognize that, after all, Gaunilo is not guilty of a self-contradiction.[22] Moreover, in siding with Anselm, Campbell flatly and unqualifiedly accuses Gaunilo of construing Anselm's "that than which nothing greater can be thought" as "that which is greatest of all things" (p. 108). Similarly, he attacks Gaunilo's theory of meaning, as elicited from *On Behalf of the Fool* 4, without calling attention to the fact that Anselm may have subscribed to this same theory (pp. 38-40). In particular, Campbell conveys the impression that Anselm, like a good Wittgensteinian, held the opinion that significance is a matter of knowing how to use words, not a matter of expressing mental events. Hereby he presents a one-sided picture of Anselm—a picture which fails to take account of the close correlation (in Anselm's theory) between the spoken word and the mental word (i.e., the image or the concept).[23] Finally, we do not definitely know that, in *Proslogion* 4, Anselm's statement "For in one way a thing is thought when the word signifying it is thought" is *not* to be construed as Gaunilo construes it in *On Behalf of the Fool* 4.[24] Indeed, in *Reply to Gaunilo* 8, Anselm instructs Gaunilo on how to conceive of God *secundum rem*; he does not quarrel with his analysis of *significatio secundum vocem*.

Campbell is equally uncharitable in his construal of Gaunilo's perfect-island counterexample: "Gaunilo speaks of an island than which *in fact* no land is greater, whereas Anselm speaks of something-than-which-nothing-greater-*can-be-thought* . . . " (p. 192). If Campbell were charitable to Gaunilo—the way he is always charitable to Anselm—he would interpret Gaunilo as speaking about an island than which none greater can be thought, and which consequently excels all other lands. I am not saying that Gaunilo's text *requires* this interpretation. (Campbell does *correct* Gaunilo to make his view accord with this interpretation.) But I am bothered by a certain unevenhandedness in Campbell's way of interpreting the debate between Anselm and Gaunilo.

III

In formulating the foregoing misgivings about Campbell's interpreta-

tion, I began with some points about translation; and I shall now conclude with a point about translation. *Proslogion* 3 opens with the words:

> *Quod utique sic vere est, ut nec cogitari possit non esse. Nam potest cogitari esse aliquid, quod non possit cogitari non esse; quod maius est quam quod non esse cogitari potest.*

Campbell translates this passage as:

> This thing so truly is that it cannot be thought not to be. For it can be thought to be something which cannot be thought not to be, which is greater than what can be thought not to be.

Now, aside from Campbell's having said " . . . so truly is that it cannot be thought . . . " instead of saying, " . . . so truly is that it cannot even be thought . . . , " I have no quarrel with this rendering. Both the Latin text and the logic of Anselm's argument are consistent with it. Nonetheless, I do not think that this reading is the preferable one; and I do have a quarrel with one of Campbell's justifications for his reading, and also with his claim about the logic of my alternative reading. I regard the above passage as saying literally:

> Assuredly, this |being| exists so truly that it cannot even be thought not to exist. For there can be thought to exist something which cannot be thought not to exist; and this thing is greater than that which can be thought not to exist.

Now, one of the reasons given by Campbell for rejecting the translation "there can be thought to exist something which . . . "[25] in favor of the translation "it can be thought to be something which . . . " is the following: "Anselm does not use '*esse*' in this generalized way with the meaning: 'there exists.' When he wanted to say *that* [my italics] in chapter II, he said '*existit*' " (p. 95). This statement of Campbell's is very naive; for Anselm does *not* regularly distinguish his use of "*esse*" from his use of "*existere*." Moreover, *Monologion* 3 should already have taught Campbell that Anselm sometimes uses "*est*" to mean "there is/there exists." But even within the *Proslogion* itself, he should have remembered Chapter 15, where Anselm wrote: "*Quoniam namque valet cogitari esse aliquid huiusmodi: si tu non es hoc ipsum, potest cogitari aliquid maius te; quod fieri nequit.*" Here "*valet cogitari esse*" must be rendered as "there can be thought to be [i.e., to exist] something of this kind," and cannot be rendered as "it can be thought to be something of this kind." For the *preceding* sentence is " . . . *non solum es quo maius cogitari nequit, sed es quiddam maius quam cogitari possit.*"[26]

So once again Campbell has been misled by his dogged desire to view Anselm as a thinker having a "keen logical sense" (pp. 102, 127, 139)— too keen a sense not to signal (by the consistent use of two different words) the difference between predication or identity, on the one hand, and existence, on the other (though he does not signal the difference between a definite and an indefinite description by the consistent use of "*id quo maius . . .* " and "*aliquid quo maius . . .* "!).

Campbell does concede the "possibility," though not the preferability, of the translation "there can be thought to exist something . . . . " But having made this concession, he saddles its adherents with the following understanding of Anselm's argument: "The argument would proceed by introducing the possible thought that there is something which cannot be thought not to be and continue by claiming that if that-than-which-a-greater-cannot-be-thought can be thought not to be, it would have been thought that something is greater than it, which is impossible" (p. 96). But this is not the way the argument would go. Anselm is not suggesting that if that than which a greater cannot be thought, could be thought not to exist, then something else[27] would be thought to be greater than it. Rather, he is maintaining that if that than which a greater cannot be thought could be thought not to exist, then *it* could be thought to be greater, because it could be thought to be something which cannot be thought not to exist. In other words, this is the very same line of reasoning as the one which Campbell himself is ascribing to Anselm! Campbell fails to realize that he is rejecting a translation which *legitimates* his own interpretation. Hence, having formulated his interpretation, he feels that he must reject this alternative translation; and he subsequently invents a dubious reason for *his* translation's being the preferable one.[28]

I have given grounds for appraising Campbell's interpretation of Anselm's *Proslogion* argument as tendentious. In the name of charitable construal, he regards Anselm as a better philosopher than he really is. This tendentious approach leads him to misread the opening prayer of *Proslogion* 2, to claim that Anselm distinguishes between *esse* and *existere* in *Proslogion* 3, and to conclude that in *Proslogion* 3 one leg of Anselm's "linch-pin" argument culminates with an appeal to an article of faith, so that Anselm escapes from the "power of the Platonic dream" (cf. p. 213). In the end, Campbell is led to wonder whether some of his own preunderstanding might not be a barrier to understanding Anselm (p. 227). And it seems to me that this query is well-placed. For Campbell,

who is a keen logician and philosopher of language, keeps wanting to understand Anselm as an equally keen logician and philosopher of language. Yet, in truth, Anselm was *not* the harbinger either of Russell or of Wittgenstein.

In last analysis, then, Campbell is wrong in believing that he has understood the structure of Anselm's argument better than anyone else between Aquinas and Charlesworth (pp. 4-5). Even apart from the many issues of translation, it should be clear to everyone that Anselm's way of dealing with the Fool's denial of God is very much different from Wittgenstein's way of dealing with a skeptic's denial of the external world. For Anselm proceeds by showing that the Fool's denial of the existence of God—whom the Fool, together with Anselm, regards as something than which a greater cannot be thought—is unintelligible because it involves a self-contradiction. By contrast, Wittgenstein at no point maintains that the skeptic's denial of the existence of the external world is unintelligible because of any self-inconsistency. Indeed, Wittgenstein's philosophical method, as well as his notion of philosophical intelligibility, is only vaguely analogous to Anselm's. Accordingly, Campbell has misconstrued not only the structure but also the relevance of Anselm's argument.[29]

II. On an Alleged Definitive Interpretation of *Proslogion* 2-4.

One may well wonder what to expect from a book which claims to provide, now at long last, a definitive interpretation of Anselm's *Proslogion* argument. Yet, this is the claim made by Gregory Schufreider in his book, *An Introduction to Anselm's Argument*.[30] "From its inception to the present day," writes Schufreider, "Anselm's own argument has never been properly understood . . . . My aim, then, is *to bring the reader into direct contact with the original argument*. This obviously cannot be accomplished through a mere presentation of the text, but requires a careful interpretation . . . " (p. xiii).

I

Schufreider's "definitive account" (p. 96) focuses on *Proslogion* 2-4, deliberately saying little about *On Behalf of the Fool* or the *Reply to Gaunilo*. Schufreider sees *Proslogion* 2 as attempting to show that something than which a greater cannot be thought exists both in the under-

standing and in reality. *Proslogion* 3, in turn, is said to argue that such a being cannot be thought not to exist, i.e., that such a being *truly* exists. This being is then affirmed by Anselm to be God because, we are told, Anselm believed that *the* distinguishing characteristic of God is to be unable to be thought not to exist (pp. 49, 61, 81). *Proslogion* 4 exhibits the sense in which the Fool both can and cannot think that God does not exist; in particular, he cannot think this insofar as he understands that God truly exists, i.e., insofar as his reason distinguishes, by means of an essential intuition, God in His singularity (p. 77). Anselm, however, is said not to expect the Fool to attain to this understanding. Indeed, Anselm does not aim to convince the Fool of anything; his argument is directed *against* the Fool, rather than being designed *for* the Fool. "Anselm's concern lies with those who are 'striving to elevate their (own) mind[s] to contemplate God' " (p. 84); for only such ardent seekers can be led, thinks Anselm, to that vision of God to which he is trying to bring them by means of *Proslogion* 2 and 3.

In sum, Schufreider's account is distinctive because of its way of handling the configuration of three issues: (1) the relationship between the reasoning of *Proslogion* 2 and the reasoning of *Proslogion* 3; (2) the analysis of the statement "God truly exists"; (3) the specification of the kind of understanding which Anselm purportedly aims at developing in those for whom he wrote down his argument. With regard to the first issue Schufreider sees *Proslogion* 2 and 3 as together constituting a single argument—complete and independent—which aims to show[31] that God truly exists. By itself *Proslogion* 2 does not establish either that *God* exists or that He *truly* exists but only that something than which a greater cannot be thought exists both in the understanding and in reality. Similarly, *Proslogion* 3 does not by itself suffice to establish that anything exists; and, *a fortiori*, it does not suffice to show that God exists or that He truly exists. Taken together, however, *Proslogion* 2 and 3 do contain, thinks Schufreider, a single valid argument for the conclusion that God truly exists. With regard to the second issue Schufreider takes "God truly exists" to mean "God so exists that He cannot be thought not to exist" (p. 60). With regard to the third issue he thinks that the Fool needs to understand, but does not, that something than which a greater cannot be thought so exists that it cannot be thought not to exist, for this is one of the things Anselm has in mind when he speaks of understanding *id quod deus est* (p. 89). But the Fool, Schufreider maintains, cannot

really understand what God is, because the Fool does not desire to emulate the contemplative. "Against the strict measure of what so exists that it cannot be thought not to exist all other beings pale, as if to nothing. And the contemplative's task is to *perform* this annulment of existing creatures so that they may fade from reason's sight. For it is through this withdrawal of all creatures that the way is cleared for a *radically purified* (rational) *vision of the matter itself* [*id ipsum quod res est*], that is, of something than which nothing greater can be thought" (p. 82, my brackets; cf. p. 78).

II

Schufreider's global interpretation is indeed intriguing, and as long as we remain at the global level it may even retain a semblance of plausibility. However, as soon as we focus upon its constituent elements, we discover a host of exegetical and hermeneutical mistakes. For example, on p. 16 we read: " . . . Anselm assumes the general principle to the effect that if something exists both in the understanding and in reality, it is greater than what exists in the understanding alone." Yet, this way of articulating Anselm's assumption is imprecise. For what Anselm assumes is, rather, that if something than which a greater cannot be thought exists both in the understanding and in reality, *it* is greater than it would be if it existed in the understanding alone. And if there is a general principle which is assumed, it is the principle that if something exists both in the understanding and in reality, *it* is greater than it would be if it existed in the understanding alone.

More importantly, in regard to *Proslogion* 3 Schufreider misinterprets both Anselm's opening sentence ("*Quod utique sic vere est, ut nec cogitari possit non esse*") and his fourth sentence ("*Sic ergo vere est aliquid quo maius cogitari non potest, ut nec cogitari possit non esse*"). For he comments:

> Let us take note of a few facts about the use of the phrase "so truly exists." The first chapter in which this phrase occurs is III, and as a matter of fact, it occurs in the very first sentence of III. This is, indeed, the first time *in* a chapter that the phrase occurs, but it does occur before this, as a chapter heading. Strangely enough, the chapter heading in which it occurs is not III . . . but rather that of II: *Quod vere sit deus*, or: That God truly exists. (p. 37)

Schufreider's mistake is to equate "so truly exists" with "truly exists." This confusion is so pervasively implanted in his mind that he actually

states above that the phrase "so truly exists" occurs in the title of *Proslogion* 2! Now, comprehending the distinction between "*sic vere est (ut) . . .* " and "*vere est*" is crucial to understanding Anselm's argument. Schufreider has taken a crucial misstep—one which shows that he is not adhering to Anselm's text. On Anselm's view a thing truly exists if it exists. Of course, for Anselm, things exist in varying degrees. Finite beings, for example, do not exist to the same extent as does God. Moreover, a finite thing exists in itself to a greater degree than it exists in our knowledge; and it exists in the Word of God to a greater degree than it exists in itself. (See *Monologion* 36.) When Anselm wants to call attention to the difference of degree in which things exist, he does so by using such phrases as "exists more truly than," "exists less than," "exists most truly of all." Thus, in *Monologion* 36, as we have just seen, a thing is said to exist more truly in itself than it exists in our knowledge of it; and in *Proslogion* 3 God is said to exist most truly of all. Where Anselm is *not* making a point about a *difference* in degree of existing, he says simply "*vere est*"; e.g., this is his expression both in *De Veritate* 7, where he is talking only about all finite beings, and in the chapter-title of *Proslogion* 2, where he is referring, uncomparatively, only to God. Now, the expression "*sic vere est (ut)* . . . " belongs to those contexts in which Anselm is indeed stressing a difference in degree of existing, as is the case in the first and the fourth sentences of *Proslogion* 3: something than which a greater cannot be thought exists *so* truly that it cannot even be thought not to exist. After having identified this being with God, Anselm writes: "Therefore, You alone exist most truly of all and thus most greatly of all; for whatever else exists does not exist as truly |as do You| and thus exists less greatly |than do You|." This passage implies that things other than God exist truly, though less truly than does God, who exists most truly of all.

Yet, with respect to the foregoing passage Schufreider falls into further error: "Anselm is *not* here saying that God exists more truly than other things . . . . What Anselm claims is not that God possesses existence more truly than all other things, but rather that God possesses existence *most* truly of all; not that God possesses existence to a higher degree, but that God possesses existence to the highest degree (or maximally). To claim, then, that God most truly of all possesses existence is not to make a claim to comparison, but to claim for God a right to distinction" (p. 63). A few pages later Schufreider asserts that, for Anselm, "to say some-

thing exists to the highest degree is *not* to say that it exists in a higher degree than other things, but to emphasize that it exists in a way wholly unlike anything else . . . " (p. 65). But, contrary to Schufreider's assertions, Anselm *is* claiming in *Proslogion* 3 that God exists more truly than all other things, as well as claiming that He exists most truly of all. For, assuredly, to say that "whatever else exists does not exist as truly |as do You|" is implicitly to say that "whatever else exists exists less truly |than do You|." We know from *Monologion* 36 that Anselm is not averse to thus comparing Creator and creature: "Now, it is evident that the more truly the Creating Being exists than does the created being, the more truly every created substance exists in the Word (i.e., in the Understanding) of the Creator than in itself." And in *Reply to Gaunilo* 5 Anselm remarks: "For that than which a greater cannot be thought can only be understood to be that which alone is greater than all |others|."[32] As in the *Monologion* and in the *Reply*, so in *Proslogion* 3 Anselm teaches both that God exists more truly than all else and that He exists more greatly than all else. In the history of philosophy Anselm dare not be confused with someone such as Nicholas of Cusa, who teaches that there is no comparative relation between Creator and creature, that God exists *most* greatly of all without existing *more* greatly than anything. Nicholas rejects the doctrine of *analogia*, substituting for it a doctrine of learned ignorance; likewise, he denies that God is conceivable nonmetaphorically (except to Himself). By contrast, Anselm of Canterbury—as is clear from *Monologion* 65-67 and *Reply to Gaunilo* 8—affirms the nonmetaphorical conceivability of God and accepts as legitimate some notion of *analogia* and some kind of comparative relation between God and creation.

Schufreider's confusion between "*vere est*" and "*sic vere est (ut)* . . . " now produces further twisting of both "*sic vere est*" and "*est non sic vere*," as they occur in *Proslogion* 3: "What we are told across these two lines [(1) "*quidquid est aliud . . . potest cogitari non esse*" and (2) "*quidquid aliud est non sic vere* . . . "] is that anything else there is can be thought not to exist, and in so far as it can be thought not to exist, exists not so truly. Put otherwise, if what so exists that it cannot be thought not to exist truly exists, then what so exists that it can be thought not to exist, in so far as it exists in this way, does not truly exist" (p. 64).[33] Yet, this restatement of the Latin—this putting the point otherwise—is another misstatement. For instead of the antecedent "what so exists that it cannot be thought not to exist *truly exists*," Schufreider

should say, more accurately, "what so exists that it cannot be thought not to exist, *most truly exists.*" And instead of the consequent "what so exists that it can be thought not to exist, in so far as it exists in this way, *does not truly exist,*" he should write "what so exists that it can be thought not to exist, in so far as it exists in this way, *does not most truly exist.*"[34] For in *Proslogion* 3 the sole occurrence of "*est non sic vere*" means "*est non verissime*" and not merely "*non vere est.*" But Schufreider is not careful in his restatement. For he wrongly conflates "*est non sic vere*" with "*non vere est,*" just as in the first and the fourth sentences of *Proslogion* 3 he confused "*sic vere est*" with "*vere est.*"[35]

Still other problems occur in Schufreider's interpretation of *Proslogion* 3. For he introduces into his analysis a consideration from *Reply to Gaunilo* 4: "*Sic igitur . . . proprium est deo non posse cogitari non esse . . . .*" This he takes to mean: "It is *the* distinguishing characteristic of God that He cannot be thought of as not existing . . . " (pp. 49, 54, 57, 61, 105n45). But this construal is tendentious. If there is one thing we learn from the *Proslogion,* it is that Anselm did not believe there to be any such thing as *the* distinguishing characteristic of God. God is distinguished from all else in multitudinous respects: He is Creator; all else is creation. He is omnipotent; all else falls short of omnipotence. He is omnipresent; all else (even a soul or an angel) exists somewhere but not everywhere. Moreover, just as God cannot rightly be thought not to exist, so He cannot rightly be thought not to be Creator, omnipotent, omnipresent, greater than can be thought, triune, and so on. The passage in *Reply to Gaunilo* 4 will thus be more correctly rendered as "it is *a* distinguishing characteristic of God not to be able to be thought not to exist . . . ." Yet, were we, *per impossibile,* somehow forced to settle upon a central distinguishing characteristic of God, from the viewpoint of the *Proslogion,* then this characteristic would more plausibly be identified as God's being Creator or as His being something than which a greater cannot be thought.

Schufreider is right about the fact that in *Proslogion* 3 Anselm *believes* that God alone exists so truly that He cannot be thought not to exist and that Anselm therefore does not hesitate to identify, as God, something than which a greater cannot be thought, having "proved" it to exist thus truly. But in *Proslogion* 3 Anselm does not *justify* this belief; i.e., it is still a matter of faith and is still in need of understanding. Indeed, Anselm can only justify this belief once his argument comes around to establish-

ing that there is only one being which is something than which a greater
cannot be thought. For if there is more than one such being, then each of
these beings will be such that it cannot be thought not to exist. Accordingly, Anselm's argument is not complete by the end of *Proslogion* 3.
And, in fact, Anselm does not attempt until *Proslogion* 5 to argue that
there is only one being than which a greater cannot be thought. There he
states that whatever *alone* exists *per se* and creates *all else* from nothing
is greater than what does not alone exist *per se* and create all else from
nothing. (For it does not share its prerogatives with any other being.)
Only at this juncture has he, from his own point of view, justified his
belief that *only one thing* cannot be thought not to exist. But he has yet to
show that this one thing is the triune Christian God, whom he is seeking.
He has yet to *understand* that the being who alone exists *per se* is also
merciful, just, impassible, triune, and "whatever else we believe about
the Divine Substance." At the end of *Proslogion* 3 his faith has not been
fully understood. He has established the existence of something which
exists so truly that it cannot be thought not to exist, and he *believes* this
something to be the God whom he is addressing and importuning. But he
knows that he (1) has not yet *shown* it to be God and therefore (2) has
not yet understood that, strictly speaking, *God* exists.[36]

Schufreider's treatment of *Proslogion* 4 is equally problematical.
Much like Campbell before him, he translates the passage

> *Deus enim est id quo maius cogitari non potest. Quod qui bene intelligit, utique
> intelligit id ipsum sic esse, ut nec cogitatione queat non esse. Qui ergo intelligit sic
> esse deum, nequit eum non esse cogitare.*

as

> For God is that than which a greater cannot be thought. Whoever really under-
> stands this understands clearly that this same being so exists that not even in
> thought can it not exist. Thus whoever understands that God exists in such a way
> cannot think of Him as not existing (p. 79).

Yet—as I myself at an earlier time did not recognize—it would be more
accurate to translate this passage as something like:

> For God is that than which a greater cannot be thought. Anyone who rightly
> understands this |i.e., rightly understands what is signified by "that than which a
> greater cannot be thought"|, surely understands that that |than which a greater
> cannot be thought| exists in such way that it cannot even conceivably not exist.
> Therefore, anyone who understands that God is such |a being| cannot think that
> He does not exist.

This difference of translation is subtle; but it has important implications for interpreting Anselm's line of reasoning. Anselm had just finished saying that no one who understands that which God is (*id quod deus est*) can think that God does not exist. And in the passage above he went on to reason as follows: that which God is is that than which a greater cannot be thought; therefore, whoever rightly understands what is signified by "that than which a greater cannot be thought" cannot think that God does not exist, because he cannot think that that than which a greater cannot be thought does not exist. By contrast, Schufreider sees Anselm as arguing: whoever understands that that than which a greater cannot be thought so exists that it cannot be thought not to exist cannot think that it does not exist (p. 80).

Moreover, nowhere in *Proslogion* 2-4 is there any mention of need for a special kind of rational insight of the sort spoken of by Schufreider. Indeed, Schufreider gets this peculiar notion (about how an understanding of Anselm's argument requires "reason's intuitive vision") from *Monologion* 10:

> *Aliter namque dico hominem, cum eum hoc nomine, quod est 'homo', significo; aliter, cum idem nomen tacens cogito; aliter, cum eum ipsum hominem mens aut per corporis imaginem aut per rationem intuetur. Per corporis quidem imaginem, ut cum eius sensibilem figuram imaginatur; per rationem vero, ut cum eius universalem essentiam, quae est 'animal rationale mortale', cogitat.*

> In one way I speak of a man when I signify him by the name "man." In another way |I speak of him| when I think this name silently. In a third way |I speak of a man| when my mind beholds him either by means of an image of a body or by means of reason—by means of an image of a body, for instance, when |my mind| imagines his perceptible shape; but by means of reason, for instance, when |my mind| thinks of his universal being, viz., *rational, mortal animal*.[31]

Here what Anselm means by "when my mind beholds him . . . by means of reason" is simply "when |my mind| thinks of his universal being, viz., *rational, mortal animal*." That is, Anselm is pointing out that when the mind thinks of a man as an *animal rationale mortale*, the *concept* of man is a "natural word," which is different from a spoken or a written word such as "*homo*" or "*anthropos*,"[38] and which is the same for all races. A similar point holds, he believes, regarding the mind's conceiving of any object in terms of that object's essential properties. Schufreider imports into *Proslogion* 4 this notion from *Monologion* 10 about the mind's beholding by means of reason. But when he does so, he suddenly begins

to speak of rational beholding as *a radically purified rational vision of the matter itself*—a vision in which existing creatures are *annulled* and are made to *fade from reason's sight* (p. 82).[39] But this contemplative approach is irrelevant to what is going on in *Proslogion* 2-4. Anselm does not know exactly how foolish and simple the Fool may be; but he does suppose that the Fool will have to be very foolish indeed not to recognize, upon reading *Proslogion* 2 and 3, that that than which a greater cannot be thought exists. For in order to attain this recognition, the Fool need only understand *to some extent* what it is for something to be that than which a greater cannot be thought.[40]

As for Anselm's alleged uniting of *logical* rigor with *mystical* insight (p. 95), Anselm does, in *Proslogion* 22, claim that God alone exists in an unqualified and proper sense of "existing." But this passage has no more to do with the argument of *Proslogion* 2-4 than does the claim in *Proslogion* 15 that God is greater than can be thought. Indeed, nowhere in the *Proslogion*, not even in *Proslogion* 22, does Anselm state (as he had in *Monologion* 28) that all things other than God, when compared with God, do not exist. What he rather emphasizes is that some created things are eternal and unlimited, even though they are not unqualifiedly so (*Proslogion* 13 and 20). And yet, the difference between the *Monologion* and the *Proslogion* in this regard is merely a matter of emphasis; for, with respect to this topic, nothing in the *Proslogion* is incompatible with *Monologion* 28. By comparison, there is also a difference of emphasis between *Monologion* 65, where God is said to be seen by us only obliquely and in a dark manner, and *Proslogion* 1, where Anselm seems to be seeking God's countenance and presence other than obliquely. Schufreider regards these two chapters as either incompatible or else a sign that Anselm changed his mind about the possibility of access to God's presence (p. 94). However, the two chapters are neither inconsistent nor indicative of Anselm's transformed thought. Even in *Proslogion* 1 Anselm recognizes that God dwells in light inaccessible and must be sought in signs and appearances. The extended argument which he formulates in the *Proslogion* furnishes him with the understanding that God is merciful, just, omnipotent, and so on. But it does not help him conceive divine mercy, justice, omnipotence, etc., *per se*. Anselm's vision of God in the *Proslogion* is not a vision of God *as He is in Himself*—just as there was also no such vision in *Monologion* 65. In the *Proslogion* Anselm identifies various attributes as God's; but he does not purport to

understand any of these attributes *proprie*, that is, properly. (Contrast Schufreider, p. 94.) Of course, he understands that God cannot be thought not to exist, and he understands why this is so: viz., because God is something than which a greater cannot be thought. Moreover, he understands that something than which a greater cannot be thought is whatever it is better to be than not to be (*Proslogion* 5). But he realizes that to understand all of this is still not to understand such a being as He is in Himself. Accordingly, even after having gone through the argumentation in *Proslogion* 2-5, he can continue to refer to God as Inaccessible Light (*Proslogion* 16) and can still lament the fact that His beauty is ineffable (*Proslogion* 17), His goodness incomprehensible (*Proslogion* 9). And in doing so, he is not blending—as Schufreider claims (p. 95)—the dimension of logic and the dimension of mysticism.

III

We are now in a position to realize that Schufreider's mistaken exegesis invalidates his global interpretation. For (1) strictly speaking, *Proslogion* 2 and 3, taken together, do not constitute a valid and independent argument for *God's* existence—whereas, less strictly speaking, *Proslogion* 2 by itself *does* constitute such an argument, given Anselm's assumption that God alone is something than which a greater cannot be thought. (Thus, the title of *Proslogion* 2 is neither misplaced nor intrinsically misleading.) *Proslogion* 3 takes over the conclusion of *Proslogion* 2 and goes on to argue that "God" exists so truly that He cannot even be thought not to exist. (2) By "God truly exists" Anselm does not mean, in the title of *Proslogion* 2, that God *so* exists that He cannot even be thought not to exist, but simply that God exists. (3) Anselm, though arousing his own mind for contemplating God, does not demand of his reader any special devotional or mystical arousal in order to understand his *reasoning*. He requires only that the reader understand to some extent what it is to be that than which a greater cannot be thought. The Fool, of course, must be intelligent enough to follow Anselm's reasoning; and his heart may need to be softened if he is to pass from understanding to faith. Anselm, as we gather from the *Reply to Gaunilo*,[41] is confident that his reflections, in *Proslogion* 2-4, can be followed by someone of ordinary intelligence; and as we know from the closing sentence of *Proslogion* 4, he does not confuse the order of understanding with the order of faith. Thus, *Proslogion* 2-4 is not only an argument directed *against*

the Fool but is also one designed *for* the Fool. For Anselm thinks that the Fool's coming to understand may well be the first step in God's bringing him to faith. The formula *"fides quaerens intellectum"* is never intended to exclude the possibility that, in the case of unbelievers, some measure of understanding is a prerequisite to faith. And though, ultimately speaking, even such understanding would rightly be regarded as a gift of grace, still there is no blending of the logical and the mystical in the *reasoning* of *Proslogion* 2-4 but only in the *style* in which the *Proslogion* is cast.

In his study of the *Proslogion* Schufreider has not done the careful and cautious job he promised us he was going to do. He has not brought us into "direct contact with the original argument"—whatever that was supposed to mean. The serious misprints and omissions[42] in the reprinted Latin passages are symptomatic of the lack of "direct" contact; and the many misreadings[43] witness to how far removed this new interpretation is from the "original." The foregoing examination has focused only upon some of the main discrepancies between Anselm's text and Schufreider's account.[44] But there should remain no doubt about the fact that Schufreider's account is definitive only in the sense that it is definitively wrong.

III. On the Interpretation and Translation of "Si enim vel in solo intellectu est potest cogitari esse et in re quod maius est" (*Proslogion* 2).

In an intrepid article entitled "Why Anselm's Proof in the *Proslogion* Is Not an Ontological Argument,"[45] G.E.M. Anscombe takes issue with the traditional reading of Anselm's text. According to this reading Anselm's proof in *Proslogion* 2 depends upon the premise that existence is a perfection; and as a result of this dependency it has been given the label "ontological argument."

I

In challenging the traditional reading, Anscombe proposes a corrected version of Anselm's proof—a version which eliminates the premise that existence is a perfection and which thereby undermines the rationale for considering the proof to be an "ontological argument." Her corrected version runs as follows:

    i. God = that than which nothing greater can be conceived.

ii. That than which nothing greater can be conceived exists at any rate in the intellect of the fool who says no such thing exists.

iii. If this does exist only in an intellect, what is greater than it can be thought to exist in reality as well.

iv. Therefore if something than which nothing greater can be conceived is only in the intellect, it is not something than which nothing greater can be conceived.

v. But this involves a contradiction.

vi. Therefore that than which nothing greater can be conceived exists in reality as well.[46]

A crucial feature of the "corrected" interpretation of Anselm's reasoning occurs in Step 3, whose formulation is based upon Anscombe's revisionist translation of "*Si enim vel in solo intellectu est potest cogitari esse et in re quod maius est*"[47] as: "For if it is only in the intellect, what is greater can be thought to be in reality as well." Now, were we to ask just what it is that Anselm is referring to as *greater*, and just what it is that is *greater* about it, then several answers stemming from Anselm's reply to Gaunilo suggest themselves. One such answer, explains Anscombe, would be the following:

> On the assumption that that than which nothing greater can be conceived is nothing outside the mind, we can certainly say that it is something that can not-exist, can be non-existent. But it is possible to think that that than which nothing greater can be conceived *does* exist. If it is thought of as existing, it must not be thought of as possibly not-existing. For it could be thought of as not possibly not-existing, and the thought of it as not possibly not-existing is obviously a thought of it as greater than if it is thought of as possibly not-existing. Thus the thought of it as existing *leads* to a thought of it as greater than what was thought of as not-existing. But there is here no suggestion that it is the *existing* that is the greater thing about what is thought to exist.[48]

So, then, Anscombe does consider Anselm to present in *Proslogion* 2 an *argument* for God's existence—but not an *ontological* argument. No doubt, she tells us, the *Proslogion* proof will need to be filled out by recourse to *Reply to Gaunilo*. And what will result, she claims, will be an argument that is more interesting and powerful than is the argument which traditionally has been ascribed to Anselm and which presumably depends upon the premise that existence is a perfection.

II

Anscombe's reinterpretation of *Proslogion* 2 rests in an essential way

upon her construal of "*Si enim vel in solo intellectu est potest cogitari esse et in re quod maius est*" as : "For if it is only in the intellect, what is greater can be thought to be in reality as well." One common way of punctuating the foregoing Latin sentence is "*Si enim vel in solo intellectu est, potest cogitari esse et in re, quod maius est.*" And this punctuation corresponds with the traditional way of rendering the Latin into English— viz., as something like: "For if it is only in the intellect, it can be thought to exist in reality as well, which is greater."[49] But Anscombe maintains that this way of punctuating and translating constitutes a "misinterpretation" (her word) and that the correct way of punctuating and translating will be without the comma after "*in re*": "*Si enim vel in solo intellectu est, potest cogitari esse et in re quod maius est*" ("For if it is only in the intellect, what is greater can be thought to be in reality as well").

Anscombe offers three reasons in support of her revisions. First of all, she points to manuscript evidence: "I have looked at many MSS of this passage and have not seen even one of such dots in this place"[50]—i.e., not even one dot of punctuation between "*in re*" and "*quod.*" Anscombe does not want to place too much emphasis upon this kind of evidence from manuscript punctuation; but she obviously supposes it to have some weight, because otherwise she would not have mentioned it at all. Yet, in dealing with the manuscript evidence, Anscombe has not looked far enough; and she has not looked at *all* the relevant passages. Now, she would not have had to look very far! For Latin Ms. Edinburgh 104 (University of Edinburgh) contains exactly the punctuation that Anscombe did not find; and this manuscript is one of the very codices explicitly compared by F. S. Schmitt in his edition of the *Opera Omnia Anselmi.* Furthermore, Anscombe, in consulting whatever manuscripts she did—and it would have been appropriate for her to cite these by name—apparently looked only at *Proslogion* 2. However, she should also have consulted two other passages: viz., (1) *Proslogion* 2 as it was recopied ("*Sumptum ex eodem libello*") for the appendix that contains the *Debate with Gaunilo*,[51] and (2) the almost exact reoccurrence—of the sentence in question—that is found in *Reply to Gaunilo* 2:12-13. As a case in point, let us take Latin Ms. Bodley 271 at Oxford University: in the sentence now under discussion no dot occurs between "*in re*" and "*quod*" either in *Proslogion* 2 or in *Sumptum ex eodem libello*; but there *is* a dot in the sentence found in *Reply* 2:12-13. As another case in point, let us take Latin Ms. Rawlinson A.392, also at Oxford University's

Bodleian Library: again, neither in *Proslogion* 2 nor in *Sumptum ex eodem libello* is there a pause between "*in re*" and "*quod*"; but, again, there *is* such a pause in *Reply* 2:12-13. By contrast, Edinburgh 104, which has the dot both in *Proslogion* 2 and in *Sumptum ex eodem libello*, does not have it in *Reply* 2:12-13.

In last analysis, the alleged evidence from manuscript punctuation can be ignored. Such punctuation was often impressionistic or impulsive; in general, it cannot be relied upon. Anscombe herself seems to put only slight credence in it. Yet, it is surprising that she even bothers to mention it at all—and still more surprising that, having mentioned it, she does not carefully explore the matter more fully, by examining all the manuscripts upon which F. S. Schmitt based his critical edition. "I have looked at many MSS of this passage and have not seen . . . " is no proper substitute for scholarly methodicalness.

A second of Anscombe's reasons in support of her revised punctuation and translation of the sentence in question is truly amazing: "If . . . you leave out that comma, you get better Latin . . . . "[52] She follows this up with "Anselm wrote beautiful Latin." There seems to be some intimation here that because Anselm wrote beautiful Latin and because you get better Latin by leaving out the comma, Anselm did not intend for there to be a comma between "*in re*" and "*quod*"—or, at least, he would not sanction any editor's or copyist's putting one there. But whether or not such a claim is intimated or implied, and whether or not Anselm is judged to have written beautiful Latin,[53] the important issue is really whether or not the disputed sentence constitutes better Latin without the comma than with it. Are we not entitled to ask?: by what plausible criteria could the sentence "*Si enim vel in solo intellectu est, potest cogitari esse et in re quod maius est*" be deemed to be *better* Latin than the sentence "*Si enim vel in solo intellectu est, potest cogitari esse et in re, quod maius est*"? Are we, perhaps, supposed to find something objectionable about a grammatical construction in which "*quod*" functions as a relative pronoun whose antecedent is an entire phrase? If so, then we would have to raise the same kind of objection regarding the use of "*quod*" in *Monologion* 7:33; 7:40; 8:51; 15:17; 18:28; 18:38; 19:30; 21:10; 21:36; 24:20; 31:13; 31:15; 32:18; 33:25; 70:23; 76:16; 78:7; 79:11—as well as in *Proslogion* 3:7; 3:12; 13:13; 13:14; 13;16, etc. And the multitude of such objections—if Anscombe were to make them—would be bound to detract from her judgment about the beauty of

Anselm's Latin. And yet, is not the following the case?: precisely because
Anselm does so frequently use "*quod*" in this free-ranging way, it is not
unnatural for us to construe "*quod*" in the same way in *Proslogion* 2. On
the other hand, if this syntactical use of "*quod*" is not what Anscombe
has in mind when she judges that on her interpretation Anselm turns out
to be writing better Latin, then she owes us an explication of her cryptic
remark.

Apparently, Anscombe entertains a third reason in support of her
revised punctuation and translation: viz., that under her interpretation
Anselm's reasoning becomes more interesting and powerful. No longer is
his reasoning deemed to rest upon the metaphysically dubious assumption that existence is a perfection—an assumption that is not explicitly
made in *Proslogion* 2. Instead, his reasoning may now be expanded—
e.g., in the way that he expands it in the *Reply to Gaunilo*—so that it
depends upon some different, but obviously true, claim: e.g., the claim
that "the thought of it [viz., of that than which nothing greater can be
conceived] as not possibly not-existing is . . . a thought of it as greater
than if it is thought of as possibly not-existing."[54] Now, Anscombe's new
way of formulating Anselm's argument may well provide us with a
proof that is philosophically superior to the traditional way of formulating
it. But the question before us is not the question of which version holds
philosophical superiority over which. The question is, which version is a
more accurate interpretation of Anselm's actual reasoning in *Proslogion*
2? And in order to answer *this* question reliably, we will need to know
what textual evidence there is in favor of Anscombe's interpretation. It
will not be enough for us merely to invoke some *a priori* principle such
as the principle of charitable construals and to urge that this principle
obliges us to put the best possible face on Anselm's reasoning. Nor will it
be acceptable to beg the interpretive question by having recourse to the
principle that Anselm was too astute a thinker not to have meant "*quod
est maius*" in Anscombe's sense rather than in the alternative sense. So
the fact that Anscombe's reading of "*quod maius est*" makes for a more
interesting and powerful argument does not, by itself, at all show that
this more powerful argument was Anselm's actual argument in *Proslogion* 2.

Anscombe offers, at most, the foregoing three defenses of her claim
that the traditional interpretation of *Proslogion* 2 is a misinterpretation.
But since the last defense (if Anscombe is really employing it) cannot

stand up by itself, and since the first two defenses are so feeble as to be discountable, Anscombe has not at all done what she set out to do: "I will now shew that the whole thing *is* a misinterpretation."[55] And having failed to fault the traditional interpretation, she has no basis for continuing to claim that her reinterpretation is superior. But might we, then, regard her not as providing a *more defensible* interpretation but as providing an *equally viable* one? Might Anselm's text be compatible with both the traditional reading and Anscombe's reading?—so that if an interpreter has a penchant for believing that Anselm was a pretty good metaphysician, he may admissibly select Anscombe's reading; and if he has a different penchant, he may select the traditional reading, though neither selection will be obviously right (or obviously wrong). To these queries the only exegetically possible answer is "absolutely not." For Anscombe's reading can itself be shown to be a misinterpretation. The evidence that refutes her comes from *Reply to Gaunilo* 2:12-13, where Anselm recapitulates the disputed segment of *Proslogion* 2:

> *Postea dixi quia si est vel in solo intellectu, potest cogitari esse et in re quod maius est. Si ergo in solo est intellectu: idipsum, scilicet quo maius non potest cogitari, est quo maius cogitari potest. Rogo quid consequentius? An enim si est vel in solo intellectu, non potest cogitari esse et in re?*[56]

The first Latin sentence, by itself, admits of being construed as Anscombe construes it. But the last Latin sentence does not admit of Anscombe's construal.[57] Now, the last sentence explicates the meaning of the first sentence; and, thus, it precludes our construing the first sentence as Anscombe does. Since the first sentence is but a restatement of the sentence in *Proslogion* 2, Anscombe's understanding of Anselm's meaning in *Proslogion* 2 is erroneous.[58]

III

There is good reason to infer that Anselm did subscribe to the metaphysical doctrine that existence is a perfection. For in *Monologion* 36 we read:

> No one doubts that created substances exist in themselves much differently from the way they exist in our knowledge. For in themselves they exist in virtue of their own being; but in our knowledge their likenesses exist, not their own being. It follows, then, that the more truly they exist anywhere by virtue of their own being than by virtue of their likenesses, the more truly they exist in themselves than in our knowledge.

Here Anselm tells us that a thing exists more truly in reality than it exists
in our mind. Now, both from *Monologion* 31 and from *Proslogion* 3:13-
15 we know that Anselm correlates *existing truly* with *existing greatly*.[59]
And in both the *Monologion* and the *Proslogion* a thing's degree of
existing greatly is correlated with its degree of perfection.[60] The clearest
statement of this correlation occurs in *Monologion* 31:

> From some substance which lives, perceives, and reasons let us mentally remove
> |first| what is rational, next what is sentient, then what is vital, and finally the
> remaining bare existence. Now, who would not understand that this substance,
> thus destroyed step by step, is gradually reduced to less and less existence—and, in
> the end, to nonexistence? Yet, those |characteristics| which when removed one at a
> time reduce a being to less and less existence increase its existence more and more
> when added |to it| again in reverse order. Therefore, it is clear that a living sub-
> stance exists more than does a nonliving one, that a sentient substance exists more
> than does a nonsentient one, and that a rational substance exists more than does a
> nonrational one. So without doubt every being exists more and is more excellent
> to the extent that it is more like that Being which exists supremely and is
> supremely excellent.[61]

So since, on Anselm's view, *existing more truly* entails *existing more
greatly*, and *existing more greatly* entails *being more excellent*, or *being
more perfect*, then just as a thing which exists in reality exists more truly
than it would if it existed only in our mind through its likeness, so too it
is more perfect than it would be if it existed only in our mind. And
Anselm's reason for affirming that it is more perfect is that he considers
its own bare existence (*nudum esse*) to be as much a perfection as are
life or sentience or rationality. Accordingly, there is no need to shy away
from the traditional interpretation of *Proslogion* 2—to do so, say, on the
alleged (*a priori*) ground that Anselm was too astute a metaphysician to
countenance the view that existence is a perfection.[62]

IV

Three other weaknesses in Anscombe's article should, perhaps, not be
left unnoticed. (1) To begin with, the article is not true to Anselm's
articulation in *Proslogion* 2—where he uses both "*aliquid quo maius
nihil cogitari potest*" and "*id quo maius cogitari nequit*." Now, although
in *Proslogion* 2 Anselm's argument begins with the *credo* that God is
something than which nothing greater can be thought, Anscombe's version of the argument begins with the *definition* of God as *that* than
which nothing greater can be conceived. Hereby the question is begged

against people such as Richard Campbell[63] when it is *assumed* that Anselm's formula *"aliquid quo . . ."* is equivalently interchangeable with his formula *"id quo . . . ."* (2) Moreover, in maintaining that Anselm's *credo* serves to enunciate a *definition* of God, Anscombe nowhere rebuts, or even takes seriously, the reasons advanced by Richard La Croix,[64] and repeated by Richard Campbell,[65] as to why Anselm ought not to be understood as setting forth a *definition* in *Proslogion* 2. (3) A further weakness is disclosed when Anscombe takes Anselm's expression *"unum argumentum,"* in the *Proslogion* preface, as meaning "single argument." "We know," she proclaims, "that Anselm wanted to give a very short single argument. And this he did." Since this knowledge can be gleaned only from Anselm's preface, we may presume that Anscombe's words "single argument" are a rendering of Anselm's *"unum argumentum."* If this presumption is correct, as it appears to be, then Anscombe has once again propounded a falsehood. For Anselm aims to find *unum argumentum quod nullo alio ad se probandum quam se solo indigeret, et solum ad astruendum quia deus vere est, et quia est summum bonum nullo alio indigens, et quo omnia indigent ut sint et ut bene sint, et quaecumque de divina credimus substantia, sufficeret."* And, assuredly, the very short single argument of *Proslogion* 2 does not suffice to do all of this.

In retrospect, Anscombe's article betrays a certain unfamiliarity not only with Anselm's texts and with the manuscript tradition but also with the secondary literature of the past fifteen years. This unfamiliarity partly occasions her scholarly sins—of omission and of commission—in promulgating a *reconstruction*-of-Anselm's-reasoning under the guise of a textually more accurate *interpretation*. But her shortcomings also partly proceed from too sympathetic an appreciation of the mind of St. Anselm. Recognizing, as she must, the problematical features of an ontological argument, and admiring, as she does, the genius of Anselm's intellect, she charitably devises a way—by expunging a single comma—to transform the dubious argument into a *prima facie* more powerful proof.

IV. On the Present Edition and Translation.

The Latin text contained in the present volume improves in only minor[66] respects upon the text edited by F. S. Schmitt in his *Opera Omnia Anselmi.*[67] Like Schmitt's edition, this one, as well, principally follows Latin Ms. Bodley 271, once at Christ Church in Canterbury, now at the

Bodleian Library of Oxford University.[68] Unlike Schmitt's edition the present one is uncritical in the sense that it makes no attempt to compare all the significant manuscripts,[69] or even all the leading ones. Yet, it is as reliable a text as is Schmitt's, which seldom veers from Bodley 271. Indeed, Bodley 271, in spite of its many erasures, is still the preeminent manuscript of Anselm's works.[70]

I

In transcribing the Latin texts, I have made various editorial decisions, three of which should be mentioned here: (1) I place the chapter-titles for the *Monologion* and for the *Proslogion* at the beginning, *before* the respective works themselves, as does Bodley 271; but I also repeat them in the Latin text, whereas Bodley 271 repeats only the chapter-numbers—placing them in the margin, while marking in the text the spot where each chapter is to begin. (2) I divide into sections the texts of the debate between Anselm and Gaunilo, even though no such divisions are found in Bodley 271. My sections correspond to Schmitt's—except for the positioning of the first numeral in the *Reply to Gaunilo*. (3) I do not reproduce—immediately prior to Gaunilo's *On Behalf of the Fool*—Chapters 2-4 of the *Proslogion,* as does Bodley 271. For even in Bodley 271 there is not a single word of difference between these chapters as they occur in the *Proslogion* proper and as they are repeated for the debate.

I cannot here signal all the intricacies of all the translation-decisions that needed to be made. Instead, I will give but two examples—a brief one and an extended one. Since Anselm does not methodically distinguish his use of "*non omnino*" from his use of "*omnino non*,"[71] a translator is completely dependent upon the context for deciding whether these always mean "not at all" or whether sometimes "*non omnino*" is being used to signify "not altogether,"—just as, at *Reply to Gaunilo* 1:59, "*non penitus*" signifies "not altogether." In particular, the translator is completely dependent upon the context with regard to the construal of "*non omnino*" at *Reply to Gaunilo* 7:11, where Anselm's point will be seen to differ crucially in relation to whichever construal is made. A similar dependence holds true for *Proslogion* 22:4, where "*non omnino*" also occurs ambiguously, but with a meaning ostensibly different from the meaning at *Reply* 7:11.

The second, more extended, example concerns the best way to translate "*aliquid quo maius nihil cogitari potest*" (or "*id quo maius . . .* "). For "*cogitare*" can be rendered into English both by "to think" and by "to think of"—even as "*dicere*" can be rendered both by "to say" and by "to speak of." So would it not be more accurate to employ the translation "something than which nothing greater can be thought of," as does G. E.M. Anscombe, than to make use of the translation "something than which a greater cannot be thought"?[72] For in the Latin expression does not "*cogitari*" have the same meaning as "*concipi*"?—i.e., as "to be conceived." And does not "to be conceived" mean "to be thought *of*"? Moreover, although Anselm on no occasion uses "*concipi*" in his expression "*aliquid quo maius . . . ,* " does not his use of both "*cogito*" and "*concipio*" in one and the same sentence at *Monologion* 65:32-35 show that in some contexts the two words are interchangeable? And is not the context of our conceiving of God just such a context?[73] Now, while not denying any of these latter considerations, I have nonetheless preferred to render "*cogitari*," in the foregoing expression, simply as "to be thought" (though elsewhere I do at times render the passive form of "*cogitare*" as " . . . thought of"[74]). Various reasons underlie this choice. Foremost among them is the conviction that Anselm's reasoning in *Proslogion* 4 and in *Reply to Gaunilo* 9 comes into English somewhat more clearly, plausibly, and accurately—or, at least, more smoothly—if the expression in question does not terminate with "of." Similarly, when in *Proslogion* 4 Anselm writes "*Aliter enim cogitatur res cum vox eam significans cogitatur . . . ,*" I render it as "For in one way a thing is thought when the word signifying it is thought . . . . " But an alternative rendering is also possible: "For in one way a thing is thought of when the word signifying it is thought . . . . "[75] (I tend to avoid this rendering, partly because it does not fit as well with my preference for "God can be thought not to exist" over "God can be thought of as not existing.")[76] However, I would deem the following alternative not to be acceptable: viz., "For in one way a thing is thought of when the word signifying it is thought of . . . . " For Anselm does not mean thinking of the word itself but rather attempting to think the word's signification.[77] After all, the Fool can think of the word "God" quite easily; but, as Anselm concedes in *Reply to Gaunilo* 7: 10-11, the Fool might not at all think the meaning (*sensus*) of the word "God".

Much of the difficulty about when to translate Anselm's Latin by

words such as "think" or "hear," rather than by words such as "think of" or "hear of," arises from the fact that Anselm does not carefully distinguish between understanding the expression "something than which a greater cannot be thought" and understanding that which is described by this expression. In *Proslogion* 2 he says: "But surely when this very same Fool hears my words 'something than which nothing greater can be thought,' he understands what he hears. And what he understands is in his understanding . . . . " Now, rightly understanding the expression seems to be the criterion for having in the understanding that which is thus described (not the criterion for having the describing words in the understanding). Hence, the corresponding Latin sentence in *Reply to Gaunilo* 2:4-5 requires an interpretive expansion, so that the entire sentence will read in English: "Next, I said that if it is understood, |what is understood| is in the understanding." Here "it" refers to the description "that than which a greater cannot be thought"; thus, the unexpanded translation would not be correct (viz., "Next, I said that if it is understood, it is in the understanding"). In any event, there is no way for a translator to escape importing interpretation into his English translation of various of Anselm's Latin sentences. For in those sentences the Latin can be translated by him only in the manner in which he understands it; and any of the alternative, linguistically admissible, understandings will constitute, necessarily, interpretation.

So readers of the present translation are cautioned that this rendition is necessarily interpretive in the ways just signaled. Yet, it is *conservatively* interpretive; and it aims at unfolding Anselm's true meaning. It may not altogether succeed; but neither does it extensively fail. The degree of its success or failure can be *argued*, in the way that I argue against the translation and the construal offered by G.E.M. Anscombe. Now, though I regard the notion of Anselm's "true meaning" as both meaningful and normative, I do not believe that there is anything such as a normative, or definitive, *translation*.[78] Nor do I know by what criteria we could decide whether or not some given *account* of one or more of Anselm's doctrines was a definitive account. The use of the epithet "definitive account" belies not only the fact of historical distance but also the fact of the cognitive distance between any two contemporary minds—indeed, the distance between one and the same individual mind at two different times. For which philosopher can give a definitive account of even his

own past thinking? Schleiermacher's slogan to the effect that the aim of interpretation is to understand an author better than he understood himself must be taken seriously. But it is not at odds with the aim to recapture the author's meaning. For the *author's* thought can be elucidated *only if it is recaptured*; and in elucidating it, an interpreter may well show that he understands it better than the author himself. Thus, a translation differs from an interpretation as such, even though the former necessarily embodies interpretive elements. For a translation does not seek to elucidate an author's meaning in the more holistic manner of an interpretation. The translation of Anselm's clause "*Aliter enim cogitatur res cum vox eam significans cogitatur . . .* " as "For in one way a thing is thought when the word signifying it is thought . . . " embodies an interpretive element insofar as it differs from the translation "For in one way a thing is thought of when the word signifying it is thought of . . . "—or insofar as it renders "*vox*" by "word" rather than by "sound." One of these translations will be better—more accurate—than the other. But each will be a *translation* of the Latin, not an *interpretation* as such. For an interpretation will do more: it will seek to elicit Anselm's view, as intimated here, about the relationship between words, thoughts, significations, and real things. And it will be forced to have recourse to other relevant texts within the Anselmian corpus—recourse that is much more elaborate than is anything required of a translator *qua* translator. Even in those cases where the differences between translating and interpreting are said to be simply "differences of degree," still—as the saying goes—differences of degree, if extended far enough, become differences of kind.[79]

So when I disagree with Campbell or Schufreider or Anscombe, I am disagreeing with their *understanding* of Anselm's line of reasoning, as well as with certain of their translations. But in so disagreeing, I am not assuming that my own translations are "something like canonical," as Schufreider querulously charges.[80] In fact, several of my criticisms of Schufreider and of Campbell are also criticisms of my own previously held views. I abandoned these views not because I authoritatively and autocratically decided one day to issue a new ruling, a *Machtspruch*, but because I came to believe them false. And some of the reasons behind my belief are discernible in, and inferable from, the present introduction, notes, text, and translation. All in all, I am willing to say with Anselm: "*Si cui vero aliter visum fuerit, nullius respuo sententiam, si vera probari*

poterit."[81] And, like Anselm, I here intend *"probari"* in a generous sense.

II

That the *Monologion* and the *Proslogion* have engendered so many different interpretive accounts is due in part to Anselm's employment of *usitatus sermo*—i.e., everyday speech, nontechnical terms. A perfect example of this usage occurs in *Monologion* 8:29-40, where he interchanges *"modus," "sensus," "significatio,"* and *"interpretatio"*—not making any special distinction between them. Likewise, in *Monologion* 19:25-38 he interchanges *"sententia," "sensus," "intellectus,"* and *"interpretatio"*— again without any special distinction between them. Nor is there a distinction between the use of *"designare"* and the use of *"significare"*[82] at *Monologion* 24:7-8. *"Essentia"* is used sometimes as a substitute for *"substantia,"* sometimes as a substitute for *"existentia."* *"Subsistens,"* as it occurs at the end of *Monologion* 6, has no different meaning from *"existens,"*[83] also found there. In *Proslogion* 14:4 *"melius"* appears in place of the more usual *"maius."*[84] Moreover, *"intelligi"* and *"cogitari"* are used interchangeably in *Proslogion* 9:43-44, even as in *Proslogion* 14:31 and *Monologion* 7:14 *"intelligi"* could equally well have been replaced by *"cogitari."* In *Reply to Gaunilo* 4 Anselm does, of course, defend his exclusive use of *"cogitari"* vis-à-vis his claim that *id quo maius cogitari nequit, non esse nequit* COGITARI. But he bases his defense upon his mistaken belief that Gaunilo is operating with a technical construal of *"intelligere."* And so, he adapts his terminology in such way as, putatively, to rebut Gaunilo.

As an example of the intellectual havoc wrought by Anselm's reliance upon *usitatus sermo*, let us look again at a section in *Monologion* 10:

Frequenti namque usu cognoscitur quia rem unam tripliciter loqui possumus. Aut enim res loquimur signis sensibilibus, id est quae sensibus corporeis sentiri possunt, sensibiliter utendo; aut eadem signa, quae foris sensibilia sunt, intra nos insensibiliter cogitando; aut nec sensibiliter nec insensibiliter his signis utendo, sed res ipsas vel corporum imaginatione vel rationis intellectu pro rerum ipsarum diversitate intus in nostra mente dicendo. Aliter namque dico hominem cum eum hoc nomine, quod est "homo," significo; aliter cum idem nomen tacens cogito; aliter cum eum ipsum hominem mens aut per corporis imaginem aut per rationem intuetur—per corporis quidem imaginem ut cum eius sensibilem figuram imaginatur; per rationem vero ut cum eius universalem essentiam, quae est animal rationale mortale, cogitat.

In the second sentence Anselm interchanges "*eadem signa . . . intra nos insensibiliter cogitando*" and "*insensibiliter his signis utendo.*" This substitution is noteworthy because it discloses that "*eadem signa . . . cogitando*" should be translated as (something like) "by thinking . . . these same signs," rather than as "by thinking of . . . these same signs." For "imperceptibly using a sign" here indicates thinking the signification of the sign, not thinking of the sign. This fact further emerges from the beginning of the third sentence: " *. . . cum eum hoc nomine, quod est 'homo,' significo . . . .* " Anselm's point here is that, in one way, I speak of a man when I signify him by means of the perceptible name "man." But Anselm goes on to state: "*aliter cum idem nomen tacens cogito . . . .*" A correct translation of this clause would be " *. . .* in another way when I think this name silently . . . ." What Anselm means by thinking the name "man" silently is *signifying a man by means of this imperceptible name.* Unless Anselm's use of language is recognized to be loose and informal—i.e., nontechnical—it can easily foster the misimpression that *eadem signa cogitando* is something other than *eisdem signis significando.* That is, someone might easily suppose that Anselm is here making a distinction which, in fact, he is not here making. For what Anselm is distinguishing between here is the proposition "*eum hoc nomine |sensibili| significo*" and the proposition "*eum hoc nomine |insensibili| significo*"—and the latter he expresses as "*idem nomen tacens cogito.*" Anselm is not careful to make his point readily clear. For he does not realize that someone might fall into confusion regarding either these foregoing two expressions or the expressions "*eadem signa . . . insensibiliter cogitando*" and "*insensibiliter his signis utendo*"—these latter being interchangeable *salva veritate* in the context at hand.

The problem that arises with respect to the foregoing pericope in *Monologion* 10 arises because the reader has a tendency to see Anselm as introducing a certain distinction—a distinction which, in actuality, he is *not* introducing.[85] However, sometimes exactly the reverse occurs: the reader, on the basis of Anselm's unembellished style, has a tendency not to see a distinction that really is being made. Such an oversight occurs, for example, in *Proslogion* 4:13-14, where Anselm switches from "*intelligit id ipsum sic esse ut . . .*" to "*intelligit sic esse deum . . . .*" Most translators take both occurrences of "*sic*" as adverbial, though the second occurrence is adjectival. In another vein, some distinctions that

were not insisted upon by Anselm should be insisted upon by us. Many translators fail to reckon with the fact that many of the sentences in *Proslogion* 2-4 (and elsewhere) should be rendered into English by the subjunctive (even though Anselm's simplified style led him to use the indicative).[86] For many of the premises are intended by Anselm to be contrary-to-fact conditional statements. And in English (as also properly in Latin) the verbs of such conditionals should be put into the subjunctive mood.[87]

Sometimes it is not clear, *prima facie*, whether Anselm is really making a distinction or not. Thus, a second look at *Proslogion* 2 is required in order to ascertain why Anselm switches from the expression "*aliquid quo maius nihil cogitari potest*" to the expression "*id quo maius cogitari nequit*" and then back again to the former. At other times Anselm is viewed by interpreters as using a term technically, when actually he is not. A. Stolz, for example, wrongly treats "*vere esse*" and its variants, as these occur in the title of *Proslogion* 2 and throughout *Proslogion* 3, as technical terms having to do with mystical theology.[88] And Kurt Flasch wrongly regards various expressions that are found in *Monologion* 1-4 as substitutes for the technical theological expression "*participare dei*," which itself is not found in *Monologion* 1-4.[89]

III

Since Anselm is not always careful in expressing his philosophical views,[90] we must be careful for him. Thus, although he does include the word "*aliud*" where it is needed in *Proslogion* 3:14 ("*quidquid aliud est . . .* "), he does not include it at *Monologion* 60:18 (" *. . . quidquid summae essentiae necesse est inesse*") or at *Reply to Gaunilo* 5:37-39 ("*Nullatenus enim potest intelligi quo maius cogitari non possit nisi id quod solum omnibus est maius*"), where it is also needed and where, assuredly, it is tacitly understood.[91] Moreover, certain of Anselm's sentences will have to be translated in such way as to bring out his points more clearly in English than they are expressed in Latin. In *Reply to Gaunilo* 1:24, for example, Anselm does not express his meaning unambiguously in speaking of that than which a greater cannot be thought: "*Si ergo cogitari potest esse, ex necessitate est.*" From a comparison of this sentence, in its immediate context, with the broader context of the *Proslogion,* we can discern that Anselm understands the signification of "*ex necessitate*" to apply to the *inference*, not to the *existence*. Accord-

ingly, instead of the contextually faulty translation "Therefore, if it can be thought to exist, it exists of necessity," a correct rendering will (perhaps) have recourse to an expansion: "Therefore, if it can be thought to exist, |there follows|, of necessity, |that| it exists."[92] (*Either* rendering—whether this correct one or the foregoing incorrect one—will, necessarily, include interpretation.) By comparison, Anselm also is not cautious in expressing his point in *Reply* 2:5-6: "*An est in nullo intellectu, quod necessario in rei veritate esse monstratum est?*" For, once again, the necessity that is signified (by "*necessario*") is intended to apply to the *inference*.

Imprecisions of other kinds are also to be found in Anselm's expressions— e.g., his ambiguous use of demonstrative and relative pronouns. In *Proslogion* 4:13 ("*Quod qui bene intelligit . . .*") the antecedent of "*Quod*" is not immediately clear. Is it the entire preceding sentence or merely the description "*id quo maius cogitari non potest*"? Only a second, more studious, look will disclose the intended scope of the reference. In this instance the translator, in his translation, need not do more than render "*Quod*" as "this," thus letting each reader come to his own decision regarding the scope of the reference. Yet, unless the translator, in his own mind, discerns correctly the intended antecedent of "*Quod*," he will more than likely *mistranslate* the sentence which succeeds "*Quod qui bene intelligit . . .*"—viz., the sentence "*Qui ergo intelligit sic esse deum, nequit eum non esse cogitare.*" Indeed, some of the mistranslations that are made by Campbell, Schufreider, and Anscombe result from misinterpretations, even as some of their misinterpretations result from mistranslations. What better evidence could there be of Anselm's imprecisions—of the fact that he did not weigh each word exactly[93]—than that his sentences could mislead these intelligent philosophers? And, yet, these very philosophers need not have been misled! For from the *Monologion*, the entire *Proslogion,* and the *Debate with Gaunilo* enough can be learned about Anselm's programmatic aims, his metaphysical assumptions, and his Latin style to allow even his imprecise expressions to be understood as he intended them to be understood.

Within the limitations established for the present Introduction, no fuller discussion of the mind of St. Anselm is possible. But enough has been said to disclose the many complexities that make Anselm's thoughts anything but easy to grasp. Though the Introduction focuses the reader's attention upon the *Proslogion* more than upon the *Monologion*, the justi-

fication for doing so is obvious: viz., that there is a more pressing exigency to rectify recent misinterpretations of Anselm's reasoning in the *Proslogion* than in the *Monologion*.[94] Nonetheless, both treatises should be studied together. For not only was the second one written with the first one in mind but both proceed via the same method of *necessariis rationibus*, as Anselm himself reminds us in *De Incarnatione Verbi* 6:

> If anyone will deign to read my two short works, viz., the *Monologion* and the *Proslogion*, which I wrote especially in order |to show| that what we hold by faith regarding the divine nature and its persons (excluding the topic of incarnation) can be proved by compelling reasons, apart from |appeal to| the authority of Scripture—if, I say, anyone is willing to read these works, then I think that he will there discover, with regard to the matter before us, arguments which he neither will be able to disprove nor will want to treat lightly.

Whether or not someone be able to disprove Anselm's arguments, surely no one with any sense would presume to treat them lightly.

PRAENOTANDA

Where, for clarification, words from the Latin text are inserted into the translation, the following rule is employed: when the Latin term is noted exactly as it appears in the Latin text, parentheses are used; when the case endings of nouns are transformed to the nominative, strokes are used.

Strokes are used in place of brackets, as an aid to readability. *English* words and phrases thus "bracketed" are supplied by the translator to fill out the meaning implied by the Latin text.

PRAENOTANDA FOR THE LATIN TEXT

The printed Latin text follows manuscript *B*. Where two folia are missing from *B*—viz., at the beginning of the *Monologion*—the text follows manuscript *T*. Where *T* is partly illegible, the printed text follows *E* and indicates in the notes the reading found in *S*.

In the text itself spelling, punctuation, and capitalization are editorialized.

In the variant readings punctuation, but not spelling, is editorialized, as is also capitalization.

OTHER PRAENOTANDA

The present bibliography is supplementary to the bibliographies contained in my previous works *A Companion to the Study of St. Anselm* and *Anselm of Canterbury: Volume Four: Hermeneutical and Textual Problems in the Complete Treatises of St. Anselm.* Accordingly, not all the entries in the present bibliography are directly relevant to the present topics and themes; and some entries that *are* directly relevant occur in the earlier bibliographies.

The numbering of the Psalms accords with the Douay Version of the Bible and, in parentheses, with the King James Version.

ABBREVIATIONS

ABBREVIATIONS IN THE BIBLIOGRAPHY AND THE ENGLISH NOTES

M	*Monologion*
P	*Proslogion*
S	*Sancti Anselmi Opera Omnia* (ed. F. S. Schmitt). E.g., 'S I, 237:7' indicates Vol. I, p. 237, line 7.
DT	*De Trinitate* (Augustine).
PF	*Ein neues unvollendetes Werk des hl. Anselm von Canterbury,* edited by F. S. Schmitt (*Beiträge zur Geschichte der Philosophie und Theologie des Mittelalters,* 33/3). Münster, Germany: Aschendorff Press, 1936.
PL	Patrologia Latina, ed. J.-P. Migne. Series published in Paris.
SB II	Raymond Foreville, editor. *Spicilegium Beccense II: Actes du colloque international du CNRS: Études anselmiennes IVe Session: Les mutations socio-culturelles au tournant des XIe - XIIe siècles.* Paris: Éditions du Centre National de la Recherche Scientifique, 1984.
CCSL	*Corpus Christianorum, Series Latina.* Series published in Turnhout, Belgium.

The standard abbreviations are used for books of the Bible.

All references to the Latin text of the *Monologion,* the *Proslogion,* and the *Debate with Gaunilo* are given in terms of the chapter and line numbers of the present edition. E.g., '*M* 3:4' stands for '*Monologion* Chap. 3, line 4.'

B	Bodleian Library Latin manuscript 271 (Oxford, England); beginning of 12th c.
E	University of Edinburgh Latin manuscript 104 (Edinburgh, Scotland); 12th c.
S	Bibliothèque Nationale de Paris Latin manuscript 13413; end of 11th c.
T	Bodleian Library Latin manuscript Rawlinson A.392 (Oxford, England); end of 11th c.

add.	*addit; addunt*
cf.	*confer*
coni.	*coniecit*
corr.	*corrigit; corrigunt*
del.	*delet; delent*
in marg.	*in margine*
lin.	*linea; lineam*
om.	*omittit; omittunt*

MONOLOGION

PROLOGUS

Quidam fratres saepe me studioseque precati sunt ut quaedam quae illis de meditanda divinitatis essentia et quibusdam aliis huiusmodi meditationi cohaerentibus usitato sermone colloquendo protuleram, sub quodam eis meditationis exemplo describerem. Cuius scilicet scribendae meditationis,
5 magis secundum suam voluntatem quam secundum rei facilitatem aut meam possibilitatem, hanc mihi formam praestituerunt: quatenus auctoritate scripturae penitus nihil in ea persuaderetur, sed quidquid per singulas investigationes finis assereret, id ita esse plano stilo et vulgaribus argumentis simplicique disputatione et rationis necessitas breviter cogeret
10 et veritatis claritas patenter ostenderet. Voluerunt etiam ut nec simplicibus paeneque fatuis obiectionibus mihi occurrentibus obviare contemnerem.

Quod quidem diu tentare recusavi, atque me cum re ipsa comparans multis me rationibus excusare tentavi. Quanto enim id quod petebant usu sibi optabant facilius, tanto illud mihi actu iniungebant difficilius.
15 Tandem tamen, victus cum precum modesta importunitate tum studii eorum non contemnenda honestate, invitus quidem propter rei difficultatem et ingenii mei imbecillitatem, quod precabantur incepi; sed libenter propter eorum caritatem quantum potui secundum ipsorum definitionem effeci. Ad quod cum ea spe sim adductus, ut quidquid facerem, illis solis
20 a quibus exigebatur, esset notum, et paulo post eisdem idipsum ut vilem rem fastidientibus contemptu esset obruendum (scio enim me in eo non tam precantibus satisfacere potuisse, quam precibus me prosequentibus finem posuisse), nescio tamen quo pacto sic praeter spem evenit ut non solum praedicti fratres sed et plures alii scripturam ipsam quisque sibi
25 eam transcribendo, in longum memoriae commendare satagerent.

Quam ego saepe retractans nihil potui invenire me in ea dixisse quod non

---

Prologus: *Folia initia desunt in B*   Incipit prologus in monologion librum Anselmi *T*
11 paeneque: peneque *habebat T, sed litterae* p *et* n *iam non plene visibiles sunt*   peneque *habent ES*
12 Quod: *abbreviatio iam non visibilis T*   Quod *habent ES*
13 multis: *litterae* tis *non plene visibiles T*   multis *ES*
19 facerem: ē *finalis iam non visibilis T*   facerem *ES*
20 idipsum: *littera* s *iam non visibilis T*   idipsum *ES*

Certain brothers have frequently and earnestly entreated me to write out for them, in the form of a meditation, certain things which I had discussed in nontechnical terms with them regarding meditating on the Divine Being[1] and regarding certain other |themes| related to a meditation of this kind. For the writing of this meditation they prescribed—in accordance more with their own wishes than with the ease of the task or with my ability—the following format: that nothing at all in the meditation would be argued on Scriptural authority, but that in unembellished style and by unsophisticated arguments and with uncomplicated disputation rational necessity would tersely prove to be the case, and truth's clarity would openly manifest to be the case, whatever the conclusion resulting from the distinct inquiries would declare. They also desired that I not disdain to refute simple and almost foolish objections which would occur to me.

For a long time I was reluctant to attempt this; and comparing myself with the task, I tried on many grounds to make excuses for myself. For the more readily they wished that what they were seeking should be of practical use to them, the more difficult they were making it for me to accomplish what they sought. But at last, overcome by the modest insistence of their entreaties as well as by the commendable probity of their earnestness, I began |to undertake| what they were entreating, |even though| I was |still| reluctant because of the difficulty of the task and the weakness of my intellectual power. But because of their love I gladly and to the best of my ability finished |it| in accordance with their prescription. I was induced to this |undertaking| by the expectation that whatever I did would be known only to those who made the request |of me| and that after a while they would overwhelm it with contempt, scorning it as a thing of little value. For in this |undertaking|, I know, I was not so much able to satisfy those who were entreating |me| as I was able to put an end to the entreaties that were pursuing me. Nevertheless, contrary to my expectation, it somehow turned out that not only the aforementioned brothers but also several others were engaged in committing this treatise to posterity by each making a copy for himself.

After frequently reexamining this treatise, I have not been able to

catholicorum patrum et maxime beati Augustini scriptis cohaereat. Quapropter si cui videbitur quod in eodem opusculo aliquid protulerim quod
aut nimis novum sit aut a veritate dissentiat, rogo ne statim me aut prae-
30 sumptorem novitatum aut falsitatis assertorem exclamet, sed prius libros
praefati doctoris Augustini *De trinitate* diligenter perspiciat, deinde
secundum eos opusculum meum diiudicet. Quod enim dixi summam
trinitatem posse dici tres substantias, Graecos secutus sum, qui confiten-
tur tres substantias in una persona, eadem fide qua nos tres personas in
35 una substantia. Nam hoc significant in deo per substantiam quod nos per
personam.

Quaecumque autem ibi dixi, sub persona secum sola cogitatione dis-
putantis et investigantis ea quae prius non animadvertisset, prolata sunt,
sicut sciebam eos velle quorum petitioni obsequi intendebam.
40 Precor autem et obsecro vehementer, si quis hoc opusculum voluerit
transcribere, ut hanc praefationem in capite libelli ante ipsa capitula studeat praeponere. Multum enim prodesse puto ad intelligenda ea quae ibi
legerit, si quis prius, qua intentione quove modo disputata sint, cognov-
erit. Puto etiam quod si quis hanc ipsam praefationem prius viderit, non
45 temere iudicabit, si quid contra suam opinionem prolatum invenerit.

30-41 assertorem . . . transcribere: *ex E transcripsi (multa verba iam non plene visibilia
sunt in T)*
38 ea quae: eaque *E*   ea que *T*

find that I said in it anything inconsistent with the writings of the Catholic Fathers—especially with Blessed Augustine's writings. Therefore, if it shall seem to anyone that in this work I have set forth some |doctrine| which either is altogether new or else departs from the truth, then I make the following request: let him not immediately declare me to be one who presumes to new |doctrines| or who teaches falsehood, but let him first look carefully at the books of *On the Trinity* by the aforementioned teacher, viz., Augustine, and then let him judge my work in the light of these books. For in stating that the Supreme Trinity can be called three substances, I have followed the Greeks, who confess |that God is| three substances in one person, by means of the same faith with which we |confess that He is| three persons in one substance.[2] For with respect to God they signify by "substance" what we |signify| by "person."

Now, whatever I have stated in this treatise I have stated in the role of one who by reflection alone investigates, and disputes with himself about, points which he had previously not considered—just as I knew was desired by those whose request I was endeavoring to oblige.

Now, I entreat and adjure anyone who wants to copy this work to make sure to append this preface at the very front thereof, before the chapter-titles themselves. For if someone knows at the outset with what intent and in what manner the disputation has been conducted, I believe that he will be greatly aided in understanding what he will read in the work itself. I also think that if someone sees this preface first, he will not be quick to pass judgment should he find presented |in the treatise| something counter to his own view.

Capitula: Incipiunt capitula *T*

Chapter Titles

1. There is something that is the best, the greatest, the highest, of all existing things.
2. The same topic continued.
3. There is a Nature which exists through itself, which is the highest of all existing things, and through which exists whatever is.
4. The same topic continued.
5. Just as this |Nature| exists through itself (*per se*) and |all| other things exist through it, so it exists from itself (*ex se*) and |all| other things exist from it.
6. This Nature was not brought into existence through any assisting cause. Nevertheless, it does not exist through nothing or from nothing. How it can be understood to exist through itself and from itself.
7. How all other things exist through and from this |Nature|.
8. How "|This Nature| made all things from nothing" is to be construed.
9. Before their creation those things which have been made from nothing were not nothing with respect to their Maker's reason.
10. This reason is an expression of things, just as a craftsman first tells himself what he is going to make.
11. Nevertheless, in this comparison there is much dissimilarity.
12. The Expression of the Supreme Being is the Supreme Being.
13. Just as all things were made through the Supreme Being, so they are sustained through it.
14. The Supreme Being exists in all things and through all things; and all things exist from it, through it, and in it.
15. What can and what cannot be predicated of the Supreme Being substantively.
16. For the Supreme Being to be *just* is the same as for it to be justice. The case is the same regarding that which can be predicated of it in a way similar |to the way in which "just" is predicated|. None of these |predicates| indicate what kind of thing it is or of what magnitude it is; instead, |they indicate| what it is.
17. |The Supreme Being| is so simple that whatever things can be predicated of its essence are one and the same thing in it. And some-

sunt, unum idemque in illa sint, et nihil de ea dici possit substantialiter nisi in eo quod quid est.

XVIII. Quod sit sine principio et sine fine.

XIX. Quomodo nihil fuit ante aut erit post illam.

XX. Quod illa sit in omni loco et tempore.

XXI. Quod in nullo sit loco aut tempore.

XXII. Quomodo sit in omni et in nullo loco et tempore.

XXIII. Quomodo melius intelligi possit esse ubique quam in omni loco.

XXIV. Quomodo melius intelligi possit esse semper quam in omni tempore.

XXV. Quod nullis mutabilis sit accidentibus.

XXVI. Quomodo illa dicenda sit esse substantia, et quod sit extra omnem substantiam et singulariter sit quidquid est.

XXVII. Quod non contineatur in communi tractatu substantiarum, et tamen sit substantia et individuus spiritus.

XXVIII. Quod idem spiritus simpliciter sit; et creata, illi comparata, non sint.

XXIX. Quod eius locutio idipsum sit quod ipse, nec tamen sint duo, sed unus spiritus.

XXX. Quod eadem locutio non constet pluribus verbis, sed sit unum verbum.

XXXI. Quod ipsum verbum non sit similitudo factorum, sed veritas essentiae, facta vero sint aliqua veritatis imitatio; et quae naturae magis sint quam aliae et praestantiores.

XXXII. Quod summus spiritus seipsum dicat coaeterno verbo.

XXXIII. Quod uno verbo dicat se et quod fecit.

XXXIV. Quomodo suo verbo videri possit dicere creaturam.

XXXV. Quod quidquid factum est, in eius verbo et scientia sit vita et veritas.

XXXVI. Quam incomprehensibili modo dicat vel sciat res a se factas.

XXXVII. Quod quidquid ipse est ad creaturam, hoc sit et verbum eius; nec tamen ambo simul pluraliter.

XXXVIII. Quod dici non possit quid duo sint, quamvis necesse sit esse duos.

XVII, 3 eo: *supra lin. T*

thing can be predicated substantively of the Supreme Being only with respect to what |this Being| is.

18. |The Supreme Being| exists without beginning and without end.
19. How nothing existed before or will exist after the Supreme Being.
20. The Supreme Being exists in every place and at all times.
21. |The Supreme Being| exists in no place at no time.
22. How |the Supreme Being| exists in every place at every time and in no place at no time.
23. How |the Supreme Being| can better be understood to exist everywhere than in every place.
24. How |the Supreme Being| can better be understood to exist always than at every time.
25. |The Supreme Being| is not mutable in virtue of any accidents.
26. In what sense |the Supreme Being| is to be called substance. It is beyond every substance. It is uniquely whatever it is.
27. |The Supreme Being| is not included in the usual classification of substances; nevertheless, it is a substance and an individual spirit.
28. This Spirit exists in an unqualified sense; compared to it created things do not exist.
29. This Spirit's Expression is the very same thing as this Spirit. Nevertheless, there are not two spirits but |only| one.
30. This Expression is not many words, but is one word.
31. This Word is not the likeness of created things but is true Existence. Created things are a likeness of this true Existence. Which natures exist more, and are more excellent, than others.
32. The Supreme Spirit speaks of itself by means of a coeternal Word.
33. By means of one Word |the Supreme Spirit| speaks both of itself and of that which it has made.
34. How |the Supreme Spirit| can be seen to speak of creatures by its own Word.
35. Whatever was made exists as life and truth in the Word and Knowledge of the Supreme Spirit.
36. In what an incomprehensible manner |the Supreme Spirit| speaks of, or knows, the things made by it.
37. Whatever the Supreme Spirit *is* in relation to creatures this Spirit's Word also is. And yet, together they are not |this relation| in a plural way.
38. It cannot be said what two they are, although they must be two.

39. This Word exists from the Supreme Spirit by being begotten.
40. The Supreme Spirit is most truly parent, and the Word is most truly offspring.
41. The Supreme Spirit most truly begets, and the Word is most truly begotten.
42. It is most truly characteristic of the one to be begetter and father, and of the other to be begotten and son.
43. Reconsideration of what is common to both and of what is proper to each.
44. How the one is the essence of the other.
45. The Son can more fittingly be called the essence of the Father than the Father |can be called the essence| of the Son. Similarly, the Son is the strength of the Father, the wisdom of the Father, and the like.
46. How various of the |statements| which are expressed in the foregoing way can also be understood in another way.
47. The Son is Understanding of Understanding, Truth of Truth, etc.
48. The Father is referred to as Memory, just as the Son is referred to as Understanding. How the Son is the Understanding (or Wisdom) of Memory, the Memory of the Father, and the Memory of Memory.
49. The Supreme Spirit loves itself.
50. This love proceeds equally from the Father and the Son.
51. The Father and the Son love themselves and each other in equal degree.
52. This Love is as great as the Supreme Spirit.
53. This Love is the same thing as the Supreme Spirit is; and yet, this Love is one spirit with the Father and the Son.
54. |This Love| proceeds as a whole from the Father and as a whole from the Son. Nevertheless, there is only one love.
55. |This Love| is not the son of the Father and of the Son.
56. Only the Father is begetter and unbegotten. Only the Son is begotten. Only their Love is neither begotten nor unbegotten.
57. This Love is uncreated and creator, even as are the Father and the Son. Nevertheless, they are together one uncreated creator and not three |uncreated creators|. This Love can be called the Spirit of the Father and of the Son.
58. Just as the Son is the essence and wisdom of the Father in the sense that He has the same essence and wisdom as the Father, so

idem spiritus sit patris et filii essentia et sapientia et similia.

LIX. Quod pater et filius et eorum spiritus pariter sint in se invicem.

LX. Quod nullus eorum alio indigeat ad memorandum vel intelligendum vel amandum, quia singulus quisque est memoria et intelligentia et amor et quidquid necesse est inesse summae essentiae.

LXI. Quod tamen non sint tres, sed unus seu pater seu filius sive utriusque spiritus.

LXII. Quomodo ex his multi filii nasci videantur.

LXIII. Quomodo non sit ibi nisi unus unius.

LXIV. Quod hoc, licet inexplicabile sit, tamen credendum sit.

LXV. Quomodo de ineffabili re verum disputatum sit.

LXVI. Quod per rationalem mentem maxime accedatur ad cognoscendum summam essentiam.

LXVII. Quod mens ipsa speculum eius et imago eius sit.

LXVIII. Quod rationalis creatura ad amandum illam facta sit.

LXIX. Quod anima semper illam amans aliquando vere beate vivat.

LXX. Quod illa se amanti seipsam retribuat.

LXXI. Quod illam contemnens aeterne misera sit.

LXXII. Quod omnis humana anima sit immortalis.

LXXIII. Quod aut semper misera aut aliquando vere beata sit.

LXXIV. Quod nulla anima iniuste privetur summo bono; et quod omnino ad ipsum nitendum sit.

LXXV. Quod summa essentia sit speranda.

LXXVI. Quod credendum sit in illam.

LXXVII. Quod in patrem et filium et eorum spiritum pariter et in singulos et simul in tres credendum sit.

LXXVIII. Quae sit viva et quae mortua fides.

LXXIX. Quid tres summa essentia quodammodo dici possit.

LXXX. Quod ipsa dominetur omnibus et regat omnia et sit solus deus.

LXX, 1 retribuat: *litterae* r¹ *et* ri *non plene legibiles* T   retribuat E

their Spirit is the essence, wisdom, and the like, of the Father and
of the Son.

59. The Father and the Son and their Spirit exist equally in one
another.

60. No one of them needs the other for remembering, understanding,
or loving—because each, distinctly, is Memory, Understanding,
Love, and whatever |else| must be present in the Supreme Being.

61. Nevertheless, there are not three |fathers or three sons or three spir-
its| but one father, one son, and one spirit common to them.

62. How from these |viz., the Father, the Son, and their Spirit| many
sons seem to be begotten.

63. How in the Supreme Spirit there is only one son and one who has
a son.

64. Although inexplicable, this |teaching| must be believed.

65. How regarding |this| ineffable matter something true was argued.

66. Through the rational mind one comes nearest to knowing the
Supreme Being.

67. The mind is the mirror and image of the Supreme Being.

68. The rational creature was made for loving the Supreme Being.

69. The soul which always loves the Supreme Being lives at some time
in true happiness.

70. The Supreme Being gives itself as a reward to |the soul| which
loves it.

71. |The soul| which despises the Supreme Being will be eternally
unhappy.

72. Every human soul is immortal.

73. |The soul| is either always unhappy or else at some time truly
happy.

74. No soul is unjustly deprived of the Supreme Good. |The soul| is
supposed to strive for the Supreme Good wholeheartedly.

75. We are to hope for the Supreme Being.

76. We are to believe in the Supreme Being.

77. We ought to believe equally in the Father, the Son, and their
Spirit—in each distinctly and in all three together.

78. Which faith is alive and which is dead.

79. What three the Supreme Being can in some respect be said to be.

80. The Supreme Being exercises dominion over all things and rules all
things and is the only God.

MONOLOGION

Quod sit quiddam optimum et maximum et
summum omnium quae sunt.

Si quis unam naturam, summam omnium quae sunt, solam sibi in
5 aeterna sua beatitudine sufficientem, omnibusque rebus aliis hoc ipsum
quod aliquid sunt aut quod aliquomodo bene sunt, per omnipotentem
bonitatem suam dantem et facientem, aliaque perplura quae de deo sive
de eius creatura necessarie credimus, aut non audiendo aut non credendo
ignorat: puto quia ea ipsa ex magna parte, si vel mediocris ingenii est,
10 potest ipse sibi saltem sola ratione persuadere. Quod cum multis modis
facere possit, unum ponam quem illi aestimo esse promptissimum. Etenim cum omnes frui solis iis appetant quae bona putant, in promptu est
ut aliquando mentis oculum convertat ad investigandum illud unde sunt
bona ea ipsa, quae non appetit nisi quia iudicat esse bona, ut deinde
15 ratione ducente et illo prosequente ad ea quae irrationabiliter ignorat,
rationabiliter proficiat. In quo tamen si quid dixero quod maior non
monstret auctoritas, sic volo accipi ut quamvis, ex rationibus quae mihi
videbuntur, quasi necessarium concludatur, non ob hoc tamen omnino
necessarium, sed tantum sic interim videri posse dicatur.
20 Facile est igitur ut aliquis sic secum tacitus dicat: cum tam innumera-
bilia bona sint, quorum tam multam diversitatem et sensibus corporeis
experimur et ratione mentis discernimus, estne credendum esse unum
aliquid, per quod unum sint bona quaecumque bona sunt, an sunt bona
alia per aliud? Certissimum quidem et omnibus est volentibus advertere
25 perspicuum quia quaecumque dicuntur aliquid, ita ut ad invicem magis
vel minus aut aequaliter dicantur, per aliquid dicuntur quod non aliud et

Monologion: Incipit monologion liber anselmi *T* (*Initia capitulorum indicantur numeris in marg. positis et signis in textu T. Titulos capitulorum, in textu non repetit T*)
I, 19 dicatur: dicat (*ex* dicatur *correctum ?*) *T* dicatur *E   totum passum om. S*
I, 21 sint: *ex* sunt *(?) corr. T*

MONOLOGION

CHAPTER ONE

There is something that is the best, the greatest,
the highest, of all existing things.

There may be someone who, as a result of not hearing or of not believing, is ignorant of the one Nature, highest of all existing things, alone sufficient unto itself in its eternal beatitude, through its own omnipotent goodness granting and causing all other things to be something and in some respect to fare well. And he may also be ignorant of the many other things which we necessarily believe about God and His creatures. If so, then I think that in great part he can persuade himself of these matters merely by reason alone—if he is of even average intelligence. Although he can do this in many ways, I shall propose one |way| which I regard as the most accessible for him. For since all men seek to enjoy only those things which they consider to be good, at some time or other he can readily turn his mind's eye to investigating that thing from whence are derived these goods which he seeks only because he judges them to be good. Thus, with reason guiding and with him following,³ he may then rationally advance to the matters of which he is unreasonably ignorant. Nevertheless, if in this |investigation| I say something that a greater authority does not teach, I want it to be accepted in such way that even if it is a necessary consequence of reasons which will seem |good| to me, it is not thereby said to be absolutely necessary, but is said only to be able to appear necessary for the time being.⁴

It is, then, easy for someone to ask himself the following question: although the good things whose very great variety we perceive by the bodily senses and distinguish by the mind's reason are so numerous, are we to believe that there is one thing through which all good things are good, or are some things good through something else?⁵ Indeed, the following is thoroughly certain and is evident to all who are willing to give heed: whatever things are said to be something in such way that they are said to be |it| either in greater or lesser or equal degree in relation to one another, are said to be |it| through something which is understood to be identical in the different things (rather than through something different

61

aliud sed idem intelligitur in diversis, sive in illis aequaliter sive inaequaliter consideretur. Nam quaecumque iusta dicuntur ad invicem, sive pariter sive magis vel minus, non possunt intelligi iusta nisi per iustitiam,
30 quae non est aliud et aliud in diversis. Ergo cum certum sit quod omnia
bona, si ad invicem conferantur, aut aequaliter aut inaequaliter sint bona,
necesse est ut omnia sint per aliquid bona, quod intelligitur idem in
diversis bonis, licet aliquando videantur bona dici alia per aliud. Per
aliud enim videtur dici bonus equus quia fortis est, et per aliud bonus
35 equus quia velox est. Cum enim dici videatur bonus per fortitudinem et
bonus per velocitatem, non tamen idem videtur esse fortitudo et velocitas. Verum si equus quia est fortis aut velox idcirco bonus est: quomodo
fortis et velox latro malus est? Potius igitur quemadmodum fortis et
velox latro ideo malus est quia noxius est, ita fortis et velox equus
40 idcirco bonus est quia utilis est. Et quidem nihil solet putari bonum nisi
aut propter aliquam utilitatem (ut bona dicitur salus et quae saluti pro-
sunt) aut propter quamlibet honestatem (sicut pulchritudo aestimatur
bona et quae pulchritudinem iuvant). Sed quoniam iam perspecta ratio
nullo potest dissolvi pacto, necesse est omne quoque utile vel honestum,
45 si vere bona sunt, per idipsum esse bona per quod necesse est esse cuncta
bona, quidquid illud sit.

Quis autem dubitet illud ipsum per quod cuncta sunt bona, esse magnum bonum? Illud igitur est bonum per seipsum, quoniam omne bonum
est per ipsum. Ergo consequitur ut omnia alia bona sint per aliud quam
50 quod ipsa sunt, et ipsum solum per seipsum. At nullum bonum quod per
aliud est, aequale aut maius est eo bono quod per se est bonum. Illud
itaque solum est summe bonum quod solum est per se bonum. Id enim
summum est quod sic supereminet aliis ut nec par habeat nec praestantius. Sed quod est summe bonum, est etiam summe magnum. Est igitur
55 unum aliquid summe bonum et summe magnum, id est summum
omnium quae sunt.

I, 30 aliud[2]: *hic, in medio capitulo, incipit B* (*Folia initialia desunt in B. Initia capitulorum indicantur numeris in marg. positis B. Titulos capitulorum, in textu non ponit B*)

in the different things), whether it is considered to be in them in equal or in unequal degree. For example, whatever things are said to be *just* in relation to one another—whether |they are said to be| equally |just| or |whether some are said to be| more just and |others| less just—can be understood to be just only through justice, which is not something different in |these| different things. Therefore, since it is certain that if compared with one another all good things are either equally or unequally good, it is necessary that all |good| things are good through something which is understood to be identical in |these| different goods—although at times, ostensibly, some things are said to be good through something else. For, ostensibly, a horse is said to be good through one thing, because it is strong, and is said to be good through another thing because it is swift. For although, ostensibly, it is said to be good through strength and good through swiftness, nevertheless strength and swiftness are seen not to be the same thing. Now, if a horse is good because it is strong or swift, how is it that a strong and swift robber is evil? Rather, then, just as a strong and swift robber is evil because he is harmful, so a strong and swift horse is good because it is useful.[6] Indeed, ordinarily, nothing is thought to be good except because of a certain usefulness (e.g., health and whatever conduces to health are called good) or because of some kind of excellence (e.g., beauty and what conduces to beauty are considered to be good). But since the reasoning already seen can in no way be faulted, it is necessary that even every useful and every excellent thing— if they are truly goods—be good through that very thing (whatever it be) through which it is necessary that all |good| things be good.

But who could doubt that that through which all |good| things are good is |itself| a great good? Therefore, it is good through itself, since every |good| thing is good through it.[7] So it follows that all other |good| things are good through something other than what they are and that this other alone |is good| through itself. But no good which is |good| through something other |than itself| is equal to or greater than that good which is good through itself. Hence, only that which alone is good through itself is supremely good; for that is supreme which so excels others that it has neither an equal nor a superior. Now, what is supremely good is also supremely great. Therefore, there is one thing which is supremely good and supremely great—i.e., |which is| the highest of all existing things.

CAPITULUM II

De eadem re.

Quemadmodum autem inventum est aliquid esse summe bonum quoniam cuncta bona per unum aliquid sunt bona, quod est bonum per
5 seipsum, sic ex necessitate colligitur aliquid esse summe magnum quoniam quaecumque magna sunt, per unum aliquid magna sunt, quod magnum est per seipsum. Dico autem non magnum spatio, ut est corpus aliquod, sed quod quanto maius tanto melius est aut dignius, ut est sapientia. Et quoniam non potest esse summe magnum nisi id quod est
10 summe bonum, necesse est aliquid esse maximum et optimum, id est summum omnium quae sunt.

CAPITULUM III

Quod sit quaedam natura per quam est, quidquid est, et
quae per se est, et est summum omnium quae sunt.

Denique non solum omnia bona per idem aliquid sunt bona, et omnia
5 magna per idem aliquid sunt magna, sed quidquid est, per unum aliquid videtur esse. Omne namque quod est, aut est per aliquid aut per nihil. Sed nihil est per nihil. Non enim vel cogitari potest ut sit aliquid non per aliquid. Quidquid est igitur, non nisi per aliquid est. Quod cum ita sit, aut est unum aut sunt plura, per quae sunt cuncta quae sunt. Sed si sunt
10 plura, aut ipsa referuntur ad unum aliquid per quod sunt, aut eadem plura singula sunt per se, aut ipsa per se invicem sunt. At si plura ipsa sunt per unum, iam non sunt omnia per plura, sed potius per illud unum, per quod haec plura sunt. Si vero ipsa plura singula sunt per se, utique est una aliqua vis vel natura existendi per se, quam habent, ut per se sint.
15 Non est autem dubium quod per id ipsum unum sint per quod habent ut sint per se. Verius ergo per ipsum unum cuncta sunt quam per plura, quae sine eo uno esse non possunt. Ut vero plura per se invicem sint, nulla patitur ratio, quoniam irrationabilis cogitatio est ut aliqua res sit per

CHAPTER TWO

The same topic continued.

Just as something has been found to be supremely good inasmuch as all good things are good through some one thing which is good through itself, so it follows necessarily that something is supremely great inasmuch as whatever things are great are great through some one thing which is great through itself. I do not mean great in size, as is a material object; but |I mean great[8] in the sense| that the greater |anything is| the better or more excellent it is—as in the case of wisdom. Now, since only what is supremely good can be supremely great, it is necessary that something be the greatest and the best, i.e., the highest, of all existing things.

CHAPTER THREE

There is a Nature which exists through itself, which is the highest of all existing things, and through which exists whatever is.

Indeed, not only are all good things good through the same thing, and all great things great through the same thing, but also whatever *is* is seen to exist through some one thing. For whatever is exists either through something or through nothing. But it is not the case that anything exists through nothing. For it cannot even be conceived that there is anything which exists other than through something. Thus, whatever is exists only through something. Accordingly, either there is one thing or there are many things through which all existing things exist. But if there are many things, then either (1) they are traced back to some one thing through which they exist, or (2) each of the many exists through itself, or (3) they exist mutually through one another. (1′) But if these many exist through one thing, then it is not, after all, the case that everything exists through the many but is rather the case that |everything exists| through that one thing through which the many exist. (2′) But if each of the many exists through itself, then surely there is some one power-(or nature)-of-existing-through-itself which they have in order to exist through themselves. And there is no doubt that they exist through this one thing through which they have the fact that they exist through themselves.[9] Thus, all things exist through this one thing more truly than through the many things which themselves are not able to exist without this one thing. (3′) But |sound| reasoning does not allow that the many exist

illud cui dat esse. Nam nec ipsa relativa sic sunt per invicem. Cum enim
20 dominus et servus referantur ad invicem, et ipsi homines qui referuntur,
omnino non sunt per invicem, et ipsae relationes quibus referuntur, non
omnino sunt per invicem, quia eaedem sunt per subiecta.

Cum itaque veritas omnimodo excludat plura esse per quae cuncta
sint, necesse est unum illud esse per quod sunt cuncta quae sunt.

25 Quoniam ergo cuncta quae sunt, sunt per ipsum unum, procul dubio
et ipsum unum est per seipsum. Quaecumque igitur alia sunt, sunt per
aliud, et ipsum solum per seipsum. At quidquid est per aliud, minus est
quam illud per quod cuncta sunt alia et quod solum est per se. Quare
illud quod est per se, maxime omnium est. Est igitur unum aliquid quod
30 solum maxime et summe omnium est. Quod autem maxime omnium est,
et per quod est quidquid est bonum vel magnum et omnino quidquid
aliquid est, id necesse est esse summe bonum et summe magnum et
summum omnium quae sunt. Quare est aliquid quod, sive essentia sive
substantia sive natura dicatur, optimum et maximum est et summum
35 omnium quae sunt.

CAPITULUM IV

De eadem re.

Amplius. Si quis intendat rerum naturas, velit nolit sentit non eas omnes
contineri una dignitatis paritate, sed quasdam earum distingui graduum
5 imparitate. Qui enim dubitat quod in natura sua ligno melior sit equus,
et equo praestantior homo, is profecto non est dicendus homo. Cum
igitur naturarum aliae aliis negari non possint meliores, nihilominus per-
suadet ratio aliquam in eis sic supereminere ut non habeat se superiorem.
Si enim huiusmodi graduum distinctio sic est infinita ut nullus ibi sit
10 gradus superior quo superior alius non inveniatur, ad hoc ratio dedu-
citur, ut ipsarum multitudo naturarum nullo fine claudatur. Hoc autem

mutually through one another, for the thought that a thing exists through that to which it gives existence is irrational. For not even relational things exist in this manner through one another. For example, when a master and a servant are referred to relatively to each other, the |two| men referred to do not at all exist through each other, nor do the relations by which they are referred to exist at all through each other (for these relations exist through their subjects).

Therefore, since the truth altogether excludes |the possibility of| there being a plurality through which all things exist, it must be the case that that through which all existing things exist is one thing.

Since, then, all existing things exist through one thing, without doubt this one thing exists through itself. Thus, all existing things other |than this one| exist through something other |than themselves|; and this one alone exists through itself. But whatever exists through something other |than itself| exists less than that which alone exists through itself and through which all other things exist. Accordingly, that which exists through itself exists most greatly of all. Therefore, there is some one thing which alone exists most greatly of all and most highly of all. But what exists most greatly of all and |is that| through which exists whatever is good and great and whatever is anything at all—necessarily, this is supremely good, supremely great, the highest of all existing things. Accordingly, there is something which—whether it is called a being, a substance, or a nature[10]—is the best, the greatest, and the highest, of all existing things.

CHAPTER FOUR

The same topic continued.

Moreover, if anyone considers the natures of things, he cannot help perceiving that they are not all of equal excellence but that some of them differ by an inequality of gradation.[11] For if anyone doubts that a horse is by nature better than a tree and that a man is more excellent than a horse, then surely this |person| ought not to be called a man. So although we cannot deny that some natures are better than others, nonetheless reason persuades us that one of them is so preeminent that no other nature is superior to it. For if such a division of gradation were so limitless that for each higher grade a still higher grade could be found, then reason would be led to the conclusion that the number of these

nemo non putat absurdum, nisi qui nimis est absurdus. Est igitur ex necessitate aliqua natura quae sic est alicui vel aliquibus superior ut nulla sit cui ordinetur inferior.

15 Haec vero natura quae talis est, aut sola est aut plures eiusmodi et aequales sunt. Verum si plures sunt et aequales: cum aequales esse non possint per diversa quaedam, sed per idem aliquid, illud unum per quod aequaliter tam magnae sunt, aut est idipsum quod ipsae sunt, id est ipsa earum essentia, aut aliud quam quod ipsae sunt. Sed si nihil est aliud 20 quam ipsa earum essentia: sicut earum essentiae non sunt plures sed una, ita et naturae non sunt plures sed una. Idem namque naturam hic intelligo quod essentiam. Si vero id, per quod plures ipsae naturae tam magnae sunt, aliud est quam quod ipsae sunt, pro certo minores sunt quam id per quod magnae sunt. Quidquid enim per aliud est magnum, minus 25 est quam id per quod est magnum. Quare non sic sunt magnae ut illis nihil sit maius aliud. Quod si nec per hoc quod sunt nec per aliud possibile est tales esse plures naturas quibus nihil sit praestantius, nullo modo possunt esse naturae plures huiusmodi. Restat igitur unam et solam aliquam naturam esse, quae sic est aliis superior, ut nullo sit inferior. Sed 30 quod tale est, maximum et optimum est omnium quae sunt. Est igitur quaedam natura, quae est summum omnium quae sunt.

Hoc autem esse non potest, nisi ipsa sit per se id quod est, et cuncta quae sunt sint per ipsam id quod sunt. Nam cum paulo ante ratio docuerit id quod per se est et per quod alia cuncta sunt, esse summum 35 omnium existentium, aut e converso id quod est summum, est per se et cuncta alia per illud, aut erunt plura summa. Sed plura summa non esse manifestum est. Quare est quaedam natura vel substantia vel essentia quae per se est bona et magna, et per se est hoc quod est, et per quam est quidquid vere aut bonum aut magnum aut aliquid est, et quae est sum- 40 mum bonum, summum magnum, summum ens sive subsistens, id est summum omnium quae sunt.

IV, 29 nullo: *cum* inferior *et ablativo et dativo utitur Anselmus*

natures is boundless. But everyone holds this |conclusion| to be absurd, except someone who himself is utterly irrational. Therefore, necessarily, there is a nature which is so superior to some |other| or some |others| that there is no |nature| to which it is ranked as inferior.

But this nature which is thus superior is singular—or else there is more than one nature of this kind, and they are equal. Assume that they are many and equal. Since they cannot be equal through different things but |only| through the same thing, this one thing through which they are equally so great either is the same thing which they are (i.e., is their essence) or else is something other than what they are. Now, if it is nothing other than their essence, then just as their essences are one rather than many, so too the natures are one rather than many. For here I am taking the nature to be identical with the essence. On the other hand, if that through which these many natures are equally great is something other than what they are, surely they are less than that through which they are great. For whatever is great through something other |than itself| is less than that |other| through which it is great. Therefore, they would not be so great that nothing else is greater than they. Now, if neither through what they are nor through something other |than what they are| it is possible for there to be many equal natures than which nothing else is more excellent, then there cannot at all be a plurality of such natures. Therefore, |the alternative which| remains is: there is only one Nature which is so superior to |all| others that it is inferior to none. Now, that which is such is the greatest, and the best, of all existing things. Thus, there is a Nature which is the highest of all existing things.

But it can be the highest only if through itself it is what it is and only if through *it* all |other| existing things are what they are. For since a few moments ago reason taught that that which exists through itself and through which all other things exist is the highest of all existing things: either, conversely,[12] that which is the highest |of all| exists through itself and all other things exist through it, or else there are many supreme beings. But it is evident that there are not many supreme beings. Hence, there is a Nature, or Substance, or Being (*essentia*)[13] which through itself is good and great and which through itself is what it is; and through this Nature exists whatever truly is good or great or something. And this Nature is the Supreme Good, the Supreme Greatness (*summum magnum*), the Supreme Being (*ens*), or Subsistence (*subsistens*)—i.e., the highest of all existing things.

Monologion

CAPITULUM V
Quod sicut illa est per se et alia per illam, ita sit ex se et alia ex illa.

Quoniam itaque placet quod inventum est, iuvat indagare utrum haec
5 ipsa natura et cuncta quae aliquid sunt, non sint nisi ex ipsa, quemadmodum non sunt nisi per ipsam. Sed liquet posse dici quia quod est ex
aliquo, est etiam per id ipsum, et quod est per aliquid, est etiam ex eo
ipso—quemadmodum quod est ex materia et per artificem, potest etiam
dici esse per materiam et ex artifice, quoniam per utrumque et ex
10 utroque, id est ab utroque, habet ut sit, quamvis aliter sit per materiam et
ex materia quam per artificem et ex artifice. Consequitur ergo ut quomodo cuncta quae sunt, per summam sunt naturam id quod sunt (et ideo
illa est per seipsam, alia vero per aliud), ita omnia quae sunt sint ex
eadem summa natura (et idcirco sit illa ex seipsa, alia autem ex alio).

CAPITULUM VI
Quod illa non sit ulla iuvante causa ducta ad esse, nec tamen sit per nihil aut ex nihilo; et quomodo intelligi possit esse per se et ex se.

5 Quoniam igitur non semper eundem habet sensum, quod dicitur esse per
aliquid aut esse ex aliquo, quaerendum est diligentius quomodo per
summam naturam vel ex ipsa sint omnia quae sunt. Et quoniam id quod
est per seipsum et id quod est per aliud, non eandem suscipiunt existendi
rationem, prius separatim videatur de ipsa summa natura, quae per se est,
10 postea de iis quae per aliud sunt.

Cum igitur constet quia illa est per seipsam quidquid est, et omnia alia
sunt per illam id quod sunt, quomodo est ipsa per se? Quod enim dicitur
esse per aliquid, videtur esse aut per efficiens aut per materiam aut per
aliquod aliud adiumentum, velut per instrumentum. Sed quidquid aliquo

CHAPTER FIVE

Just as this |Nature| exists through itself (*per se*)
and |all| other things exist through it, so it exists from itself (*ex se*)
and |all| other things exist from it.

Since, then, what has been ascertained commends itself, it is agreeable to investigate whether this Nature and all that is something exist only *from* this Nature, even as they exist only *through* this Nature. Clearly, we can say that what exists from a thing exists also through it and that what exists through a thing exists also from it. For example, what exists from a material and through a craftsman can also be said to exist through a material and from a craftsman. For through both and from both (i.e., by both) it has its existence, even though it exists through a material and from a material in a way other than |the way it exists| through a craftsman and from a craftsman. As a logical consequence, then: just as through the Supreme Nature all existing things are what they are (and, thus, this Nature exists through itself, whereas |all| other things exist through something other |than themselves|), so all existing things exist from the Supreme Nature (and, thus, this Nature exists from itself, whereas |all| other things exist from something other |than themselves|).

CHAPTER SIX

This Nature was not brought into existence through any assisting
cause. Nevertheless, it does not exist through nothing or from
nothing. How it can be understood to exist through itself and from itself.

Therefore, since "to exist through something" or "to exist from something" does not always retain the same meaning, we must inquire more carefully about how all existing things exist through and from the Supreme Nature. And since what exists through itself does not have the same mode of existing as what exists through something other |than itself|, let me separately examine first the Supreme Nature, which exists through itself, and afterwards those things which exist through something other |than themselves|.

Therefore, since it is evident that through itself this |Nature| is whatever it is and that through it all other things are what they are, in what manner does this |Nature| exist through itself? For what is said to exist through something seems to exist either through something efficient or through a material or through some other aid, as through an instru-

15 ex his tribus modis est, per aliud est et posterius et aliquomodo minus est
eo per quod habet ut sit. At summa natura nullatenus est per aliud, nec
est posterior aut minor seipsa aut aliqua alia re. Quare summa natura nec
a se nec ab alio fieri potuit, nec ipsa sibi nec aliud aliquid illi materia
unde fieret fuit, aut ipsa se aliquomodo aut aliqua res illam ut esset quod
20 non erat, adiuvit.

Quid igitur? Quod enim non est, a quo faciente aut ex qua materia aut
quibus adiumentis ad esse pervenerit, id videtur aut esse nihil aut, si
aliquid est, per nihil esse et ex nihilo. Quae licet, ex iis quae rationis luce
de summa iam animadverti substantia, putem nullatenus in illam posse
25 cadere, non tamen negligam huius rei probationem contexere. Quoniam
namque ad magnum et delectabile quiddam me subito perduxit haec
mea meditatio, nullam vel simplicem paeneque fatuam obiectionem dis-
putanti mihi occurrentem negligendo volo praeterire. Quatenus et ego
nihil ambiguum in praecedentibus relinquens certior valeam ad sequentia
30 procedere, et si cui forte quod speculor persuadere voluero, omni vel
modico remoto obstaculo quilibet tardus intellectus ad audita facile possit accedere.

Quod igitur illa natura, sine qua nulla est natura, sit nihil, tam falsum
est quam absurdum erit si dicatur quidquid est nihil esse. Per nihil vero
35 non est, quia nullo modo intelligi potest ut quod aliquid est, sit per nihil.
At si quo modo est ex nihilo: aut per se, aut per aliud, aut per nihil est ex
nihilo.

Sed constat quia nullo modo aliquid est per nihil. Si igitur est aliquomodo ex nihilo: aut per se aut per aliud est ex nihilo. Per se autem nihil
40 potest esse ex nihilo, quia si quid est ex nihilo per aliquid, necesse est ut

ment.[14] But whatever exists in any of these three modes exists through something other |than itself| and is later, and somehow less, than this other through which it has its existence. Yet, the Supreme Nature does not at all exist through something other |than itself|; nor is it later or less than either itself or any other thing. Accordingly, the Supreme Nature could not have been |efficiently| caused to exist either by itself or by something other |than itself|; nor was it itself or anything else the material from which it was made; nor did it somehow aid itself (nor did some |other| thing aid it) to become what previously it was not.

What |shall I say| then? For that which does not exist by anything's making or from any material, or that which did not come to exist by any assisting |factors| seems either to be nothing or, if it is something, to exist through nothing (*per nihil*) and from nothing (*ex nihilo*). Although (on the basis of what I have already noticed about the Supreme Substance by the light of reason) I think that these |implications| cannot at all apply to this |Substance|, nonetheless I will not neglect constructing a proof of this point. For since this meditation of mine has led me all of a sudden to a certain important and interesting point, I do not want to pass carelessly over even some simple, almost foolish, objection occurring to me as I am disputing. |My purpose is twofold: viz.,| so that in leaving nothing doubtful in the preceding |arguments|, I myself can advance more assuredly to the succeeding ones and so that (if I wish to convince someone of what I observe) by my removing every obstacle, even a small one, anyone who is slow to understand can have easy access to what he has heard.

Therefore, |to say| that this Nature (in the absence of which no nature would exist) is nothing is as false as it would be absurd to say that whatever exists is nothing. Moreover, |this Nature| does not exist *through* nothing, since it is altogether unintelligible that what is something exists through nothing. Yet, if |this Nature| somehow existed *from* nothing, then it would exist from nothing either (1) through itself or (2) through something other |than itself| or (3) through nothing.

(NOT *3*) Now, it is evident that something does not at all exist *through* nothing. So if |this Nature| somehow existed *from* nothing, it would exist from nothing either through itself or through something other |than itself|. (NOT *1*) But a thing cannot through itself exist from nothing; for if a thing existed from nothing through something, then that |something| through which it existed would have to be prior |to it|. Therefore, since

id per quod est prius sit. Quoniam igitur haec essentia prior seipsa non est, nullo modo est ex nihilo per se.

At si dicitur per aliam aliquam naturam extitisse ex nihilo, non est summa omnium, sed aliquo inferior; nec est per se hoc quod est, sed per 45 aliud. Item si per aliquid est ipsa ex nihilo: id per quod est, magnum bonum fuit, cum causa tanti boni fuit. At nullum bonum potest intelligi ante illud bonum sine quo nihil est bonum. Hoc autem bonum sine quo nullum est bonum, satis liquet hanc esse summam naturam, de qua agitur. Quare nulla res vel intellectu praecessit, per quam ista ex nihilo 50 esset.

Denique si haec ipsa natura est aliquid aut per nihil aut ex nihilo, procul dubio aut ipsa non est per se et ex se quidquid est, aut ipsa dicitur nihil. Quod utrumque superfluum est exponere, quam falsum sit. Licet igitur summa substantia non sit per aliquid efficiens aut ex aliqua materia 55 nec aliquibus sit adiuta causis ut ad esse perduceretur, nullatenus tamen est per nihil aut ex nihilo, quia per seipsam et ex seipsa est quidquid est.

Quomodo ergo tandem esse intelligenda est per se et ex se, si nec ipsa se fecit, nec ipsa sibi materia extitit, nec ipsa se quolibet modo, ut quod non erat esset, adiuvit? Nisi forte eo modo intelligendum videtur quo 60 dicitur quia lux lucet vel lucens est per seipsam et ex seipsa. Quemadmodum enim sese habent ad invicem lux et lucere et lucens, sic sunt ad se invicem essentia et esse et ens, hoc est existens sive subsistens. Ergo summa essentia et summe esse et summe ens, id est summe existens sive summe subsistens, non dissimiliter sibi convenient quam lux et lucere et 65 lucens.

this Being is not prior to itself, it is not the case that *through itself* it somehow exists from nothing.

(NOT 2) On the other hand, if |this Nature| is said to have come from nothing through some other nature, then |this Nature| would not be the highest of all things but would be inferior to some |other| thing; moreover it would not through itself be what it is, but |would be it| through something other |than itself|. Likewise, if this Nature existed from nothing through something |else|, then this |something| through which it existed would have been a great good since it would have been the cause of such great good. But no good could conceivably |have existed| before the Good without which nothing |at all| would be good. Now, it is clear enough that this Good, without which nothing |at all| would be good, is identical with the Supreme Nature which is under discussion. Hence, it is not even conceivable that this |Nature| was preceded by some other thing through which it existed from nothing.[15]

Finally, if this Nature were something either *through* nothing or *from* nothing, then without doubt either it would not be through and from itself whatever it is or else it would |have to| be said to be nothing. But it is superfluous to discuss how false each |of these alternatives| is. Therefore, even though the Supreme Substance does not exist through anything efficient or from any material, and was not helped to begin existing by any |instrumental| causes, nevertheless it does not at all exist through nothing or from nothing, because whatever it is it is through and from itself.

How, then, in last analysis, ought this |Nature| to be understood to exist through itself and from itself if it did not |efficiently| cause itself and was not its own material and did not somehow aid itself to become what earlier it was not? Should one perhaps understand how, by comparison with one's saying that through itself and from itself light shines (or is shining)? For in the way that *light* and *to shine* and *shining* are related to one another, so *being* and *to be* and *be-ing* (i.e., *existing*, or *subsisting*)[16] are related to one another. Thus, *supreme being* and *supremely to be* and *supremely be-ing* (i.e., *supremely existing*, or *supremely subsisting*) are related to one another analogously to *light* and *to shine* and *shining*.

Quomodo omnia alia sint per illam et ex illa.

Restat nunc, de rerum earum universitate quae per aliud sunt, discutere quomodo sint per summam substantiam: utrum quia ipsa fecit universa 5 aut quia materia fuit universorum. Non enim opus est quaerere utrum ideo sint universa per ipsam quia alio faciente aut alia materia existente illa tantum quolibet modo ut res omnes essent adiuverit, cum repugnet iis quae iam supra patuerunt si secundo loco et non principaliter sint per ipsam quaecumque sunt.

10 Primum itaque mihi quaerendum esse puto utrum universitas rerum quae per aliud sunt, sit ex aliqua materia. Non autem dubito omnem hanc mundi molem cum partibus suis sicut videmus formatam, constare ex terra et aqua et aëre et igne, quae scilicet quattuor elementa aliquomodo intelligi possunt sine his formis quas conspicimus in rebus forma- 15 tis, ut eorum informis aut etiam confusa natura videatur esse materia omnium corporum suis formis discretorum; non inquam hoc dubito, sed quaero unde haec ipsa quam dixi mundanae molis materia sit. Nam si huius materiae est aliqua materia, illa verius est corporeae universitatis materia. Si igitur universitas rerum, seu visibilium seu invisibilium, est ex 20 aliqua materia, profecto non solum non potest esse sed nec dici potest esse ex alia materia quam ex summa natura, aut ex seipsa, aut ex aliqua tertia essentia, quae utique nulla est. Quippe nihil omnino vel cogitari potest esse praeter illud summum omnium, quod est per seipsum, et universitatem eorum quae non per se sed per idem summum sunt. Quare 25 quod nullo modo aliquid est, nullius rei materia est. Ex sua vero natura rerum universitas, quae per se non est, esse non potest; quoniam si hoc esset, aliquomodo esset per se et per aliud quam per id per quod sunt cuncta, et non esset solum id per quod cuncta sunt—quae omnia falsa

CHAPTER SEVEN
How all other things exist through and from this |Nature|.

Now, with regard to all the things which exist through something other |than themselves|, there remains to discuss how they exist through the Supreme Substance: |do they exist through it| (A) because it |efficiently| caused them all or (B) because it was the material of them all? There is no need to ask whether or not all these things exist through this Substance only by virtue of its having in some way aided them to exist, while something other than this Substance created them or was the material |out of which they were made. We need not pursue such an inquiry| because were it the case that whatever |all these things| are they are |only| secondarily, and not principally, through this |Substance|, then what has already been proved would be contradicted.

So I think that I must first ask whether everything which exists through something other |than itself| (B) exists from some material. I do not doubt that the world's entire mass, as we see it formed with its parts, consists of earth, water, air, and fire. These four elements somehow can be conceived apart from the forms which we see in formed things, so that the unformed, or even mingled, nature of these elements is seen to be the material of all corporeal objects which exist separately, each having its own form. Although I do not doubt any of these facts, I do ask: whence exists the aforementioned material of the massive world? For if this material exists from some other material, then that other is more truly the material of every corporeal thing. Thus, if all things, whether visible or invisible, exist from some material, then surely they can exist, and be said to exist, only from the material (B.1) of the Supreme Nature or (B.2) of themselves, or (B.3) of some third being. (NOT B.3) But, assuredly, a third being does not exist. Indeed, nothing at all can even be thought to exist except the Supreme Being (which exists through itself) and all |other| things (which exist through the Supreme Being rather than through themselves). Consequently, what in no way is something is not the material of anything. (NOT B.2) Moreover, the universe, which does not exist through itself, cannot exist from out of its own nature. For if it existed from out of its own nature, it *would* in some way exist through itself and |thus| through something other than that through which all things exist, and that through which all things exist would not be singular. But these |consequences| are false. Moreover, everything that

sunt. Item omne quod ex materia est, ex alio est et eo posterius. Quo-
30 niam igitur nihil est aliud a seipso vel posterius seipso, consequitur ut
nihil sit materialiter ex seipso.

At si ex summae naturae materia potest esse aliquid minus ipsa, summum bonum mutari et corrumpi potest—quod nefas est dicere. Quapropter quoniam omne quod aliud est quam ipsa, minus est ipsa, impos-
35 sibile est aliquid aliud hoc modo esse ex ipsa. Amplius. Dubium non est
quia nullatenus est bonum per quod mutatur vel corrumpitur summum
bonum. Quod si qua minor natura est ex summi boni materia: cum nihil
sit undecumque nisi per summam essentiam, mutatur et corrumpitur
summum bonum per ipsam. Quare summa essentia, quae est ipsum
40 summum bonum, nullatenus est bonum—quod est inconveniens. Nulla
igitur minor natura materialiter est ex summa natura. Cum igitur eorum
essentiam quae per aliud sunt, constet non esse velut ex materia ex
summa essentia, nec ex se, nec ex alio, manifestum est quia ex nulla
materia est.

45 Quare quoniam quidquid est, per summam essentiam est, nec per
ipsam aliud aliquid esse potest nisi ea aut faciente aut materia existente,
consequitur ex necessitate ut praeter ipsam nihil sit nisi ea faciente. Et
quoniam nihil aliud est vel fuit nisi illa et quae facta sunt ab illa, nihil
omnino facere potuit per aliud vel instrumentum vel adiumentum quam
50 per seipsam. At omne quod fecit, sine dubio aut fecit ex aliquo velut ex
materia, aut ex nihilo. Quoniam ergo certissime patet quia essentia
omnium quae praeter summam essentiam sunt, ab eadem summa essentia facta est, et quia ex nulla materia est, procul dubio nihil apertius
quam quia illa summa essentia tantam rerum molem, tam numerosam
55 multitudinem, tam formose formatam, tam ordinate variatam, tam convenienter diversam sola per seipsam produxit ex nihilo.

VII, 31 sit: *supra lin. B²*

is from |any| material is from something other |than itself| and is later than that other. Therefore, since no thing is other than itself or later than itself, it follows that no thing exists materially from itself.

(NOT B.1) But if from the "material" of the Supreme Nature there could be something less than the Supreme Nature, then the Supreme Good could be changed and corrupted—something abominable to say. Thus, since everything other than the Supreme Nature is less than it is, something other |than it| cannot exist materially from it. Furthermore, assuredly, that through which the Supreme Good would be changed or corrupted would itself not at all be good. But if any nature inferior |to the Supreme Nature| existed from the "material" of the Supreme Good, then since whatever exists from anywhere at all exists only through the Supreme Being, the Supreme Good would be changed and corrupted through the Supreme Being. Thus, the Supreme Being, which is the Supreme Good, would not be a good at all—an inconsistency. Therefore, no nature inferior |to the Supreme Nature| exists materially from the Supreme Nature. Since, then, it is evident that the being of those things which exist through something other |than themselves| does not exist "materially" from the Supreme Being or materially from itself or materially from some third thing, it is obvious that (NOT B) it does not exist from any material at all.

Therefore, since whatever exists exists through the Supreme Being, and since all things other |than the Supreme Being| can exist through it only if it either |efficiently| causes them or else is the material |out of which they are made|, necessarily nothing besides it exists except (A) by its |efficient| causing. And since there neither is nor was anything except this Being and the things made by it, |this Being| was not able to make anything at all through anything else (be it |merely| an instrument or an aid) than through itself. Yet, everything that it made it made, without doubt, either (A.1) materially from something, or else (A.2) from nothing. Therefore, since it is most assuredly evident that the being of all existing things (other than the Supreme Being) has been made by the Supreme Being and (NOT A.1) exists from no material, assuredly nothing is more clear than that the Supreme Being through itself and by itself produced (A.2) from nothing (*ex nihilo*) so great a complex of things—so vastly numerous, so beautifully formed, so well-ordered in their variety, so harmonious in their diversity.

Quomodo intelligendum sit quia fecit omnia ex nihilo.

Sed occurrit quiddam de nihilo. Nam ex quocumque fit aliquid, id causa
est eius quod ex se fit, et omnis causa necesse est aliquod ad essentiam
5 effecti praebeat adiumentum. Quod sic omnes tenent experimento ut et
nulli rapiatur contendendo, et vix ulli surripiatur decipiendo. Si ergo
factum est ex nihilo aliquid, ipsum nihil causa fuit eius quod ex ipso
factum est. Sed quomodo id quod nullum habebat esse, adiuvit aliquid,
ut perveniret ad esse? Si autem nullum adiumentum de nihilo provenit
10 ad aliquid, cui aut qualiter persuadeatur quia ex nihilo aliquid efficiatur?
　　Praeterea "nihil" aut significat aliquid aut non significat aliquid. Sed si
nihil est aliquid, quaecumque facta sunt ex nihilo, facta sunt ex aliquo. Si
vero nihil non est aliquid: quoniam intelligi non potest ut ex eo quod
penitus non est, fiat aliquid, nihil fit ex nihilo, sicut vox omnium est quia
15 de nihilo nihil. Unde videtur consequi ut quidquid fit, fiat ex aliquo. Aut
enim fit de aliquo aut de nihilo. Sive igitur nihil sit aliquid sive nihil non
sit aliquid, consequi videtur ut quidquid factum est, factum sit ex aliquo.
Quod si verum esse ponitur, omnibus quae supra disposita sunt opponitur. Unde quoniam quod erat nihil aliquid erit, id quod maxime erat
20 aliquid nihil erit. Ex eo namque quod quandam substantiam maxime
omnium existentem inveneram, ad hoc, ut omnia alia sic facta essent ab
ea ut nihil esset unde facta essent, ratiocinando perveneram. Quare si
illud unde facta sunt, quod putabam esse nihil, est aliquid: quidquid
inventum aestimabam de summa essentia, est nihil.
25　　Quid igitur intelligendum est de nihilo? Nam nihil quod videam obici
posse vel paene fatuum, iam statui in hac meditatione negligere. Tribus
itaque ut puto modis, quod ad praesentis impedimenti sufficit expedi-
mentum, exponi potest, si qua substantia dicitur esse facta ex nihilo.
Unus quidem modus est quo volumus intelligi penitus non esse factum,

VIII, 3 Sed: *hic incipit capitulum 8 in ES　totum folium deest in T*　　Nam: *hic incipit capitulum 8 in B*

CHAPTER EIGHT
How "|This Nature| made all things from nothing" is to be construed.

But a |problem| occurs about *nothing*. For that from which a thing is made is a cause of the thing made from it; and, necessarily, every cause contributes some assistance to the effect's existence. On the basis of their experience all men accept this |principle|—to such an extent that it can be wrested from no one through debate and removed from scarcely no one through deception. Hence, if something were made from nothing, nothing was a cause of what was made from it. Yet, how could that which had no existence have aided something |else| to begin to exist? But if no aid comes to something from nothing, who would be persuaded, and how would he be persuaded, that something is made from nothing?

Moreover, either "nothing" signifies something or it does not signify something. But if nothing is something, then whatever is made from nothing is made from something. But if nothing is not something, then from nothing nothing is made; for it is inconceivable that anything be made from nothing at all. (As the truism goes: "From nothing nothing comes.") Therefore, it seems to follow that whatever is made is made from something. For |a thing| is made either from something or from nothing. Therefore, whether nothing is something or whether it is not something, there seems to follow that whatever is made is made from something. However, if |this conclusion| is posited as true, it opposes all |the conclusions| previously reached. Accordingly, since what was nothing would be something, that which was most greatly something would be nothing. For from the fact that I found a certain Substance which exists most greatly of all, I rationally inferred that all things other |than this Substance| were made by it in such way that they were made from nothing. Therefore, if that from which they were made (which I believed to be nothing) is something, then all that I thought I had concluded about the Supreme Being is nothing.

What, then, must be understood regarding *nothing*? For I have already determined not to neglect in this meditation any objection which I see to be possible—even an almost foolish objection. So if any substance is said to have been made from nothing, |this statement|, it seems to me, can be interpreted in three ways; and these |interpretations| suffice to resolve the present difficulty. One way is that by which we want it understood that what is said to have been made from nothing has not at

30 quod factum dicitur ex nihilo. Cui simile est, cum quaerenti de tacente, unde loquatur, respondetur "de nihilo"—id est, non loquitur. Secundum quem modum de ipsa summa essentia et de eo quod penitus nec fuit nec est, quaerenti unde factum sit, recte responderi potest "de nihilo"—id est, nequaquam factum est. Qui sensus de nullo eorum quae facta sunt, intel-
35 ligi potest. Alia significatio est quae dici quidem potest, vera tamen esse non potest: ut si dicatur aliquid sic esse factum ex nihilo ut ex ipso nihilo, id est ex eo quod penitus non est, factum sit—quasi ipsum nihil sit aliquid existens, ex quo possit aliquid fieri. Quod quoniam semper falsum est: quotiens esse ponitur, impossibilis inconvenientia consequitur.
40 Tertia interpretatio qua dicitur aliquid esse factum de nihilo, est cum intelligimus esse quidem factum, sed non esse aliquid unde sit factum. Per similem significationem dici videtur, cum homo contristatus sine causa dicitur contristatus de nihilo. Secundum igitur hunc sensum si intelligatur quod supra conclusum est, quia praeter summam essentiam
45 cuncta quae sunt, ab eadem ex nihilo facta sunt—id est, non ex aliquo: sicut ipsa conclusio praecedentia convenienter consequetur, ita ex eadem conclusione nihil inconveniens subsequetur.

Quamvis non inconvenienter et sine omni repugnantia ea quae facta sunt a creatrice substantia, dici possint esse facta ex nihilo, eo modo quo
50 dici solet dives ex paupere, et recepisse quis sanitatem ex aegritudine. Id est, qui prius pauper erat, nunc est dives, quod antea non erat; et qui prius habebat aegritudinem, nunc habet sanitatem, quam antea non habebat. Hoc igitur modo non inconvenienter intelligi potest, si dicitur creatrix essentia universa fecisse de nihilo, sive quod universa per illam facta
55 sint de nihilo—id est, quae prius nihil erant, nunc sunt aliquid. Hac ipsa quippe voce qua dicitur quia illa fecit, sive quia ista facta sunt, intelligitur quia cum illa fecit, aliquid fecit, et cum ista facta sunt, nonnisi aliquid facta sunt. Sic enim aspicientes aliquem de valde humili fortuna

all been made. Similar to this is the case in which one asks about another, who is silent, "Of what is he speaking?" and is given the reply "Of nothing"; that is, |the other| is not speaking. In this way one who asks with regard to the Supreme Being or with regard to something which has not at all existed and does not at all exist, "From what was it made?", can correctly be answered "From nothing." That is, it was not made at all. This sense can be understood of none of the things which have been made. Secondly, there is a signification |of "from nothing"| which can be expressed but yet which cannot be the case. For example, something may be said to have been made from nothing in that it was made from nothing itself (i.e., was made from what does not at all exist), as if nothing itself were an existing thing from which some |other| thing could be made.[17] But since |this statement| is always false, a contradiction ensues as often as |the statement| is asserted. The third interpretation by which something is said to have been made from nothing is when we understand that it has indeed been made but that there is not anything from which it was made. The signification is seen to be similar when of a man who is saddened without reason we say, "He is saddened from nothing." Therefore, if we construe in this third sense our previous conclusion that except for the Supreme Being all existing things have been made by the Supreme Being from nothing—i.e., not from anything— then just as that conclusion follows consistently from the preceding |considerations|, so from that conclusion nothing inconsistent follows.

Nonetheless, we can say suitably and without any inconsistency that those things which have been made by the Creative Substance were made from nothing in the way that a rich man is commonly said by us |to have been made| from a poor man, or that from sickness a man has regained health. That is, he who previously was poor is now rich—something which he was not beforehand; and he who previously was sick is now healthy— something which he was not beforehand. In this |same| manner, then, we can suitably understand the following statements: "The Creative Being made all things from nothing" and "Through the Creative Being all things were made from nothing"—that is, things that once were nothing are now something. Indeed, in saying that the Creative Being *made* or that all other things *were made*, we mean that when the Creative Being made, it made something, and that when the other things were made, they were made only something. Thus, when we observe a man of very meager means who has been elevated by a second man to

multis opibus ab aliquo honoribusve exaltatum dicimus: "ecce fecit ille
60 istum de nihilo" aut "factus est iste ab illo de nihilo"—id est, iste qui
prius quasi nihilum deputabatur, nunc illo faciente vere aliquid existimatur.

CAPITULUM IX

Quod ea quae facta sunt de nihilo, non nihil erant,
antequam fierent, quantum ad rationem facientis.

Verum videor mihi videre quiddam quod non negligenter discernere cogit
5 secundum quid ea quae facta sunt, antequam fierent, dici possint fuisse
nihil. Nullo namque pacto fieri potest aliquid rationabiliter ab aliquo, nisi
in facientis ratione praecedat aliquod rei faciendae quasi exemplum, sive
aptius dicitur forma, vel similitudo, aut regula. Patet itaque quoniam
priusquam fierent universa, erat in ratione summae naturae, quid aut
10 qualia aut quomodo futura essent. Quare cum ea quae facta sunt, clarum
sit nihil fuisse, antequam fierent, quantum ad hoc quia non erant quod
nunc sunt, nec erat ex quo fierent; non tamen nihil erant quantum ad
rationem facientis, per quam et secundum quam fierent.

CAPITULUM X

Quod illa ratio sit quaedam rerum locutio, sicut faber
prius apud se dicit quod facturus est.

Illa autem rerum forma quae in eius ratione res creandas praecedebat:
5 quid aliud est quam rerum quaedam in ipsa ratione locutio, veluti cum
faber facturus aliquod suae artis opus prius illud intra se dicit mentis
conceptione? Mentis autem sive rationis locutionem hic intelligo, non
cum voces rerum significativae cogitantur, sed cum res ipsae vel futurae
vel iam existentes acie cogitationis in mente conspiciuntur. Frequenti
10 namque usu cognoscitur quia rem unam tripliciter loqui possumus. Aut
enim res loquimur signis sensibilibus, id est quae sensibus corporeis sen-

great wealth or honor, we say "The second man made the first man from nothing," or "The first man was made from nothing by the second man." That is, the first man, who formerly was regarded as nothing, is now esteemed as truly something because of the making of the second man.

CHAPTER NINE

Before their creation those things which have been made from nothing were not nothing with respect to their Maker's reason.

But I seem to see a certain |point| which requires |me| to distinguish carefully the respect in which those things which have been made can be said to have been nothing before they were made. For by no means can anything reasonably be made by anyone unless beforehand there is in the maker's reason a certain pattern, as it were, of the thing to be made—or more fittingly put, a form or likeness or rule. Thus, it is evident that before all things were made there was in the Supreme Nature's reason what they were going to be or what kind they were going to be or how they were going to be.[18] Therefore, although it is clear that before they were made, those things which have been made were nothing—with respect to the fact that they were not then what they are now and that there was not anything from which they were made— nevertheless they were not nothing with respect to their Maker's reason, through which and according to which they were made.

CHAPTER TEN

This reason is an expression of things, just as a craftsman first tells himself what he is going to make.

But what is this form of things, which in the Maker's reason preceded the things to be created, other than an expression-of-things in the Maker's reason?—just as when a craftsman[19] who is about to make a work from his craft first speaks of it within himself by a mental conception? Now, by "mental expression" or "rational expression" I do not mean here thinking the words which are significative of things; I mean, rather, viewing mentally, with the acute gaze of thought, the things themselves which already exist or are going to exist. For in ordinary usage we recognize that we can speak of a single object in three ways. For we speak of objects either (1) by perceptibly employing perceptible signs

tiri possunt, sensibiliter utendo; aut eadem signa, quae foris sensibilia
sunt, intra nos insensibiliter cogitando; aut nec sensibiliter nec insensibiliter his signis utendo, sed res ipsas vel corporum imaginatione vel ratio-
15 nis intellectu pro rerum ipsarum diversitate intus in nostra mente
dicendo. Aliter namque dico hominem cum eum hoc nomine, quod est
"homo," significo; aliter cum idem nomen tacens cogito; aliter cum eum
ipsum hominem mens aut per corporis imaginem aut per rationem
intuetur—per corporis quidem imaginem ut cum eius sensibilem figuram
20 imaginatur; per rationem vero ut cum eius universalem essentiam, quae
est animal rationale mortale, cogitat.

Hae vero tres loquendi varietates singulae verbis sui generis constant.
Sed illius quam tertiam et ultimam posui locutionis verba, cum de rebus
non ignoratis sunt, naturalia sunt et apud omnes gentes sunt eadem. Et
25 quoniam alia omnia verba propter haec sunt inventa: ubi ista sunt, nullum aliud verbum est necessarium ad rem cognoscendam; et ubi ista esse
non possunt, nullum aliud est utile ad rem ostendendam. Possunt etiam
non absurde dici tanto veriora, quanto magis rebus quarum sunt verba
similia sunt et eas expressius signant. Exceptis namque rebus illis quibus
30 ipsis utimur pro nominibus suis ad easdem significandas, ut sunt quaedam voces velut "a" vocalis—exceptis inquam his nullum aliud verbum
sic videtur rei simile cuius est verbum, aut sic eam exprimit, quomodo
illa similitudo quae in acie mentis rem ipsam cogitantis exprimitur. Illud
igitur iure dicendum est maxime proprium et principale rei verbum.
35 Quapropter si nulla de qualibet re locutio tantum propinquat rei, quantum illa quae huiusmodi verbis constat, nec aliquid aliud tam simile rei
vel futurae vel iam existentis in ratione alicuius potest esse: non immerito
videri potest apud summam substantiam, talem rerum locutionem et
fuisse antequam essent ut per eam fierent, et esse cum factae sunt ut per
40 eam sciantur.

X, 33 exprimitur: exprimit *B*   exprimitur *EST*
X, 39 factae: facta *BEST*   *ad* factae *mutavi*

(i.e., |signs| which can be perceived by the bodily senses) or (2) by imperceptibly thinking to ourselves these same signs, which are perceptible outside us, or (3) neither by perceptibly nor by imperceptibly employing these signs, but by inwardly and mentally speaking of the objects themselves—in accordance with their variety—either through the imagination of bodies or through rational discernment.[20] For example, in one way I speak of a man when I signify him by the name "man." In another way |I speak of him| when I think this name silently. In a third way |I speak of a man| when my mind beholds him either by means of an image of a body or by means of reason—by means of an image of a body, for instance, when |my mind| imagines his perceptible shape; but by means of reason, for instance, when |my mind| thinks of his universal being, viz., *rational, mortal animal*.[21]

Each of these three kinds of speaking has its corresponding kind of words. Yet, words of that |kind of| speaking which I mentioned third, and last, are natural and are the same for all races, if they are not words for unknown things.[22] And since all other words have been formulated because of these |natural words|, wherever *these* are no other word is needed for recognizing an object; and where *they* cannot be, no other |word| is useful for manifesting the object. Moreover, |these natural words| can without absurdity be called truer the more they resemble, and the more expressly they signify, the objects for which they are words. Except for those things which we use as names for themselves in order to signify themselves (e.g., certain sounds such as the vowel *a*)—except for these, I say, no other word seems so similar to the object for which it is a word, and |no other word| so expresses that object, as does that likeness which is expressed in the acute gaze of the mind as it conceives the object itself. Therefore, the natural word is rightly to be called the principal and most proper word for an object. No expression of anything whatsoever approximates an object as closely as does that expression which consists of words of this kind; and in no one's reason can there be anything else which is so similar to an object, whether already existing or going to exist. Consequently, in the case of the Supreme Substance such an Expression of objects can justifiably be seen (1) to have existed before these objects, in order that they might be made through it, and (2) to exist now that they have been made, in order that they may be known through it.

CAPITULUM XI
Quod tamen multa sit in hac similitudine dissimilitudo.

Sed quamvis summam substantiam constet prius in se quasi dixisse cunc-
tam creaturam quam eam secundum eandem et per eandem suam inti-
5 mam locutionem conderet, quemadmodum faber prius mente concipit
quod postea secundum mentis conceptionem opere perficit: multam
tamen in hac similitudine intueor dissimilitudinem. Illa namque nihil
omnino aliunde assumpsit, unde vel eorum quae factura erat formam in
seipsa compingeret, vel ea ipsa hoc quod sunt perficeret. Faber vero
10 penitus nec mente potest aliquid corporeum imaginando concipere, nisi
id quod aut totum simul aut per partes ex aliquibus rebus aliquomodo
iam didicit, nec opus mente conceptum perficere, si desit aut materia aut
aliquid sine quo opus praecogitatum fieri non possit. Quamquam enim
homo tale aliquod animal possit cogitando sive pingendo quale nusquam
15 sit confingere, nequaquam tamen hoc facere valet nisi componendo in eo
partes, quas ex rebus alias cognitis in memoriam attraxit. Quare in hoc
differunt ab invicem illae in creatrice substantia et in fabro suorum operum
faciendorum intimae locutiones: quod illa nec assumpta nec adiuta aliunde, sed prima et sola causa sufficere potuit suo artifici ad suum opus
20 perficiendum, ista vero nec prima nec sola nec sufficiens est ad suum
incipiendum. Quapropter ea quae per illam creata sunt, omnino non sunt
aliquid quod non sunt per illam; quae vero fiunt per istam, penitus non
essent, nisi essent aliquid quod non sunt per ipsam.

CAPITULUM XII
Quod haec summae essentiae locutio sit summa essentia.

Sed cum pariter ratione docente certum sit quia quidquid summa substantia fecit, non fecit per aliud quam per semetipsam, et quidquid fecit,

CHAPTER ELEVEN
Nevertheless, in this comparison there is much dissimilarity.

It is evident that within itself the Supreme Substance "spoke," as it were, of all creatures before it created them through and according to its own inmost Expression—just as a craftsman first conceives mentally what he subsequently produces in accordance with his mental conception. Nevertheless, I detect in this comparison much dissimilarity |between the Supreme Substance and an ordinary craftsman|. For the Supreme Substance did not from anywhere borrow anything at all whereby to fashion within itself the form of the creatures which it was going to make, or whereby to make these creatures what they are. By contrast, a craftsman cannot at all conceive in his mind, imaginatively, any material object except one which he has already in some way experienced (either in its entirety all at once or through parts from various objects);[23] moreover, a craftsman cannot produce the work conceived in his mind if he lacks either the materials or any thing without which the preconceived work cannot be accomplished. For example, although a man can form the concept or the image of some kind of animal which nowhere exists, he can do so only by therein putting together parts which he has drawn into his memory from objects previously experienced.[24] Hence, these two inner expressions of their respective works to be made—viz., |the Expression| in the Creative Substance and |the expression| in a craftsman—differ from each other in the following respect: The former was neither borrowed from anywhere nor aided from anywhere; as first and only cause it was able to suffice its Craftsman for accomplishing His work. By contrast, the latter is neither the first cause, the sole cause, nor the sufficient cause for |the craftsman's| commencing his |work|. Therefore, those things which have been created through the Expression |in the Creative Substance| are wholly through this Expression whatever they are, whereas the things made through |the craftsman's| expression would not at all exist unless they were something more than what they are through his expression.

CHAPTER TWELVE
The Expression of the Supreme Being is the Supreme Being.

But it is equally certain, as reason teaches, that (1) whatever the Supreme Substance made, it made through no other than through itself

5 per suam intimam locutionem fecit, sive singula singulis verbis, sive
potius uno verbo simul omnia dicendo: quid magis necessarium videri
potest quam hanc summae essentiae locutionem non esse aliud quam
summam essentiam? Non igitur negligenter praetereundam huius locutionis considerationem puto; sed priusquam de illa possit tractari diligen-
10 ter, eiusdem summae substantiae proprietates aliquas studiose investi-
gandas existimo.

CAPITULUM XIII

Quod sicut omnia per summam essentiam facta sunt,
ita vigeant per ipsam.

Constat ergo per summam naturam esse factum, quidquid non est idem
5 illi. Dubium autem non nisi irrationabili menti esse potest, quod cuncta
quae facta sunt, eodem ipso sustinente vigent et perseverant esse quamdiu sunt, quo faciente de nihilo habent esse quod sunt. Simili namque per
omnia ratione qua collectum est omnia quae sunt esse per unum aliquid,
unde ipsum solum est per seipsum et alia per aliud—simili inquam ratione
10 potest probari quia quaecumque vigent per unum aliquid vigent, unde
illud solum viget per seipsum et alia per aliud. Quod quoniam aliter esse
non potest, nisi ut ea quae sunt facta vigeant per aliud, et id a quo sunt
facta vigeat per seipsum: necesse est ut sicut nihil factum est nisi per
creatricem praesentem essentiam, ita nihil vigeat nisi per eiusdem ser-
15 vatricem praesentiam.

CAPITULUM XIV

Quod illa sit in omnibus et per omnia, et omnia sint
ex illa et per illam et in illa.

Quod si ita est—immo quia ex necessitate sic est—consequitur ut ubi
5 ipsa non est, nihil sit. Ubique igitur est et per omnia et in omnibus. At

and that (2) whatever it made, it made through its own inmost Expression (whether by uttering different things with different words or else by uttering all things at once with a single word). Accordingly, what |view| can be seen to be more necessary than that the Expression of the Supreme Being is not other than the Supreme Being? Therefore, I think that examination of this Expression must not be passed over lightly. But before this topic can be developed critically, several properties of the Supreme Substance must be carefully examined, it seems to me.

CHAPTER THIRTEEN
Just as all things were made through the Supreme Being,
so they are sustained through it.

Therefore, it is evident that whatever is not identical with the Supreme Nature was made through the Supreme Nature. Only an irrational mind can doubt that all created things endure and continue to exist as long as they do because they are sustained by the same one who made |them| from nothing and from whom they have their being what they are. For we can prove that whatever things are sustained |in existence| are sustained by some one thing and, hence, it alone is sustained through itself, whereas |all| other things |are sustained| through something other |than themselves. We can prove this| by |using| an argument similar in every respect |to the argument| by which we inferred that all existing things exist through some one thing and, hence, it alone exists through itself, whereas |all| other things exist through something other |than themselves|. Since it can only be the case that |all| the things which have been made are sustained through something other |than themselves| and that the thing by which they have been made is sustained through itself, it must be the case that just as nothing was made except through the creative and present Being, so nothing is sustained except through the conserving presence of this same |Being|.

CHAPTER FOURTEEN
The Supreme Being exists in all things and through all things;
and all things exist from it, through it, and in it.

But if |the foregoing consideration| is true—or, rather, because it must be true—it follows that where the Supreme Being does not exist, nothing exists. Therefore, |the Supreme Being| exists everywhere and through all

quoniam absurdum est ut scilicet quemadmodum nullatenus aliquid creatum potest exire creantis et foventis immensitatem, sic creans et fovens
nequaquam valeat aliquomodo excedere factorum universitatem: liquet
quoniam ipsa est quae cuncta alia portat et superat, claudit, et penetrat.
10 Si igitur haec illis quae superius sunt inventa iungantur, eadem est quae
in omnibus est et per omnia, et ex qua et per quam et in qua omnia.

CAPITULUM XV

Quid possit aut non possit dici de illa substantialiter.

Iam non immerito valde moveor quam studiose possum inquirere, quid
omnium quae de aliquo dici possunt, huic tam admirabili naturae queat
5 convenire substantialiter. Quamquam enim mirer si possit in nominibus
vel verbis quae aptamus rebus factis de nihilo reperiri, quod digne
dicatur de creatrice universorum substantia, tentandum tamen est ad
quid hanc indagationem ratio perducet. Itaque de relativis quidem nulli
dubium, quia nullum eorum substantiale est illi de quo relative dicitur.
10 Quare si quid de summa natura dicitur relative, non est eius significati-
vum substantiae. Unde hoc ipsum quod summa omnium sive maior
omnibus quae ab illa facta sunt, seu aliud aliquid similiter relative dici
potest: manifestum est quoniam non eius naturalem designat essentiam.
Si enim nulla earum rerum umquam esset, quarum relatione summa et
15 maior dicitur, ipsa nec summa nec maior intelligeretur; nec tamen
idcirco minus bona esset aut essentialis suae magnitudinis in aliquo detrimentum pateretur. Quod ex eo manifeste cognoscitur quoniam ipsa,
quidquid boni vel magni est, non est per aliud quam per seipsam. Si
igitur summa natura sic potest intelligi non-summa ut tamen nequaquam
20 sit maior aut minor quam cum intelligitur summa omnium, manifestum
est quia "summum" non simpliciter significat illam essentiam quae

things and in all things. Now, it is absurd |to think| that just as a created thing cannot at all exceed the greatness of the Creating and Sustaining |Being|, so the Creating and Sustaining |Being| cannot at all exceed the totality of created things. Consequently, it is clear that this |Being| is what sustains, excels, encompasses, and pervades all other things. Therefore, if these |conclusions| are conjoined with the ones discovered earlier, then |one and| the same |Being| exists in and through all |other| things and is that from which, through which, and in which all |other| things |exist|.[25]

CHAPTER FIFTEEN
What can and what cannot be predicated
of the Supreme Being substantively.

Now, I am especially and not unjustifiably moved to inquire, as earnestly as I can, into what (from among whatever is predicable of something) can substantively besuit such a marvelous Nature as this. For although I would be surprised if among the names or words which we apply to things made from nothing, there could be found a |word| that would appropriately be predicated of the Substance which created all |other| things, nevertheless I must try to ascertain to what end reason will direct this investigation. Now, about relational |words|—no one doubts that none of them apply to the substance of the thing of which they are predicated relationally.[26] Therefore, if some |word| is predicated of the Supreme Nature relationally, |this word| does not signify its substance. Thus, although |the Supreme Nature| can be spoken of relationally as *supreme* over, or as *greater* than, all the things that it made (or can be spoken of relationally in some other similar way), |these utterances| do not, it is obvious, designate its natural being. For if there never existed any of the things in relation to which it is called supreme and greater, then it would not be understood to be either supreme or greater. Nevertheless, it would not for that reason be less good or would not at all undergo detriment with respect to its essential greatness. We recognize this plainly from the fact that through no other than through itself is this Being as good as it is or as great as it is. So if the Supreme Nature can so be understood to be not-supreme that it is still |understood to be| no greater or lesser than when it is understood to be supreme over all things, clearly "supreme" does not signify unqualifiedly *that* Being which

omnimodo maior et melior est quam quidquid non est quod ipsa. Quod autem ratio docet de "summo," non dissimiliter invenitur in similiter relativis.

25 Illis itaque quae relative dicuntur omissis, quia nullum eorum simpliciter demonstrat alicuius essentiam, ad alia discutienda se convertat intentio. Equidem si quis singula diligenter intueatur: quidquid est praeter relativa, aut tale est ut ipsum omnino melius sit quam non-ipsum, aut tale ut non-ipsum in aliquo melius sit quam ipsum. "Ipsum" autem et 30 "non-ipsum" non aliud hic intelligo quam verum, non-verum; corpus, non-corpus; et his similia. Melius quidem est omnino aliquid quam non-ipsum, ut sapiens quam non-ipsum-sapiens; id est, melius est sapiens quam non-sapiens. Quamvis enim iustus non-sapiens melior videatur quam non-iustus sapiens, non tamen est melius simpliciter non-sapiens 35 quam sapiens. Omne quippe non-sapiens simpliciter, inquantum non-sapiens est, minus est quam sapiens—quia omne non-sapiens melius esset, si esset sapiens. Similiter omnino melius est verum quam non-ipsum, id est quam non-verum; et iustum quam non-iustum; et vivit quam non-vivit. Melius autem est in aliquo non-ipsum quam ipsum, ut 40 non-aurum quam aurum. Nam melius est homini esse non-aurum quam aurum, quamvis forsitan alicui melius esset aurum esse quam non-aurum, ut plumbo. Cum enim utrumque, scilicet homo et plumbum, sit non-aurum: tanto melius aliquid est homo quam aurum, quanto inferioris esset naturae, si esset aurum; et plumbum tanto vilius est, quanto pretio-45 sius esset, si aurum esset.

Patet autem, ex eo quod summa natura sic intelligi potest non-summa ut nec summum omnino melius sit quam non-summum, nec non-summum alicui melius quam summum, multa relativa esse quae nequaquam hac contineantur divisione. Ultrum vero aliqua contineantur, 50 inquirere supersedeo, cum ad propositum sufficiat, quod de illis notum est: nullum scilicet eorum designare simplicem summae naturae substantiam. Cum igitur quidquid aliud est, si singula dispiciantur, aut sit melius

in every way is greater and better than whatever is not what it is. Now, that which reason teaches regarding "supreme" holds equally true for similar relational |words|.

And so, leaving aside those |words| which are predicated relationally (since none of them unqualifiedly exhibit the essence of anything), let me turn my attention to the discussion of other |words|. Surely, if someone carefully examines them one at a time, |he will see that| whatever nonrelational |words| there are, |each one| either is such that |what| it |signifies| is in every respect better than |what| its negation |signifies| or else is such that its negation is in some respect better than it. (By "it" and "its negation" I mean here only *true* and *not-true, material object* and *not-material-object*, and the like). Indeed, |in some cases| something is in every respect better than its negation—as, for example, *wise* than *not-wise*; i.e., *wise* is better than *not-wise*. (For although someone who is just without being wise seems better than someone who is wise without being just, nevertheless *not-wise* is not unqualifiedly better than *wise*. Indeed, whatever is not-wise is, insofar as it is not wise, unqualifiedly inferior to what is wise; for whatever is not wise would be better if it were wise. Similarly, *true* is in every respect better than not-itself, i.e., than *not-true*; and *just* |is in every respect better| than *not-just*; and *lives* |is in every respect better| than *not-lives*. But |in some cases| the negation is in some respect the better; for example, *not-gold* |is in some respect better| than *gold*. For it is better for a man to be not-gold than to be gold, even though for something |else| it might be better to be gold than not-gold (e.g., for lead). For although neither a man nor a piece of lead is gold, still, the more inferior in nature |a man| would become if he were gold, the better thing a man is than gold; and the more valuable a piece of lead would become if it were gold, the more inferior lead is |to gold|.

From the fact that the Supreme Nature can be understood to be not-supreme in such way that (1) |for it to be| supreme is in no respect better than |for it to be| not-supreme and (2) |for it to be| not-supreme is not in some respect better than |for it to be| supreme, clearly there are many relational |words| which are not at all encompassed by the above classification. I forego inquiring about whether some |relational words| *are* |so| encompassed, because for my purposes what has |already| been learned about them suffices, viz., that none of these |words| designate the simple substance of the Supreme Nature. Since, then, if we look separately at whatever else there is |i.e., at whatever is signified by nonrelational

quam non-ipsum, aut non-ipsum in aliquo sit melius quam ipsum: sicut
nefas est putare quod substantia supremae naturae sit aliquid quo melius
55 sit aliquomodo non-ipsum, sic necesse est ut sit quidquid omnino melius
est quam non-ipsum. Illa enim sola est qua penitus nihil est melius et
quae melior est omnibus quae non sunt quod ipsa est. Non est igitur
corpus vel aliquid eorum quae corporei sensus discernunt. Quippe his
omnibus melius est aliquid quod non est quod ipsa sunt. Mens enim
60 rationalis, quae nullo corporeo sensu quid vel qualis vel quanta sit percipitur: quanto minor esset, si esset aliquid eorum quae corporeis sensibus
subiacent, tanto maior est quam quodlibet eorum. Penitus enim ipsa
summa essentia tacenda est esse aliquid eorum quibus est aliquid, quod
non est quod ipsa sunt, superius; et est omnino, sicut ratio docet, dicenda
65 quodlibet eorum quibus est omne, quod non est quod ipsa sunt, inferius.
Quare necesse est eam esse viventem, sapientem, potentem et omnipotentem, veram, iustam, beatam, aeternam, et quidquid similiter absolute
melius est quam non-ipsum. Quid ergo quaeratur amplius quid summa
illa sit natura, si manifestum est quid omnium sit aut quid non sit?

CAPITULUM XVI

Quod idem sit illi esse iustam quod est esse iustitiam;
et eodem modo de iis quae similiter de illa dici possunt; et quod
nihil horum monstret, qualis illa vel quanta sit, sed quid sit.

5 Sed fortasse cum dicitur iusta vel magna vel aliquid similium, non osten-
ditur quid sit, sed potius qualis vel quanta sit. Per qualitatem quippe vel
quantitatem quodlibet horum dici videtur. Omne namque quod iustum
est, per iustitiam iustum est. Et alia huiusmodi similiter. Quare ipsa
summa natura non est iusta nisi per iustitiam. Videtur igitur partici-
10 patione qualitatis, iustitiae scilicet, iusta dici summe bona substantia.
Quod si ita est, per aliud est iusta, non per se. At hoc contrarium est

words, each is something which| either it is better to be than not to be or else in some respect it is better not to be than to be: just as it is blasphemous to suppose that the substance of the Supreme Nature is something which in some respect it would be better not to be, so this substance must be whatever in every respect it is better to be than not to be. For this substance alone is that than which nothing at all is better; and it alone is better than all things which are not what it is. Hence, it is not a material object or one of the things which the bodily senses detect. (Indeed, there is something better than all these |material objects|— something which is not what they are. For |consider| a rational mind, whose nature, quality, or quantity is perceived by no bodily sense: the more inferior a rational mind would become if it were one of those things which are subject to the bodily senses, the greater it is than any of those things.) For the Supreme Being must in no respect be said to be one of those things to which something that is not what they are is superior. And the Supreme Being (as reason teaches) must unqualifiedly be said to be each of those things to which whatever is not what they are is inferior.[27] Therefore, necessarily, the Supreme Being is living, wise, powerful and all-powerful, true, just, blessed, eternal, and whatever similarly is in every respect better than its negation. Why, then, should I continue to ask what this Supreme Nature is, if whatever it is or is not is evident?

CHAPTER SIXTEEN

For the Supreme Being to be *just* is the same as for it to be justice.
The case is the same regarding that which can be predicated of it
in a way similar |to the way in which "just" is predicated|.
None of these |predicates| indicate what kind of thing it is or of what
magnitude it is; instead, |they indicate| what it is.

*not accidents
but rather
essence !
divine*

But when we call |the Supreme Being| *just* or great (or any such thing), perhaps we are indicating not what it is but rather what kind of thing it is or of what magnitude it is. Indeed, each of these |predicates, viz., "just" and "great"| seems to be predicated with respect to quality or to quantity; for whatever is just is just through justice (and likewise for other |predicates| of this kind). Therefore, the Supreme Nature is just only through justice. Hence, it seems that the supremely good Substance is called just by participation in a quality, viz., justice. But if so, |i.e., if the Supreme Substance were just in this way|, then |the Supreme Sub-

veritati perspectae: quia—bona vel magna vel subsistens—quod est, omnino per se est, non per aliud. Si igitur non est iusta nisi per iustitiam, nec iusta potest esse nisi per se: quid magis conspicuum, quid magis
15 necessarium, quam quod eadem natura est ipsa iustitia; et cum dicitur esse iusta per iustitiam, idem est quod per se; et cum iusta per se dicitur esse, non aliud intelligitur quam per iustitiam? Quapropter si quaeratur quid sit ipsa summa natura de qua agitur, quid verius respondetur quam "iustitia"? Videndum igitur quomodo intelligendum sit, quando illa na-
20 tura, quae est ipsa iustitia, dicitur iusta.

Quoniam enim homo non potest esse iustitia, sed habere potest iusti- tiam: non intelligitur iustus homo existens iustitia, sed habens iustitiam. Quoniam igitur summa natura non proprie dicitur quia habet iustitiam, sed existit iustitia: cum dicitur iusta, proprie intelligitur existens iustitia,
25 non autem habens iustitiam. Quare si cum dicitur existens iustitia, non dicitur qualis est sed quid est, consequitur ut cum dicitur iusta, non dicatur qualis sit sed quid sit. Deinde quoniam de illa suprema essentia idem est dicere quia est iusta, et quia est existens iustitia, et cum dicitur "est existens iustitia," non est aliud quam "est iustitia": nihil differt in illa
30 sive dicatur "est iusta," sive "est iustitia." Quapropter cum quaeritur de illa quid est, non minus congrue respondetur "iusta" quam "iustitia."

Quod vero in exemplo iustitiae ratum esse conspicitur, hoc de omni- bus quae similiter de ipsa summa natura dicuntur, intellectus sentire per rationem constringitur. Quidquid igitur eorum de illa dicatur: non qualis
35 vel quanta, sed magis quid sit monstratur. Sed palam est quia quodlibet bonum summa natura sit, summe illud est. Illa igitur est summa essentia, summa vita, summa ratio, summa salus, summa iustitia, summa sapien- tia, summa veritas, summa bonitas, summa magnitudo, summa pulchri- tudo, summa immortalitas, summa incorruptibilitas, summa immutabili-

stance| would be just not through itself but through something other |than itself|. But this |view| is contrary to the truth which we have already seen, viz., that whether good or great or existing—what |the Supreme Nature| is, it is completely through itself and not through something other |than itself|. So if it is just only through justice, and if it can be just only through itself, what is more clear and more necessary than that this Nature *is* justice? And when it is said to be just through justice, is not this the same as |being just| through itself? And when it is said to be just through itself, what else is meant other than |that it is just| through justice?[28] Therefore, if someone asks "What is this Supreme Nature which is being investigated?" is there a truer answer than "justice"? So I must look into how we are to understand the statement that this Nature (which *is* justice) is just.

For since a man cannot be justice but can have justice, a just man is not understood to be a man who *is* justice but to be a man who *has* justice. So since the Supreme Nature is not properly said to have justice but rather to be justice, then when |this Nature| is said to be just, it is properly understood to be |a Nature| which is justice rather than to be |a Nature| which has justice. Hence, if when we say that it is |a Nature| which is justice we are saying not what kind of thing it is but rather what it is, then (by logical inference) when we say that it is just, we are saying not what kind of thing it is but what it is. Or again, with regard to the Supreme Being: since to say that it is just is the same as saying that it is what is justice, and since to say that it is what is justice is not other than saying that it is justice, it makes no difference, with regard to this Nature, whether we say "It is just" or "It is justice." Therefore, when someone asks regarding this Nature "What is it?" the answer "just" is no less appropriate than the answer "justice."

The intellect is bound to discern rationally that what is seen to have been established in the case of justice also holds true for all the things predicated similarly of the Supreme Nature. Hence, whichever of these is predicated of this Nature, they tell neither what kind of thing this Nature is nor of what magnitude it is but rather what it is. But obviously the Supreme Nature is supremely whatever good thing it is. Therefore, the Supreme Nature is Supreme Being (*summa essentia*), Supreme Life (*summa vita*), Supreme Reason, Supreme Refuge, Supreme Justice, Supreme Wisdom, Supreme Truth, Supreme Goodness, Supreme Greatness, Supreme Beauty, Supreme Immortality, Supreme Incorruptibility,

40 tas, summa beatitudo, summa aeternitas, summa potestas, summa unitas—
quod non est aliud quam summe ens, summe vivens, et alia similiter.

CAPITULUM XVII

Quod ita sit simplex ut omnia quae de eius essentia
dici possunt, unum idemque in illa sint, et nihil de ea
dici possit substantialiter nisi in eo quod quid est.

5 Quid ergo? Si illa summa natura tot bona est, eritne composita tam
pluribus bonis, an potius non sunt plura bona, sed unum bonum, tam
pluribus nominibus significatum? Omne enim compositum ut subsistat,
indiget iis ex quibus componitur; et illis debet quod est, quia quidquid
est, per illa est, et illa quod sunt, per illud non sunt; et idcirco penitus
10 summum non est. Si igitur illa natura composita est pluribus bonis, haec
omnia quae omni composito insunt, in illam incidere necesse est. Quod
nefas falsitatis aperta ratione destruit et obruit tota quae supra patuit
necessitas veritatis. Cum igitur illa natura nullo modo composita sit, et
tamen omnimodo tot illa bona sit, necesse est ut illa omnia non plura sed
15 unum sint. Idem igitur est quodlibet unum eorum quod omnia, sive
simul sive singula—ut cum dicitur iustitia vel essentia, idem significat
quod alia, vel omnia simul vel singula. Quemadmodum itaque unum est
quidquid essentialiter de summa substantia dicitur, ita ipsa uno modo,
una consideratione, est quidquid est essentialiter. Cum enim aliquis
20 homo dicatur et corpus et rationalis et homo, non uno modo vel consideratione haec tria dicitur. Secundum aliud enim est corpus, et secundum aliud rationalis, et singulum horum non est totum hoc quod est
homo. Illa vero summa essentia nullo modo sic est aliquid ut illud idem
secundum alium modum aut secundum aliam considerationem non sit,
25 quia quidquid aliquomodo essentialiter est, hoc est totum quod ipsa est.
Nihil igitur quod de eius essentia vere dicitur, in eo quod qualis vel

Supreme Immutability, Supreme Beatitude, Supreme Eternity, Supreme Power, Supreme Oneness. And |all| these |descriptions| are the same as |the descriptions| Supremely Being (*summe ens*), Supremely Living (*summe vivens*), and so forth.

CHAPTER SEVENTEEN

|The Supreme Being| is so simple that whatever things can be predicated of its essence are one and the same thing in it. And something can be predicated substantively of the Supreme Being only with respect to what |this Being| is.

What, then? If the Supreme Nature is so many goods, will it be composed of so many goods, or are they, rather than being many goods, |only| one good signified by so many names? For everything composite needs for its existence the parts of which it is composed; and what it is it owes to its parts. For through them it is whatever it is, whereas what they are they are not through it; and so, it is not at all supreme. Hence, if the Supreme Nature were composed of many goods, then what holds true of everything composite would also have to hold true of it. But the whole necessity of previously established truth destroys and overthrows, by means of clear reasoning, this blasphemous falsity. Therefore, since this Nature is in no respect composite and yet is in every respect those very many goods |listed above|, all those goods must be one rather than many.[29] Hence, each one of them is the same as all |the others|— whether they be considered distinctly or all together. For example, when |this Nature| is said to be justice or being, |these predicates| signify the same thing as do the other |predicates|, whether considered distinctly or all together. Thus, even as whatever is predicated essentially of the Supreme Substance is one, so whatever the Supreme Substance is essentially it is in one way, in one respect. For when a man is said to be a body and rational and a man, these three things are not said in a single way, in a single respect. For in one respect he is a body, in another rational; and neither of these constitutes the whole of what a man is. By contrast, it is not at all the case that the Supreme Being is something in such way that in some manner or respect it is not this thing; for whatever |the Supreme Being| in some respect essentially is is the whole of what it is. Therefore, whatever is predicated truly of its essence applies to what it is, not to what kind of thing it is or to of what magnitude it is.[30]

quanta, sed in eo quod quid sit, accipitur. Quidquid enim est quale vel quantum, est etiam aliud in eo quod quid est; unde non simplex, sed compositum est.

CAPITULUM XVIII
Quod sit sine principio et sine fine.

Ex quo igitur haec tam simplex natura creatrix et vigor omnium fuit, vel usquequo futura est? An potius nec ex quo nec usquequo est, sed sine
5 principio et sine fine est? Si enim principium habet, aut ex se vel per se hoc habet, aut ex alio vel per aliud, aut ex nihilo vel per nihil. Sed constat per veritatem iam perspectam quia nullo modo ex alio vel ex nihilo, aut per aliud vel per nihil, est. Nullo igitur modo per aliud vel ex alio, aut per nihil vel ex nihilo, initium sortita est. Ex seipsa vero vel per
10 se initium habere non potest, quamquam ex seipsa et per seipsam sit. Sic enim est ex se et per se ut nullo modo sit alia essentia quae est per se et ex se, et alia per quam et ex qua est. Quidquid autem ex aliquo vel per aliquid incipit esse, non est omnino idem illi ex quo vel per quod incipit esse. Summa igitur natura non incepit per se vel ex se. Quoniam igitur
15 nec per se nec ex se, nec per aliud nec ex alio, nec per nihil nec ex nihilo habet principium: nullo modo habet principium.

Sed neque finem habebit. Si enim finem habitura est, non est summe immortalis et summe incorruptibilis. Sed constat quia est summe et immortalis et incorruptibilis. Non habebit igitur finem. Amplius. Si finem
20 habitura est, aut volens aut nolens deficiet. Sed pro certo non est simplex bonum, cuius voluntate perit summum bonum. At ipsa est verum et simplex bonum. Quare sua sponte non deficiet ipsa, quam certum est esse summum bonum. Si vero nolens peritura est, non est summe potens

For whatever is |subject to| a quality or a quantity is something else with respect to what it is |i.e., with respect to its essence| and, thus, is not simple but is composite.

|The Supreme Being| exists without beginning and without end.

From what time, then, did this so simple Nature—Creator and Sustainer of all things—first exist? And when will it cease to exist? Or does |this Nature| exist neither from a beginning point nor to an end point but rather as beginningless and endless? For were it to have a beginning it would have a beginning either (1) from or through itself, (2) from or through something other |than itself|, or (3) from or through nothing. But from the truth already seen, clearly |this Nature| does not in any way exist either from something other |than itself| or from nothing, either through something other |than itself| or through nothing. Therefore, it did not at all have a beginning from or through something other |than itself|, from or through nothing. Moreover, it could not have had a beginning from or through itself, even though it exists from itself and through itself. For |this Nature| exists from and through itself in such way that there is not at all one being which exists from and through itself and another being through which and from which the first being exists. Now, whatever begins to exist from something or through something is not at all the same thing as that from which or through which it begins to exist. Therefore, the Supreme Nature did not begin |to exist| through itself or from itself. Thus, since it has no beginning either from or through itself, either from or through something other |than itself|, either from or through nothing, it has no beginning at all.

On the other hand, |the Supreme Nature| will also have no end. For if it were going to have an end, it would not be supremely immortal and supremely incorruptible. But it is evident[31] that it is both supremely immortal and supremely incorruptible. Hence, it will not have an end. Furthermore, if it were going to have an end, it would come to an end either willingly or unwillingly.[32] But surely that |Being| by means of whose will the Supreme Good perished would not be a simple good. But the Supreme Nature *is* a true and simple good. Hence, this Nature, which is assuredly the Supreme Good, would not come to an end willingly. Yet, if it were going to come to an end unwillingly, it would not

nec omnipotens. Sed rationis necessitas asseruit eam esse summe poten-
25 tem et omnipotentem. Non ergo nolens deficiet. Quare si nec volens nec
nolens summa natura finem habebit, nullo modo finem habebit.

Amplius. Si summa illa natura principium vel finem habet, non est
vera aeternitas, quod esse supra inexpugnabiliter inventum est. Deinde
cogitet qui potest, quando incepit aut quando non fuit hoc verum: scilicet
30 quia futurum erat aliquid; aut quando desinet et non erit hoc verum:
videlicet quia praeteritum erit aliquid. Quodsi neutrum horum cogitari
potest, et utrumque hoc verum sine veritate esse non potest, impossibile
est vel cogitare quod veritas principium aut finem habeat. Denique si
veritas habuit principium vel habebit finem: antequam ipsa inciperet,
35 verum erat tunc quia non erat veritas; et postquam finita erit, verum erit
tunc quia non erit veritas. Atqui verum non potest esse sine veritate. Erat
igitur veritas antequam esset veritas; et erit veritas postquam finita erit
veritas—quod inconvenientissimum est. Sive igitur dicatur veritas habere,
sive intelligatur non habere, principium vel finem: nullo claudi potest
40 veritas principio vel fine. Quare idem sequitur de summa natura, quia
ipsa summa veritas est.

CAPITULUM XIX

Quomodo nihil fuit ante aut erit post illam.

Sed ecce iterum insurgit nihil, et quaecumque hactenus ratio veritate et
necessitate concorditer attestantibus disseruit, asserit esse nihil. Si enim
5 ea quae supra digesta sunt, necessariae veritatis munimine firmata sunt,
non fuit aliquid ante summam essentiam nec erit aliquid post eam.
Quare nihil fuit ante eam, et nihil erit post eam. Nam aut aliquid aut
nihil necesse est praecessisse vel subsecuturum esse. Qui autem dicit quia
nihil fuit ante ipsam et nihil erit post ipsam, id pronuntiare videtur quia

be supremely powerful or all-powerful. But rational necessity has already declared that it is supremely powerful and all-powerful. Hence, it would not come to an end unwillingly. Consequently, if the Supreme Nature shall not have an end either willingly or unwillingly, it shall not at all have an end.

Moreover, if the Supreme Nature were to have a beginning or an end it would not be true eternity—something which it has already uncontestably been found to be.[33] Or again, let anyone who can, try to conceive of when it began to be true, or was ever not true, that something was going to exist.[34] Or |let him try to conceive of| when it will cease being true and will not be true that something has existed in the past. Now, if neither of these things can be conceived, and if both |statements| can be true only if there is truth, then it is impossible even to think that truth has a beginning or an end. Indeed, suppose that truth had had a beginning, or suppose that it would at some time come to an end: then even before truth had begun to be, it would have been true that there was no truth; and even after truth had come to an end, it would still be true that there would no longer be truth. But it could not be true without truth. Hence, there would have been truth before truth came to be, and there would still be truth after truth had ceased to be. But these |conclusions| are self-contradictory. Therefore, whether truth is said to have a beginning or an end, or whether it is understood not to have a beginning or an end, truth cannot be confined by any beginning or end. Consequently, the same |conclusion| holds with regard to the Supreme Nature, because the Supreme Nature is the Supreme Truth.

CHAPTER NINETEEN

How nothing existed before or will exist after the Supreme Being.

But, behold, *nothing* once again rises up; and it alleges to be nothing all that reason has thus far discussed and all that truth and necessity have given consistent witness to. For if those things which have been explained above have been made secure by the fortification of necessary truth, then there was not anything earlier than the Supreme Being nor will there be anything later than the Supreme Being. Hence, nothing was before it, and nothing will be after it. For, necessarily, either something or nothing preceded it and is going to succeed it. But anyone who says that nothing was before it and that nothing will be after it seems to be saying that (1)

10 fuit ante ipsam quando nihil erat, et erit post ipsam quando nihil erit.
Quando ergo nihil erat, illa non erat; et quando nihil erit, illa non erit.
Quomodo ergo non incepit ex nihilo, aut quomodo non deveniet ad
nihilum, si illa nondum erat cum iam erat nihil, et eadem iam non erit
cum adhuc erit nihil? Quid igitur molita est tanta moles argumentorum,
15 si tam facile demolitur nihilum molimina eorum? Si namque constituitur
ut summum esse nihilo et praecedenti succedat et subsequenti decedat:
quidquid supra statuit verum necesse, destituitur per inane nihilum. An
potius repugnandum est nihilo, ne tot structurae necessariae rationis
expugnentur a nihilo, et summum bonum quod lucerna veritatis quaesi-
20 tum et inventum est, amittatur pro nihilo?

Potius igitur asseratur, si fieri potest, quia nihil non fuit ante summam
essentiam nec erit post illam quam, dum locus datur ante vel post illam
nihilo, per nihilum reducatur ad nihil illud esse quod per seipsum con-
duxit id quod erat nihil ad esse. Duplicem namque una pronuntiatio
25 gerit sententiam, cum dicitur quia nihil fuit ante summam essentiam.
Unus enim est eius sensus quia priusquam summa essentia esset, fuit cum
erat nihil; alter vero eius est intellectus quia ante summam essentiam non
fuit aliquid. Veluti si dicam "nihil me docuit volare," hoc aut sic expo-
nam quia "ipsum nihil" (quod significat non aliquid) docuit me volare
30 (et erit falsum) aut quia non me docuit aliquid volare (quod est verum).
Prior itaque sensus est quem sequitur supra tractata inconvenientia, et
omnimoda ratione pro falso repellitur; alter vero est qui superioribus
perfecta cohaeret convenientia, et tota illorum contextione verus esse
compellitur. Quare cum dicitur quia nihil fuit ante illam, secundum pos-
35 teriorem intellectum accipiendum est; nec sic est exponendum ut intelligatur aliquando fuisse quando illa non erat et nihil erat, sed ita ut intelli-

before the Supreme Being there was a time when nothing existed and that (2) after the Supreme Being there will be a time when nothing will exist. Consequently, when nothing existed, the Supreme Being did not exist; and when nothing will exist, the Supreme Being will not exist. So if when nothing already existed the Supreme Being did not yet exist, and if the Supreme Being will no longer exist when nothing will still exist, how is it that |the Supreme Being| did not begin |to exist| from nothing, or how is it that it will not come to nothing? What, then, did such an array of arguments accomplish if nothing so easily destroys their effi-cacy? For if it be established that the Supreme Being is subsequent to nothing, which precedes it, and ceases prior to nothing, which succeeds it, then all that necessary truth determined above is destroyed through a mere nothing. Or must this *nothing* be opposed, lest so many necessary structures of reason be overthrown by nothing and lest the Supreme Good, which by the light of truth has been sought-after and found, be lost for nothing?

Therefore, if possible, let us deny the proposition "Nothing existed before and will exist after the Supreme Being" rather than, while giving place to nothing before and after the Supreme Being, to reduce to nothing through nothing this Being, which through itself brought into existence what had been nothing. For the one expression—viz., "Nothing existed before the Supreme Being"—has a twofold meaning. For one meaning of it is that before the Supreme Being existed there was a time when nothing existed; but the other meaning of it is: it is not the case that there was anything before the Supreme Being. Similarly, if I were to say "Nothing taught me to fly," I might construe this |statement| to mean that *nothing itself* (in the sense of *not-something*) taught me to fly—|an assertion| which would be false. Or |I might construe it to mean| that it is not the case that anything taught me to fly—|an asser-tion| which is true.[35] And so, the first construal is that from which there follows the inconsistency discussed above; and |this construal| is rejected as in every respect false. But the second |construal| is perfectly consistent with the earlier |conclusions| and is of necessity true in conjunction with them. Therefore, when it is said that nothing existed before the Supreme Being, the statement must be taken in accordance with the second mean-ing. It must not be construed to mean that there was a time when nothing existed and the Supreme Being did not exist; rather, |it must be construed| to mean that it is not the case that there was anything before

gatur quia ante illam non fuit aliquid. Eadem ratio est duplicis intellectus,
si nihil dicatur post illam esse futurum. Si ergo haec interpretatio quae
facta est de nihilo diligenter discernitur, verissime nec aliquid nec nihil
40 summam essentiam aut praecessisse aut subsecuturum esse, et nihil fuisse
ante vel post illam esse secuturum concluditur; et tamen nulla iam consti-
tutorum soliditas nihili inanitate concutitur.

CAPITULUM XX

Quod illa sit in omni loco et tempore.

Quamquam autem supra conclusum sit quia creatrix haec natura ubique
et in omnibus et per omnia sit, et ex eo quia nec incepit nec desinet esse,
5 consequatur quia semper fuit et est et erit: sentio tamen quiddam contra-
dictionis summurmurare, quod me cogit diligentius ubi et quando illa sit
indagare. Itaque summa essentia aut ubique et semper est, aut tantum
alicubi et aliquando, aut nusquam et numquam. Quod dico aut in omni
loco vel tempore, aut determinate in aliquo, aut in nullo.
10   Sed quid videtur repugnantius quam ut quod verissime et summe est,
id nusquam et numquam sit? Falsum est igitur nusquam vel numquam
illam esse. Deinde quoniam nullum bonum nec penitus aliquid est sine
ea: si ipsa nusquam vel numquam est, nusquam vel numquam aliquod
bonum est, et nusquam vel numquam omnino aliquid est. Quod quam
15 falsum sit, nec dicere opus est. Falsum igitur est et illud: quod illa nusquam et numquam sit. Aut est ergo determinate alicubi et aliquando, aut
ubique et semper. At si determinate est in aliquo loco vel tempore: ibi et
tunc tantum, ubi et quando ipsa est, potest aliquid esse; ubi vero et
quando ipsa non est, ibi et tunc penitus nulla est essentia, quia sine ea
20 nihil est. Unde consequetur ut sit aliquis locus et aliquod tempus ubi et
quando nihil omnino est. Quod quoniam falsum est—ipse namque locus
et ipsum tempus aliquid est—non potest esse summa natura alicubi vel

the Supreme Being. The same kind of twofold meaning occurs if we say that nothing will exist after the Supreme Being. Accordingly, if we examine carefully the construal which has been given concerning |the word| "nothing," then we conclude very truly that neither something nor nothing preceded or will succeed the Supreme Being and that nothing existed before it or will exist after it. And nevertheless, the stability of our previously established conclusions is not at all shaken by a mere nothing.

CHAPTER TWENTY
The Supreme Being exists in every place and at all times.

It was concluded above[36] that this Creative Nature exists everywhere, in all things and through all things; and the fact that it neither began to exist nor will cease to exist entails that it always was, is, and will be.[37] Nonetheless, I detect a murmur of contradiction which requires me to investigate more closely where and when the Supreme Being exists. Accordingly, the Supreme Being exists either (1) everywhere and always or (2) only in some place and at some time or (3) nowhere and never— in other words, either (1) in every place and at every time or (2) |only| in a delimited way in some place and at some time or (3) in no place and at no time.

But what is more obviously objectionable than |supposing| that what exists supremely and most truly, exists nowhere and never? Therefore, it is false that the Supreme Being exists nowhere and never. Moreover, without this Being there would exist neither any good nor anything at all. Hence, if it existed nowhere or never, there would nowhere or never be anything good and nowhere or never be anything at all. (It is not necessary to discuss how false this |consequence| is.) (NOT *3*) So it is false that the Supreme Being nowhere and never exists. Hence, either it exists |only| in a delimited way in some place and at some time or else it exists everywhere and always. Assume that it exists only in a delimited way in some place and at some time. Then, only where and when it existed could anything exist; where and when it did not exist, no being would exist—because without the Supreme Being there would be nothing. Thus, it would follow that there is a place and a time at which there would not exist anything at all. But this |consequence| is false; for that place and that time would be something. (NOT *2*) Therefore, the Supreme

aliquando determinate. Quod si dicitur quia determinate ipsa per se alicubi et aliquando est, sed per potentiam suam est ubicumque vel quan
25 documque aliquid est, non est verum. Quoniam enim potentiam eius nihil aliud quam ipsam esse manifestum est, nullo modo potentia eius sine ipsa est. Cum ergo non sit alicubi vel aliquando determinate, necesse est ut sit ubique et semper, id est in omni loco vel tempore.

CAPITULUM XXI

Quod in nullo sit loco aut tempore.

Quod si ita est, aut tota est in omni loco vel tempore, aut tantum quaelibet pars eius, ut altera pars sit extra omnem locum et tempus. Si vero
5 partim est et partim non est in omni loco vel tempore, partes habet— quod falsum est. Non igitur partim est ubique et semper. Tota autem quomodo est ubique et semper? Aut enim sic est intelligendum ut tota semel sit in omnibus locis vel temporibus et per partes in singulis, aut sic ut tota sit etiam in singulis. Verum si per partes est in singulis, non effugit
10 partium compositionem et divisionem—quod valde alienum a summa natura inventum est. Quapropter non est ita tota in omnibus locis aut temporibus ut per partes sit in singulis. Restat altera pars discutienda: scilicet qualiter summa natura tota sit in omnibus et singulis locis vel temporibus. Hoc nimirum esse non potest nisi aut simul aut diversis tem
15 poribus. Sed quoniam ratio loci ac ratio temporis, quas hactenus simul progressas eisdem vestigiis una potuit indagare prosecutio, hic ab invicem digredientes disputationem videntur diversis quasi fugere anfractibus, singulatim suis investigentur discussionibus. Primum ergo videatur si

Nature cannot exist |only| in a delimited way in some place and at some time. Now, if it be said that through itself this Nature exists in a delimited way in some place and at some time but that through its power it exists wherever and whenever something is—|this statement| would not be true. For since, clearly, this Nature's power is nothing other than itself, its power exists in no way apart from itself. (1) Therefore, since |this Nature| does not exist in a delimited way in any place or at any time, it is necessary that it exist everywhere and always, i.e., in every place and at every time.

CHAPTER TWENTY-ONE

|The Supreme Being| exists in no place at no time.

But if |the above conclusion| holds, then either |the Supreme Being| exists as a whole in every place and at every time or else only a part of it |occupies every place and time|, with the result that the rest of it exists beyond every place and time.[38] But if it partly were and partly were not in every place and at every time, then it would have parts—|a consequence| which is false. Hence, it is not the case that only a part of it exists everywhere and always. But how does it exist as a whole everywhere and always? We must understand this either (1) in such way that the whole of it once occupies every place and time through its parts which are present in each place and at each time, or else (2) in such way that it exists as a whole even in each place and at each time. But if through its parts it is present in each place at each time, |this Nature| would not escape composition from parts and division into parts—something which has been found to be totally foreign to the Supreme Nature. Hence, it does not exist as a whole in all places or at all times in such way that through parts it is in each place and at each time. |So| the second alternative remains to be discussed, viz., how the Supreme Nature exists as a whole in each and every place and at each and every time. Now, without doubt, this can occur |i.e., the Supreme Nature can exist in each and every place and at each and every time| only at the same time or else at different times. But since the law of place and the law of time (which hitherto one procedure was able to examine, because these |laws| moved forward together on the same footing) here diverge from each other and seem to "shun" (as it were) disputation by |taking| different routes, let each be examined distinctly in a discussion of its own. So first

summa natura tota possit esse in singulis locis aut simul aut per diversa
20 tempora. Deinde id ipsum in temporibus inquiratur.

Si igitur tota est simul in singulis locis, per singula loca sunt singulae
totae. Sicut enim locus a loco distinguitur, ut singula loca sint, ita id
quod totum est in uno loco, ab eo quod eodem tempore totum est in alio
loco distinguitur, ut singula tota sint. Nam quod totum est in aliquo loco,
25 nihil eius est quod non sit in ipso loco. At de quo nihil est quod non sit
in aliquo loco, nihil est de eo quod sit eodem tempore extra eundem
locum. Quod igitur totum est in aliquo loco, nihil eius est quod eodem
tempore sit extra ipsum locum. Sed de quo nihil est extra quemlibet
locum, nihil eius est eodem tempore in alio loco. Quare quod totum est
30 in quolibet loco, nihil eius est simul in alio loco. Quod igitur totum est in
aliquo loco, quomodo totum quoque est simul in alio loco, si nihil de eo
potest esse in alio loco? Quoniam igitur unum totum non potest esse
simul in diversis locis totum, consequitur ut per singula loca singula sint
tota, si in singulis locis simul aliquid est totum. Quapropter si summa
35 natura tota est uno tempore in singulis omnibus locis, quot singula loca
esse possunt, tot singulae summae naturae sunt—quod irrationabile est
opinari. Non est igitur tota uno tempore in singulis locis.

At vero si diversis temporibus tota est in singulis locis: quando est in
uno loco, nullum bonum et nulla essentia est interim in aliis locis, quia
40 sine ea prorsus aliquid non existit. Quod absurdum esse vel ipsa loca
probant, quae non nihil sed aliquid sunt. Non est itaque summa natura
tota in singulis locis diversis temporibus.

Quod si nec eodem tempore nec diversis temporibus tota est in singulis locis, liquet quia nullo modo est tota in singulis omnibus locis.

let it be seen whether the Supreme Nature can exist in each *place* as a whole—either at the same time or at different times. Then, let the same question be posed about |different| *times* |viz., the question whether at each *time* the Supreme Nature can exist as a whole—either at each time at once or else at each time successively|.

If, then, |the Supreme Nature| were to exist as a whole in each *place* at once, these wholes would be distinct in the distinct places. For just as one place is distinct from another (so that they are different places), so what exists as a whole in one place is distinct from what at the same time exists as a whole in another place (so that they are different wholes). For none of what exists as a whole in a given place fails to exist in that place. And if none of a thing fails to exist in a given place, none of it exists at the same time anywhere besides in that place. Therefore, none of what exists wholly in a given place exists at the same time outside that place. But if none of it exists outside a given place, none of it exists at the same time in some other place. Thus, that which exists as a whole in any place does not at all exist at the same time in another place. Accordingly, with regard to whatever exists as a whole in some place, how would it likewise exist as a whole in another place at the same time—if none of it can exist in another place? Therefore, inasmuch as one whole cannot at the same time exist as a whole in different places, it follows that in the distinct places there would be distinct wholes—if in each place there were something existing as a whole at the same time. Thus, if the Supreme Nature were to exist as a whole in every single place at the same time, there would be as many distinct supreme natures as there can be distinct places—|a conclusion| which it is unreasonable to believe. Therefore, it is not the case that |the Supreme Nature| exists as a whole in each place at the same time.

On the other hand, if |the Supreme Nature| were to exist as a whole in each place at different times, then while it existed in one place no good and no being would be present in other places, because without the Supreme Being not anything at all exists. But these very places, which are something rather than nothing, prove this |alternative| to be absurd. Thus, it is not the case that the Supreme Nature exists as a whole in each place at different times.

But if it does not exist in each place as a whole either at the same time or at different times, clearly it does not at all exist as a whole in every single place.

45 Nunc est indagandum si eadem summa natura sit tota in singulis temporibus, aut simul aut distincte per singula tempora. Sed quomodo est aliquid totum simul in singulis temporibus, si ipsa tempora simul non sunt? Si vero separatim et distincte tota est in singulis temporibus, quemadmodum aliquis homo totus est heri et hodie et cras, proprie dici-

50 tur quia fuit et est et erit. Ergo eius aetas, quae nihil aliud est quam eius aeternitas, non est tota simul, sed est partibus extensa per temporum partes. At eius aeternitas nihil aliud est quam ipsa. Summa igitur essentia erit divisa per partes secundum temporum distinctiones. Si enim eius aetas per temporum cursus producitur, habet cum ipsis temporibus

55 praesens, praeteritum, et futurum. Quid autem aliud est eius vel aetas vel existendi diuturnitas quam eius aeternitas? Ergo cum eius aeternitas nihil aliud sit quam eius essentia, sicut supra digesta ratio indubitabiliter probat: si eius aeternitas habet praeteritum, praesens, et futurum, consequenter quoque eius essentia habet praeteritum, praesens, et futurum. At quod

60 praeteritum est, non est praesens vel futurum; et quod praesens est, non est futurum nec praeteritum; et quod futurum est, non est praeteritum vel praesens. Quomodo igitur stabit, quod supra rationabili et perspicua necessitate claruit—scilicet quia illa summa natura nullo modo composita sed summe simplex est et summe incommutabilis—si aliud et aliud

65 est in diversis temporibus et per tempora distributas habet partes? Aut potius si illa vera sunt—immo quia liquida vera sunt—quomodo haec possibilia sunt? Nullo igitur modo creatrix essentia aut aetas aut aeternitas eius recipit praeteritum vel futurum. (Praesens enim quomodo non habet, si vere est?) Sed "fuit" significat praeteritum, et "erit" futurum.

70 Numquam igitur illa fuit vel erit. Quare non est distincte, sicut nec simul, tota in diversis singulis temporibus.

Si igitur, sicut discussum est, nec sic est tota in omnibus locis vel temporibus ut semel sit tota in omnibus et per partes in singulis, nec sic

I must now investigate whether this Supreme Nature exists as a whole at each *time*—either |existing| at each time at once or else |existing| at each time successively. But how would anything exist as a whole at each time at once, if these |different| times are not simultaneous? On the other hand, if |this Nature| were to exist as a whole distinctly and successively at each time (as a man exists as a whole yesterday, today, and tomorrow), then |this Nature| would properly be said to have existed, to exist, and to be going to exist. Therefore, its lifetime—which is nothing other than its eternity—would not exist as a whole at once but would be extended by parts throughout the parts of time. Now, its eternity is nothing other than itself. Hence, the Supreme Being would be divided into parts according to the divisions of time. For if its lifetime were produced throughout the course of time, it would together with time have a past, a present, and a future. But what is its lifetime or its length of existing other than its eternity? Consequently, since its eternity is nothing other than its essence (as unhasty reasoning unassailably proved in the foregoing |discussion|),[39] if its eternity had a past, a present, and a future its essence would also have to have a past, a present, and a future. Now, what is past is not present or future; and what is present is not past or future; and what is future is not past or present. Therefore, if the Supreme Nature were different things at different times and if it had temporally distributed parts, how would there remain firm what was previously shown[40] by clear and rational necessity—viz., that the Supreme Nature is in no way composite but is supremely simple and supremely immutable? Or rather, if those |conclusions| are true |viz., that the Supreme Nature is supremely simple and immutable|—indeed, since they are clear truths—how are these |conclusions| possible |viz., that the Supreme Nature is different things at different times and has temporal parts|? Hence, neither the Creative Being, its lifetime, nor its eternity admits in any way of a past or a future. (But if |this Being| truly |i.e., really| *is*, how would it fail to have a present?) Yet, "it was" signifies a past; and "it will be" signifies a future. Therefore, it never was and never will be. Consequently, it no more exists as a whole at each different time successively than it exists as a whole at each different time at once.

If, then, (as was argued), the Supreme Being does not exist as a whole in every place and at every time (1) in such way that the whole of it once occupies every |place and time| through its parts, which are present

ut tota sit in singulis, manifestum est quoniam non est ullo modo tota in
75 omni loco vel tempore. Et quoniam similiter pervisum est quia non sic
est in omni loco vel tempore ut pars sit in omni et pars sit extra omnem
locum aut tempus, impossibile est ut sit ubique et semper. Nullatenus
enim potest intelligi esse ubique et semper nisi aut tota aut pars. Quod si
nequaquam est ubique et semper, aut erit determinate in aliquo loco vel
80 tempore, aut in nullo. Determinate autem eam in aliquo non posse esse
iam discussum est. In nullo igitur loco vel tempore, id est nusquam et
numquam, est. Non enim potest esse nisi aut in omni aut in aliquo.

Sed rursus cum constet inexpugnabiliter non solum quia est per se et
sine principio et sine fine, sed quia aliquid sine ea nec usquam nec
85 umquam est, necesse est illam esse ubique et semper.

CAPITULUM XXII

Quomodo sit in omni et in nullo loco et tempore.

Quomodo ergo convenient haec tam contraria secundum prolationem, et
tam necessaria secundum probationem? Fortasse quodam modo est
5 summa natura in loco vel tempore, quo non prohibetur sic esse simul
tota in singulis locis vel temporibus ut tamen non sint plures totae sed
una sola tota, nec eius aetas, quae non est nisi vera aeternitas, non sit
distributa in praeteritum, praesens, et futurum. Non enim videntur hac
lege loci ac temporis cogi nisi ea quae sic sunt in loco vel tempore ut loci
10 spatium aut temporis diuturnitatem non excedant. Quare sicut de iis
quae huiusmodi sunt, unum idemque totum simul non posse esse totum
in diversis locis et temporibus omni veritate asseritur, ita in iis quae

in each |place| and at each |time|, and |if it does| not |exist in each place and at each time| (2) in such way that it exists as a whole in each |place| and at each |time|, then clearly the Supreme Nature does not at all exist as a whole in every place and at every time. And since we have also seen that |the Supreme Nature| does not exist in every place and at every time in such way that part of it occupies every |place and time| while part of it is beyond every place and time, *it is impossible that* |the Supreme Nature| *exist everywhere and always.* For it could not at all be thought to exist everywhere and always except either as a whole or as a part. Now, if it does not at all exist everywhere and always, it |must| exist either in a delimited way in some place and at some time or else in no |place and| at no |time|. But I have already argued[41] that it cannot exist in a delimited way in some |place| or at some |time|. Therefore, it |must| exist in no place and at no time, i.e., nowhere and never; for it could not exist except either in every |place| and |at every time| or else in some |place| and at some |time|.

On the other hand, since it is uncontestably evident[42] not only (1) that |the Supreme Nature| exists through itself without beginning and end but also (2) that if it did not exist nothing would ever exist anywhere, *it is necessary that the Supreme Nature exist everywhere and always.*

CHAPTER TWENTY-TWO

How |the Supreme Being| exists in every place at every time
and in no place at no time.

How, then, are these |two conclusions| (so contradictory according to their utterance, so necessary according to their proof) consistent with each other? Well, perhaps the Supreme Nature does exist in place and time in a way which does not prevent it from so existing as a whole in each place at once and as a whole at each time at once that, nonetheless, it is not many wholes, but only one, and its lifetime (which is only its true eternity) is not divided into a past, a present, and a future. For only those things which exist in place or time in such way that they do not transcend spatial extension or temporal duration are bound by the law of place and the law of time. Therefore, just as for things which do not transcend place and time it is said in all truth that one and the same whole cannot exist as a whole in different places at once and cannot exist as a whole at different times at once, so for those things which do

huiusmodi non sunt, id ipsum nulla necessitate concluditur. Iure namque
dici videtur quod tantum eius rei sit aliquis locus cuius quantitatem locus
15 circumscribendo continet et continendo circumscribit, et quod eius
solum rei sit aliquod tempus cuius diuturnitatem tempus metiendo aliquomodo terminat et terminando metitur. Quapropter cuius amplitudini
aut diuturnitati nulla meta vel a loco vel a tempore opponitur, illi nullum
esse locum vel tempus vere proponitur. Quoniam namque nec locus illi
20 facit quod locus, nec tempus quod tempus, non irrationabiliter dicitur
quia nullus locus est eius locus, et nullum tempus est eius tempus. Quod
vero nullum locum aut tempus habere conspicitur, id profecto nullatenus
loci aut temporis legem subire convincitur. Nulla igitur lex loci aut temporis naturam ullam aliquomodo cogit, quam nullus locus ac tempus
25 aliqua continentia claudit.

Quaenam autem rationalis consideratio omnimoda ratione non excludat ut creatricem summamque omnium substantiam, quam necesse est
alienam esse et liberam a natura et iure omnium quae ipsa de nihilo fecit,
ulla loci cohibitio vel temporis includat, cum potius eius potentia, quae
30 nihil est aliud quam eius essentia, cuncta a se facta sub se continendo
concludat? Quomodo quoque non est impudentis imprudentiae dicere
quod summae veritatis aut locus circumscribat quantitatem aut tempus
metiatur diuturnitatem, quae nullam penitus localis vel temporalis disten-
tionis magnitudinem suscipit vel parvitatem?
35   Quoniam itaque loci haec est et temporis conditio, ut tantummodo
quidquid eorum metis clauditur, nec partium fugiat rationem (vel qualem suscipit locus eius secundum quantitatem vel qualem patitur tempus
eius secundum diuturnitatem), nec ullo modo possit totum a diversis
locis vel temporibus simul contineri; quidquid vero loci vel temporis
40 continentia nequaquam coërcetur, nulla locorum vel temporum lege ad
partium multiplicitatem cogatur, aut praesens esse totum simul pluribus
locis aut temporibus prohibeatur—quoniam inquam haec est conditio
loci ac temporis, procul dubio summa substantia, quae nulla loci vel
temporis continentia cingitur, nulla eorum lege constringitur. Quare
45 quoniam summam essentiam totam et inevitabilis necessitas exigit nulli

transcend place and time the above statement need not hold true. For the following statements are seen to be correct: "A thing has a place only if a place contains the thing's size by delimiting it and delimits the thing's size by containing it"; and "A thing has a time only if a time somehow limits the thing's duration by measuring it and measures the thing's duration by limiting it." Therefore, if something's size or duration has no spatial or temporal limitation, then |that thing| is truly stated to have no place and no time. For since place does not affect it in the way that place does |affect things|, and since time |does not affect it| in the way that time |does affect things|, we may reasonably say that no place is its place and that no time is its time. But what is seen to have no place or time is shown assuredly to be not at all subject to the law of place or the law of time. Therefore, no law of place or of time in any way restricts a nature which place and time do not at all confine by any containment.

But which rational reflection does not exclude, in every respect, |the possibility| that some spatial or temporal restriction confines the Creative and Supreme Substance, which must be other than, and free from, the nature and the law of all things which it made from nothing? For, rather, the Supreme Substance's power (which is nothing other than its essence) confines, by containing beneath itself, all the things which it made. How is it not also a mark of shameless ignorance to say that place delimits the greatness (*quantitatem*)—or that time measures the duration—of the Supreme Truth, which does not at all admit of greatness or smallness of spatial or temporal extension?

It is, then, a determining condition of place and of time that only whatever is bounded by their limits cannot escape the relatedness of parts—whether the kind of relatedness that its place undergoes with respect to size or the kind of relatedness that its time undergoes with respect to duration. Nor can this thing in any way be contained as a whole by different places at once, nor as a whole by different times at once. (But whatever is not at all bound by the containment of place and of time is not bound by the law of place or the law of time with respect to multiplicity of parts, or is not prevented from being present as a whole at the same time in many places or at many times.) Since this, I say, is a determining condition of place and time, without doubt the Supreme Substance—which is not bound by any containment of place and of time—is not bound by the law of place and the law of time. Therefore, since an inescapable necessity demands that the Supreme Being be pres-

loco vel tempori deesse, et nulla ratio loci aut temporis prohibet omni
loco vel tempori simul totam adesse, necesse est eam simul totam omnibus et singulis locis et temporibus praesentem esse. Non enim quia huic
loco vel tempori praesens est, idcirco prohibetur illi vel illi loco aut tem-
50 pori simul et similiter praesens esse; nec quoniam fuit aut est aut erit,
ideo aeternitatis eius aliquid evanuit a praesenti tempore cum praeterito
quod iam non est, aut transit cum praesenti quod vix est, aut venturum
est cum futuro quod nondum est. Nullatenus namque cogitur vel prohibetur lege locorum aut temporum alicubi aut aliquando esse vel non esse,
55 quod nullo modo intra locum vel tempus claudit suum esse. Nam si ipsa
summa essentia dicitur esse in loco aut tempore: quamvis de illa et de
localibus sive temporalibus naturis una sit prolatio propter loquendi con-
suetudinem, diversus tamen est intellectus propter rerum dissimilitudinem. In illis namque duo quaedam eadem prolatio significat: id est, quia
60 et praesentia sunt locis et temporibus in quibus esse dicuntur, et quia
continentur ab ipsis. In summa vero essentia unum tantum percipitur: id
est, quia praesens est, non etiam quia continetur.

   Unde si usus loquendi admitteret, convenientius dici videretur esse
cum loco vel tempore quam in loco vel tempore. Plus enim significatur
65 contineri aliquid cum dicitur esse in alio, quam cum dicitur esse cum
alio. In nullo itaque loco vel tempore proprie dicitur esse, quia omnino a
nullo alio continetur; et tamen in omni loco vel tempore suo quodam
modo dici potest esse, quoniam quidquid aliud est ne in nihilum cadat ab
ea praesente sustinetur. In omni loco et tempore est, quia nulli abest; et
70 in nullo est, quia nullum locum aut tempus habet. Nec in se recipit
distinctiones locorum aut temporum, ut hic vel illic vel alicubi, aut nunc

ent as a whole in every place and at every time, and since no law of place or of time prohibits the Supreme Being from being present as a whole in every place at once or from being present as a whole at every time at once, the Supreme Being must be present as a whole in each and every place at once and present as a whole at each and every time at once. Its being present at one place or time does not prevent it from being simultaneously and similarly present at another place or time. Nor is it the case that because it was or is or will be, something of its eternity (*a*) has vanished from the temporal present along with the past, which no longer exists, or (*b*) fades with the present, which scarcely exists, or (*c*) is going to come with the future, which does not yet exist. For the law of place and the law of time do not in any way compel to exist or not to exist in any place or at any time (and do not in any way prevent from existing or not existing in any place or at any time) that which does not in any way confine its own existence within place and time. For if the Supreme Being is said to be in place or time, then even though on account of our customary way of speaking |this| one utterance applies both to the Supreme Being and to spatial and temporal natures, nonetheless on account of the dissimilarity of these beings the meaning |of the utterance| is different |in the two cases|. For in the case of spatial and temporal natures the one utterance signifies two things: (1) that they are present in the places and at the times they are said to be present; and (2) that |these natures| are contained by these places and times. By contrast, in the case of the Supreme Being only one thing is understood, viz., that the Supreme Being is present—not, in addition, that it is contained.[43]

Therefore, if our ordinary way of speaking were to permit, |the Supreme Being| would seem more suitably said to be *with* a place or *with* a time than to be *in* a place or *in* or *at* a time. For when something is said to be *in* something else, it is signified to be contained—more than |it is thus signified| when it is said to be *with* something else. Therefore, |the Supreme Being| is not properly said to be *in* any place or time, because |the Supreme Being| is not at all contained by anything else. And yet, in its own way, it can be said to be in every place and time, inasmuch as all other existing things are sustained by its presence in order that they not fall away into nothing.[44] |The Supreme Being| is in every place and time because it is absent from none; and it is in no |place or time| because it has no place or time. It does not receive into itself distinctions of place

vel tunc vel aliquando; nec secundum labile praesens tempus quo utimur
est, aut secundum praeteritum vel futurum fuit aut erit, quoniam haec
circumscriptorum et mutabilium propria sunt, quod illa non est; et tamen
75 haec de ea quodammodo dici possunt, quoniam sic est praesens omnibus
circumscriptis et mutabilibus ac si illa eisdem circumscribatur locis et
mutetur temporibus. Patet itaque, quantum sat est ad dissolvendam quae
insonabat contrarietatem, qualiter summa omnium essentia ubique et
semper et nusquam et numquam, id est in omni et nullo loco aut tem-
80 pore, sit, iuxta diversorum intellectuum concordem veritatem.

CAPITULUM XXIII

Quomodo melius intellegi possit esse ubique quam in omni loco.

Verum cum constet eandem summam naturam non magis esse in omnibus locis quam in omnibus quae sunt, non velut quae contineatur, sed
5 quae penetrando cuncta contineat, cur non dicatur esse ubique hoc sensu
ut potius intelligatur esse in omnibus quae sunt, quam tantum in omnibus locis, cum hunc intellectum et rei veritas exhibeat, et ipsa localis
verbi proprietas nequaquam prohibeat? Solemus namque saepe localia
verba irreprehensibiliter attribuere rebus quae nec loca sunt nec circum-
10 scriptione locali continentur. Velut si dicam ibi esse intellectum in anima,
ubi est rationalitas. Nam cum "ibi" et "ubi" localia verba sint, non tamen
locali circumscriptione aut anima continet aliquid, aut intellectus vel
rationalitas continentur. Quare summa natura secundum rei veritatem
aptius dicitur esse ubique secundum hanc significationem ut intelligatur
15 esse in omnibus quae sunt, quam si intelligitur tantum in omnibus locis.
Et quoniam sicut supra expositae rationes docent, aliter esse non potest,
necesse est eam sic esse in omnibus quae sunt, ut una eademque perfecte
tota simul sit in singulis.

and time—as, for example, *here, there,* and *somewhere,* or *now, then,* and *sometime.* Nor does it exist in the fleeting temporal present which we experience, nor did it exist in the past, nor will it exist in the future. For these are distinguishing properties of delimited and mutable things; but it is neither delimited nor mutable. Nevertheless, these |temporal modes| can in a sense be predicated of the Supreme Being, inasmuch as it is present to all delimited and mutable things just as if it were delimited by the same places |as they are| and were changed during the same times |as they are|. And so, we see clearly (as clearly as is necessary for resolving what sounded contradictory) how according to the consistent truth of |two| different meanings the Supreme Being exists everywhere and always, nowhere and never—i.e., in every place and time, and in no place or time.

CHAPTER TWENTY-THREE

How |the Supreme Being| can better be understood to exist everywhere than in every place.

But since it is evident[45] that the Supreme Nature exists in all existing things as well as in all places (|in these things| not as what is contained but as what contains all things by its pervasive presence), why is |this Nature| not said to exist everywhere in the sense that it is understood to exist in all existing things rather than |being understood to exist| merely in all places? For the truth of the matter exhibits this understanding, and the proper meaning of spatial discourse does not at all preclude it. For it is our irreproachable practice often to predicate spatial words of things which neither are places nor are contained by spatial limits. For example, I might say that the intellect[46] is *there* in the soul *where* rationality is. Now, although "there" and "where" are spatial words, nonetheless the soul does not contain something within spatial limits, nor is the intellect or rationality thus contained. Therefore, according to the truth of the matter, the Supreme Nature is more fittingly said to exist everywhere in the sense that it exists in all existing things than merely in the sense that it exists in all places. And it is necessary that the Supreme Nature exist in all existing things in such way that one and the same |Nature| exists as completely whole in each thing at once—since (as the reasons presented earlier teach) |the case| cannot be otherwise.

Quomodo melius intelligi possit esse semper quam in omni tempore.

Eandem quoque summam substantiam constat sine principio et fine esse, nec habere praeteritum aut futurum nec temporale, hoc est labile, praesens
5 quo nos utimur—quoniam aetas sive aeternitas eius, quae nihil aliud est quam ipsa, immutabilis et sine partibus est. Nonne ergo "semper," quod videtur designare totum tempus, multo verius (si de illa dicitur) intelligitur significare aeternitatem, quae sibi ipsi numquam est dissimilis, quam temporum varietatem, quae sibi semper in aliquo est non similis?
10 Quare si dicitur semper esse: quoniam idem est illi esse et vivere, nihil melius intelligitur quam aeterne esse vel vivere, id est interminabilem vitam perfecte simul totam obtinere. Videtur enim eius aeternitas esse interminabilis vita simul perfecte tota existens. Cum enim supra iam satis liqueat quod eadem substantia non sit aliud quam vita sua et aeternitas
15 sua, nec sit aliquomodo terminabilis, nec nisi simul et perfecte tota: quid aliud est vera aeternitas, quae illi soli convenit, quam interminabilis vita simul et perfecte tota existens? Nam vel hoc solo veram aeternitatem soli illi inesse substantiae, quae sola non facta sed factrix esse inventa est, aperte percipitur: quoniam vera aeternitas principii finisque meta carere
20 intelligitur; quod nulli rerum creatarum convenire, eo ipso quod de nihilo factae sunt, convincitur.

Quod nullis mutabilis sit accidentibus.

Sed haec essentia quam patuit omnimode sibi esse eandem substantialiter: nonne aliquando est a se diversa vel accidentaliter? Verum quomodo
5 est summe incommutabilis, si per accidentia potest (non dicam esse, sed) vel intelligi variabilis? Et econtra, quomodo non est particeps accidentis, cum hoc ipsum quod maior est omnibus aliis naturis et quod illis dissimilis est, illi videatur accidere?

CHAPTER TWENTY-FOUR
How |the Supreme Being| can better be understood
to exist always than to exist at every time.

It is also evident[47] that (1) the Supreme Substance exists without beginning and without end and (2) that it does not have a past, a future, or a temporal (i.e., a fleeting) present such as we experience; for its lifetime, or eternity, which is nothing other than itself, is immutable and without parts. Consequently, if |the word| "always"—which seems to indicate time as a whole—is predicated of the Supreme Being, is not |this word| much more truly understood to signify eternity (which is never unlike itself) than |it is understood to signify| temporal modalities (which in some respect are always unlike one another)? Hence, if |the Supreme Being| is said always to exist, then since for it to exist is the same as for it to live, nothing better is understood |by "always existing"| than eternally existing, or eternally living—i.e., having an unending life which at once is completely whole. For its eternity is seen to be an unending life existing as completely whole at once.[48] It is already sufficiently evident above[49] that the Supreme Substance is nothing other than its own life and its own eternity, in no respect having boundaries, and existing only as completely whole at once. Hence, what else is true eternity, besuiting the Supreme Being alone, other than unending life that exists as completely whole at once? For by the fact alone that true eternity is present only in the Supreme Substance (which alone was found not to be made but to be the Maker) we discern clearly that true eternity is understood to be unlimited by a beginning and an end. |But| that this |unlimitedness| does not befit any of the created things is demonstrated by the fact that they have been created from nothing.

CHAPTER TWENTY-FIVE
|The Supreme Being| is not mutable in virtue of any accidents.

But at some time is not the Supreme Being—which was clearly seen[50] to be in every respect substantially identical with itself—at least accidentally different from itself? Yet, how is it supremely immutable if it can (I will not say *be* but) even be *thought to be* changeable through accidents? On the other hand, how would it fail to participate in an accident since its being greater than all other natures and its being unlike them seem to *happen* to it?

Sed quid repugnant quorundam quae accidentia dicuntur susceptibili-
10 tas et naturalis incommutabilitas, si ex eorum assumptione nulla substantiam consequatur variabilitas? Omnium quippe quae accidentia dicuntur,
alia non nisi cum aliqua participantis variatione adesse et abesse posse
intelliguntur, ut omnes colores; alia nullam omnino vel accedendo vel
recedendo mutationem circa id de quo dicuntur efficere noscuntur, ut
15 quaedam relationes. Constat namque quia homini post annum praesentem nascituro nec maior nec minor nec aequalis sum nec similis. Omnes
autem has relationes utique cum natus fuerit, sine omni mei mutatione
ad illum habere potero et amittere, secundum quod crescet vel per quali-
tates diversas mutabitur. Palam itaque fit, quia eorum quae accidentia
20 dicuntur, quaedam aliquatenus attrahant commutabilitatem, quaedam
vero nullatenus subtrahant immutabilitatem.

Sicut igitur summa natura accidentibus mutationem efficientibus numquam in sua simplicitate locum tribuit, sic secundum ea quae nullatenus
summae incommutabilitati repugnant, aliquando dici aliquid non respuit,
25 et tamen aliquid eius essentiae unde ipsa variabilis intelligi possit non
accidit. Unde hoc quoque concludi potest: quia nullius accidentis susceptibilis est. Quippe quemadmodum illa accidentia quae mutationem aliquam accendendo vel recedendo faciunt, ipso suo effectu vere accidere
rei quam mutant perpenduntur, sic illa quae a simili effectu deficiunt,
30 improprie dici accidentia deprehenduntur. Sicut ergo semper sibi est
omnimodo eadem substantialiter, ita numquam est a se diversa ullo
modo vel accidentaliter. Sed quoquo modo sese habeat ratio de proprie-
tate nominis accidentium, illud sine dubio verum est: quia de summe
incommutabili natura nihil potest dici, unde mutabilis possit intelligi.

CAPITULUM XXVI

Quomodo illa dicenda sit esse substantia, et quod sit
extra omnem substantiam et singulariter sit quidquid est.

Sed si ratum est quod de huius naturae simplicitate perspectum est,
5 quomodo substantia est? Nam cum omnis substantia admixtionis differ-

But why would natural immutability be inconsistent with a suscepti-
bility to certain |traits| which are called accidents—provided that no
change in substance follows from the acquisition of these accidents?[51]
Indeed, of all the things which are called accidents some (e.g., all colors)
are understood to be able to be present or absent only in conjunction
with some change in their participating |subject|. Others (e.g., certain
relations) are known to cause, by their coming and going, no change at
all with regard to that object to which they are ascribed. For example, it
is evident that I am not taller than, shorter than, equal to, or similar to a
man who will be born after the present year. But after he is born, I will
surely be able to have and to lose all of these relations to him—
according as he will grow or will change in various of his qualities—
without any change in myself. So it is evident that of those |traits| which
are called accidents, some bring change to some extent, whereas others
do not at all diminish immutability.

   Therefore, just as the Supreme Nature never in its simplicity admits of
accidents which cause change, so it does not repudiate something's sometimes being predicated in accordance with those things which are not at
all incompatible with its supreme immutability. And yet, there does not
happen, to its being, anything in terms of which the Supreme Nature can
be regarded as mutable. Hence, we can also conclude that |this Nature|
does not admit of any accident. Indeed, just as those accidents which
cause some change by their coming and going are regarded as really
happening, by their own effect, to the thing which they change, so those
|properties| which do not have any such effect are found to be called
accidents improperly. Therefore, just as the |Supreme Being| is always in
every respect substantially identical to itself, so it is never in any respect
even accidentally different from itself. But whatever may be the correct
analysis of the proper meaning of the word "accidents," it is certainly
true that with regard to the supremely immutable Nature nothing can be
said on the basis of which |this Nature| can be understood to be mutable.

CHAPTER TWENTY-SIX
In what sense |the Supreme Being| is to be called substance.
It is beyond every substance. It is uniquely whatever it is.

But if what has been discerned about the simplicity of the Supreme
Nature is right, how is it that the Supreme Nature is a substance? For

entiarum vel mutationis accidentium sit susceptibilis, huius immutabilis sinceritas omnimodae admixtioni sive mutationi est inaccessibilis. Quomodo ergo obtinebitur eam esse quamlibet substantiam, nisi dicatur "substantia" pro "essentia," et sic sit extra sicut est supra omnem sub-
10 stantiam? Nam quantum illud esse quod per se est quidquid est, et de nihilo facit omne aliud esse, diversum est ab eo esse quod per aliud fit de nihilo quidquid est: tantum omnino distat summa substantia ab iis quae non sunt idem quod ipsa. Cumque ipsa sola omnium naturarum habeat a se sine alterius naturae auxilio esse quidquid est, quomodo non est singu-
15 lariter absque suae creaturae consortio quidquid ipsa est? Unde si quando illi est cum aliis nominis alicuius communio, valde procul dubio intelligenda est diversa significatio.

CAPITULUM XXVII

Quod non contineatur in communi tractatu substantiarum,
et tamen sit substantia et individuus spiritus.

Constat igitur quia illa substantia nullo communi substantiarum tractatu
5 includitur, a cuius essentiali communione omnis natura excluditur. Nempe cum omnis substantia tractetur aut esse universalis (quae pluribus substantiis essentialiter communis est, ut hominem esse commune est singulis hominibus) aut esse individua (quae universalem essentiam communem habet cum aliis, quemadmodum singuli homines commune
10 habent cum singulis, ut homines sint), quomodo aliquis summam naturam in aliarum substantiarum tractatu contineri intelligit, quae nec in plures substantias se dividit, nec cum alia aliqua per essentialem communionem se colligit? Quoniam tamen ipsa non solum certissime existit, sed etiam summe omnium existit, et cuiuslibet rei essentia dici solet substantia:
15 profecto si quid digne dici potest, non prohibetur dici substantia. Et quoniam non noscitur dignior essentia quam spiritus aut corpus, et ex his spiritus dignior est quam corpus, utique eadem asserenda est esse spiritus, non corpus. Quoniam autem nec ullae partes sunt eiusdem spiritus, nec

although every substance is capable of having a mixture of differentiae or of undergoing a change of accidents, the immutable integrity of the Supreme Nature does not admit of any kind of mixture or change. How, then, shall one maintain that it is some kind of substance—unless "substance" stands for "being," and so |this Nature| is both beyond and above every substance? Now, the Being which through itself is whatever it is and which makes from nothing every other being is different from that being which through another and from nothing is made whatever it is. As different |as this one Being is from the other|, so altogether different is the Supreme Substance from those things which are not identical to it. And since of all natures this one alone has from itself, without the aid of another nature, its being whatever it is, how would it fail to be uniquely whatever it is and to have nothing in common with its creature? Hence, if it ever has some name in common with other things, without any doubt a very different signification must be understood |in its case|.

CHAPTER TWENTY-SEVEN

|The Supreme Being| is not included in the usual classification
of substances; nevertheless, it is a substance and an individual spirit.

Therefore, it is evident that this Substance, from which every |other| nature is excluded from having anything essentially in common, is not included in the usual classification of substances. To be sure, every substance is classified either as a universal, which is essentially common to many substances (as to-be-a-man is common to individual men), or else as a particular (*individua*), which has a universal essence in common with other |particulars| (as individual men have in common the fact that they are men). So how would anyone understand the Supreme Nature to be contained in the |same| classification as other substances? For neither is it common to many substances, nor does it have anything essentially in common with any other |substance|. Nevertheless, since it not only most certainly exists but even exists supremely, and since the being of any thing is usually called substance, surely if |the Supreme Being| can be acceptably called anything, there is no reason not to call it a substance. And since no more excellent being is known than spirit or body, and since of these |two| spirit is more excellent than body, surely the Supreme Being must be called spirit, not body. However, since this Spirit

plures esse possunt eiusmodi spiritus, necesse est ut sit omnino individuus
20 spiritus. Quoniam enim, sicut supra constat, nec partibus est compositus,
nec ullis differentiis vel accidentibus intelligi potest esse mutabilis, impossibile est ut qualibet sectione sit divisibilis.

CAPITULUM XXVIII

Quod idem spiritus simpliciter sit;
et creata, illi comparata, non sint.

Videtur ergo consequi ex praecedentibus quod iste spiritus, qui sic suo
5 quodam mirabiliter singulari et singulariter mirabili modo est, quadam
ratione solus sit, alia vero quaecumque videntur esse, huic collata, non
sint. Si enim diligenter intendatur, ille solus videbitur simpliciter et perfecte et absolute esse, alia vero omnia fere non esse et vix esse. Quoniam
namque idem spiritus propter incommutabilem aeternitatem suam nullo
10 modo secundum aliquem motum dici potest quia fuit vel erit, sed simpliciter est; nec mutabiliter est aliquid quod aliquando aut non fuit aut
non erit; neque non est quod aliquando fuit aut erit, sed quidquid est,
semel et simul et interminabiliter est—quoniam inquam huiusmodi est
eius esse, iure ipse simpliciter et absolute et perfecte dicitur esse.
15   Quoniam vero alia omnia mutabiliter secundum aliquid aliquando aut
fuerunt aut erunt quod non sunt, aut sunt quod aliquando non fuerunt
vel non erunt, et quoniam hoc quia fuerunt iam non est, illud autem
scilicet quia erunt nondum est, et hoc quod in labili brevissimoque et vix
existente praesenti sunt vix est—quoniam ergo tam mutabiliter sunt, non
20 immerito negantur simpliciter et perfecte et absolute esse, et asseruntur
fere non esse et vix esse. Deinde cum omnia quaecumque aliud sunt
quam ipse, de non-esse venerint ad esse non per se sed per aliud, et cum
de esse redeant ad non-esse quantum ad se nisi sustineantur per aliud,
quomodo illis convenit simpliciter aut perfecte sive absolute esse et non
25 magis vix esse aut fere non esse?

XXVIII, 7 videbitur: *ex* videtur *corr.* (bi *supra lin.*) *B²*
XXVIII, 17 erunt: *ex* erut *corr.* (n *supra lin.*) *B*

has no parts, and since there cannot be more than one such spirit, necessarily |this Spirit| is an altogether individual spirit.[52] For as is evident above,[53] |this Spirit| is not composed of parts, nor can it be understood to be changeable by means of any differentiae or accidents. Therefore, it is impossible for it to be divided in any way.

CHAPTER TWENTY-EIGHT

This Spirit exists in an unqualified sense; compared
to it created things do not exist.

Therefore, from the foregoing |considerations| it is seen to follow that this Spirit, which exists in such a marvelously unique and uniquely marvelous way of its own, in a certain sense alone exists—while by comparison to it other things, whatever they are seen to be, do not exist.[54] For if we take a close look, only this Spirit will be seen to exist in an unqualified sense and completely and absolutely; and everything else |will be seen| almost not to exist and scarcely to exist. On account of its immutable eternity this Spirit can be said unqualifiedly to exist; it cannot at all be said, in accordance with some alteration, to have existed or to be going to exist. Nor is it, mutably, anything which at some time it either was not or will not be; nor does it fail to be something which it once was or once will be. Rather, whatever it is it is at one and the same time and endlessly. Since, I say, its being is of this kind, this Spirit is rightly said to exist in an unqualified sense and absolutely and completely.

All other things in some respect and at some time and mutably either were or will be what they now are not, or else they now are what at some time they were not or will not be. Moreover, their past being no longer exists; their future being does not yet exist; and what they are in the fleeting, momentary, and scarcely existing present scarcely exists. Therefore, since they exist so mutably, they are justifiably denied to exist in an unqualified sense and completely and absolutely, and are said almost not to exist and scarcely to exist. Or again, all things other than this Spirit come from not-being into being through something other than through themselves; and with respect to their own power, they would return from being to not-being unless they were sustained through something other |than themselves|. Therefore, how would it besuit them to exist in an unqualified sense or completely or absolutely instead of scarcely existing or almost not existing?

Cumque esse solius eiusdem ineffabilis spiritus nullo modo intelligi possit aut ex non-esse inceptum, aut aliquem pati posse ex eo quod est in non-esse defectum, et quidquid ipse est non sit per aliud quam per se (id est, per hoc quod ipse est), nonne huius esse merito solum intelligitur
30 simplex perfectumque et absolutum? Quod vero sic simpliciter et omnimoda ratione solum est perfectum, simplex, et absolutum: id nimirum quodam modo iure dici potest solum esse. Et econtra, quidquid per superiorem rationem nec simpliciter nec perfecte nec absolute esse sed vix esse aut fere non esse cognoscitur, id utique aliquomodo recte non
35 esse dicitur. Secundum hanc igitur rationem solus ille creator spiritus est, et omnia creata non sunt; nec tamen omnino non sunt, quia per illum, qui solus absolute est, de nihilo aliquid facta sunt.

CAPITULUM XXIX
Quod eius locutio idipsum sit quod ipse,
nec tamen sint duo, sed unus spiritus.

Iam vero iis quae de proprietatibus huius summae naturae ad praesens
5 mihi ducem rationem sequenti occurrerunt perspectis, opportunum existimo ut de eius locutione, per quam facta sunt omnia, si quid possum considerem. Etenim cum omnia quae de illa supra potui animadvertere, rationis robur inflexibile teneant, illud me maxime cogit de illa diligentius discutere, quia idipsum quod ipse summus spiritus est probatur esse.
10 Si enim ille nihil fecit nisi per seipsum, et quidquid ab eo factum est per illam est factum, quomodo illa est aliud quam quod est idem ipse? Amplius. Asserunt utique inexpugnabiliter ea quae iam inventa sunt, quia nihil omnino potuit umquam aut potest subsistere praeter creantem spiritum et eius creaturam. Hanc vero spiritus eiusdem locutionem
15 impossibile est inter creata contineri, quoniam quidquid creatum subsistit per illam factum est, illa vero per se fieri non potuit. Nihil quippe per seipsum fieri potest, quia quidquid fit, posterius est eo per quod fit, et

The existence of this sole ineffable Spirit can in no way be understood either to have begun from not-being or to be able to undergo any falling away (from that which it is) into not-being; moreover, whatever this Spirit is it is through no other than through itself—i.e., through that which it itself is. Therefore, is not its existence alone justifiably understood to be simple, complete, and absolute? But surely what exists so unqualifiedly and what alone is in every respect complete, simple, and absolute can in a certain respect rightly be said alone to exist. On the other hand, surely whatever through the above reasoning is known not to exist in an unqualified sense and completely and absolutely, but to exist scarcely at all or almost not to exist, is in a certain respect rightly said not to exist. So according to this reasoning the sole Creator-Spirit exists, and all created things do not exist. Nevertheless, created things do not altogether lack existence, since from nothing they have been made something through this Spirit, which alone exists absolutely.

CHAPTER TWENTY-NINE

This Spirit's Expression is the very same thing as this Spirit. Nevertheless, there are not two spirits but |only| one.

But having examined these |topics| which have presently occurred to me (as I am following the guidance of reason) concerning the properties of the Supreme Nature, I |now| think it useful to consider, as best I can, the Supreme Nature's Expression, through which all things were made. For although all the |points| which I was able to notice earlier[55] concerning this Expression possess the inflexible strength of reason, the fact that this Expression is proved to be the same thing that the Supreme Spirit is imposes a special requirement upon me to discuss this Expression the more carefully. For if the Supreme Spirit made all other things only through itself, and if whatever was made by it was made through its Expression, how is this Expression anything other than what the Supreme Spirit itself is? Moreover, assuredly those truths which have already been discovered[56] declare uncontestably that nothing at all was ever able or is ever able to exist besides the Creating Spirit and its creatures. Now, it is impossible that the Expression of this Spirit would be in the class of created things. For whatever is created is made through this Expression; but this Expression could not have been made through itself. Indeed, nothing can be made through itself, because whatever is made exists later

nihil est posterius seipso. Relinquitur itaque ut haec summi spiritus locutio, cum creatura esse non possit, non sit aliud quam summus spiritus.

20 Denique haec ipsa locutio nihil aliud potest intelligi quam eiusdem spiritus intelligentia, qua cuncta intelligit. Quid enim est aliud illi rem loqui aliquam hoc loquendi modo quam intelligere? Nam non ut homo non semper dicit quod intelligit. Si igitur summe simplex natura non est aliud quam quod est sua intelligentia, quemadmodum est idem quod est

25 sua sapientia: necesse est ut similiter non sit aliud quam quod est sua locutio. Sed quoniam iam manifestum est summum spiritum unum tantum esse et omnimode individuum, necesse est ut sic illi haec sua locutio sit consubstantialis ut non sint duo, sed unus spiritus.

CAPITULUM XXX
Quod eadem locutio non constet pluribus verbis,
sed sit unum verbum.

Cur igitur dubitem quod supra dubium dimiseram, scilicet utrum haec
5 locutio in pluribus verbis an in uno verbo consistat? Nam si sic est summae naturae consubstantialis ut non sint duo, sed unus spiritus: utique sicut illa summe simplex est, ita et ista. Non igitur constat pluribus verbis, sed est unum verbum per quod facta sunt omnia.

CAPITULUM XXXI
Quod ipsum verbum non sit similitudo factorum,
sed veritas essentiae, facta vero sint aliqua veritatis imitatio;
et quae naturae magis sint quam aliae et praestantiores.

5 Sed ecce videtur mihi suboriri nec facilis nec ullatenus sub ambiguitate relinquenda quaestio. Etenim omnia huiusmodi verba quibus res quaslibet mente dicimus, id est cogitamus, similitudines et imagines sunt rerum quarum verba sunt; et omnis similitudo vel imago tanto magis vel minus est vera, quanto magis vel minus imitatur rem cuius est similitudo.
10 Quid igitur tenendum est de verbo, quo dicuntur et per quod facta sunt omnia? Erit aut non erit similitudo eorum quae per ipsum facta sunt? Si

than that through which it is made, and nothing exists later than itself. Thus, |the other alternative| holds, viz., that the Expression of the Supreme Spirit—since it cannot be a creature—is none other than the Supreme Spirit.

Indeed, this Expression can be understood to be nothing other than the understanding of the Supreme Spirit by which |the Supreme Spirit| understands all things. For what else is it for this Spirit to speak of a thing (in this way of speaking) than for it to understand it? For unlike a man, the Supreme Spirit never fails to express what it understands. Therefore, if the supremely simple Nature is none other than what its understanding is—just as it is the same thing that its wisdom is—then, necessarily, it is also none other than what its Expression is. But since it is already evident[57] that the Supreme Spirit is only singular and is in every respect an individual,[58] necessarily its Expression is so consubstantial with it that there is one Spirit rather than two.

CHAPTER THIRTY
This Expression is not many words, but is one word.

Why, then, should I continue to doubt what I earlier[59] left in doubt, viz., whether this Expression is one word or many words? For if |the Expression of the Supreme Nature| is so consubstantial with it that there is one Spirit rather than two, then surely just as the Supreme Nature is supremely simple, so too is this Expression. Therefore, it is not many words but is one word, through which all things have been made.[60]

CHAPTER THIRTY-ONE
This Word is not the likeness of created things but is true Existence.
Created things are a likeness of this true Existence.
Which natures exist more, and are more excellent, than others.

But, lo, a difficult question seems to me to arise—a question not to be left in any ambiguity. For all such words by which we mentally speak of objects (i.e., by which we think them) are likenesses and images of those objects for which they are words.[61] And every likeness and image is true in proportion to the exactness with which it imitates the thing whose likeness it is. What, then, must be believed about the Word by which all things are spoken of and through which all things were made? Will it or will it not be the likeness of those things which were made through it?

enim ipsum est vera mutabilium similitudo, non est consubstantiale
summae incommutabilitati—quod falsum est. Si autem non omnino vera
sed qualiscumque similitudo mutabilium est, non est verbum summae
15 veritatis omnino verum—quod absurdum est. At si nullam mutabilium
habet similitudinem, quomodo ad exemplum illius facta sunt?

Verum forsitan nihil huius remanebit ambiguitatis, si quemadmodum
in vivo homine veritas hominis esse dicitur, in picto vero similitudo sive
imago illius veritatis, sic existendi veritas intelligatur in verbo cuius
20 essentia sic summe est ut quodam modo illa sola sit; in iis vero quae in
eius comparatione quodam modo non sunt, et tamen per illud et secundum illud facta sunt aliquid, imitatio aliqua summae illius essentiae per-
pendatur. Sic quippe verbum summae veritatis, quod et ipsum est
summa veritas, nullum augmentum vel detrimentum sentiet secundum
25 hoc quod magis vel minus creaturis sit simile; sed potius necesse erit
omne quod creatum est tanto magis esse et tanto esse praestantius,
quanto similius est illi quod summe est et summe magnum est. Hinc
etenim fortasse—immo non fortasse sed pro certo—hinc omnis intellectus iudicat naturas quolibet modo viventes praestare non-viventibus, sen-
30 tientes non-sentientibus, rationales irrationalibus. Quoniam enim summa
natura suo quodam singulari modo non solum est, sed et vivit et sentit et
rationalis est, liquet quoniam omnium quae sunt, id quod aliquomodo
vivit, magis est illi simile quam id quod nullatenus vivit; et quod modo
quolibet vel corporeo sensu cognoscit aliquid, magis quam quod nihil
35 omnino sentit; et quod rationale est, magis quam quod rationis capax
non est. Quoniam vero simili ratione quaedam naturae magis minusve
sint quam aliae, perspicuum est. Quemadmodum enim illud natura
praestantius est quod per naturalem essentiam propinquius est praestan-
tissimo, ita utique illa natura magis est, cuius essentia similior est summae
40 essentiae.

Quod sic quoque facile animadverti posse existimo. Nempe si cuilibet

For (1) if it is a true likeness of |those| mutable things, then it is not consubstantial with the Supreme Immutability—|a consequence| which is false. (2) On the other hand, if it is not in every respect a true likeness of mutable things but is a likeness |only| in some respects, then the Supreme Truth's Word is not altogether true—|a consequence| which is absurd. (3) Or if it has no likeness to mutable things, how were they made according to its form?

But perhaps no ambiguity will remain if |we make use of the following comparison|. The living man is said to be the true man; but the likeness, or image, of a true man is said to be in a portrait |of this man|. By comparison, the Word is understood to be true Existence, for the being of the Word exists so supremely that, in a way, it alone exists; but a kind of likeness of this Supreme Being is understood to be in those things which, in a way, by comparison with it, do not exist—even though they have been made something through it and in accordance with it. Thus, Supreme Truth's Word, which Word is itself the Supreme Truth, will not become something greater or something lesser by virtue of a greater or lesser degree of likeness to creatures. Rather, it must be the case that every created thing both exists and is excellent in proportion to its likeness to what exists supremely and is supremely great. For this reason, perhaps—or rather not perhaps but certainly—every intellect judges that natures which are in any way alive excel nonliving |natures|, and that sentient natures excel nonsentient |natures|, and that rational natures excel nonrational |ones|. For since the Supreme Nature in its own unique way not only exists but also lives and perceives and reasons, clearly whatever existing thing in some respect lives is more like the Supreme Nature than what does not at all live. And what in any way (be it even by a bodily sense) recognizes an object |is| more |like the Supreme Nature| than what does not at all perceive. And what is rational |is| more |like the Supreme Nature| than what has no rational capacity. By a similar consideration it is clear that some natures exist more than others or less than others. For just as that is naturally more excellent which, with respect to its natural being, more closely approximates what is most excellent, so indeed that nature exists more whose being is more like the Supreme Being.[62]

I think that this |same point| can also be readily seen by means of the following |consideration|. From some substance which lives, perceives,

substantiae, quae et vivit et sensibilis et rationalis est, cogitatione auferatur quod rationalis est, deinde quod sensibilis, et postea quod vitalis, postremo ipsum nudum esse quod remanet: quis non intelligat quod illa 45 substantia, quae sic paulatim destruitur, ad minus et minus esse, et ad ultimum ad non-esse gradatim perducitur? Quae autem singulatim absumpta quamlibet essentiam ad minus et minus esse deducunt, eadem ordinatim assumpta illam ad magis et magis esse perducunt. Patet igitur quia magis est vivens substantia quam non-vivens, et sensibilis quam 50 non-sensibilis, et rationalis quam non-rationalis. Non est itaque dubium quod omnis essentia eo ipso magis est et praestantior est, quo similior est illi essentiae, quae summe est et summe praestat. Satis itaque manifestum est in verbo, per quod facta sunt omnia, non esse ipsorum similitudinem sed veram simplicemque essentiam, in factis vero non esse simplicem 55 absolutamque essentiam sed verae illius essentiae vix aliquam imitationem. Unde necesse est non idem verbum secundum rerum creatarum similitudinem magis vel minus esse verum, sed omnem creatam naturam eo altiori gradu essentiae dignitatisque consistere, quo magis illi propinquare videtur.

CAPITULUM XXXII

Quod summus spiritus seipsum dicat coaeterno verbo.

Sed cum ita sit, quomodo illud quod simplex est veritas, potest esse verbum eorum quorum non est similitudo, cum omne verbum quo ali-5 qua res sic mente dicitur, similitudo sit rei eiusdem? Et si non est verbum eorum quae facta sunt per ipsum, quomodo constabit quia sit verbum? Nempe omne verbum, alicuius rei verbum est. Denique si numquam creatura esset, nullum eius esset verbum. Quid igitur? An concludendum est quia si nullo modo esset creatura, nequaquam esset verbum illud 10 quod est summa et nullius indigens essentia? Aut fortasse ipsa summa essentia, quae verbum est, essentia quidem esset aeterna, sed verbum non esset, si nihil umquam per illam fieret? Eius enim quod nec fuit nec est nec futurum est, nullum verbum esse potest. Verum secundum hanc ratio-

and reasons let us mentally remove |first| what is rational, next what is sentient, then what is vital, and finally the remaining bare existence. Now, who would not understand that this substance, thus destroyed step by step, is gradually reduced to less and less existence—and, in the end, to nonexistence? Yet, those |characteristics| which when removed one at a time reduce a being to less and less existence increase its existence more and more when added |to it| again in reverse order. Therefore, it is clear that a living substance exists more than does a nonliving one, that a sentient substance exists more than does a nonsentient one, and that a rational substance exists more than does a nonrational one. So without doubt every being exists more and is more excellent to the extent that it is more like that Being which exists supremely and is supremely excellent. Thus, it is quite evident that in the Word, through which all things were made, there is no likeness of created things but is, rather, true and simple Existence—whereas in created things there is not simple and absolute existence but a meager imitation of this true Existence. Hence, it must be the case that this Word is not more or less true according to a likeness to created things, but rather that every created nature has a higher degree of existence and excellence to the extent that it is seen to approximate this Word.

CHAPTER THIRTY-TWO

The Supreme Spirit speaks of itself by means of a coeternal Word.

Accordingly, how can what is simple Truth be the Word |or Image|[63] of those things whose likeness it is not? For every word by which an object is thus mentally spoken of is a likeness of that object. And if |this Word| is not a word |or an image| of these things that were made through itself, then how would it be true that it is a word? Without doubt, every word |or image| is a word |or an image| of some thing;[64] indeed, if there never existed a creature, then there would exist no word |or image| of a creature. What then? Must one conclude that if no creature in any respect existed, then the Word, which is the Supreme Being, in need of nothing |else|, would not at all exist? Or |are we to think|, perhaps, |that| the Supreme Being, which the Word is, would indeed be an eternal being but would not be a word if nothing were ever made through it? For there can be no word |or image| of that which neither did exist, does exist, nor will exist. But according to this reasoning,[65] if there never

nem, si numquam ulla praeter summum spiritum esset essentia, nullum
15 omnino esset in illo verbum. Si nullum in illo verbum esset, nihil apud se
diceret. Si nihil apud se diceret: cum idem sit illi sic dicere aliquid quod
est intelligere, non aliquid intelligeret. Si nihil intelligeret, ergo summa
sapientia, quae non est aliud quam idem spiritus, nihil intelligeret—quod
absurdissimum est. Quid ergo? Si enim nihil intelligeret, quomodo esset
20 summa sapientia?

Aut si nullo modo aliquid esset praeter illam, quid illa intelligeret? Sed
numquid seipsam non intelligeret? At quomodo vel cogitari potest quod
summa sapientia se aliquando non intelligat, cum rationalis mens possit
non solum suimet sed et ipsius summae sapientiae reminisci, et illam et
25 se intelligere? Si enim mens humana nullam eius aut suam habere memoriam
aut intelligentiam posset, nequaquam se ab irrationalibus creaturis et
illam ab omni creatura, secum sola tacite disputando, sicut nunc mens
mea facit, discerneret. Ergo summus ille spiritus sicut est aeternus, ita
aeterne sui memor est et intelligit se ad similitudinem mentis rationalis—
30 immo non ad ullius similitudinem, sed ille principaliter et mens rationalis
ad eius similitudinem. At si aeterne se intelligit, aeterne se dicit. Si
aeterne se dicit, aeterne est verbum eius apud ipsum. Sive igitur ille
cogitetur nulla alia existente essentia, sive aliis existentibus, necesse est
verbum illius coaeternum illi esse cum illo.

CAPITULUM XXXIII
Quod uno verbo dicat se et quod fecit.

Sed ecce quaerenti mihi de verbo quo creator dicit omnia quae fecit,
obtulit se verbum quo seipsum dicit, qui omnia fecit. An ergo alio verbo

existed any being besides the Supreme Spirit, there would not at all be a word in this Spirit. And if there were no word in this Spirit, this Spirit would not speak within itself. And if it did not speak within itself, then it would not understand anything—since for it in this way to speak of something is for it to understand something. And if it understood nothing, then Supreme Wisdom, which is none other than this Spirit, would understand nothing—an utterly absurd |consequence|. What |follows|, then? For if the |Supreme Spirit| were to understand nothing, how would it be Supreme Wisdom?

Or again, if there in no way existed anything other than Supreme Wisdom, what would this Wisdom understand? Would it |in that case| fail to understand itself? But how can we even think that Supreme Wisdom ever fails to understand itself, since a rational |human| mind can remember[66] not only itself but also the Supreme Wisdom, and can understand itself and the Supreme Wisdom? (For if the human mind could not have remembrance or understanding either of itself or of the Supreme Wisdom, then it would not be able—by disputing silently with itself, just as my mind is now doing—to distinguish itself from irrational creatures and to distinguish the Supreme Wisdom from all its creatures.) Hence, just as the Supreme Spirit is eternal, so it eternally remembers itself and understands itself similarly to the way the rational mind |remembers itself and understands itself|. Or better, |it remembers itself and understands itself| according to no likeness but rather principally; and the rational mind |remembers itself and understands itself| in a way similar to this Spirit's |remembering itself and understanding itself|. But if |the Supreme Spirit| understands itself eternally, it speaks of itself eternally. And if it speaks of itself eternally, its Word is eternally with it. Consequently, whether this Spirit be thought of as not having any creatures or whether it be thought of as having creatures, its coeternal Word must be with it.

CHAPTER THIRTY-THREE
By means of one Word |the Supreme Spirit| speaks
both of itself and of that which it has made.

But, lo, as I was inquiring just now about the Word by which the Creator speaks of all that it has made, I was confronted with the Word by

5 dicit se ipsum, et alio ea quae facit; aut potius eodem ipso verbo quo dicit se ipsum, dicit quaecumque facit? Nam hoc quoque verbum quo se ipsum dicit, necesse est idipsum esse quod ipse est, sicut constat de verbo illo quo dicit ea quae a se facta sunt. Cum enim etiam si nihil umquam aliud esset nisi summus ille spiritus, ratio tamen cogat verbum illud quo 10 se dicit ex necessitate esse: quid verius quam hoc verbum eius non esse aliud quam quod ipse est? Ergo si et se ipsum et ea quae facit consub-stantiali sibi verbo dicit, manifestum est quia verbi quo se dicit, et verbi quo creaturam dicit, una substantia est. Quomodo ergo si una substantia est, duo verba sunt? Sed forsitan non cogit identitas substantiae, verbi 15 unitatem admittere. Nam idem ipse qui his verbis loquitur, eandem illis habet substantiam, et tamen verbum non est.

Sed utique verbum quo se dicit summa sapientia, convenientissime dici potest verbum eius secundum superiorem rationem, quia eius perfec-tam tenet similitudinem. Nam nulla ratione negari potest, cum mens 20 rationalis seipsam cogitando intelligit, imaginem ipsius nasci in sua cogitatione—immo ipsam cogitationem sui esse suam imaginem ad eius similitudinem tamquam ex eius impressione formatam. Quamcumque enim rem mens seu per corporis imaginationem seu per rationem cupit veraciter cogitare, eius utique similitudinem quantum valet in ipsa sua 25 cogitatione conatur exprimere. Quod quanto verius facit, tanto verius rem ipsam cogitat. Et hoc quidem cum cogitat aliquid aliud quod ipsa non est, et maxime cum aliquod cogitat corpus, clarius perspicitur. Cum enim cogito notum mihi hominem absentem, formatur acies cogitationis meae in talem imaginem eius, qualem illam per visum oculorum in 30 memoriam attraxi. Quae imago in cogitatione verbum est eiusdem hominis, quem cogitando dico. Habet igitur mens rationalis, cum se cogi-tando intelligit, secum imaginem suam ex se natam, id est cogitationem

which the Creator of all things speaks of itself. Does |the Creator|, then, speak of itself by means of one word and speak of its creation by means of another? Or does |the Creator| by means of the same Word by which it speaks of itself speak of whatever it makes? For, necessarily, the Word by which |the Creator| speaks of itself is what the Creator is, just as is evident in the case of the Word by which |the Creator| speaks of the things made by it.[67] For since—even if nothing were ever to exist except the Supreme Spirit—reason would require |the conclusion| that the Word by which |this Spirit| speaks of itself cannot fail to exist, what is more true than that the Word |or Image| of this Spirit[68] is not anything other than what this Spirit is? Hence, if by a Word consubstantial with itself this Spirit speaks of itself and of those things which it makes, then clearly the substance of the Word by which |this Spirit| speaks of itself is one with the substance of the Word by which it speaks of creatures. So if there is |only| one substance, how would there be two words? On the other hand, perhaps the identity of substance does not require us to admit a oneness of word. For this Spirit, which speaks by means of these words, has the same substance as they do; but nevertheless this Spirit is not a word.

Assuredly, the Word by which Supreme Wisdom speaks of itself can most suitably, according to the foregoing reasoning, be called the Word |or Image| of this Wisdom; for it has a perfect likeness to this Wisdom. For we cannot at all deny that when a rational mind understands itself by thinking of itself, an image of the mind is begotten in the mind's thought—or better, the mind's thought of itself is its own image, formed according to the likeness of the mind and formed, as it were, from an "impression" of the mind. For as best it can the mind tries to express in its thought a likeness of whatever thing it desires to think of truly (whether through imagining a material object or through reason). The more truly it expresses this likeness, the more truly it thinks of the object itself. Indeed, this |fact| is noticed more clearly in cases where |the mind| thinks of something other than itself—especially when it thinks of a material object. For example, when in his absence I think of a man whom I know, the acute gaze of my thought is formed into that kind of image of him which I brought into my memory through the vision of my eyes. This mental image is a word |or likeness| of this man whom I speak of by thinking of him. Therefore, when a rational mind understands itself by thinking of itself, it has with itself an image of itself begotten from itself—i.e., it has a thought of itself, formed after the likeness of itself and

sui ad suam similitudinem quasi sua impressione formatam—quamvis ipsa se a sua imagine non nisi ratione sola separare possit. Quae imago
35 eius verbum eius est.

Hoc itaque modo quis neget summam sapientiam, cum se dicendo intelligit, gignere consubstantialem sibi similitudinem suam, id est verbum suum? Quod verbum, licet de re tam singulariter eminenti proprie aliquid satis convenienter dici non possit, non tamen inconvenienter sicut
40 similitudo ita et imago et figura et caracter eius dici potest. Verbum autem quo creaturam dicit, nequaquam similiter est verbum creaturae, quia non est eius similitudo, sed principalis essentia. Consequitur igitur ut ipsam creaturam non dicat verbo creaturae. Cuius ergo verbo eam dicit, si non eam dicit verbo eius? Nam quod dicit, verbo dicit; et ver-
45 bum, alicuius est verbum, id est similitudo. Sed si nihil aliud dicit quam se aut creaturam, nihil dicere potest nisi aut suo aut eius verbo. Si ergo nihil dicit verbo creaturae: quidquid dicit, verbo suo dicit. Uno igitur eodemque verbo dicit seipsum et quaecumque fecit.

CAPITULUM XXXIV

Quomodo suo verbo videri possit dicere creaturam.

Sed quomodo tam differentes res, scilicet creans et creata essentia, dici possunt uno verbo, praesertim cum verbum ipsum sit dicenti coaeter-
5 num, creatura autem non sit illi coaeterna? Forsitan quia ipse est summa sapientia et summa ratio, in qua sunt omnia quae facta sunt—quemadmodum opus quod fit secundum aliquam artem, non solum quando fit, verum et antequam fiat et postquam dissolvitur, semper est in ipsa arte non aliud quam quod est ars ipsa—idcirco cum ipse summus spiritus
10 dicit seipsum, dicit omnia quae facta sunt. Nam et antequam fierent, et cum iam facta sunt, et cum corrumpuntur seu aliquomodo variantur:

formed from its own "impression" of itself, as it were. Yet, only through its reason can a mind distinguish itself from its own image. And this image of the mind is a word |or likeness| of the mind.

So who would deny that in this way Supreme Wisdom begets its own consubstantial likeness, i.e., its Word, when it understands itself by speaking of itself? Although nothing can properly or suitably enough be said of a thing so uniquely excellent, nevertheless the Word can (not unsuitably) be called the image, figure, and form (*caracter*)⁶⁹—as well as the likeness—of the Supreme Wisdom. Yet, |this| Word, by which |Supreme Wisdom| speaks of creatures, is not at all likewise a word |or an image| of creatures—because this Word is not the likeness of creatures but is rather the principal Existence. Thus, it follows that |Supreme Wisdom| does not speak of creatures by a word |or an image| of creatures. By what word, then, does it speak of creatures if it does not speak of them by a word |or an image| of creatures? For that of which |Supreme Wisdom| speaks, it speaks of by a word; and a word is a word—i.e., a likeness—of something. But if |Supreme Wisdom| speaks of nothing other than either of itself or of its creatures, then it can speak of something only by the Word |or Image| of itself or else by a word |or an image| of creatures. Therefore, if it does not speak of anything by a word |or an image| of creatures, then whatever it speaks of it speaks of by its own Word. Consequently, by one and the same Word it speaks of itself and of whatever it has made.

CHAPTER THIRTY-FOUR
How |the Supreme Spirit| can be seen
to speak of creatures by its own Word.

But how can such different things, viz., the Creating Being and the created being, be spoken of by one word?—especially since this Word is co-eternal with the Speaker, whereas the creation is not coeternal therewith. Perhaps when the Supreme Spirit speaks of itself it speaks of all created things *because* it itself is the Supreme Wisdom and Supreme Reason, in which all created things exist (just as an object which is made according to some craft exists always—i.e., not only upon being made, but even before being made and after having perished—in the craft itself, as identical with what the craft itself is.)⁷⁰ For before |created things| were made and once they have been made and after they have perished or have changed in some manner, they always exist in this Spirit as what

semper in ipso sunt, non quod sunt in seipsis, sed quod est idem ipse. Etenim in seipsis sunt essentia mutabilis secundum immutabilem rationem creata; in ipso vero sunt ipsa prima essentia et prima existendi veri-
15 tas, cui prout magis utcumque illa similia sunt, ita verius et praestantius existunt. Hoc itaque modo non irrationabiliter asseri potest, quia cum seipsum dicit summus ille spiritus, dicit etiam quidquid factum est uno eodemque verbo.

CAPITULUM XXXV

Quod quidquid factum est, in eius verbo
et scientia sit vita et veritas.

Verum cum constet quia verbum eius consubstantiale illi est et perfecte
5 simile, necessario consequitur ut omnia quae sunt in illo, eadem et eodem modo sint in verbo eius. Quidquid igitur factum est—sive vivat sive non vivat, aut quomodocumque sit in se—in illo est ipsa vita et veritas. Quoniam autem idem est summo spiritui scire quod intelligere sive dicere, necesse est ut eodem modo sciat omnia quae scit, quo ea
10 dicit aut intelligit. Quemadmodum igitur sunt in verbo eius omnia vita et veritas, ita sunt in scientia eius.

CAPITULUM XXXVI

Quam incomprehensibili modo dicat vel sciat res a se factas.

Qua ex re manifestissime comprehendi potest, quomodo dicat idem spiritus vel quomodo sciat ea quae facta sunt, ab humana scientia compre-
5 hendi non posse. Nam nulli dubium creatas substantias multo aliter esse in seipsis quam in nostra scientia. In seipsis namque sunt per ipsam suam essentiam; in nostra vero scientia non sunt earum essentiae, sed earum similitudines. Restat igitur ut tanto verius sint in seipsis quam in nostra scientia, quanto verius alicubi sunt per suam essentiam quam per suam
10 similitudinem. Cum ergo et hoc constet, quia omnis creata substantia tanto verius est in verbo (id est, in intelligentia) creatoris quam in seipsa,

this Spirit is, rather than as what they are in themselves.[71] For in themselves they are a mutable being, created according to immutable Reason. But in this Spirit they are the primary Being and the primary true Existence; and the more created things |in themselves| are in any way like this true Existence, the more truly and excellently they exist. And so, in this way one can, not unreasonably, maintain that when the Supreme Spirit speaks of itself, it also speaks, by one and the same Word, of whatever has been made.

CHAPTER THIRTY-FIVE

Whatever was made exists as life and truth
in the Word and Knowledge of the Supreme Spirit.

But since it is evident that the Word |or Image| of the Supreme Spirit is consubstantial with it and perfectly similar to it, necessarily all things existing in this Spirit exist also, in the same way, in its Word. Therefore, whatever was made—whether it lives or does not live, or howsoever it exists in itself—exists as life itself and truth itself in the Supreme Spirit.[72] But since for the Supreme Spirit to know is the same thing as for it to understand or to speak, all the things that it knows it must know in the same way in which it speaks of them or understands them. Therefore, just as all things exist as life and truth in the Word of this Spirit, so they |also| exist |as life and truth| in this Spirit's Knowledge.

CHAPTER THIRTY-SIX

In what an incomprehensible manner |the Supreme Spirit|
speaks of, or knows, the things made by it.

From the foregoing can be most clearly comprehended that human knowledge cannot comprehend how the Supreme Spirit speaks of, or knows, those things which have been made. For no one doubts that created substances exist in themselves much differently from the way they exist in our knowledge. For in themselves they exist in virtue of their own being; but in our knowledge their likenesses exist, not their own being. It follows, then, that the more truly they exist anywhere by virtue of their own being than by virtue of their likenesses, the more truly they exist in themselves than in our knowledge. Now, it is evident that the more truly the Creating Being exists than does the created being, the more truly every created substance exists in the Word (i.e., in the

quanto verius existit creatrix quam creata essentia: quomodo compre-
hendat humana mens cuiusmodi sit illud dicere, et illa scientia, quae sic
longe superior et verior est creatis substantiis, si nostra scientia tam longe
15 superatur ab illis, quantum earum similitudo distat ab earum essentia?

CAPITULUM XXXVII
Quod quidquid ipse est ad creaturam, hoc sit et
verbum eius; nec tamen ambo simul pluraliter.

Verum cum manifeste rationes superiores doceant summum spiritum per
5 verbum suum fecisse omnia, numquid non et ipsum verbum fecit eadem
omnia? Quoniam enim illi est consubstantiale, cuius est verbum, necesse
est ut sit summa essentia. Summa autem essentia non est nisi una, quae
sola creatrix et solum principium est omnium quae facta sunt. Ipsa
namque sola fecit non per aliud quam per se omnia ex nihilo. Quare
10 quaecumque summus spiritus facit, eadem et verbum eius facit et similiter. Quidquid igitur summus spiritus est ad creaturam, hoc et verbum
eius est et similiter; nec tamen ambo simul pluraliter, quia non sunt
plures creatrices summae essentiae. Sicut igitur ille est creator rerum et
principium, sic et verbum eius; nec tamen sunt duo, sed unus creator et
15 unum principium.

CAPITULUM XXXVIII
Quod dici non possit quid duo sint,
quamvis necesse sit esse duos.

Studiose itaque attendendum est quiddam quod valde insolitum rebus
5 aliis, in summo spiritu et verbo eius videtur evenire. Nam certum est sic
unicuique singulatim et utrisque simul inesse, quidquid sunt in essentia et
quidquid sunt ad creaturam, ut et singulatim perfectum sit ambobus, et
tamen pluralitatem non admittat in duobus. Licet enim singulatim et ille
perfecte sit summa veritas et creator, et verbum eius sit summa veritas et
10 creator, non tamen ambo simul sunt duae veritates aut duo creatores.
Sed cum haec ita sint, miro tamen modo apertissimum est quia nec ille

Understanding) of the Creator than in itself. Therefore, how would the human mind comprehend what that kind of speaking and knowledge is which is so vastly superior to and truer than created substances, if our knowledge is as vastly surpassed by these |created| things as their likenesses are different from their being?

CHAPTER THIRTY-SEVEN
Whatever the Supreme Spirit *is* in relation to creatures this Spirit's Word also is. And yet, together they are not |this relation| in a plural way.

Since, plainly, the foregoing rational considerations teach that the Supreme Spirit made all things through its own Word, did not its Word also make all |these| same things? For since |the Word| is consubstantial with that of which it is the Word |or Image|, the Word must be the Supreme Being. But the Supreme Being is only one |being|, which is the sole Creator and only Beginning of all that has been made. For it alone, through no other than through itself, made all things from nothing. Wherefore, whatever things the Supreme Spirit makes, its Word also makes in the same way.[73] And so, whatever the Supreme Spirit is in relation to creatures its Word also is in the same way; and yet, together they are not |this relation| in a plural way, for there are not many creating and supreme beings. Thus, just as this Spirit is the Creator and the Beginning of |all| things, so also is its Word. And yet, they are not two, but are one Creator and one Beginning.

CHAPTER THIRTY-EIGHT
It cannot be said what two they are, although they must be two.

Thus, we must carefully give heed to something which, though very uncommon in the case of created things, is seen to hold true of the Supreme Spirit and its Word. Assuredly, whatever they are essentially and whatever they are in relation to creatures is present to each individually and to both together in such way that it is wholly in each of the two without being more than one. For although this Spirit is itself completely the Supreme Truth and completely the Creator, and although its Word is also itself completely the Supreme Truth and completely the Creator, nevertheless both together are not two truths or two creators. But even though these |observations| are correct, still in a remarkable

cuius est verbum, potest esse verbum suum, nec verbum potest esse ille cuius est verbum. Ut in eo quod significat vel quid sint substantialiter vel quid sint ad creaturam, semper individuam teneant unitatem; in eo
15 vero quod ille non est ex isto, hoc autem est ex illo, ineffabilem admittant pluralitatem. Ineffabilem certe. Quamvis enim necessitas cogat ut sint duo, nullo tamen modo exprimi potest, quid duo sint. Nam et si forte duo pares aut aliquid aliud similiter ad invicem possint dici; in his ipsis tamen relativis si quaeratur quid sit illud de quo dicuntur, non poterit
20 dici pluraliter, quemadmodum dicuntur duae pares lineae aut duo similes homines. Quippe nec sunt duo pares spiritus nec duo pares creatores nec duo aliquid, quod significet eorum aut essentiam aut habitudinem ad creaturam. Sed nec duo aliquid quod designet propriam habitudinem alterius ad alterum, quia nec duo verba nec duae imagines. Verbum
25 namque hoc ipsum quod verbum est aut imago, ad alterum est, quia non nisi alicuius verbum est aut imago; et sic propria sunt haec alterius ut nequaquam alteri coaptentur. Nam ille cuius est verbum aut imago, nec imago nec verbum est. Constat igitur quia exprimi non potest, quid duo sint summus spiritus et verbum eius, quamvis quibusdam singulorum
30 proprietatibus cogantur esse duo. Etenim proprium est unius esse ex altero, et proprium est alterius alterum esse ex illo.

CAPITULUM XXXIX

Quod idem verbum sit a summo spiritu nascendo.

Quod ipsum nullo utique verbo videtur familiarius posse proferri quam si dicatur proprium esse unius nasci ex altero, et proprium alterius nasci
5 alterum ex ipso. Certum namque iam constat quia verbum summi spiritus non sic est ex eo, quemadmodum ea quae ab illo facta sunt, sed quemadmodum creator de creatore, summum de summo, et—ut plena brevitate omnimoda absolvatur similitudo—penitus idem ipsum est de

way it is perfectly clear that the Supreme Spirit, of which there is a Word |or an Image|, cannot be its own word; nor can the Word be this Spirit, of which it is the Word |or Image|. Thus, with respect to signifying what |this Spirit and its Word| are substantively and what they are in relation to creatures, they are always an individual oneness. But with respect to the fact that the Supreme Spirit is not of the Word but that the Word is of the Supreme Spirit, they are an ineffable plurality. To be sure, ineffable—because although necessity requires that they be two, what two they are cannot at all be expressed.[74] For even if in relation to each other they could possibly be called two equals, or some such thing, still if we ask regarding these relational |words| "What is that of which they are predicated?" we cannot answer in the plural—as |we can| when we are talking about two equal *lines* or two similar *men*. Indeed, they are not two equal spirits or two equal creators or two of anything which signifies either their essence or their relation to creatures. Nor are they two of anything which designates the distinguishing relation of the one to the other, for there are not two words or two images. For the Word, with respect to the fact that it is a word or an image, is related to the Supreme Spirit, for a word or an image is |the word or image| only of something; and being a word or an image is so proper to the Word that |this same characterization| does not at all fit the Supreme Spirit. For this Spirit, of which there is a Word or an Image, is itself neither word nor image. Therefore, it is evident that there cannot be expressed what two the Supreme Spirit and its Word are, even though it is necessary that they be two because of certain distinguishing properties which each has. For it is the distinguishing property of the one to exist from the other; and it is the distinguishing property of the other that this one exist from it.

CHAPTER THIRTY-NINE

This Word exists from the Supreme Spirit by being begotten.

There surely seems to be no more ready way to put this matter than to say that it is the distinguishing property of the one to be *begotten* from the other, and is the property of the other that this one be begotten from it. For it is already certain[75] that the Word of the Supreme Spirit does not exist from the Supreme Spirit in the same way as do the things made by the Supreme Spirit. Rather, it exists as Creator from Creator, as the Supreme from the Supreme. Or, to sum up the full likeness in a few

eodem ipso, et ita ut nullatenus sit nisi ex eo. Cum igitur pateat verbum
10 summi spiritus sic esse ex ipso solo ut perfectam eius quasi proles parentis teneat similitudinem, nec sic esse ex ipso ut fiat ab eo, profecto nullo
modo convenientius cogitari potest esse ex illo quam nascendo. Nempe
si innumerabiles res indubitanter dicuntur nasci ex iis ex quibus habent ut
sint, cum nullam eorum de quibus nasci dicuntur teneant similitudinem,
15 sicut proles parentis (dicimus enim capillos nasci de capite et poma ex
arbore, licet nec illi capitis nec ista arboris similia sint)—si inquam multa
huiusmodi non absurde dicuntur nasci: tanto congruentius dici potest
verbum summi spiritus ex illo existere nascendo, quanto perfectius quasi
proles parentis trahit eius similitudinem ex illo existendo.

CAPITULUM XL

Quod verissime ille sit parens et illud proles.

Quodsi convenientissime dicitur nasci, et tam simile est illi de quo nascitur, cur aestimetur simile quasi proles parenti, et non potius asseratur
5 quia tanto verior est ille parens et istud proles, quanto magis et ille ad
huius nativitatis perfectionem solus sufficit et quod nascitur eius similitudinem exprimit? Namque in rebus aliis quas parentis prolisque certum
est habitudinem habere, nulla sic gignit ut omnino nullius indigens sola
per se ad gignendam prolem sufficiat; nulla sic gignitur ut nulla admixta
10 dissimilitudine omnimodam similitudinem parentis exhibeat. Si ergo verbum summi spiritus sic est omnino ex ipsius sola essentia, et sic singulariter est illi simile ut nulla proles sic sit omnino ex sola parentis essentia,
aut sic similis parenti: profecto nullis rebus tam convenienter videtur
aptari habitudo parentis et prolis quam summo spiritui et verbo eius.

XL, 11 est: *ex ? corr. B²*

words: the same thing exists altogether from the same thing—and in such way that it does not at all exist except from this thing. Therefore, since it is clear that (1) the Word of the Supreme Spirit exists from it alone, in such way as to possess its perfect likeness—as of offspring to parent—and since (2) the Word does not exist from the Supreme Spirit as something made by it, surely in no way can |the Word| more suitably be thought to exist from the Supreme Spirit than by being begotten. Indeed, countless items are said, without qualm, to be begotten from those things to which they owe their existence. |We speak this way even in cases| where things do not at all, analogously to an offspring and its parent, resemble that from which they are said to be begotten. For example, we say that hair is begotten from a head and fruit from a tree, even though hair does not resemble a head nor fruit a tree. If, then, many such things are not absurdly said to be begotten, then the more perfectly |the Word of the Supreme Spirit| resembles the Supreme Spirit, like offspring to parent, by existing from it, the more appropriately the Word of the Supreme Spirit can be said to exist from it by being begotten.

CHAPTER FORTY

The Supreme Spirit is most truly parent,
and the Word is most truly offspring.

But if |the Word| is most suitably said to be begotten, and if it is so like the Supreme Spirit from whom it is begotten, then why would we think that |the Word is| *like* an offspring to its parent? Why would we not rather maintain that the more the Supreme Spirit alone suffices for effecting this begottenness and the more what is begotten expresses the Supreme Spirit's likeness, the truer parent the Supreme Spirit is and the truer offspring the Word is? For with regard to other things which assuredly are related as parent and offspring, none begets in such way that it alone needs no one else but is completely sufficient by itself to beget offspring; and none is begotten in such way that, having no dissimilarity admixed, it resembles its parent in every respect. Therefore, if the Word of the Supreme Spirit exists so entirely from this Spirit's essence alone, and resembles this Spirit so uniquely, that no offspring exists as completely only from the essence of its parent or resembles its parent as much, surely the relationship of offspring to parent is seen to befit nothing as suitably as |it befits| the Supreme Spirit and its Word. Hence,

15 Quapropter illius est proprium verissimum esse parentem, istius vero verissimam esse prolem.

CAPITULUM XLI
Quod ille verissime gignat, illud gignatur.

At hoc constare non poterit, nisi pariter ille verissime gignat, et istud verissime gignatur. Sicut igitur illud est perspicuum, ita hoc esse certissi-
5 mum necesse est. Quare summi spiritus est verissime gignere, et verbi eius verissime gigni.

CAPITULUM XLII
Quod alterius verissime sit esse genitorem et patrem,
alterius genitum et filium.

Vellem iam quidem et forte possem illum esse verissime patrem, hoc
5 vero esse verissime filium, concludere; sed nec hoc negligendum existimo, an patris et filii, an matris et filiae magis illis apta sit appellatio, cum in eis nulla sit sexus discretio. Nam si idcirco convenienter est ille pater et proles eius filius, quia uterque est spiritus, cur non pari ratione alteri convenit esse matrem, alteri filiam, quia uterque est veritas et
10 sapientia? An quia in iis naturis quae sexus habent differentiam, melioris sexus est patrem esse vel filium, minoris vero matrem vel filiam? Est hoc quidem naturaliter in pluribus; in quibusdam vero e contrario, ut in quibusdam avium generibus, in quibus femininus sexus semper maior et validior est, masculinus vero minor et infirmior.
15 Aut certe idcirco magis convenit summo spiritui patrem dici quam matrem, quia prima et principalis causa prolis semper est in patre. Nam si maternam causam quolibet modo semper paterna praecedit, nimis incongruum est ut illi parenti aptetur nomen matris, cui ad gignendam

XLII, 12 in³: *supra lin. B*

the Supreme Spirit has the distinguishing property of being the most true parent, and the Word has the distinguishing property of being the most true offspring.

CHAPTER FORTY-ONE

The Supreme Spirit most truly begets,
and the Word is most truly begotten.

But this |conclusion above| will not be able to stand unless, likewise, (1) the Supreme Spirit most truly begets and (2) the Word is most truly begotten. Therefore, just as the first is clearly true, so must the second be completely certain. Hence, it is the distinguishing property of the Supreme Spirit most truly to beget and the distinguishing property of the Word most truly to be begotten.

CHAPTER FORTY-TWO

It is most truly characteristic of the one to be begetter and father,
and of the other to be begotten and son.

I would now like to infer, if I can, that the Supreme Spirit most truly is father and that the Word most truly is son. Yet, I think I ought not to by-pass |the following question|: is the appellation "father and son" or the appellation "mother and daughter" more befitting for them?, for there is no sexual distinction in the Supreme Spirit and the Word. For if the Supreme Spirit is suitably |called| father and its offspring suitably |called| son because each is spirit, then why is it not suitable, by parity of reasoning, for the one to be |called| mother and the other to be |called| daughter because each is truth and wisdom?[76] Is it |preferable to call them father and son| because among those natures which have a difference of sex it is characteristic of the better sex to be father or son and of the inferior sex to be mother or daughter? Now, although this is by nature the case for many |beings|, for others the reverse holds true. For example, in some species of birds the female sex is always larger and stronger, the male sex smaller and weaker.

But, surely, the Supreme Spirit is more suitably called father than mother because the first and principal cause of offspring is always in the father. For if the paternal |cause| always in some way precedes the maternal cause, then it is exceedingly inappropriate for the name "mother" to be applied to that parent whom no other cause either joins or pre-

prolem nulla alia causa aut sociatur aut praecedit. Verissimum igitur est
20 summum spiritum patrem esse prolis suae. Quod si filius semper similior
est patri quam filia, nihil autem similius est alteri quam summo patri
proles sua: verissimum est hanc prolem non esse filiam, sed filium. Sicut
igitur proprium est illius verissime gignere, istius vero gigni, sic proprium
est illius verissimum esse genitorem, istius vero verissimum genitum. Et
25 sicut alter est verissimus parens, alter verissima proles, sic alter est verissimus pater, alter verissimus filius.

CAPITULUM XLIII

Retractatio communionis amborum et proprietatum singulorum.

Inventis tot et tantis singulorum proprietatibus, quibus mira quaedam
tam ineffabilis quam inevitabilis in summa unitate probatur esse plurali-
5 tas: valde mihi videtur delectabile retractare saepius tam impenetrabile
secretum. Ecce enim cum sic impossibile sit eundem esse eum qui gignit
et eum qui gignitur, atque eundem esse parentem et prolem, ut necesse
sit alium esse genitorem, alium genitum, et alium esse patrem, alium
filium: sic tamen necesse est idem esse illum qui gignit et illum qui gigni-
10 tur, necnon parentem et prolem, ut impossibile sit aliud esse genitorem
quam quod est genitus, aliud esse patrem quam quod filius. Et cum ita sit
alius ille et alius ille ut omnino pateat quod duo sint, sic tamen
unum et idipsum est id quod est ille et ille ut penitus lateat quid
duo sint. Nam sic est alius pater, alius filius ut cum ambos dixerim,
15 videam me duos dixisse; et sic est idipsum quod est et pater et filius, ut
non intelligam quid duos dixerim. Quamvis namque singulus pater sit
perfecte summus spiritus et singulus filius sit perfecte summus spiritus, sic
tamen unum idemque est spiritus pater et spiritus filius ut pater et filius
non sint duo spiritus, sed unus spiritus. Ut sicut singula propria singul-

cedes for the begetting of offspring. Therefore, it is most true that the Supreme Spirit is father of its own offspring. But if a son is always more like a father than is a daughter, and if no one thing is more like another than this offspring is like the Supreme Father, it is most true that this offspring is a son, not a daughter. Therefore, just as this Spirit has the distinguishing property of most truly begetting and this offspring of most truly being begotten, so the former has the distinguishing property of being the most true begetting one and the latter of being the most true begotten one. And just as the one is the most true parent and the other the most true offspring, so the one is the most true father and the other the most true son.

CHAPTER FORTY-THREE

Reconsideration of what is common to both
and of what is proper to each.

Having now discovered so many, and such important, properties of each[77]—|properties| by which a certain remarkable plurality, as ineffable as it is necessary, is proved to exist in supreme oneness—I find it especially delightful to reflect more frequently upon such an impenetrable mystery. For, lo, it is so impossible for the one who begets and the one who is begotten to be the same, and so impossible for the parent and the offspring to be the same, that it is necessary for the Begetter to be other than the Begotten and for the Father to be other than the Son. And yet, it is so necessary for the one who begets and the one who is begotten to be the same, and so necessary for the parent and the offspring to be the same, that it is impossible for the Begetter to be other than what the Begotten is or for the Father to be other than what the Son is. Although both exist distinctly in such way that the fact of their being two is perfectly clear, nonetheless what each of them is is so one and the same |as what the other is| that what two they are is thoroughly hidden.[78] For the Father and the Son are so distinct that when I speak of both I see that I have spoken of two; yet, what the Father and the Son are is so identical that I do not understand what I have called two. For although the Father, considered distinctly, is completely the Supreme Spirit and although the Son, considered distinctly, is completely the Supreme Spirit, nevertheless the Spirit who is Father and the Spirit who is Son are so one and the same that the Father and the Son are not two spirits but one. Thus, just as the proper-

20 orum non recipiunt pluralitatem quia non sunt duorum, ita id quod commune est amborum, individuam teneat unitatem, quamvis totum sit singulorum. Nam sicut non sunt duo patres aut duo filii, sed unus pater et unus filius, quoniam singula sunt singulorum propria: ita non sunt duo sed unus spiritus, quamvis et singuli patris et singuli filii sit perfectum
25 esse spiritum. Sic sunt oppositi relationibus ut alter numquam suscipiat proprium alterius; sic sunt concordes natura ut alter semper teneat essentiam alterius. Sic enim diversi sunt per hoc quod alter est pater, alter filius, ut numquam dicatur aut pater filius aut filius pater; et sic idem sunt per substantiam ut semper sit in patre essentia filii et in filio essentia
30 patris. Est enim non diversa, sed eadem, non plures, sed una utriusque essentia.

CAPITULUM XLIV
Quomodo alter alterius sit essentia.

Unde etiam si alter alterius dicatur essentia, non erratur a veritate, sed summa unitas simplicitasque commendatur communis naturae. Non
5 enim quemadmodum intelligitur sapientia hominis, per quam homo sapiens est, qui per se non potest esse sapiens, ita intelligi potest, si dicatur pater essentia filii et filius essentia patris, ut eo modo sit filius existens per patrem et pater per filium, quasi non possit alter existens esse nisi per alterum, sicut homo non potest esse sapiens nisi per sapien-
10 tiam. Sicut namque summa sapientia semper sapit per se, ita summa essentia semper est per se. Est autem perfecte summa essentia pater et perfecte summa essentia filius. Pariter ergo perfectus pater per se est et perfectus filius per se est, sicut uterque sapit per se. Non enim idcirco minus perfecta est essentia vel sapientia filius, quia est essentia nata de
15 patris essentia et sapientia de sapientia; sed tunc minus perfecta essentia

ties which are unique to each do not admit of plurality because they do not belong to both, so what is common to both constitutes an individual oneness even though the whole of it belongs to each. For just as there are not two fathers or two sons but |only| one father and one son since the distinguishing properties of the Father are distinct from the distinguishing properties of the Son, so there are not two spirits but |only| one even though it is true of both Father and Son that each is completely spirit. |The Father and the Son| are so opposite in relation that the one never sustains the distinguishing property of the other; and they are so concordant in nature that the one always has the essence of the other. For with respect to the fact that the one is the Father and the other is the Son they are so different that the Father is never called the Son nor the Son called the Father; and with respect to their substance they are so identical that the essence of the Son is always in the Father and the essence of the Father is always in the Son. For their essence is the same rather than different, one rather than many.

How the one is the essence of the other.

So also, to say that the one is the essence of the other involves no departure from the truth; rather, it indicates the supreme oneness and supreme simplicity of a common nature. For it is not the case that just as we understand a man's wisdom, through which a man is wise, who cannot be wise through himself, so we can understand (if the Father is said to be the essence of the Son, and the Son to be the essence of the Father) that, similarly, the Son is existent through the Father, and the Father through the Son—as if the one could not be existent except through the other, even as a man cannot be wise except through wisdom. For just as Supreme Wisdom is always wise through itself, so the Supreme Being always exists through itself. But the Father is completely the Supreme Being, and the Son is completely the Supreme Being. Therefore, the complete Father exists through Himself, and likewise the complete Son exists through Himself—even as each is wise through Himself. For it is not the case that the Son is less perfect existence (*essentia*) or wisdom because He is existence begotten from the existence of the Father and wisdom |begotten| from the wisdom |of the Father|. (But |the Son| *would* be less perfect existence or wisdom if He did not exist

aut sapientia esset, si non esset per se aut non saperet per se. Nequaquam
enim repugnant ut filius et per se subsistat et de patre habeat esse. Sicut
enim pater habet essentiam et sapientiam et vitam in semetipso, ut non
per alienam sed per suam essentiam sit, per suam sapientiam sapiat, per
20 suam vitam vivat: ita gignendo dat filio habere essentiam et sapientiam et
vitam in semetipso, ut non per extraneam sed per suam essentiam,
sapientiam, et vitam subsistat, sapiat, et vivat. Alioquin non erit idem
esse patris et filii, nec erit par patri filius. Quod quam falsum sit, liquidis-
sime superius pervisum est.

25   Quare non repugnat filium et subsistere per se et esse de patre, quia
hoc ipsum, id est per seipsum posse subsistere, necesse est illum habere
ex patre. Nam si quis sapiens suam me sapientiam cuius prius expers
essem doceret, utique hoc ipsa sapientia eius facere non incongrue diceretur.
Sed quamvis mea sapientia ab illius sapientia haberet esse et sapere,
30 tamen cum iam esset, non nisi sua essentia esset nec saperet nisi seipsa.
Multo igitur magis aeterni patris coaeternus filius, qui sic habet a patre
esse ut non sint duae essentiae, per se subsistit, sapit, et vivit. Non igitur
sic intelligi potest quod pater filii aut filius patris sit essentia, quasi alter
non possit subsistere per se sed per alterum; sed ad significandam quam
35 habent communionem summe simplicis summeque unius essentiae, sic
congrue dici et intelligi potest quia sic est alter idipsum quod alter, ut
alter habeat essentiam alterius. Hac itaque ratione, quoniam utrique non
aliud est habere essentiam quam essentiam esse: sicut habet alter alterius
essentiam, ita est alter essentia alterius; id est idem esse est alteri quod
40 alteri.

through Himself or were not wise through Himself.) For there is no inconsistency at all involved in the Son's existing through Himself and His having existence (*esse*) from the Father. For the Father has existence, wisdom, and life in Himself, so that He exists through His own being, is wise through His own wisdom, and lives through His own life (rather than through another's being, wisdom, or life). Similarly, by begetting |the Son| he bestows on Him the having of existence, wisdom, and life in Himself |i.e., in the Son Himself|, so that the Son exists through His own being, is wise through His own wisdom, and lives through His own life (rather than through someone else's being, wisdom, or life).[79] Otherwise, the existence (*esse*) of the Father and of the Son would not be identical, nor would the Son be equal to the Father. But we have already seen[80] most clearly how false |this consequence| is.

So, then, the fact that the Son exists from the Father is not inconsistent with the fact that the Son exists through Himself. For it is necessary that He have from the Father the very ability to exist through Himself. If some wise man were to teach me his wisdom which previously I lacked, surely his wisdom would not inappropriately be said to do this |i.e., to cause my wisdom|. But although my wisdom would owe its existence and its being-wise to his wisdom, nevertheless once my wisdom existed it would exist only by its own being and would be wise only by itself. Therefore, it is all the more true that the eternal Father's co-eternal Son—who has existence from the Father in such way that they are not two beings—exists, is wise, and lives through Himself. Therefore, "the Father is the essence of the Son" or "the Son is the essence of the Father" cannot be understood as if the one were |able to exist| through the other but not able to exist through Himself. Rather, in order to signify their commonness of supremely simple and supremely singular essence, it can be appropriately said and understood that the one so is the very same thing as the other that the one has the essence of the other. And so, on the basis of the fact that, for either of them, to have an essence is not other than to be an essence: just as the one has the essence of the other, so the one is the essence of the other—i.e., the one has the same being (*esse*) as the other.

CAPITULUM XLV

Quod aptius dici possit filius essentia patris quam pater filii;
et quod similiter sit filius patris virtus et sapientia et similia.

Quod licet secundum perspectam rationem verum sit, valde tamen magis
5 congruit filium dici essentiam patris quam patrem essentiam filii. Quoniam namque pater a nullo habet essentiam nisi a seipso, non satis apte
dicitur habere essentiam alicuius nisi suam. Quia vero filius essentiam
suam habet a patre et eandem quam habet pater, aptissime dici potest
habere essentiam patris. Quare quoniam neuter aliter habet essentiam
10 quam existendo essentia: sicut satis aptius intelligitur habere filius patris
essentiam quam pater filii, ita convenientius dici potest filius patris essentia quam pater filii. Nam haec una si fiat prolatio, satis acuta brevitate
commendat filium non solum eandem essentiam habere cum patre, sed
hanc ipsam habere de patre. Ut hoc sit, "filius est essentia patris" quod
15 est, "filius est non differens essentia de patris essentia" (immo "de patre
essentia"). Similiter ergo est filius patris virtus et sapientia seu veritas, et
iustitia, et quidquid summi spiritus convenit essentiae.

CAPITULUM XLVI

Quomodo quaedam ex iis quae sic proferuntur
aliter quoque possint intelligi.

Videntur tamen quaedam ex iis quae sic proferri et intelligi possunt,
5 aliam quoque non incongruam sub hac ipsa pronuntiatione intelligentiam
suscipere. Liquet enim filium esse verum verbum, id est perfectam intelligentiam sive perfectam totius paternae substantiae cognitionem et scientiam et sapientiam, id est quae ipsam patris essentiam intelligit et cognoscit et scit et sapit. Si igitur hoc sensu filius dicatur patris intelligentia et

CHAPTER FORTY-FIVE

The Son can more fittingly be called the essence
of the Father than the Father |can be called the essence|
of the Son. Similarly the Son is the strength of the Father,
the wisdom of the Father, and the like.

Although according to the aforeseen reasoning this |last conclusion| is
true, nevertheless for the Son to be called the essence of the Father is
much more appropriate than for the Father |to be called| the essence of
the Son. For since the Father has His essence from no one except Himself, He is not very fittingly said to have anyone's essence except His
own. But because the Son has His essence from the Father and because
He has the same |essence| as the Father has, the Son can very fittingly be
said to have the Father's essence. Therefore, since neither |the Father nor
the Son| has an essence otherwise than by being an essence: just as the
Son is much more fittingly understood to have the Father's essence than
the Father |to have| the Son's |essence|, so the Son can more suitably be
said to be the essence of the Father than the Father |can be said to be the
essence| of the Son. For when this one utterance is made, it indicates
sufficiently, by its terseness, that the Son not only has the same essence
as the Father but also that He has this |essence| from the Father. Thus, to
say that the Son is the essence of the Father is to say that the Son is not
a different essence from the essence of the Father—or better, |is not
different| from the Father-essence. Similarly, therefore, the Son is the
Father's strength, wisdom, truth, justice, and whatever else besuits the
essence of the Supreme Spirit.

CHAPTER FORTY-SIX

How various of the |statements| which are expressed
in the foregoing way can also be understood in another way.

Nevertheless, various of the |statements| which can be expressed and
understood in the foregoing way are seen to admit also of another mean-
ing which is not inconsistent with the present construal. For, clearly, the
Son is the true Word—i.e., the perfect Understanding, Cognition,
Knowledge, and Wisdom—of the whole paternal substance. That is, the
Son understands, cognizes, knows, and comprehends the essence of the
Father. Therefore, if the Son is called the Understanding, Wisdom,

10 sapientia et scientia et cognitio sive notitia, quoniam intelligit, sapit, scit, et novit patrem: nequaquam a veritate disceditur. Veritas quoque patris aptissime dici potest filius, non solum eo sensu quia est eadem filii veritas quae est et patris, sicut iam perspectum est, sed etiam hoc sensu ut in eo intelligatur non imperfecta quaedam imitatio sed integra veritas paternae
15 substantiae, quia non est aliud quam quod est pater.

CAPITULUM XLVII
Quod filius sit intelligentia intelligentiae et veritas
veritatis et similiter de similibus.

At si ipsa substantia patris est intelligentia et scientia et sapientia et veri-
5 tas, consequenter colligitur quia sicut filius est intelligentia et scientia et sapientia et veritas paternae substantiae, ita est intelligentia intelligentiae, scientia scientiae, sapientia sapientiae, veritas veritatis.

CAPITULUM XLVIII
Quod in memoria intelligatur pater, sicut in intelligentia
filius; et quomodo filius sit intelligentia vel sapientia
memoriae et memoria patris et memoriae.

5 De memoria vero quid sentiendum est? An aestimandus est filius intelligentia memoriae, sive memoria patris, aut memoria memoriae? Equidem cum summa sapientia sui memor esse negari non possit: nihil competentius quam in memoria pater, sicut in verbo filius, intelligitur, quoniam de memoria nasci verbum videtur. Quod clarius in nostra mente percipitur.
10 Quoniam namque mens humana non semper se cogitat, sicut sui semper meminit: liquet cum se cogitat quia verbum eius nascitur de memoria. Unde apparet quia si semper se cogitaret, semper verbum eius de memoria nasceretur. Rem etenim cogitare cuius memoriam habemus, hoc est mente eam dicere; verbum vero rei est ipsa cogitatio ad eius similitudi-
15 nem ex memoria formata. Hinc itaque liquido animadverti potest de

Knowledge, and Cognition, or Conception, of the Father in the sense that He understands, comprehends, knows, and cognizes the Father, there is no departure at all from the truth. Moreover, the Son can very fittingly be called the truth of the Father—not only in the sense that the truth of the Son is identical with |the truth| of the Father (as we have already seen),[81] but also in the sense that in the Son there is understood to be (not an imperfect image of the paternal substance but) the whole truth of the paternal substance, for the Son is the same as what the Father is |i.e., the same essence|.

CHAPTER FORTY-SEVEN
The Son is Understanding of Understanding, Truth of Truth, etc.

But if the substance of the Father is understanding, knowledge, wisdom, and truth, it follows that as the Son is the Understanding, Knowledge, Wisdom, and Truth of the paternal substance, so He is Understanding of Understanding, Knowledge of Knowledge, Wisdom of Wisdom, Truth of Truth.

CHAPTER FORTY-EIGHT
The Father is referred to as Memory, just as the Son
is referred to as Understanding. How the Son is
the Understanding (or Wisdom) of Memory, the Memory
of the Father, and the Memory of Memory.

But what are we to believe about memory? Ought the Son to be thought to be the Understanding of Memory, or the Memory of the Father, or the Memory of Memory? Indeed, since we cannot deny that Supreme Wisdom remembers[82] itself, nothing is more fitting than that just as the Son is referred to as the Word, so the Father is referred to as Memory— for the word seems to be born from memory, as we observe more clearly in regard to our own minds. For since the human mind does not always think of itself (as it does always remember itself), it is clear that when it thinks of itself the word |or image| of itself is begotten from memory. Apparently, then, if |the mind| were always to think of itself, the word |or image| of itself would always be born from memory. For to think of a thing which we remember is to speak of this thing mentally; but this thought formed from memory and formed in the thing's likeness is the word |or image| of the thing. Herefrom, then, we can see clearly—regarding

summa sapientia, quae sic semper se dicit sicut semper sui memor est, quia de aeterna memoria eius coaeternum verbum nascitur. Sicut igitur verbum congrue intelligitur proles, ita memoria parentis nomen aptissime suscipit. Si ergo proles, quae omnino de solo summo spiritu nata
20 est, proles est memoriae eius: nihil consequentius quam quia memoria sua est idem ipse. Quippe non, in eo quod sui memor est, sic est in sua memoria velut alia res in alia, quemadmodum ea quae sic sunt in humanae mentis memoria ut non sint ipsa nostra memoria; sed sic est memor sui ut ipse memoria sua sit. Consequitur itaque ut quomodo filius
25 est intelligentia sive sapientia patris, ita sit et paternae memoriae. At quidquid filius sapit aut intelligit, eius similiter et meminit. Est igitur filius memoria patris et memoria memoriae, id est memoria memor patris qui est memoria, sicut est sapientia patris et sapientia sapientiae, id est sapientia sapiens patrem sapientiam. Et filius quidem memoria nata
30 de memoria, sicut sapientia nata de sapientia; pater vero de nullo nata memoria vel sapientia.

CAPITULUM XLIX
Quod summus spiritus se amet.

Sed ecce, dum huius patris filiique proprietates communionemque delectabiliter intueor, nihil delectabilius in illis contemplandum invenio quam
5 mutui amoris affectum. Quam enim absurde negetur summus spiritus se amare, sicut sui memor est et se intelligit—cum et mens rationalis se et illum amare posse convincatur, ex eo quia sui et illius memor esse et se et illum intelligere potest? Otiosa namque et penitus inutilis est memoria et intelligentia cuiuslibet rei, nisi prout ratio exigit res ipsa ametur aut
10 reprobetur. Amat ergo seipsum summus spiritus, sicut sui meminit et se intelligit.

the Supreme Wisdom, which always speaks of itself as well as always remembering itself—that the Coeternal Word is begotten from the Eternal Memory. Therefore, as the Word is appropriately understood to be an offspring, so Memory is very fittingly called a parent. Hence, if an offspring begotten completely from the Supreme Spirit alone is an offspring of this Spirit's memory, nothing |follows| more consistently than that the Supreme Spirit is its own memory. Indeed, with respect to |the Supreme Spirit's| remembering itself, the Supreme Spirit is not in its own memory as one thing is in another—as is the case with those |remembrances| which exist in the human mind's memory in such way that they are not our memory itself. Rather, this Spirit remembers itself in such way that it is its memory of itself. Hence, it follows that as the Son is the Understanding and Wisdom of the Father, so He is |the Understanding and Wisdom| of the paternal memory. Now, whatever the Son comprehends or understands, He likewise remembers. Therefore, the Son is the Memory of the Father and the Memory of Memory (i.e., Memory remembering the Father, who is Memory), even as He is the Wisdom of the Father and the Wisdom of Wisdom (i.e., Wisdom comprehending the Father, who is Wisdom). And, indeed, the Son |is| Memory begotten from Memory—just as |He is| Wisdom begotten from Wisdom. But the Father |is| Memory and Wisdom begotten from no |other|.

CHAPTER FORTY-NINE
The Supreme Spirit loves itself.

But, lo, as I am contemplating with delight the distinguishing properties of the Father and the Son, together with what they have in common, I find in the Father and the Son nothing more delightful to reflect upon than the affection of mutual love. For how absurd it would be to deny that the Supreme Spirit loves itself as well as remembering and understanding itself—since even a rational |human| mind, from the fact that it can remember and understand both itself and this Spirit, is proved to be able to love both itself and this Spirit. For the remembrance and understanding of any thing whatsoever is in vain, and is altogether useless, unless this thing be loved or condemned to the extent that reason requires. Therefore, the Supreme Spirit loves itself, even as it remembers and understands itself.

CAPITULUM L

Quod idem amor pariter procedat a patre et filio.

Palam certe est rationem habenti eum non idcirco sui memorem esse aut se intelligere quia se amat, sed ideo se amare quia sui meminit et se
5 intelligit; nec eum se posse amare, si sui non sit memor aut se non intelligat. Nulla enim res amatur sine eius memoria aut intelligentia; et multa tenentur memoria et intelliguntur, quae non amantur. Patet igitur amorem summi spiritus ex eo procedere quia sui memor est et se intelligit. Quod si in memoria summi spiritus intelligitur pater, in intelligentia filius: man-
10 ifestum est quia a patre pariter et filio summi spiritus amor procedit.

CAPITULUM LI

Quod uterque pari amore diligat se et alterum.

Sed si se amat summus spiritus, procul dubio amat se pater, amat se filius, et alter alterum—quia singulus pater est summus spiritus, et singu-
5 lus filius summus spiritus, et ambo simul unus spiritus, et quia uterque pariter sui et alterius meminit, et se et alterum intelligit. Et quoniam omnino idipsum est quod amat vel amatur in patre, et quod in filio, necesse est ut pari amore uterque diligat se et alterum.

CAPITULUM LII

Quod tantus sit ipse amor, quantus est summus spiritus.

Quantus ergo est amor iste summi spiritus sic communis patri et filio? Sed si tantum se diligit, quantum sui meminit et se intelligit, tantum
5 autem sui memor est et intelligit se, quanta est eius essentia, quod aliter esse non potest: profecto tantus est amor eius, quantus ipse est.

L, 4 se¹: *supra lin. B*

This love proceeds equally from the Father and the Son.

To one who is rational it is surely clear that the Supreme Spirit does not remember itself and understand itself because it loves itself but rather loves itself because it remembers itself and understands itself. |Clearly,| moreover, this Spirit cannot love itself unless it remembers itself or understands itself. For nothing is loved without being remembered or understood,[83] whereas many things are remembered and understood without being loved. So, clearly, the Supreme Spirit's love proceeds from its remembering itself and understanding itself. But if the Father is referred to as the Memory of the Supreme Spirit, and if the Son |is referred to| as the Understanding |of the Supreme Spirit|, then it is evident that the love of the Supreme Spirit proceeds equally from the Father and the Son.[84]

The Father and the Son love themselves and
each other in equal degree.

But if the Supreme Spirit loves itself, then without doubt the Father loves Himself, the Son loves Himself, and the Father and the Son love each other. For the Father, considered distinctly, is the Supreme Spirit; and the Son, considered distinctly, is the Supreme Spirit; and both together are one spirit. Moreover, |they love themselves and each other| because each remembers and understands both Himself and the other in equal degree. And since what loves and is loved is wholly the same for the Father and for the Son, it is necessarily the case that each loves Himself and the other in equal degree.

This Love is as great as the Supreme Spirit.

How great, then, is the Supreme Spirit's love—|a love| so mutual to the Father and the Son? If the Supreme Spirit loves itself to the extent that it remembers and understands itself, and if it remembers and understands itself in proportion to its essence—as cannot fail to be the case—then surely the Supreme Spirit's love is as great as this Spirit itself.

Quod idem amor sit idipsum quod est summus spiritus,
et tamen ipse cum patre et filio unus spiritus.

Verum quid potest esse par summo spiritui nisi summus spiritus? Iste
5 itaque amor est summus spiritus. Denique si nulla umquam creatura, id
est si nihil umquam aliud esset quam summus spiritus pater et filius,
nihilominus seipsos et invicem pater et filius diligerent. Consequitur
itaque hunc amorem non esse aliud quam quod est pater et filius, quod
est summa essentia. At quoniam summae essentiae plures esse non pos-
10 sunt: quid magis necessarium quam patrem et filium et utriusque amorem
unam esse summam essentiam? Est igitur idem amor summa sapientia,
summa veritas, summum bonum, et quidquid de summi spiritus substantia dici potest.

Quod totus procedat a patre, totus a filio,
et tamen non sit nisi unus amor.

Intuendum est diligenter utrum sint duo amores, unus a patre procedens,
5 alter a filio; an unus non totus ab uno procedens, sed partim a patre,
partim a filio; an nec plures nec unus partim procedens a singulis, sed
unus totus a singulis et idem totus a duobus simul. Sed huius dubitationis
certitudo hinc indubitanter cognoscitur: quia non ex eo procedit in quo
plures sunt pater et filius, sed ex eo in quo unum sunt. Nam non ex
10 relationibus suis, quae plures sunt—alia est enim relatio patris, alia filii—
sed ex ipsa sua essentia, quae pluralitatem non admittit, emittunt pater et
filius pariter tantum bonum. Sicut ergo singulus pater est summus spiritus, et singulus filius est summus spiritus, et simul pater et filius non duo
sed unus spiritus: ita a singulo patre manat totus amor summi spiritus, et
15 a singulo filio totus, et simul a patre et filio non duo toti, sed unus
idemque totus.

CHAPTER FIFTY-THREE

This Love is the same thing that the Supreme Spirit is; and yet, this Love is one spirit with the Father and the Son.

But what can be equal to the Supreme Spirit except the Supreme Spirit? Hence, this Love is the Supreme Spirit. Indeed, if there never had been a creature—i.e., if nothing had ever existed other than the Supreme Spirit, who is Father and Son—nonetheless, the Father and the Son would still have loved themselves and each other. Hence, it follows that this Love is identical with what the Father and the Son are, viz., the Supreme Being. Now, since there cannot be many supreme beings, what is more necessary than that the Father, the Son, and their Love be one Supreme Being? Therefore, this Love is the Supreme Wisdom, the Supreme Truth, the Supreme Good, and whatever |else| can be predicated of the substance of the Supreme Spirit.

CHAPTER FIFTY-FOUR

|This Love| proceeds as a whole from the Father and as a whole from the Son. Nevertheless, there is only one love.

We must consider closely whether there are (1) two loves—one proceeding from the Father and the other |proceeding| from the Son—or (2) one |love| proceeding not as a whole from |either|one but |proceeding| partly from the Father and partly from the Son or (3) neither two |loves| nor one |love| which proceeds partly from the Father and partly from the Son but rather one and the same |love proceeding| as a whole from each distinctly and as a whole from both together. Now, the solution to this question is unquestionably recognized from the following |consideration: the Supreme Spirit's Love| does not proceed |from the Father and the Son| with respect to the fact that they are two but with respect to the fact that they are one. For the Father and the Son equally send forth such a great good not from their relations, which are plural (the one relation is that of father, the other that of son), but from their essence, which does not admit of plurality.[85] Therefore, just as the Father, considered distinctly, is the Supreme Spirit and just as the Son, considered distinctly, is the Supreme Spirit, and yet the Father and the Son together are not two spirits but are one spirit, so the Supreme Spirit's Love proceeds as a whole from the Father, considered distinctly, and as a whole from the Son, considered distinctly, and as one and the same whole (not as two wholes) from the Father and the Son together.

CAPITULUM LV
Quod non sit eorum filius.

Quid ergo? Cum hic amor pariter habeat esse a patre et filio, et sic similis sit ambobus ut nullatenus dissimilis sit illis, sed omnino idem sit
5 quod illi: numquid filius eorum aut proles aestimandus est? Sed sicut verbum, mox consideratur, se prolem eius esse a quo est, evidentissime probat, promptam praeferendo parentis imaginem: sic amor aperte se prolem negat, quia dum a patre et filio procedere intelligitur, non statim tam perspicuam exhibet se contemplanti eius ex quo est similitudinem—
10 quamvis ipsum considerata ratio doceat omnino idipsum esse quod est pater et filius. Denique si proles eorum est: aut alter eorum erit pater eius, alter mater, aut uterque pater sive mater est—quae omnia veritati repugnare videntur. Quoniam namque nullatenus aliter a patre procedit quam a filio, nulla veritas patitur ut dissimili vocabulo ad illum pater et
15 filius referantur. Non est igitur alter pater eius, alter mater. Ut autem duo aliqua sint, quae singula perfectam et nulla consideratione differentem habeant pariter ad aliquid unum patris aut matris habitudinem: nulla natura aliquo monstrari concedit exemplo. Ergo non est uterque, scilicet pater et filius, pater aut mater amoris a se manantis. Nequaquam itaque
20 videtur veritati convenire ut idem amor, eorum filius sit aut proles.

CAPITULUM LVI
Quod solus pater sit genitor et ingenitus, solus filius genitus, solus amor nec genitus nec ingenitus.

Sed videtur tamen amor idem nec omnino secundum communis locutio-
5 nis usum dici posse ingenitus, nec ita proprie sicut verbum genitus. Solemus enim saepe dicere aliquid gigni ex ea re de qua existit—ut cum dicimus calorem aut splendorem gigni ab igne, seu aliquod effectum ex

LV, 5 proprie: propriae *B*   proprie *EST*
LV, 6 mox: mox *hic significat idem cum* mox ut; *cf. Gaunilo pro Insipiente* **2** 16

CHAPTER FIFTY-FIVE
|This Love| is not the son of the Father and of the Son.

What then? Since this Love has its existence equally from the Father and the Son, and since it is so like them that it is in no respect unlike them but is in every respect the same thing that they are, must it be regarded as their son or their offspring? Now, as soon as contemplated, the Word evidences most clearly, by manifesting the clear image of its parent, that it is the offspring of the one from whom it exists. By comparison, |the Supreme Spirit's| Love clearly denies that it is an offspring, because when it is understood to proceed from the Father and the Son, it does not immediately exhibit, to one contemplating it, as clear a likeness of the one from whom it exists—even though reflective reason teaches that this Love is in every respect the very thing that the Father and the Son are. Indeed, if |this Love| were the offspring of the Father and the Son, one of the two would be the father of this Love and the other would be the mother, or else both would be its father or both would be its mother—all |three of| which |alternatives| are seen to be counter to the truth. On the one hand, since |this Love| does not proceed at all differently from the Father than from the Son, it is inadmissible to refer to the Father and the Son differently in relation to this Love; thus, it is not the case that the one is its father and the other its mother. On the other hand, there is no precedent in nature for supposing that there are two things each of which has, equally, a perfect and an exactly similar relation of father or mother to some one thing. Thus, it is not the case that both the Father and the Son are father or mother of this Love which proceeds from them. Therefore, that the Love |of the Father and the Son| is their son or their offspring is seen not to agree in any respect with the truth.

CHAPTER FIFTY-SIX
Only the Father is begetter and unbegotten. Only the Son is begotten. Only their Love is neither begotten nor unbegotten.

But in accordance with our practice in ordinary discourse, this Love (it seems) cannot at all be called unbegotten; nor |can it be called| begotten, as properly as can the Word. For we are accustomed frequently to say that a thing is begotten from that from which it exists—as when we say that heat or brightness is begotten from fire or that an effect |is begotten|

causa sua. Secundum hanc igitur rationem amor a summo spiritu exiens non omnino asseri potest ingenitus. Ita vero proprie sicut verbum dici
10 genitus non potest, quia verbum verissimam esse prolem et verissimum filium, amorem vero nullatenus filium aut prolem esse manifestum est. Potest itaque—immo debet—dici solus ille cuius verbum est genitor et ingenitus, quia solus est pater et parens, et nullo modo ab alio est. Solum autem verbum genitum, quia solum filius et proles est. Solus vero amor
15 utriusque nec genitus nec ingenitus, quia nec filius est nec proles est, nec omnino non est ab alio.

CAPITULUM LVII

Quod amor idem sic sit increatus et creator sicut pater
et filius, et tamen ipse cum illis non tres, sed unus increatus
et unus creator; et quod idem possit dici spiritus patris et filii.

5 Quoniam autem idem amor singulus est summa essentia, sicut pater et filius, et tamen simul pater et filius et utriusque amor non plures sed una summa essentia, quae, sola a nullo facta, non per aliud quam per se omnia fecit: necesse est ut quemadmodum singulus pater et singulus filius est increatus et creator, ita et amor singulus sit increatus et creator,
10 et tamen omnes tres simul non plures sed unus increatus et unus creator. Patrem itaque nullus facit sive creat aut gignit. Filium vero pater solus non facit, sed gignit. Pater autem pariter et filius non faciunt neque gignunt, sed quodam modo, si sic dici potest, spirant suum amorem. Quamvis enim non nostro modo spiret summe incommutabilis essentia, tamen
15 ipsum suum amorem a se ineffabiliter procedentem non discedendo ab illa sed existendo ex illa, forsan non alio modo videtur posse dici aptius ex se emittere quam spirando.

Quod si dici potest: sicut verbum summae essentiae filius est eius, ita eiusdem amor satis convenienter appellari potest spiritus eius. Ut cum

LVII, 8 ut: *ex* aut *corr. B*

from its cause. According to this reasoning, then, the Love which proceeds from the Supreme Spirit cannot at all be called unbegotten; on the other hand, it cannot as properly be called begotten as can the Word. For clearly the Word is the most true offspring and the most true son; but clearly this Love is not at all a son or an offspring. Thus, only He of whom the Word |or Image| is, can be called—or, rather, ought to be called—begetter and unbegotten; for He alone is father and parent and in no way exists from another. And only the Word |should be called| begotten, since it alone is son and offspring. And only the Father and the Son's Love |should be called| neither begotten nor unbegotten, since (1) it is neither son nor offspring and (2) it does not altogether escape existing from someone |else|.

CHAPTER FIFTY-SEVEN

This Love is uncreated and creator, even as are the Father
and the Son. Nevertheless, they are together one uncreated
creator and not three |uncreated creators|. This Love
can be called the Spirit of the Father and of the Son.

This Love, considered distinctly, is the Supreme Being, even as are the Father and the Son; and yet, the Father and the Son and their Love are not many, but are one Supreme Being, which alone is not made by anyone |else| but which made all |else| only through itself. Therefore, we must infer that just as the Father, considered distinctly, is uncreated and creator, and just as the Son, considered distinctly, is uncreated and creator, so their Love, considered distinctly, is uncreated and creator. Nevertheless, all three together are one uncreated creator and not three |uncreated creators|. Thus, no one makes or creates or begets the Father. And only the Father begets (but does not create) the Son. And the Father and the Son neither create nor beget their Love; but in some way—if it can be thus expressed—they equally breathe out their Love. For although the supremely immutable Being does not breathe in the manner that we do, still perhaps it cannot at all more fittingly be said to send from itself its own Love (which proceeds ineffably from it by existing from it rather than by parting from it) than by breathing.

Furthermore (if we may speak this way), just as the Word of the Supreme Being is its son, so the Love of the Supreme Being can quite suitably be called its spirit.[86] Thus, although this Love is essentially spirit,

20 essentialiter ipse sit spiritus, sicut pater et filius, illi non putentur alicuius spiritus, quia nec pater ab ullo alio est, nec filius a patre quasi spirante nascitur, iste autem aestimetur spiritus utriusque, quia ab utroque suo quodam inenarrabili modo spirante mirabiliter procedit. Qui etiam ex eo quia est communio patris et filii, non absque ratione quasi proprium
25 assumere posse videtur aliquod nomen, quod patri filioque commune sit, si proprii nominis exigit indigentia. Quod quidem, si fiat scilicet ut ipse amor nomine "spiritus," quod substantiam pariter patris et filii significat, quasi proprio designetur: ad hoc quoque non inutiliter valebit, ut per hoc idipsum esse quod est pater et filius, quamvis ab illis esse suum habeat,
30 intimetur.

CAPITULUM LVIII

Quod sicut filius est essentia vel sapientia patris
eo sensu quia habet eandem essentiam vel sapientiam
quam pater, sic idem spiritus sit patris
et filii essentia et sapientia et similia.

Potest quoque, quemadmodum filius est substantia et sapientia et virtus patris eo sensu quia habet eandem essentiam et sapientiam et virtutem quam pater, ita utriusque spiritus intelligi essentia vel sapientia vel virtus patris et filii, quia habet omnino eandem quam habent illi.

CAPITULUM LIX

Quod pater et filius et eorum spiritus pariter sint in se invicem.

Iucundum est intueri in patre et filio et utriusque spiritu quomodo sint in se invicem tanta aequalitate ut nullus alium excedat. Praeter hoc enim
5 quia unusquisque illorum sic est perfecte summa essentia ut tamen omnes tres simul non sint nisi una summa essentia, quae nec sine se vel extra se nec maior vel minor seipsa esse potest, per singulos tamen idipsum non minus valet probari. Est etenim totus pater in filio et communi

even as the Father and the Son |are essentially spirit|, nevertheless the Father and the Son are not thought to be anyone's spirit—because the Father is not from anyone else, nor is the Son begotten from the Father's breathing |Him| out, as it were. Rather, this Love may be thought to be the spirit of the Father and of the Son because it marvelously proceeds from both, who breathe |it| out in a certain unique and ineffable way. Moreover, because this Love is common to the Father and the Son, it is reasonably regarded as able to take as its own a name which is common to the Father and the Son, if there is pressing need of a proper name. But, indeed, should it happen that this Love is referred to by the proper name "Spirit"—|a name| which signifies the substance of the Father and of the Son equally—then |this name| will also usefully serve to indicate through itself that |this Love| is what the Father and the Son are, even though it has its own existence from them.

CHAPTER FIFTY-EIGHT
Just as the Son is the essence and wisdom of the Father
in the sense that He has the same essence and wisdom as
the Father, so their Spirit is the essence, wisdom,
and the like, of the Father and of the Son.

Just as the Son is the substance, wisdom, and strength of the Father in the sense that He has the same essence, wisdom, and strength as the Father, so their Spirit can also be understood to be the essence, wisdom, and strength of the Father and of the Son in that He has exactly the same |essence, wisdom, and strength| as they do.

CHAPTER FIFTY-NINE
The Father and the Son and their Spirit
exist equally in one another.

It is pleasing to contemplate with regard to the Father, the Son, and their Spirit how they exist in one another with such great equality that no one of them excels the other. For aside from the fact that each of them is so perfectly the Supreme Being that all three together are only one Supreme Being which cannot be separate from itself or beyond itself or greater-or-lesser than itself, this very same |fact|[87] can equally well be proved with respect to each, considered distinctly. For the Father as a whole exists in the Son and in the Spirit common |to Him and the Son|; and

spiritu, et filius in patre et eodem spiritu, et idem spiritus in patre et filio,
10 quia memoria summae essentiae tota est in eius intelligentia et in amore,
et intelligentia in memoria et in amore, et amor in memoria et intelligentia. Totam quippe suam memoriam summus spiritus intelligit et amat, et
totius intelligentiae meminit et totam amat, et totius amoris meminit et
totum intelligit. Intelligitur autem in memoria pater, in intelligentia filius,
15 in amore utriusque spiritus. Tanta igitur pater et filius et utriusque spiritus aequalitate sese complectuntur et sunt in se invicem ut eorum nullus
alium excedere aut sine eo esse probetur.

CAPITULUM LX

Quod nullus eorum alio indigeat ad memorandum vel intelligendum vel
amandum, quia singulus quisque est memoria et intelligentia et
amor et quidquid necesse est inesse summae essentiae.

5 Sed in his nullatenus negligenter memoriae commendandum, quod
intuenti mihi occurrit, existimo. Sic enim necesse est ut pater intelligatur
memoria, filius intelligentia, spiritus amor: ut nec pater indigeat filio aut
communi spiritu, nec filius patre vel eodem spiritu, sive idem spiritus
patre aut filio, quasi pater per se meminisse solum possit, intelligere
10 autem non nisi per filium, et amare non nisi per suum filiique spiritum;
et filius per se intelligere tantum queat, per patrem autem memor sit, et
per spiritum suum amet; et idem spiritus per se non aliud quam amare
valeat, sed pater illi sit memor, et filius illi intelligat. Nam cum in his
tribus unusquisque singulus sit summa essentia et summa sapientia sic
15 perfecta ut ipsa per se memor sit et intelligat et amet, necesse est ut
nullus horum trium alio indigeat aut ad memorandum aut ad intelligendum aut ad amandum. Singulus enim quisque essentialiter est et memoria
et intelligentia et amor et quidquid summae essentiae necesse est inesse.

the Son as a whole exists in the Father and in this same Spirit; and this same Spirit as a whole exists in the Father and in the Son. For the Supreme Being's Memory as a whole exists in its Understanding and in its Love; and its Understanding |as a whole exists| in its Memory and in its Love; and its Love |as a whole exists| in its Memory and in its Understanding. Indeed, the Supreme Spirit understands and loves the whole of its Memory; and it remembers and loves the whole of its Understanding; and it remembers and understands the whole of its Love. But the Father is referred to as Memory, the Son as Understanding, and their Spirit as Love. Therefore, the Father, the Son, and their Spirit so equally encompass one another and so equally exist in one another that no one of them can excel the other or exist without Him.

CHAPTER SIXTY

No one of them needs the other for remembering, understanding,
or loving—because each, distinctly, is Memory, Understanding,
Love, and whatever |else| must be present in the Supreme Being.

But in regard to these |three| I think that what occurs to me as I investigate must be carefully kept in mind. The Father must be understood as Memory, the Son as Understanding, and the Spirit as Love in such way that the Father does not need either the Son or the Spirit common |to them|, the Son |does| not |need| the Father or this same Spirit, and this Spirit |does| not |need| the Father or the Son. We must not suppose that (1) the Father can only remember through Himself, while being able to understand only through the Son and to love only through His and the Son's Spirit, or (2) that the Son can only understand through Himself, while remembering through the Father and loving through His own Spirit, or (3) that this same Spirit can only love through Himself, while the Father remembers for Him and the Son understands for Him. For with regard to these three each, distinctly, is the Supreme Being and Supreme Wisdom so perfectly that this Being and Wisdom remembers, understands, and loves through itself. Consequently, none of these three could possibly need one of the others in order to remember or understand or love. For each, distinctly, is essentially memory, understanding, love, and whatever |else| must be present in the Supreme Being.

CAPITULUM LXI

Quod tamen non sint tres, sed unus seu pater
seu filius sive utriusque spiritus.

Quandam hic video quaestionem occurrere. Nam si pater ita est intelli-
5 gentia et amor sicut est memoria, et filius sic est memoria et amor quomodo est intelligentia, et utriusque spiritus non minus est memoria et
intelligentia quam amor: quomodo non est pater filius et alicuius spiritus;
et quare non est filius pater et spiritus alicuius; et cur non est idem
spiritus alicuius pater et alicuius filius? Sic quippe intelligebatur quod
10 memoria esset pater, filius intelligentia, utriusque spiritus amor. Verum
haec questio non difficile solvitur, si ea quae iam ratione inventa sunt,
considerentur. Idcirco enim non est pater filius aut alterius spiritus, licet
sit intelligentia et amor, quia non est intelligentia genita aut amor ab
aliquo procedens; sed quidquid est, gignens est tantum, et a quo procedit
15 alius. Filius quoque ideo non est pater aut alicuius spiritus, quamvis
seipso et memor sit et amet, quia non est memoria gignens aut amor ab
alio ad similitudinem sui spiritus procedens; sed quidquid existit, tantum
gignitur, et est a quo spiritus procedit. Spiritum quoque non cogit esse
patrem aut filium hoc quia contentus est memoria aut intelligentia sua,
20 cum non sit memoria gignens aut intelligentia genita, sed solum quidquid
est procedat. Quid igitur prohibet concludi quia unus tantum est in
summa essentia pater, unus filius, unus spiritus, et non tres patres aut filii
aut spiritus?

CAPITULUM LXII

Quomodo ex his multi filii nasci videantur.

Sed ne forte repugnet huic assertioni quod intueor. Nam dubium esse
non debet quia pater et filius et eorum spiritus unusquisque seipsum et
5 alios ambos dicit, sicut se et alios intelligit. Quod si ita est: quomodo non
sunt in summa essentia tot verba, quot sunt dicentes et quot sunt qui

---

LXII, 6 quot¹: *ex* quod *(?) corr. B*   quot²: *ex* quod *(?) corr. B*

CHAPTER SIXTY-ONE
Nevertheless, there are not three |fathers or three sons
or three spirits| but one father, one son,
and one spirit common to them.

I notice that at this point a question arises. For if the Father is understanding and love as well as Memory, and if the Son is memory and love
as well as Understanding, and if their Spirit is memory and understanding as well as Love (indeed, such was the manner in which we understood that the Father is Memory, the Son Understanding, and their Spirit
Love), then how does the Father avoid being a son and someone's spirit?
And why is the Son not a father and someone's spirit? And why is their
Spirit not someone's father and someone's son? Now, these questions are
not difficult to answer provided we reflect upon the |conclusions| already
discovered by reason. Although the Father is understanding and love, He
is not a son or anyone's spirit, because He is not understanding as begot-
ten from someone |else| or love as proceeding from someone |else|.
Whatever He is He is only as one who begets and as one from whom
someone else proceeds. Moreover, although the Son by Himself remem-
bers and loves, He is not a father or anyone's spirit, because He is not
memory which begets or love which proceeds from someone else in the
way that His Spirit does. Whatever He is is only begotten and is that
from which a spirit proceeds. Moreover, the fact that the Spirit is com-
prised of memory or understanding does not require that He be also a
father or a son, because |the Spirit| is not memory which begets or
understanding which is begotten. Rather, whatever He is only proceeds.
Therefore, what prevents us from concluding that there is only one
Father, one Son, and one Spirit in the Supreme Being—not three fathers
or three sons or three spirits?

CHAPTER SIXTY-TWO
How from these |viz., the Father, the Son, and
their Spirit| many sons seem to be begotten.

But let what I now see not perchance contradict this assertion |above|.
For there ought to be no doubt that the Father and the Son and their
Spirit each speaks of Himself and of the other two (just as each |also|
understands Himself and the other two). But if so, how is it that in the
Supreme Being there are not as many words as there are ones speaking

dicuntur? Si enim plures homines unum aliquid cogitatione dicant: tot
eius videntur esse verba, quot sunt cogitantes, quia in singulorum cogitationibus verbum eius est. Item si unus homo cogitet plura aliqua, tot
10 verba sunt in mente cogitantis, quot sunt res cogitatae. Sed in hominis
cogitatione cum cogitat aliquid quod extra eius mentem est, non nascitur
verbum cogitatae rei ex ipsa re, quoniam ipsa absens est a cogitationis
intuitu, sed ex rei aliqua similitudine vel imagine quae est in cogitantis
memoria, aut forte quae tunc cum cogitat per corporeum sensum ex re
15 praesenti in mentem attrahitur. In summa vero essentia sic sibi semper
sunt praesentes pater et filius et eorum spiritus—est enim, sicut iam perspectum est, unusquisque non minus in aliis quam in seipso—ut cum
invicem se dicunt, sic videatur idem ipse qui dicitur gignere verbum
suum, quemadmodum cum a seipso dicitur. Quomodo ergo nihil gignit
20 filius aut eius patrisque spiritus, si unusquisque eorum verbum suum gignit,
cum a se dicitur vel ab alio? Quot autem verba probari possunt de
summa nasci substantia, tot eam necesse est secundum superiorem considerationem filios gignere, et tot emittere spiritus. Hac itaque ratione
videntur in illa esse non solum multi patres et filii et procedentes, sed et
25 aliae necessitudines.

CAPITULUM LXIII

Quomodo non sit ibi nisi unus unius.

Aut certe pater et filius et eorum spiritus, de quibus iam certissimum est
quia vere existunt, non sunt tres dicentes, quamvis singulus quisque sit
5 dicens; nec sunt plura quae dicuntur, cum unusquisque seipsum et alios
duos dicit. Sicut enim summae sapientiae inest scire et intelligere, ita
utique aeternae incommutabilisque scientiae et intelligentiae naturale est
semper id praesens intueri quod scit et intelligit. Nihil autem aliud est

and ones being spoken of? For if several men utter one thing mentally, there seem to be as many words |or images| of this thing as there are thinkers, because a word |or an image| of this thing is in each one's thought. Likewise, if one man thinks of several things, there are as many words in his mind as there are things thought of. But in a man's thought when he thinks of something which is outside his mind, the word |or image| of the object thought of is not begotten from the object itself, since the object itself is not present in the mental vision. Rather, |the word is begotten in his thought| from a likeness or an image of the object—either |an image| which is in the memory of the one thinking, or else possibly |an image| which, during the time that the person is thinking, is conducted from the object which is present, into the mind by means of the bodily senses. Yet, in the Supreme Being the Father and the Son and their Spirit are always so present to one another (for, as already noted,[88] each of them exists no less in the others than in Himself) that when they speak of one another, the one who is spoken of seems to beget His own word, just as when He speaks of Himself. Therefore, if each one of them begets His own word when He speaks of Himself or is spoken of by one of the others, how is it that the Son, or how is it that the Spirit of the Father and of the Son, fails to beget anything? Moreover, according to the above reasoning the Supreme Substance must beget as many sons and send forth as many spirits as there are words which can be proved to be begotten from it. Consequently, by this reasoning, there seem to be in the Supreme Being not only many fathers and sons and proceeding |spirits| but also other relations.

CHAPTER SIXTY-THREE
How in the Supreme Spirit there is only
one son and one who has a son.[89]

On the other hand, surely the Father and the Son and their Spirit (all of whom, it is already most certain, really exist) are not three speakings—even though each, considered distinctly, speaks. Nor is more than one thing spoken of when each speaks of Himself and of the other two. For just as it belongs to the Supreme Wisdom to know and to understand, so it is surely the nature of eternal and immutable Knowledge and Understanding always to behold as present that which it knows and understands. Yet, for the Supreme Spirit to speak in such way is simply for it

summo spiritui huiusmodi dicere quam quasi cogitando intueri, sicut
10 nostrae mentis locutio non aliud est quam cogitantis inspectio. Certissimum autem iam consideratae rationes reddiderunt: quidquid summae
naturae inest essentialiter, id perfecte convenire patri et filio et eorum
spiritui singulatim, et tamen idipsum si simul dicatur de tribus, non
admittere pluralitatem. Cum ergo constet quia sicut pertinet ad eius
15 essentiam scientia et intelligentia, sic eius scire et intelligere non est aliud
quam dicere (id est, semper praesens intueri) quod scit et intelligit:
necesse est ut quemadmodum singulus pater et singulus filius et singulus
eorum spiritus est sciens et intelligens, et tamen hi tres simul non sunt
plures scientes aut intelligentes, sed unus sciens, unus intelligens, ita singulus
20 quisque sit dicens, nec tamen omnes simul tres dicentes, sed unus dicens.
Hinc illud quoque liquide cognosci potest: quia cum hi tres dicuntur, vel
a seipsis vel ab invicem, non sunt plura quae dicuntur. Quid namque ibi
dicitur nisi eorum essentia? Si ergo illa una sola est, unum solum est
quod dicitur. Ergo si unum est in illis quod dicit, et unum quod dicitur—
25 una quippe sapientia est quae in illis dicit, et una substantia quae
dicitur—consequitur non ibi esse plura verba sed unum. Licet igitur
unusquisque seipsum et omnes invicem se dicant, impossibile tamen est
esse in summa essentia verbum aliud praeter illud de quo iam constat
quod sic nascitur ex eo cuius est verbum ut et vera eius dici possit imago
30 et vere filius eius sit.

In quo mirum quiddam et inexplicabile video. Ecce enim cum manifestum sit unumquemque, scilicet patrem et filium et patris filiique spiritum, pariter se et ambos alios dicere, et unum solum ibi esse verbum:
nullatenus tamen ipsum verbum videtur posse dici verbum omnium
35 trium, sed tantum unius eorum. Constat enim ipsum esse imaginem et
filium eius cuius est verbum; et patet quia nec imago nec filius, suimet
aut a se procedentis spiritus, congrue dici potest. Nam nec ex seipso nec

LXIII, 27 se: *ex* si *corr. B*

mentally to see, as it were—even as our own mental speaking is nothing other than a mental seeing. Now, reasons already considered[90] have made it most certain that whatever belongs to the Supreme Nature essentially, perfectly besuits the Father, considered distinctly, the Son, considered distinctly, and their Spirit, considered distinctly; and yet, that very |characteristic| does not admit of plurality if it is predicated of the three together. Now, it is evident[91] that just as knowledge and understanding pertain to the essence of the Supreme Spirit, so the Supreme Spirit's knowing and understanding are the same as its speaking (i.e., the same as its always beholding as present) what it knows and understands. Consequently, it is necessary that just as the Father, considered distinctly, the Son, considered distinctly, and their Spirit, considered distinctly, know and understand, and nevertheless these three together are not several knowings or understandings but one knowing and understanding, so each |of them|, considered distinctly, speaks, and nevertheless all of them together are not three speakings but one speaking. Hence, we can also recognize clearly that when these three |viz., the Father, the Son, and their Spirit| are spoken of—whether each speaks of Himself or whether they speak of one another—there are not many |beings| which are spoken of. For what is spoken of *there* except their essence? Hence, if this essence is only singular, then what is spoken of is only singular. Thus, if what speaks is one in them, and if what is spoken of is one (indeed, what speaks in them is one wisdom, and what is spoken of is one substance), necessarily there are not many words in the Supreme Spirit but |only| one word. Consequently, although each |speaks of| Himself and all speak of one another, still in the Supreme Being there cannot be any other word than the Word which (I have proved)[92] is so begotten from the one whose word it is that it can be called this one's true image and is truly His son.

In this |fact| I see something marvelous and inexplicable. For, lo, although it is clear that (1) the Father, the Son, and the Spirit of the Father and of the Son each speaks equally of Himself and of the other two, and that (2) there is only one word in the Supreme Spirit, nevertheless this Word cannot in any way, it seems, be called the word of all three but |can be called the word| only of one of them. For it is evident[93] that the Word is the image and the son of the one whose word it is; and, clearly, |the Word| cannot appropriately be called the image or the son either of itself or of the spirit proceeding from it. For |the Word| is not

ex procedente a se nascitur, nec seipsum aut procedentem a se existendo imitatur. Seipsum quippe non imitatur nec a se trahit existendi similitu-
40 dinem, quia imitatio et similitudo non est in uno solo, sed in pluribus. Illum vero non imitatur nec ad eius similitudinem existit, quia iste non habet ab illo esse, sed ille ab isto. Restat igitur hoc solum verbum illius solius esse de quo nascendo habet esse, et ad cuius omnimodam simili-tudinem existit. Unus ergo pater, non plures patres, unus filius, non
45 plures filii, unus procedens spiritus, non plures procedentes spiritus sunt in summa essentia. Qui cum ita tres sint ut numquam pater sit filius aut procedens spiritus, nec filius aliquando sit pater aut spiritus procedens, nec umquam spiritus patris et filii sit pater aut filius, et singulus quisque sic sit perfectus ut nullo indigeat: id tamen quod sunt sic est unum ut
50 sicut de singulis pluraliter dici non potest, ita nec de tribus simul. Et cum pariter unusquisque seipsum et omnes invicem se dicant, non tamen sunt ibi plura verba sed unum; et ipsum non singulorum aut omnium simul, sed unius tantum.

CAPITULUM LXIV

Quod hoc, licet inexplicabile sit, tamen credendum sit.

Videtur mihi huius tam sublimis rei secretum transcendere omnem intel-lectus aciem humani, et idcirco conatum explicandi qualiter hoc sit con-
5 tinendum puto. Sufficere namque debere existimo rem incomprehensibi-lem indaganti, si ad hoc ratiocinando pervenerit ut eam certissime esse cognoscat, etiamsi penetrare nequeat intellectu quomodo ita sit; nec idcirco minus iis adhibendam fidei certitudinem, quae probationibus necessariis nulla alia repugnante ratione asseruntur, si suae naturalis alti-

begotten from itself and is not begotten from |the spirit| which proceeds from it; nor does |the Word| through existing imitate either itself or the one proceeding from it. Indeed, |the Word| does not imitate itself or contract from itself the likeness of existing, because there is no imitation and no similarity with regard to a single thing alone but |only| with regard to more than one thing |viz., the imitating and the imitated|. On the other hand, |the Word| does not imitate the proceeding Spirit, nor |does the Word| exist in His likeness—because the Son does not exist from the proceeding Spirit but, rather, the Spirit exists from the Son. Therefore, |the alternative| remains that this Word alone is |the word| only of Him from whom it has its existence by being begotten and in whose complete likeness it exists. Therefore, in the Supreme Being there is one father, one son, and one proceeding spirit—rather than more than one father, son, or proceeding spirit. And these are so three that the Father is never the Son or the proceeding Spirit; nor is the Son ever the Father or the proceeding Spirit; nor is the Spirit of the Father and of the Son ever the Father or the Son. Moreover, each |of these three|, considered distinctly, is so complete that He needs no |other|. Nonetheless, what |the three| are is so one that just as it cannot be predicated plurally of each, considered distinctly, so |it can| not |be predicated plurally| of the three together. And although in equal measure each of them |speaks of| Himself and all speak of one another, nevertheless in the Supreme Being there are not many words but |only| one. And this Word is |the word| not of each distinctly or of all together but of one |of them| alone.

CHAPTER SIXTY-FOUR

Although inexplicable, this |teaching| must be believed.

The hiddenness of so sublime a matter seems to me to surpass the entire acute gaze of the human intellect; and so, I think that I ought to refrain from attempting to explain how this doctrine is true. For I think that anyone who is investigating an incomprehensible doctrine should be content if by rational inference he comes to recognize that this doctrine is most certainly true—even if he is unable to comprehend how it could be true. And |I think that| to these |doctrines| which are asserted |to be true| on the basis of compelling proofs (with no other rational consideration opposing) the certitude of faith ought no less to be assigned if because of |the doctrines'| naturally deep incomprehensibility they can-

10 tudinis incomprehensibilitate explicari non patiantur. Quid autem tam
incomprehensibile, tam ineffabile, quam id quod super omnia est? Quapropter si ea quae de summa essentia hactenus disputata sunt, necessariis
sunt rationibus asserta: quamvis sic intellectu penetrari non possint ut et
verbis valeant explicari, nullatenus tamen certitudinis eorum nutat solidi-
15 tas. Nam si superior consideratio rationabiliter comprehendit incomprehensibile esse quomodo eadem summa sapientia sciat ea quae fecit, de
quibus tam multa nos scire necesse est: quis explicet quomodo sciat aut
dicat seipsam, de qua aut nihil aut vix aliquid ab homine sciri possibile
est? Ergo si in eo quod seipsam dicit, generat pater et generatur filius:
20 "generationem eius quis ennarrabit?"

CAPITULUM LXV

Quomodo de ineffabili re verum disputatum sit.

Sed rursum si ita se ratio ineffabilitatis illius habet—immo quia sic est—
quomodo stabit quidquid de illa secundum patris et filii et procedentis
5 habitudinem disputatum est? Nam si vera illud ratione explicitum est,
qualiter est illa ineffabilis? Aut si ineffabilis est, quomodo est ita sicut est
disputatum? An quodamtenus de illa potuit explicari, et ideo nihil prohibet esse verum quod disputatum est; sed quia penitus non potuit comprehendi, idcirco est ineffabilis? Sed ad illud, quid responderi poterit,
10 quod iam supra in hac ipsa disputatione constitit: quia sic est summa
essentia supra et extra omnem aliam naturam ut si quando de illa dicitur
aliquid verbis quae communia sunt aliis naturis, sensus nullatenus sit
communis? Quem enim sensum, in omnibus iis verbis quae cogitavi,
intellexi nisi communem et usitatum? Si ergo usitatus sensus verborum
15 alienus est ab illa, quidquid ratiocinatus sum non pertinet ad illam.
Quomodo igitur verum est inventum esse aliquid de summa essentia, si
quod est inventum longe diversum est ab illa?
Quid ergo? An quodam modo inventum est aliquid de incomprehen-

not be explained. But what is so incomprehensible, so ineffable, as that which is higher than all |other| things? Therefore, if the claims hitherto made about the Supreme Being have been asserted on the basis of compelling reasons, then the firm certainty of these |statements| is not at all shaken, even though they cannot be comprehended to the point that they can be explained in words.[94] For if my previous reflection rationally comprehends that it is incomprehensible how the Supreme Wisdom knows the things it made (about which things it is necessary that we know so much), who could explain how |this Wisdom| knows itself or speaks of itself (about which |Wisdom| either nothing or nearly nothing is possible to be known by man)? Therefore, if by virtue of |Supreme Wisdom's| speaking of itself the Father generates and the Son is generated, "who shall explain His generation?"[95]

CHAPTER SIXTY-FIVE

How regarding |this| ineffable matter something true was argued.

But on the other hand, if such is the manner of the Supreme Wisdom's ineffability—or rather, *because* it is such—how will there hold true what was argued about the Supreme Wisdom in regard to the relation of Father and of Son and of proceeding |Spirit|? For if that |which was argued| was explained by sound reasoning, then how is the Supreme Wisdom ineffable? Or if |the Supreme Being| is ineffable, how is |the matter| such as it was argued to be? |Is not the case as follows?|: to some extent an explanation regarding Supreme Wisdom was able to be given, and so nothing precludes the truth of what was argued; but because |this Wisdom| was not at all able to be comprehended, it is ineffable. But what can be said about that which was established in the preceding[96] disputation?: viz., that the Supreme Being is so above and beyond every other nature that whenever something is predicated of it in words which are also applied to other natures, the meaning |of these words| is not at all the same in the two cases. For in all those words which I thought, did I understand any meaning except the customary and ordinary meaning? So if the ordinary meaning of |these| words does not apply to the Supreme Being, none of my previous inferences apply to it. Therefore, how is it true that something was discovered about the Supreme Being if what was discovered is far different from the Supreme Being?

What then? |Could it be that| in one respect something was dis-

sibili re, et quodam modo nihil perspectum est de ea? Saepe namque
20 multa dicimus quae proprie sicut sunt non exprimimus, sed per aliud
significamus id quod proprie aut nolumus aut non possumus depromere—
ut cum per aenigmata loquimur. Et saepe videmus aliquid non proprie,
quemadmodum res ipsa est, sed per aliquam similitudinem aut imaginem—
ut cum vultum alicuius consideramus in speculo. Sic quippe unam ean-
25 demque rem dicimus et non dicimus, videmus et non videmus. Dicimus
et videmus per aliud; non dicimus et non videmus per suam proprietatem. Hac itaque ratione nihil prohibet et verum esse quod disputatum est
hactenus de summa natura et ipsam tamen nihilominus ineffabilem per-
sistere, si nequaquam illa putetur per essentiae suae proprietatem expressa,
30 sed utcumque per aliud designata. Nam quaecumque nomina de illa natura dici posse videntur, non tam mihi eam ostendunt per proprietatem
quam per aliquam innuunt similitudinem. Etenim cum earundem vocum
significationes cogito, familiarius concipio mente quod in rebus factis
conspicio quam id quod omnem humanum intellectum transcendere
35 intelligo. Nam valde minus aliquid—immo longe aliud—in mente mea
sua significatione constituunt quam sit illud ad quod intelligendum per
hanc tenuem significationem mens ipsa mea conatur proficere. Nam nec
nomen sapientiae mihi sufficit ostendere illud per quod omnia facta sunt
de nihilo et servantur a nihilo; nec nomen essentiae mihi valet exprimere
40 illud quod per singularem altitudinem longe est supra omnia et per
naturalem proprietatem valde est extra omnia. Sic igitur illa natura et
ineffabilis est, quia per verba sicuti est nullatenus valet intimari; et falsum
non est si quid de illa ratione docente per aliud velut in aenigmate potest
aestimari.

CAPITULUM LXVI

Quod per rationalem mentem maxime accedatur
ad cognoscendum summam essentiam.

Cum igitur pateat quia nihil de hac natura possit percipi per suam pro-
5 prietatem sed per aliud, certum est quia per illud magis ad eius cognitio-

covered about an incomprehensible thing, whereas in another respect nothing was discerned about it? For we often speak of many things which we do not express properly, as they are.[97] Instead, we signify obliquely (*per aliud*) that which we either cannot, or else do not want to, express properly (e.g., when we speak symbolically). And often we see a thing, though not properly (i.e., not as the object itself is) but rather by means of a likeness or an image (e.g., when we see someone's face in a mirror). Thus, we do and do not speak of one and the same thing; we do and do not see one and the same object. We speak of and see obliquely; we do not speak of and do not see in accordance with the respective reality. So in this manner, if the Supreme Nature is not at all assumed to be expressed in accordance with the reality of its essence but |is assumed to be| somehow or other designated obliquely, then nothing precludes the truth of all that was hitherto argued about the Supreme Nature, and yet nothing prevents this Nature from remaining as ineffable as ever. For whatever words seem to be predicable of this Nature do not so much reveal it to me in its reality as hint at |it| through a likeness.[98] For when I think the significations of these words, I more readily conceive of what I observe in created things than of that |Being| which I understand to transcend all human understanding. For by their respective significations |these words| form in my mind something much less than—indeed, something far different from—that toward which my mind, by means of these inadequate meanings, tries to advance in order to understand. For example, not even the word "wisdom" suffices for disclosing to me this |Being| through which all things were made from nothing and are kept from |falling away into| nothing. Nor can the word "being" express to me that |Reality| which is far above all things by virtue of its unique loftiness and which is far removed from all things by virtue of its own nature. So, then, this Nature is ineffable, because words cannot at all express it as it is; and yet, if under the instruction of reason we can obliquely, as in a dark manner,[99] think something regarding it, |this thought| is not false.

CHAPTER SIXTY-SIX

Through the rational mind one comes nearest
to knowing the Supreme Being.

Therefore, since it is evident that something about this Nature can be perceived not with respect to its reality but |only| obliquely (*per aliud*),

nem acceditur quod illi magis per similitudinem propinquat. Quidquid
enim inter creata constat illi esse similius, id necesse est esse natura
praestantius. Quapropter id et per maiorem similitudinem plus iuvat
mentem indagantem summae veritati propinquare, et per excellentiorem
10 creatam essentiam plus docet, quid de creante mens ipsa debeat aestimare. Procul dubio itaque tanto altius creatrix essentia cognoscitur,
quanto per propinquiorem sibi creaturam indagatur. Nam quod omnis
essentia in quantum est in tantum sit summae similis essentiae, ratio iam
supra considerata dubitare non permittit. Patet itaque quia sicut sola est
15 mens rationalis inter omnes creaturas, quae ad eius investigationem
assurgere valeat, ita nihilominus eadem sola est per quam maxime
ipsamet ad eiusdem inventionem proficere queat. Nam iam cognitum est
quia haec illi maxime per naturalis essentiae propinquat similitudinem.
Quid igitur apertius quam quia mens rationalis quanto studiosius ad se
20 discendum intendit, tanto efficacius ad illius cognitionem ascendit, et
quanto seipsam intueri negligit, tanto ab eius speculatione descendit?

CAPITULUM LXVII

Quod mens ipsa speculum eius et imago eius sit.

Aptissime igitur ipsa sibimet esse velut speculum dici potest, in quo spe-
culetur, ut ita dicam, imaginem eius, quam facie ad faciem videre nequit.
5 Nam si mens ipsa sola ex omnibus quae facta sunt, sui memor et intelligens et amans esse potest, non video cur negetur esse in illa vera imago
illius essentiae quae per sui memoriam et intelligentiam et amorem in
trinitate ineffabili consistit. Aut certe inde verius esse illius se probat
imaginem: quia illius potest esse memor, illam intelligere et amare. In
10 quo enim maior est et illi similior, in eo verior illius esse imago cognoscitur. Omnino autem cogitari non potest rationali creaturae naturaliter
esse datum aliquid tam praecipuum tamque simile summae sapientiae
quam hoc: quia potest reminisci et intelligere et amare id quod optimum

LXVI, 12 propinquiorem: propinquiorem (p² *supra lin.*) B
LXVI, 19 quanto: quanto (n *supra lin.*) B

it is certain that one more closely approaches a knowledge of it through that which more closely approximates it in likeness. For among created things whatever is shown to be more similar to the Supreme Nature must be more excellent by nature. Therefore, by virtue of its greater likeness this |created thing| more greatly aids the inquiring mind to approach the Supreme Truth, and by virtue of its more excellent created being it more fully teaches what the mind ought to think regarding the Creator. Hence, without doubt, the more the Creative Being is investigated by reference to a creature more near to itself, the more thoroughly this Being is known. For the argument considered earlier[100] leaves no doubt that every being in the degree to which it exists is in that degree similar to the Supreme Being. Clearly, then, just as the rational mind alone of all creatures is able to mount an investigation of the Supreme Being, so equally the rational mind alone is that through which the rational mind itself is most able to advance toward finding the Supreme Being. For we already know[101] that the rational mind most nearly approximates the Supreme Nature through a likeness of natural being. Therefore, what is clearer than that (1) the more earnestly the rational mind attends to knowing itself, the more effectively it ascends to knowledge of the Supreme Being, and (2) the more it neglects inspecting itself, the more it wanes from contemplating the Supreme Being?

CHAPTER SIXTY-SEVEN

The mind is the mirror and image of the Supreme Being.

The mind, then, can very fittingly be called its own mirror, as it were, in which it beholds, so to speak, the image of this Being which it cannot see face to face.[102] For if of all created things the mind alone can remember itself,[103] understand, and love, then I do not see why we should deny that there is in it the true image of this Being, which exists as an ineffable trinity of self-remembrance, understanding, and love. Indeed, by the fact that |the mind| can remember, understand, and love the Supreme Being it proves the more truly that it is the image of the Supreme Being. For the greater |the mind| is and the more similar it is to the Supreme Being, the truer image of the Supreme Being it is known to be. Yet, there cannot at all be thought to be naturally bestowed upon the rational creature anything as excellent and as similar to the Supreme Wisdom as is the ability to remember, to understand, and to love that which is the greatest and

et maximum est omnium. Nihil igitur aliud est inditum alicui creaturae
15 quod sic praeferat imaginem creatoris.

Quod rationalis creatura ad amandum illam facta sit.

Consequi itaque videtur quia rationalis creatura nihil tantum debet stu-
dere quam hanc imaginem, sibi per naturalem potentiam impressam, per
5 voluntarium effectum exprimere. Etenim praeter hoc quia creanti se,
debet hoc ipsum quod est: hinc quoque quia nil tam praecipuum posse
quam reminisci et intelligere et amare summum bonum cognoscitur,
nimirum nihil tam praecipue debere velle convincitur. Quis enim neget
quaecumque meliora sunt in potestate, ea magis esse debere in voluntate?
10   Denique rationali naturae non est aliud esse rationalem quam posse
discernere iustum a non-iusto, verum a non-vero, bonum a non-bono,
magis bonum a minus bono. Hoc autem posse omnino inutile illi est et
supervacuum nisi quod discernit amet aut reprobet secundum verae discretionis iudicium. Hinc itaque satis patenter videtur omne rationale ad
15 hoc existere: ut sicut ratione discretionis aliquid magis vel minus bonum
sive non-bonum iudicat, ita magis vel minus id amet aut respuat. Nihil
igitur apertius quam rationalem creaturam ad hoc esse factam ut summam essentiam amet super omnia bona, sicut ipsa est summum bonum—
immo ut nihil amet nisi illam aut propter illam, quia illa est bona per se,
20 et nihil aliud est bonum nisi per illam. Amare autem eam nequit nisi eius
reminisci et eam studuerit intelligere. Clarum ergo est rationalem creaturam totum suum posse et velle ad memorandum et intelligendum et
amandum summum bonum impendere debere, ad quod ipsum esse
suum se cognoscit habere.

best of all. Therefore, on no creature is there bestowed anything else which so displays the image of the Creator.

CHAPTER SIXTY-EIGHT

The rational creature was made for loving the Supreme Being.

And so, it seems to follow that the rational creature ought earnestly to desire nothing as much as to express, as a voluntary effect, this image impressed on it as a natural ability. For aside from the rational creature's owing what he is to his Creator: from the fact that he is known to be able |to do| nothing as excellent as remembering, understanding, and loving the Supreme Good, he is proved without doubt to be under obligation to will nothing as principally |as the Supreme Good|. For who would deny that the better things over which we have power ought more to be willed?

Indeed, for a rational nature to be rational is nothing other than for it to be able to discriminate what is just from what is not just, what is true from what is not true, what is good from what is not good, what is more good from what is less good. But the ability |to make these discriminations| is thoroughly useless and superfluous to rational nature unless what it distinguishes it |also| loves or disapproves in accordance with the dictates of correct discrimination. Herefrom, then, we see quite clearly that every rational |being| exists for the following purpose: viz., that even as by rational discrimination he judges a thing to be more or less good, or else to be no good at all, so he might love that thing in proportionately greater or lesser degree, or else reject it. Therefore, nothing is clearer than that the rational creature was made for this end: viz., to love above all |other| goods the Supreme Being, inasmuch as it is the Supreme Good. Or better, |he was made| so that he might love nothing except the Supreme Being or on account of the Supreme Being—since the Supreme Being is good through itself and nothing else is good except through it. Yet, |the rational creature| cannot love the Supreme Being without striving to remember it and to understand it. Clearly, then, the rational creature ought to devote his entire ability and his entire will to |the end of| remembering, understanding, and loving the Supreme Good—to which end he knows that he has his existence.

Quod anima semper illam amans aliquando vere beate vivat.

Dubium autem non est humanam animam esse rationalem creaturam. Ergo necesse est eam esse factam ad hoc: ut amet summam essentiam. 5 Necesse est igitur eam esse factam aut ad hoc ut sine fine amet, aut ad hoc ut aliquando vel sponte vel violenter hunc amorem amittat. Sed nefas est aestimare summam sapientiam ad hoc eam fecisse: ut aliquando tantum bonum aut contemnat, aut volens tenere aliqua violentia perdat. Restat igitur eam esse factam ad hoc: ut sine fine amet summam essen- 10 tiam. At hoc facere non potest nisi semper vivat. Sic igitur est facta ut semper vivat, si semper velit facere ad quod facta est. Deinde inconveniens nimis est summe bono summeque sapienti et omnipotenti creatori ut quod fecit esse ad se amandum, id faciat non esse, quamdiu vere amaverit, et quod sponte dedit non amanti ut semper amaret, id auferat 15 vel auferri permittat amanti, ut ex necessitate non amet—praesertim cum dubitari nullatenus debeat quod ipse omnem naturam se vere amantem amet. Quare manifestum est humanae animae numquam auferri suam vitam, si semper studeat amare summam vitam.

Qualiter ergo vivet? Quid enim magnum est longa vita, nisi sit a 20 molestiarum incursione vere secura? Quisquis enim dum vivit aut timendo aut patiendo molestiis subiacet aut falsa securitate fallitur, quid nisi misere vivit? Si quis autem ab iis liber vivit, beate vivit. Sed absurdissimum est ut aliqua natura semper amando illum qui est summe bonus et omnipotens, semper misere vivat. Liquet igitur humanam animam 25 huiusmodi esse ut si servet id ad quod est, aliquando vere secura ab ipsa morte et omni alia molestia beate vivat.

CHAPTER SIXTY-NINE

The soul which always loves the Supreme Being
lives at some time in true happiness.

But without doubt the human soul is a rational creature. Hence, it must
have been made for the purpose of loving the Supreme Being. Necessar-
ily, then, it was made either so that it might love |this Being| endlessly or
else so that it might at some time lose this love either freely or by force.
But it is blasphemous to think that Supreme Wisdom created the soul so
that the soul might sometime despise such a great good or else might
lose it by force, while willing to keep it. Thus, |the alternative| remains
that the soul was created for loving the Supreme Being endlessly. How-
ever, the soul cannot do this |viz., love endlessly,| unless it always lives.
So, then, it was created so that it might always live—provided it would
always will to do that for which it was made. Moreover, it would be
altogether unbesuiting to the omnipotent, supremely good, and supremely
wise Creator to cause not to exist, while it was truly loving |Him|, a
thing which He made to exist for the purpose of loving Him. And |it
would be altogether unbesuiting to Him| to remove or to permit to be
removed from a being which loved |Him| the gift which He freely gave
to this being when it did not love |Him| so that it might always love
|Him|—a removal which would necessitate this being's not loving |Him.
This possibility seems| all the more |unsuitable| since we ought in no
way to doubt that the Creator loves every nature which truly loves Him.
Therefore, it is evident that the human soul's life will never be removed
from it—provided it always earnestly desire to love the Supreme Life.

What kind of life, then, will the soul have? For of what value is a long
life unless it is truly free from distressful intrusions? For whoever during
his lifetime is subject to distress either because of fear or of suffering, or
whoever is deceived because of a false security—how does he live except
unhappily? By contrast, if someone lives free of these |conditions|, he
lives happily. But it is thoroughly absurd that a nature would, while
always loving Him who is both omnipotent and supremely good, always
live unhappily. Clearly, then, the human soul is such that if it keeps that
end for which it exists, it will at some time live happily—truly free from
death itself and every other form of distress.

Quod illa se amanti seipsam retribuat.

Denique nullatenus verum videri potest ut iustissimus et potentissimus nihil retribuat amanti se perseveranter, cui non amanti tribuit essentiam
5 ut amans esse posset. Si enim nihil retribuit amanti, non discernit iustissimus inter amantem et contemnentem id quod summe amari debet; nec amat amantem se; aut non prodest ab illo amari—quae omnia ab illo dissonant. Retribuit igitur omni se amare perseveranti.

Quid autem retribuit? Si nihilo dedit rationalem essentiam ut amans
10 esset, quid dabit amanti si amare non cesset? Si tam grande est quod amori famulatur, quam grande est quod amori recompensatur? Et si tale est amoris fulcimentum, quale est amoris emolumentum? Nam si rationalis creatura, quae sibi inutilis est sine hoc amore, sic eminet in omnibus creaturis: utique nihil potest esse praemium huius amoris nisi quod
15 supereminet in omnibus naturis. Etenim idem ipsum bonum quod sic se amari exigit, non minus se ab amante desiderari cogit. Nam quis sic amet iustitiam, veritatem, beatitudinem, incorruptibilitatem ut iis frui non appetat? Quid ergo summa bonitas retribuet amanti et desideranti se, nisi seipsam? Nam quidquid aliud tribuat, non retribuit, quia nec compen-
20 satur amori nec consolatur amantem nec satiat desiderantem.

Aut si se vult amari et desiderari, ut aliud retribuat: non se vult amari et desiderari propter se sed propter aliud, et sic non se vult amari sed aliud—quod cogitare nefas est. Nihil ergo verius quam quod omnis anima rationalis, si quemadmodum debet studeat amando desiderare

LXX, 7 non: *supra lin.* B

CHAPTER SEVENTY
The Supreme Being gives itself as a reward
to |the soul| which loves it.

Indeed, we cannot at all regard as true |the supposition| that the most just and most powerful |Bcing| givcs no reward to |a soul| loving it perseveringly—|a soul| to which, not loving |it|, it gave existence so that this soul could love |it|. For were |this Being| to give no reward to |a soul| loving it, Supreme Justice would not be distinguishing between |a soul| that loves what ought to be loved supremely and |a soul| that despises what ought to be loved supremely. Moreover, either Supreme Justice would not be loving |a soul| which was loving it, or else to be loved by Supreme Justice would be of no advantage. But these |consequences| are all incompatible with Supreme Justice. Therefore, it rewards every |soul| that perseveres in loving it.

But what does |Supreme Justice| give as a reward? If to what was nothing it gave a rational being, so that |this being| would love |it|, what will it give to |a soul| which loves |it| without ceasing to love |it|? If the |initial| assistance to love is so great, how great is the recompense to love? And if such is the supporting of love, what will be the nature of love's gain? For if the rational creature, which without this love is useless to itself, is so eminent among all creatures, surely nothing can be this love's reward except what is preeminent among all natures. For the Supreme Good, which thus demands to be loved, requires equally that it be desired by |the soul| loving it. For who could love justice, truth, happiness, and incorruptibility in such way as not to desire to enjoy them? Therefore, with what shall Supreme Goodness reward |the soul| which loves and desires it if not with itself?[104] For whatever else it bestows it does not bestow as a reward, because |any other bestowal| would neither compensate the love nor console the loving |soul| nor satisfy its desires.

On the other hand, if |Supreme Goodness| willed to be loved and desired in order to give some other reward, then Supreme Goodness would will to be loved and desired not for its own sake but for the sake of something else. And so, it would not will that it itself be loved but would will that this other thing |be loved|—something blasphemous to think. Therefore, nothing is truer than that every rational soul at some time shall receive the Supreme Beatitude to enjoy—provided |the soul|

25 summam beatitudinem, aliquando illam ad fruendum percipiat. Ut quod
nunc videt quasi "per speculum et in aenigmate," tunc videat "facie ad
faciem." Utrum autem ea sine fine fruatur, dubitare stultissimum est,
quoniam illa fruens nec timore torqueri poterit nec fallaci securitate
decipi, nec eius indigentiam iam experta illam poterit non amare; nec illa
30 deseret amantem se; nec aliquid erit potentius quod eas separet invitas.
Quare quaecumque anima summa beatitudine semel frui coeperit, aeterne
beata erit.

CAPITULUM LXXI

Quod illam contemnens aeterne misera sit.

Hinc utique consequenter colligitur quod illa quae summi boni amorem
contemnit, aeternam miseriam incurrat. Nam si dicitur quod pro tali con-
5 temptu sic iustius puniatur ut ipsum esse vel vitam perdat, quia se non
utitur ad id ad quod facta est, nullatenus hoc admittit ratio: ut post
tantam culpam pro poena recipiat esse quod erat ante omnem culpam.
Quippe antequam esset, nec culpam habere nec poenam sentire poterat.
Si ergo anima contemnens id ad quod facta est, sic moritur ut nihil
10 sentiat aut ut omnino nihil sit: similiter se habebit et in maxima culpa et
sine omni culpa, nec discernet summe sapiens iustitia inter id quod nullum bonum potest et nullum malum vult, et id quod maximum bonum
potest et maximum malum vult. At hoc satis patet, quam inconveniens
sit. Nihil igitur videri potest consequentius et nihil credi debet certius,
15 quam hominis animam sic esse factam ut si contemnat amare summam
essentiam, aeternam patiatur miseriam. Ut sicut amans aeterno gaudebit
praemio, ita contemnens aeterna poena doleat. Et sicut illa sentiet suffi-
cientiam immutabilem, ita ista sentiat inconsolabilem indigentiam.

LXXI, 18 immutabilem: immutabilem (bi *supra lin.*) B

strive as it should to desire Supreme Beatitude out of love for it. As a result, what |the soul| now sees as if through a glass, darkly, it shall then see face to face.[105] But to question whether or not |the rational soul| will enjoy Supreme Beatitude endlessly would be very foolish. For while enjoying this Beatitude |the soul| cannot be tormented by fear or deceived by a false security. Nor having experienced the need of this Beatitude can |the soul| keep from loving it.[106] Nor will Supreme Beatitude forsake |a soul| which loves it. Nor will there be anything more powerful which will separate it and the soul against their wills. Therefore, any soul which once begins to enjoy Supreme Beatitude will be eternally happy.

CHAPTER SEVENTY-ONE

|The soul| which despises the Supreme Being
will be eternally unhappy.

Assuredly, from these |conclusions| we can consistently infer that the soul which despises loving the Supreme Good will incur eternal unhappiness. Now, if someone were to say, "For such contempt |the soul| would be more justly punished by losing its existence, or life, since |the soul| does not use itself for that end for which it was made," then reason would not at all allow |the supposition| that |the soul|, after such great guilt, should be punished by becoming what it was before any guilt. Indeed, before |the soul| existed it was not able to have guilt or to be aware of punishment. Therefore, if after despising the end for which it was made the soul were to die in such way that it did not experience anything or in such way that it were absolutely nothing, its condition would be the same in the case of greatest guilt as in the case of no guilt; moreover, supremely wise Justice would not be discriminating between (1) what can |do| no good and will no evil, and (2) what can |do| the greatest good but wills the greatest evil. But how unsuitable this |consequence| is is quite plain. So, then, nothing can be seen |to follow| more consistently, and nothing ought to be believed more assuredly, than that man's soul was made in such way that if it despises loving the Supreme Being it will suffer eternal unhappiness. Consequently, just as the loving |soul| will rejoice in an eternal reward, so the despising |soul| will grieve in eternal punishment. And as the former will experience immutable sufficiency, so the latter will experience inconsolable need.

CAPITULUM LXXII
Quod omnis humana anima sit immortalis.

Sed nec amantem animam necesse est aeterne beatam esse nec contemnentem miseram, si sit mortalis. Sive igitur amet sive contemnat id ad
5 quod amandum creata est, necesse est eam immortalem esse. Si autem
aliquae sunt animae rationales, quae nec amantes nec contemnentes iudicandae sint—sicut videntur esse animae infantum—quid de iis sentiendum est? Sunt mortales an immortales? Sed procul dubio omnes humanae
animae eiusdem naturae sunt. Quare quoniam constat quasdam esse
10 immortales, necesse est omnem humanam animam esse immortalem.

CAPITULUM LXXIII
Quod aut semper misera aut aliquando vere beata sit.

Verum cum omne quod vivit aut numquam aut aliquando sit vere secu-
rum ab omni molestia, nihilominus est necesse omnem humanam ani-
5 mam aut semper miseram esse aut aliquando vere beatam.

CAPITULUM LXXIV
Quod nulla anima iniuste privetur summo bono;
et quod omnino ad ipsum nitendum sit.

Quae vero animae incunctanter iudicandae sint sic amantes id ad quod
5 amandum factae sunt ut illo quandoque frui, quae autem sic contemnentes ut illo semper indigere mereantur, aut qualiter quove merito illae
quae nec amantes nec contemnentes dici posse videntur, ad beatitudinem
aeternam miseriamve distribuantur: aliquem mortalium disputando posse
comprehendere, procul dubio aut difficillimum aut impossibile existimo.
10 Quod tamen a summe iusto summeque bono creatore rerum nulla eo
bono ad quod facta est iniuste privetur, certissime est tenendum; et ad
idem ipsum bonum est omni homini toto corde, tota anima, tota mente
amando et desiderando nitendum.

CHAPTER SEVENTY-TWO
Every human soul is immortal.

But if |the soul| were mortal: then, necessarily, the soul which loves |the Supreme Being| would not be eternally happy; and |the soul| which despises |the Supreme Being would| not |be eternally| unhappy. Thus, whether |the soul| loves or despises that which it was created to love, necessarily the soul is immortal. Now, if there are any rational souls which must be deemed to be neither loving nor despising—as the souls of infants seem to be—what must be believed about them? Are they mortal or immortal? Well, without doubt, all human souls are of the same nature. Therefore, since it is evident that some |of them| are immortal, it is necessary that every human soul be immortal.

CHAPTER SEVENTY-THREE
|The soul| is either always unhappy or else
at some time truly happy.

But since any living thing either is never, or else is at some time, truly free from all distress, it is no less necessary that every human soul either be always unhappy or else be at some time truly happy.

CHAPTER SEVENTY-FOUR
No soul is unjustly deprived of the Supreme Good. |The soul|
is supposed to strive for the Supreme Good wholeheartedly.

I think that it is certainly either very difficult or else impossible for any mortal man to be able to ascertain by disputing[107] (1) which souls are unhesitantly to be deemed as so loving the end which they were created to love that they deserve at some time to enjoy this end, (2) which |souls| so despise this end that they deserve always to be in need of it, and (3) in what manner or by what merit the souls which apparently can be called neither loving nor despising are assigned to eternal happiness or eternal unhappiness. Nevertheless, we must most certainly maintain that the supremely just and supremely good Creator of things does not unjustly deprive any |soul| of that good for which it was made; moreover, every man is supposed to strive for this same good by loving and desiring it with all his heart, all his soul, and all his mind.[108]

CAPITULUM LXXV

Quod summa essentia sit speranda.

Sed in hac intentione humana anima nullatenus se poterit exercere, si desperet quo intendit se posse pervenire. Quapropter quantum illi est
5 utile studium annitendi, tantum necessaria est spes pertingendi.

CAPITULUM LXXVI

Quod credendum sit in illam.

Amare autem aut sperare non potest, quod non credit. Expedit itaque eidem humanae animae summam essentiam et ea sine quibus illa amari
5 non potest credere, ut illa credendo tendat in illam. Quod idem apte breviusque significari posse puto, si pro eo quod est "credendo tendere in summam essentiam," dicatur "credere in summam essentiam." Nam si quis dicat se credere in illam, satis videtur ostendere et per fidem quam profitetur ad summam se tendere essentiam, et illa se credere quae ad
10 hanc pertinent intentionem. Nam non videtur credere in illam sive qui credit quod ad tendendum in illam non pertinet, sive qui per hoc quod credit non ad illam tendit.

Et fortasse indifferenter dici potest credere in illam et ad illam, sicut pro eodem accipi potest "credendo tendere in illam" et " . . . ad illam,"
15 nisi quia quisquis tendendo ad illam pervenerit, non extra illam remanebit, sed intra illam permanebit; quod expressius et familiarius significatur, si dicitur tendendum esse in illam, quam si dicitur ad illam. Hac itaque ratione puto congruentius posse dici credendum esse in illam quam ad illam.

We are to hope for the Supreme Being.

But the human soul would not at all be able to engage in this endeavor if it despaired of being able to attain what it was striving for. Therefore, the hope of attaining is as much necessary to the human soul as the desire to strive for is useful.

We are to believe in the Supreme Being.

But that which does not believe cannot love or hope. Therefore, it is advantageous for the human soul to believe the Supreme Being and the things without which the Supreme Being cannot be loved, so that the soul by believing may strive unto the Supreme Being. Yet, I think that this same |idea| can be conveyed fittingly and more tersely if instead of saying "by believing, to strive unto the Supreme Being" we say |simply| "to believe in the Supreme Being." For if someone declares that he believes in the Supreme Being, he seems sufficiently enough to indicate |thereby| that (1) he strives for the Supreme Being through the faith which he is professing and that (2) he believes those things which pertain to this endeavor. For someone who believes what does not pertain to striving unto the Supreme Being or who does not strive for the Supreme Being through what he believes does not seem to believe in the Supreme Being.

Presumably, it makes no difference whether we say "to believe *in* the Supreme Being" or "to believe *on* the Supreme Being"—just as we can accept as the same the expressions "by believing, to strive *unto* the Supreme Being" and "by believing, to strive *for* it."[109] Yet, whoever by striving for it will arrive, will remain within it rather than remaining outside it; and this |idea| is more explicitly and more readily indicated by saying that |the soul| ought to "strive unto the Supreme Being" than by saying that |the soul| ought to "strive for the Supreme Being." And so, for this reason I think that "|The soul| ought to believe *in* the Supreme Being" can be said more appropriately than "|The soul| ought to believe *on* the Supreme Being."

CAPITULUM LXXVII

Quod in patrem et filium et eorum spiritum pariter
et in singulos et simul in tres credendum sit.

Credendum igitur est pariter in patrem et filium et eorum spiritum, et in
5 singulos et simul in tres—quia et singulus pater et singulus filius et singulus eorum spiritus est summa essentia, et simul pater et filius cum suo
spiritu sunt una eademque summa essentia, in quam solam omnis homo
debet credere, quia est solus finis quem in omni cogitatu actuque suo per
amorem debet intendere. Unde manifestum est quia sicut in illam tendere
10 nisi credat illam nullus potest, ita illam credere, nisi tendat in illam, nulli
prodest.

CAPITULUM LXXVIII

Quae sit viva et quae mortua fides.

Quapropter quantacumque certitudine credatur tanta res: inutilis erit
fides et quasi mortuum aliquid, nisi dilectione valeat et vivat. Etenim
5 nullatenus fidem illam, quam competens comitatur dilectio, si se oppor-
tunitas conferat operandi, otiosam esse sed magna se quadam operum
exercere frequentia—quod sine dilectione facere non posset—vel hoc
solo probari potest: quia quod summam iustitiam diligit, nihil iustum
contemnere, nihil valet iniustum admittere. Ergo quoniam quod aliquid
10 operatur, inesse sibi vitam, sine qua operari non valeret, ostendit: non
absurde dicitur et operosa fides vivere, quia habet vitam dilectionis sine
qua non operaretur, et otiosa fides non vivere, quia caret vita dilectionis
cum qua non otiaretur. Quare si "caecus" dicitur non tantum qui perdidit visum, sed qui cum debet habere non habet: cur non similiter potest
15 dici fides sine dilectione "mortua" non quia vitam suam (id est, dilectionem) perdiderit, sed quia non habet, quam semper habere debet?
Quemadmodum igitur illa fides quae per dilectionem operatur, viva esse

LXXVIII, 6 quadam: *ex* quodam *corr.* B²
LXXVIII, 12 operaretur: *ex* operatur *corr.* (re *supra lin.*) B²

CHAPTER SEVENTY-SEVEN
We ought to believe equally in the Father, the Son, and
their Spirit—in each distinctly and in all three together.

Therefore, we ought to believe equally in the Father, the Son, and their
Spirit—in each distinctly and in all three together. For the Father, considered distinctly, is the Supreme Being; the Son, considered distinctly, is
the Supreme Being; and their Spirit, considered distinctly, is the Supreme
Being. And the Father and the Son, together with their Spirit, are
together one and the same Supreme Being in which alone every man
ought to believe, since this is the singular end which |each man| out of
love ought to strive unto in every thought and deed. Hence, it is evident
that just as a man can strive unto the Supreme Being only if he believes
|in| this Being, so believing |in| this Being is of no avail to anyone unless
he strives thereunto.

CHAPTER SEVENTY-EIGHT
Which faith is alive and which is dead.

Therefore, with whatever degree of certainty so important a matter is
believed, |this| faith will be useless and as something dead unless it is
made alive and strong by love. Indeed, this faith, which its corresponding love accompanies, is not at all idle—provided the opportunity to
use |it| arises. Rather, |this faith| exercises itself in a great number of
works—something which it could not do in the absence of love. |These
claims| can be proved by the solitary fact that what loves Supreme Jus-
tice can neither despise anything just nor admit of anything unjust.
Therefore, since that which accomplishes something shows |thereby| that
it possesses the vital force without which it could not accomplish |what it
did|, we may without absurdity say |the following|: (1) working faith is
alive because it has the vital force of love, in whose absence it would not
accomplish |what it does|, and that (2) idle faith is not alive because it
lacks the vital force of love, in whose presence it would not be idle.
Thus, if we call *blind* not only someone who has lost his sight but also
someone who does not have sight when he ought to have it, why can we
not likewise call faith without love *dead*—not because it has lost its vital
force (i.e., its love) but because it does not have |the vital force| which it
ought always to have?[110] Therefore, just as faith which works through
love[111] is recognized to be living faith, so faith which is idle through

cognoscitur, ita illa quae per contemptum otiatur, mortua esse convincitur. Satis itaque convenienter dici potest viva fides credere in id in
20 quod credi debet, mortua vero fides credere tantum id quod credi debet.

CAPITULUM LXXIX

Quid tres summa essentia quodammodo dici possit.

Ecce patet omni homini expedire ut credat in quandam ineffabilem trinam unitatem et unam trinitatem—unam quidem et unitatem propter
5 unam essentiam, trinam vero et trinitatem propter tres nescio quid. Licet
enim possim dicere trinitatem propter patrem et filium et utriusque spiritum, qui sunt tres, non tamen possum proferre uno nomine propter quid
tres—velut si dicerem propter tres personas, sicut dicerem unitatem
propter unam substantiam. Non enim putandae sunt tres personae, quia
10 omnes plures personae sic subsistunt separatim ab invicem ut tot necesse
sit esse substantias quot sunt personae—quod in pluribus hominibus, qui
quot personae tot individuae substantiae sunt, cognoscitur. Quare in
summa essentia sicut non sunt plures substantiae, ita nec plures personae.
Si quis itaque inde velit alicui loqui: quid tres dicet esse patrem et
15 filium et utriusque spiritum, nisi forte indigentia nominis proprie conve-
nientis coactus, elegerit aliquod de illis nominibus quae pluraliter in
summa essentia dici non possunt, ad significandum id quod congruo
nomine dici non potest—ut si dicat illam admirabilem trinitatem esse
unam essentiam vel naturam et tres personas sive substantias? Nam haec
20 duo nomina aptius eliguntur ad significandam pluralitatem in summa
essentia, quia "persona" non dicitur nisi de individua rationali natura, et
"substantia" principaliter dicitur de individuis, quae maxime in pluralitate
consistunt. Individua namque maxime substant, id est subiacent, accidentibus, et ideo magis proprie substantiae nomen suscipiunt. Unde iam
25 supra manifestum est summam essentiam, quae nullis subiacet accidentibus, proprie non posse dici substantiam, nisi "substantia" ponatur pro
"essentia." Potest ergo hac necessitatis ratione irreprehensibiliter illa
summa et una trinitas sive trina unitas dici una essentia et tres personae
sive tres substantiae.

LXXIX, 16 pluraliter: pluraliter (li *supra lin.*) B

contemptuousness is shown to be dead. Thus, living faith can quite suitably be said to believe *in* what ought to be believed in, whereas dead faith |can be said| merely to believe what ought to be believed.

CHAPTER SEVENTY-NINE

What three the Supreme Being can in some respect be said to be.

Lo, it is clearly advantageous for every man to believe in an ineffable Oneness which is trine and Trinity which is one. Indeed, |this Being is| one and a oneness by virtue of one essence; but I do not know by virtue of what three it is trine and a trinity. For although I can speak of a trinity because of the Father, the Son, and their Spirit, who are three, nevertheless I cannot in a single word name that by virtue of which they are three (as if I were to say "|a trinity| by virtue of three *persons*," as I might say "a oneness by virtue of one *substance*"). For they must not be thought to be three persons, because in cases where there are more persons than one, they all exist so independently of one another that there must be as many substances as there are persons—something which we recognize in the case of a plurality of men, who are as many individual substances as they are persons. Therefore, just as there are not many substances in the Supreme Being, so there are not many persons.

Thus, if someone wanted to speak to someone |else| about the Trinity, what three would he say that the Father, the Son, and their Spirit are?— unless perhaps, compelled by the lack of a properly suitable word, he were to choose a word from among those which cannot be predicated plurally of the Supreme Being |and were to use this word| for signifying what cannot be said by an appropriate word. For instance, he might say that this wonderful Trinity is one being or nature and three *persons* or *substances*. For these last two words are quite fittingly selected for signifying a plurality in the Supreme Being, since "person" is predicated only of an *individual* rational nature[112] and "substance" is predicated mainly of *individual* things, which, especially, are a plurality. For individuals, especially, support accidents—i.e., are subject to accidents; and so, individuals are quite properly called substances. (Accordingly, we have already seen[113] that the Supreme Being, which is subject to no accidents, cannot *properly* be called a substance—except where "substance" is a substitute for "being.") Therefore, on the basis of this necessity, the Supreme Trinity which is one, or Supreme Oneness which is trine, can irreproachably be called one being and three *persons* or three *substances*.

CAPITULUM LXXX

Quod ipsa dominetur omnibus et regat omnia et sit solus deus.

Videtur ergo—immo incunctanter asseritur—quia nec nihil est id quod dicitur deus, et huic soli summae essentiae proprie nomen dei assignatur.

5 Quippe omnis qui deum esse dicit, sive unum sive plures, non intelligit nisi aliquam substantiam quam censet supra omnem naturam quae deus non est, ab hominibus et venerandam propter eius eminentem dignitatem et exorandam contra sibi quamlibet imminentem necessitatem. Quid autem tam pro sua dignitate venerandum et pro qualibet re deprecandum

10 quam summe bonus et summe potens spiritus, qui dominatur omnibus et regit omnia? Sicut enim constat quia omnia per summe bonam summeque sapientem omnipotentiam eius facta sunt et vigent, ita nimis inconveniens est si aestimetur quod rebus a se factis ipse non dominetur, sive quod factae ab illo ab alio minus potente minusve bono vel sapiente,

15 aut nulla penitus ratione sed sola casuum inordinata volubilitate, regantur; cum ille solus sit, per quem cuilibet et sine quo nulli bene est et ex quo et per quem et in quo sunt omnia. Cum igitur solus ipse sit non solum bonus creator, sed et potentissimus dominus et sapientissimus rector omnium: liquidissimum est hunc solum esse quem omnis alia natura

20 secundum totum suum posse debet diligendo venerari et venerando diligere, de quo solo prospera sunt speranda, ad quem solum ab adversis fugiendum, cui soli pro quavis re supplicandum. Vere igitur hic est non solum deus, sed solus deus ineffabiliter trinus et unus.

LXXX, 23 unus: Explicit monologion liber anselmi cantuariensis archiepiscopi *add.* B

CHAPTER EIGHTY
The Supreme Being exercises dominion over all things and
rules all things and is the only God.

Therefore, it seems—or rather, it is unhesitatingly affirmed—that this
|Being| which we call God is not nothing and that the name "God" is
properly assigned to this Supreme Being alone. Indeed, everyone who
affirms that a God exists (whether one God or more than one) under-
stands |thereby| nothing other than a Substance which he believes to be
above every nature that is not God—|a Substance which| men are to
worship because of its excellent worthiness and which they are to entreat
against lurking misfortune. What, though, is so to be worshipped
because of its worthiness and implored in regard to any matter whatsoever as is the supremely good and supremely powerful Spirit, which
exercises dominion over all things and rules all things? For just as it is
evident[114] that all things were made through, and are sustained by, this
Spirit's supremely good and supremely wise omnipotence, so it would be
altogether unsuitable to think that (1) this Spirit does not have dominion
over the things made by it or that (2) the things made by it are governed
by some other less powerful, less good, or less wise being—or (3) governed by no rational principle at all but only by a random changing, due
to chance occurrences. For this Spirit alone is the one through whom
anything fares well and without whom not anything fares well—and from
whom, through whom, and in whom all things exist. Therefore, since
this Spirit alone is not only the good Creator but also both the most
powerful Lord and the wisest Ruler of all, it alone (we see most clearly)
is the one whom every other nature to its full ability ought to worship
lovingly and love worshipfully. |And, most clearly, this Spirit is the one|
from whom alone good fortune is to be hoped for, to whom alone flight
from adversity is to be taken, and of whom alone supplication is to be
made for anything whatsoever. Truly, then, this Spirit not only is God
but is the only God—ineffably three and one.

PROSLOGION

Postquam opusculum quoddam velut exemplum meditandi de ratione
fidei, cogentibus me precibus quorundam fratrum, in persona alicuius
tacite secum ratiocinando quae nesciat investigantis, edidi: considerans
illud esse multorum concatenatione contextum argumentorum, coepi
5 mecum quaerere si forte posset inveniri unum argumentum quod nullo
alio ad se probandum quam se solo indigeret, et solum ad astruendum
quia deus vere est, et quia est summum bonum nullo alio indigens, et
quo omnia indigent ut sint et ut bene sint, et quaecumque de divina
credimus substantia, sufficeret. Ad quod cum saepe studioseque cogitati-
10 onem converterem, atque aliquando mihi videretur iam posse capi quod
quaerebam, aliquando mentis aciem omnino fugeret: tandem desperans
volui cessare velut ab inquisitione rei quam inveniri esset impossibile.
Sed cum illam cogitationem, ne mentem meam frustra occupando ab
aliis in quibus proficere possem impediret, penitus a me vellem exclu-
15 dere: tunc magis ac magis nolenti et defendenti se coepit cum importunitate quadam ingerere. Cum igitur quadam die vehementer eius importu-
nitati resistendo fatigarer, in ipso cogitationum conflictu sic se obtulit
quod desperaveram, ut studiose cogitationem amplecterer quam sollicitus
repellebam. Aestimans igitur quod me gaudebam invenisse, si scriptum
20 esset, alicui legenti placiturum: de hoc ipso et de quibusdam aliis sub
persona conantis erigere mentem suam ad contemplandum deum et
quaerentis intelligere quod credit, subditum scripsi opusculum. Et quoniam nec istud nec illud cuius supra memini, dignum libri nomine aut
cui auctoris praeponeretur nomen iudicabam, nec tamen eadem sine ali-
25 quo titulo, quo aliquem, in cuius manus venirent, quodam modo ad se
legendum invitarent, dimittenda putabam: unicuique suum dedi titulum,
ut prius *Exemplum meditandi de ratione fidei*, et sequens *Fides quaerens
intellectum* diceretur. Sed cum iam a pluribus cum his titulis utrumque

Upon the insistent adjurations of certain brothers I wrote a work—as an example of meditating about the rational basis of faith—in the role of someone who by arguing silently with himself investigates what he does not yet know. Afterwards,[1] considering this |work| to be composed of a chain of many arguments, I began to ask myself whether perhaps a single consideration could be found which would require nothing other than itself for proving itself and which would suffice by itself to demonstrate (1) that God truly |i.e., really| exists and (2) that He is the Supreme Good (needing no one else, yet needed by all |else| in order to exist and to fare well) and whatever |else| we believe about the Divine Substance. I often and eagerly directed my thinking to this |goal|. At times what I was in quest of seemed to me to be apprehensible; at times it completely eluded the acute gaze of my mind. At last, despairing, I wanted to desist, as though from pursuit of a thing which was not possible to be found. But just when I wanted completely to exclude from myself this thinking—lest by occupying my mind in vain, it would keep |me| from other |projects| in which I could make headway—just then it began more and more to force itself insistently upon me, unwilling and resisting |as I was|. Then one day when I was tired as a result of vigorously resisting its entreaties, what I had despaired of |finding| appeared in my strife-torn mind in such way that I eagerly embraced the |line-of-| thinking which I, as one who was anxious, had been warding off. Supposing, then, that if what I rejoiced to have discovered were written down it would please its readers, I wrote the following work on this |subject|, and on various others, in the role of someone endeavoring to elevate his mind toward contemplating God and in the role of someone seeking to understand what he believes. And I deemed neither this present |writing| nor the one mentioned above to be worthy to be called a treatise or to be something to which the name of the author should be prefixed; and, nevertheless, I thought that they should not be circulated without titles, by which in some way they would issue to anyone into whose hands they came an invitation to read them. Hence, I gave a title to each, so that the first was called *An Example of Meditating about the Rational Basis of Faith* and the second was called *Faith Seeking Understanding*.[2] But after several people had already copied both |works| under these

transcriptum esset, coegerunt me plures (et maxime reverendus archie-
30 piscopus Lugdunensis, Hugo nomine, fungens in Gallia legatione Apostolica, qui mihi hoc ex Apostolica praecepit auctoritate) ut nomen meum
illis praescriberem. Quod, ut aptius fieret, illud quidem *Monologion*, id
est soliloquium, istud vero *Proslogion*, id est alloquium, nominavi.

CAPITULA

    I. Excitatio mentis ad contemplandum deum.

    II. Quod vere sit deus.

    III. Quod non possit cogitari non esse.

    IV. Quomodo insipiens dixit in corde quod cogitari non potest.

    V. Quod deus sit quidquid melius est esse quam non esse; et solus existens per se omnia alia faciat de nihilo.

    VI. Quomodo sit sensibilis, cum non sit corpus.

    VII. Quomodo sit omnipotens, cum multa non possit.

    VIII. Quomodo sit misericors et impassibilis.

    IX. Quomodo totus iustus et summe iustus parcat malis; et quod iuste misereatur malis.

    X. Quomodo iuste puniat et iuste parcat malis.

    XI. Quomodo "universae viae domini misericordia et veritas," et tamen "iustus dominus in omnibus viis suis."

    XII. Quod deus sit ipsa vita qua vivit, et sic de similibus.

    XIII. Quomodo solus sit incircumscriptus et aeternus, cum alii spiritus sint incircumscripti et aeterni.

    XIV. Quomodo et cur videtur et non videtur deus a quaerentibus eum.

    XV. Quod maior sit quam cogitari possit.

    XVI. Quod haec sit lux inaccessibilis quam inhabitat.

    XVII. Quod in deo sit harmonia, odor, sapor, lenitas, pulchritudo, suo ineffabili modo.

Capitula: Incipunt capitula *B* (*In textu initia capitulorum indicantur numeris in marg. positis. Titulos capitulorum, in textu non repetit B*)

|respective| titles, I was urged by several to prefix my name to these |writings—urged| especially by Hugh,[3] the reverend archbishop of Lyons, who was serving as apostolic legate in Gaul and who on the basis of his apostolic authority directed me to do this. In order for the |affixing of my name| to be done more fittingly, I retitled the former |writing| *Monologion*, i.e., a soliloquy, and the present |writing| *Proslogion*, i.e., an address.

Chapter Titles

1. Arousal of the mind for contemplating God.
2. God truly |i.e., really| exists.
3. |God| cannot be thought not to exist.
4. How the Fool said in his heart that which cannot be thought.
5. God is whatever it is better to be than not to be. Alone existing through Himself, He makes all other things from nothing.
6. How God is able to perceive even though He is not something corporeal.
7. How He is omnipotent even though He cannot do many things.
8. How He is merciful and impassible.
9. How He who is completely and supremely just spares those who are evil. He is justly merciful to them.
10. How He justly punishes and justly spares those who are evil.
11. How "all the ways of the Lord are mercy and truth," and yet, "the Lord is just in all His ways."
12. God is the life by which He lives, and similarly for similar |attributes|.
13. How He alone is unlimited and eternal, although other spirits are |also| unlimited and eternal.
14. How and why God is both seen and not seen by those who seek Him.
15. He is greater than can be thought.
16. This is the inaccessible light in which He dwells.
17. Harmony, fragrance, succulence, softness, and beauty are present in God in their own ineffable manner.

XXVI, 1 dominus: Expliciunt capitula *B*

18. There are no parts in God or in the eternity which He is.
19. He is not in place or in time; but all things are in Him.
20. He is before and beyond all things—even eternal things.
21. Whether this |eternity| is one aeon or more than one.
22. He alone is what He is and who He is.
23. The Father, the Son, and the Holy Spirit are equally this |supreme| good. It is the one necessary |Being|, which is every good, complete good, and the only good.
24. A conjecture about what kind of good this is and about how great it is.
25. The kinds and the quantity of goods for those who enjoy this |Good|.
26. Whether this is the full joy which the Lord promises.

PROSLOGION

CAPITULUM I
Excitatio mentis ad contemplandum deum.

Eia nunc, homuncio, fuge paululum occupationes tuas; absconde te mod-
icum a tumultuosis cogitationibus tuis. Abice nunc onerosas curas, et
5 postpone laboriosas distentiones tuas. Vaca aliquantulum deo, et requiesce
aliquantulum in eo. Intra in cubiculum mentis tuae; exclude omnia
praeter deum et quae te iuvent ad quaerendum eum; et clauso ostio
quaere eum. Dic nunc, totum cor meum, dic nunc deo: quaero vultum
tuum; vultum tuum, domine, requiro. Eia nunc ergo tu, domine deus
10 meus, doce cor meum ubi et quomodo te quaerat, ubi et quomodo te
inveniat. Domine, si hic non es, ubi te quaeram absentem? Si autem
ubique es, cur non video praesentem? Sed certe habitas lucem inaccessibilem. Et ubi est lux inaccessibilis? Aut quomodo accedam ad lucem
inaccessibilem? Aut quis me ducet et inducet in illam, ut videam te in
15 illa? Deinde quibus signis, qua facie te quaeram? Numquam te vidi,
domine deus meus; non novi faciem tuam. Quid faciet, altissime domine,
quid faciet iste tuus longinquus exsul? Quid faciet servus tuus, anxius
amore tui et longe proiectus a facie tua? Anhelat videre te, et nimis abest
illi facies tua. Accedere ad te desiderat, et inaccessibilis est habitatio tua.
20 Invenire te cupit, et nescit locum tuum. Quaerere te affectat, et ignorat
vultum tuum. Domine, deus meus es, et dominus meus es, et numquam
te vidi. Tu me fecisti et refecisti, et omnia mea bona tu mihi contulisti, et
nondum novi te. Denique ad te videndum factus sum, et nondum feci
propter quod factus sum.
25   O misera sors hominis, cum hoc perdidit ad quod factus est! O durus
et dirus casus ille! Heu quid perdidit et quid invenit; quid abscessit et quid
remansit! Perdidit beatitudinem ad quam factus est, et invenit miseram

Proslogion: Incipit proslogion (s *supra lin.*) liber anselmi cantuariensis archiepiscopi *B*
I, 7 ostio: hostio *B*
I, 11 si[1]: *ex* sic *corr. B*

PROSLOGION

CHAPTER ONE

Arousal of the mind for contemplating God.

Come now, insignificant man, leave behind for a time your preoccupations; seclude yourself for a while from your disquieting thoughts. Turn aside now from heavy cares, and set aside your wearisome tasks. Make time for God, and rest a while in Him. Enter into the inner chamber of your mind; shut out everything except God and what is of aid to you in seeking Him; after closing the chamber door, seek Him out.⁴ Speak now, my whole heart; speak now to God: I seek Your countenance; Your countenance, O Lord, do I seek.⁵ So come now, Lord my God, teach my heart where and how to seek You, where and how to find You. If You are not here, O Lord, where shall I seek You who are absent? But if You are everywhere, why do I not behold You as present? But surely You dwell in light inaccessible.⁶ Yet, where is light inaccessible? Or how shall I approach unto light inaccessible? Or who will lead me to and into this |light| so that in it I may behold You? Furthermore, by what signs, by what facial appearance shall I seek You? Never have I seen You, O Lord my God; I am not acquainted with Your face. What shall this Your distant exile do? What shall he do, O most exalted Lord? What shall Your servant do, anguished out of love for You and cast far away from Your face?⁷ He pants to see You, but Your face is too far removed from him. He desires to approach You, but Your dwelling place is inaccessible. He desires to find You but does not know Your abode. He longs to seek You but does not know Your countenance. O Lord, You are my God, and You are my Lord; yet, never have I seen You. You have created me and created me anew and have bestowed upon me whatever goods I have; but I am not yet acquainted with You. Indeed, I was made for seeing You; but not yet have I done that for which I was made.

O the unhappy fate of man when he lost that |end| for which he was made! O that hard and ominous fall! Alas, what he lost and what he found, what vanished and what remained! He lost the happiness for which he was made and found an unhappiness for which he was not

221

propter quam factus non est. Abscessit sine quo nihil felix est, et remansit quod per se nonnisi miserum est. Manducabat tunc homo panem angel-
30 orum, quem nunc esurit; manducat nunc panem dolorum, quem tunc nesciebat. Heu publicus luctus hominum, universalis planctus filiorum Adae! Ille ructabat saturitate; nos suspiramus esurie. Ille abundabat; nos mendicamus. Ille feliciter tenebat et misere deseruit; nos infeliciter ege-mus et miserabiliter desideramus, et heu vacui remanemus. Cur non
35 nobis custodivit, cum facile posset, quo tam graviter careremus? Quare sic nobis obseravit lucem, et obduxit nos tenebris? Ut quid nobis abstulit vitam, et inflixit mortem? Aerumnosi, unde sumus expulsi; quo sumus impulsi! Unde praecipitati; quo obruti! A patria in exsilium, a visione dei in caecitatem nostram. A iucunditate immortalitatis in amaritudinem et
40 horrorem mortis. Misera mutatio de quanto bono in quantum malum! Grave damnum, gravis dolor, grave totum!

Sed heu me miserum, unum de aliis miseris filiis Evae elongatis a deo: quid incepi; quid effeci? Quo tendebam; quo deveni? Ad quid aspirabam; in quibus suspiro? Quaesivi bona, et ecce turbatio! Tendebam in deum,
45 et offendi in me ipsum. Requiem quaerebam in secreto meo, et tribulatio-nem et dolorem inveni in intimis meis. Volebam ridere a gaudio mentis meae, et cogor rugire a gemitu cordis mei. Sperabatur laetitia, et ecce unde densentur suspiria! Et o tu, domine, usquequo? Usquequo, domine, obliviscaris nos, usquequo avertis faciem tuam a nobis? Quando respicies
50 et exaudies nos? Quando illuminabis oculos nostros et ostendes nobis faciem tuam? Quando restitues te nobis? Respice, domine, exaudi, illumina nos, ostende nobis teipsum. Restitue te nobis, ut bene sit nobis, sine quo tam male est nobis. Miserare labores et conatus nostros ad te, qui nihil vale-mus sine te. Invitas nos; adiuva nos. Obsecro, domine, ne desperem sus-
55 pirando, sed respirem sperando. Obsecro, domine: amaricatum est cor meum sua desolatione: indulca illud tua consolatione. Obsecro, domine: esuriens incepi quaerere te: ne desinam ieiunus de te. Famelicus accessi;

made. That without which nothing is happy vanished, and there remained what through itself is only unhappy. Man then ate the bread-of-angels[8] for which he now hungers; and now he eats the bread-of-sorrows,[9] which then he did not know. Alas, the common mourning of men, the universal lament of the sons of Adam! Adam burped with satiety; we sigh with hunger. He abounded; we go begging. He happily possessed and unhappily deserted; we unhappily lack and unhappily desire, while, alas, remaining empty. Why did he not, when easily able, keep for us that of which we were so gravely deprived? Why did he block off from us the light and enshroud us in darkness? Why did he take away from us life and inflict death? Wretched |creatures that we are|, expelled from that home, impelled to this one!, cast down from that abode, sunken to this one! |We have been banished| from our homeland into exile, from the vision of God into our own blindness, from the delight of immortality into the bitterness and horror of death. O miserable transformation from such great good into such great evil! What a grievous loss, a heavy sorrow, an unmitigated plight!

But, alas, unhappy me, one of the other unhappy sons of Eve who are far removed from God: what did I set out to do?, what have I achieved? For what was I striving?, where have I arrived? To what was I aspiring?, for what do I sigh? I sought after good things[10] and, behold, |here is| turmoil.[11] I was striving unto God but collided with myself. I was seeking rest in my inner recesses but found tribulation and grief[12] in my inmost being. I wanted to laugh from joy of mind but am constrained to cry out from groaning of heart.[13] I hoped for gladness, but, lo, as a result, my sighs increase! O Lord, how long? How long, O Lord, will You forget us? How long will You turn away Your face from us?[14] When will You look upon us and hear us? When will You enlighten our eyes[15] and show us Your face?[16] When will You restore Yourself to us? Look upon us, O Lord; hear us, enlighten us, reveal Yourself unto us. Restore unto us Yourself—without whom we fare so badly—so that we may fare well. Have compassion upon the efforts and attempts which we, who can do nothing without You, direct toward You. |As| You summon us, |so| aid us.[17] I beseech |You|, O Lord, that I may not despair with sighing but may revive in hoping. I beseech You, O Lord: my heart is made bitter by its own desolation; sweeten it by Your consolation. I beseech You, O Lord, that having begun in hunger to seek You, I may not finish without partaking of You. I set out famished; let me not return still unfed. I came as

ne recedam impastus. Pauper veni ad divitem, miser ad misericordem; ne redeam vacuus et contemptus. Et si antequam comedam suspiro, da vel
60 post suspiria quod comedam. Domine, incurvatus non possum nisi deorsum aspicere; erige me ut possim sursum intendere. Iniquitates meae supergressae caput meum obvolvunt me, et sicut onus grave gravant me. Evolve me, exonera me, ne urgeat puteus earum os suum super me. Liceat mihi suspicere lucem tuam, vel de longe vel de profundo. Doce
65 me quaerere te, et ostende te quaerenti—quia nec quaerere te possum nisi tu doceas, nec invenire nisi te ostendas. Quaeram te desiderando; desiderem quaerendo. Inveniam amando; amem inveniendo.

· Fateor, domine, et gratias ago quia creasti in me hanc imaginem tuam, ut tui memor [sim], te cogitem, te amem. Sed sic est abolita attritione
70 vitiorum, sic est offuscata fumo peccatorum, ut non possit facere ad quod facta est, nisi tu renoves et reformes eam. Non tento, domine, penetrare altitudinem tuam, quia nullatenus comparo illi intellectum meum; sed desidero aliquatenus intelligere veritatem tuam, quam credit et amat cor meum. Neque enim quaero intelligere ut credam, sed credo
75 ut intelligam. Nam et hoc credo: quia nisi credidero, non intelligam.

CAPITULUM II

Quod vere sit deus.

Ergo, domine, qui das fidei intellectum, da mihi ut, quantum scis expedire, intelligam quia es, sicut credimus, et hoc es quod credimus. Et
5 quidem credimus te esse aliquid quo nihil maius cogitari possit. An ergo non est aliqua talis natura, quia dixit insipiens in corde suo "non est deus"? Sed certe ipse idem insipiens, cum audit hoc ipsum quod dico, "aliquid quo maius nihil cogitari potest," intelligit quod audit; et quod intelligit in intellectu eius est, etiam si non intelligat illud esse. Aliud
10 enim est rem esse in intellectu, aliud intelligere rem esse. Nam cum pic-

I, 69 sim: *supplevi*

one who is poor to one who is rich, as one who is unhappy to one who is merciful; let me not return empty and spurned. And if before I eat I sigh,[18] grant at least after the sighs that which I may eat. O Lord, bent over |as I am| I can look only downwards; straighten me so that I can look upwards. Having mounted above my head, my iniquities cover me over; and as a heavy burden they weigh me down.[19] Deliver me |from them|; unburden me, so that the abyss of iniquities does not engulf me.[20] Permit me, at least from afar or from the deep, to look upwards toward Your light. Teach me to seek You, and reveal Yourself to me as I seek; for unless You teach |me| I cannot seek You, and unless You reveal Yourself I cannot find You. Let me seek You in desiring You; let me desire You in seeking You. Let me find |You| in loving |You|; let me love |You| in finding |You|.

O Lord, I acknowledge and give thanks that You created in me Your image so that I may remember,[21] contemplate, and love You. But |this image| has been so effaced by the abrasion of transgressions, so hidden from sight by the dark billows of sins, that unless You renew and refashion it, it cannot do what it was created to do. O Lord, I do not attempt to gain access to Your loftiness, because I do not at all consider my intellect to be equal to this |task|. But I yearn to understand some measure of Your truth, which my heart believes and loves. For I do not seek to understand in order to believe, but I believe in order to understand. For I believe even this: that unless I believe, I shall not understand.[22]

CHAPTER TWO

God truly |i.e., really| exists.

Therefore, O Lord, You who give understanding to faith, grant me to understand—to the degree You know to be advantageous—that You exist, as we believe,[23] and that You are what we believe |You to be|. Indeed, we believe You to be something than which nothing greater can be thought. Or is there, then, no such nature |as You|, for the Fool has said in his heart that God does not exist?[24] But surely when this very same Fool hears my words "something than which nothing greater[25] can be thought," he understands what he hears. And what he understands is in his understanding,[26] even if he does not understand |i.e., judge| it to exist. For that a thing is in the understanding is distinct from understanding that |this| thing exists. For example, when a painter envisions

tor praecogitat quae facturus est, habet quidem in intellectu, sed nondum intelligit esse, quod nondum fecit. Cum vero iam pinxit, et habet in intellectu, et intelligit esse, quod iam fecit. Convincitur ergo etiam insipiens esse vel in intellectu aliquid quo nihil maius cogitari potest, quia hoc

15 cum audit intelligit, et quidquid intelligitur in intellectu est. Et certe id quo maius cogitari nequit, non potest esse in solo intellectu. Si enim vel in solo intellectu est, potest cogitari esse et in re—quod maius est. Si ergo id quo maius cogitari non potest, est in solo intellectu: id ipsum quo maius cogitari non potest, est quo maius cogitari potest. Sed certe hoc

20 esse non potest. Existit ergo procul dubio aliquid quo maius cogitari non valet, et in intellectu et in re.

CAPITULUM III
Quod non possit cogitari non esse.

Quod utique sic vere est ut nec cogitari possit non esse. Nam potest cogitari esse aliquid quod non possit cogitari non esse, quod maius est

5 quam quod non esse cogitari potest. Quare si id quo maius nequit cogitari, potest cogitari non esse: id ipsum quo maius cogitari nequit, non est id quo maius cogitari nequit—quod convenire non potest. Sic ergo vere est aliquid quo maius cogitari non potest ut nec cogitari possit non esse. Et hoc es tu, domine deus noster. Sic ergo vere es, domine deus meus, ut

10 nec cogitari possis non esse. Et merito. Si enim aliqua mens posset cogitare aliquid melius te, ascenderet creatura super creatorem et iudicaret de creatore—quod valde est absurdum. Et quidem quidquid est aliud praeter te solum, potest cogitari non esse. Solus igitur verissime omnium, et ideo maxime omnium, habes esse—quia quidquid aliud est, non sic

15 vere, et idcirco minus, habet esse. Cur itaque dixit insipiens in corde suo

what he is about to paint:[27] he indeed has in his understanding that which he has not yet made, but he does not yet understand that it exists. But after he has painted |it|: he has in his understanding that which he has made, and he understands that it exists. So even the Fool is convinced that something than which nothing greater can be thought is at least in his understanding; for when he hears of this |being|, he understands |what he hears|, and whatever is understood is in the understanding. But surely that than which a greater cannot be thought cannot be only in the understanding. For if it were only in the understanding, it could be thought to exist also in reality—something which is greater |than existing only in the understanding|. Therefore, if that than which a greater cannot be thought were only in the understanding, then that than which a greater *cannot* be thought would be that than which a greater *can* be thought! But surely this |conclusion| is impossible. Hence, without doubt, something than which a greater cannot be thought exists both in the understanding and in reality.[28]

CHAPTER THREE
|God| cannot be thought not to exist.

Assuredly, this |being| exists so truly |i.e., really| that it cannot even be thought not to exist. For there can be thought to exist something which cannot be thought not to exist; and this thing is greater than that which can be thought not to exist. Therefore, if that than which a greater cannot be thought could be thought not to exist, then that than which a greater cannot be thought would not be that than which a greater cannot be thought—|a consequence| which is contradictory. Hence, something than which a greater cannot be thought exists so truly that it cannot even be thought not to exist. And You are this |being|, O Lord our God. Therefore, O Lord my God, You exist so truly that You cannot even be thought not to exist. And this is rightly the case. For if any mind could think of something better than You, the creature would rise above the Creator and would sit in judgment over the Creator—something which is utterly absurd. Indeed, except for You alone, whatever else exists can be thought not to exist. Therefore, You alone exist most truly of all and thus most greatly of all; for whatever else exists does not exist as truly |as do You| and thus exists less greatly |than do You|.[29] Since, then, it is so readily clear to a rational mind that You exist most greatly of all, why did the

"non est deus," cum tam in promptu sit rationali menti te maxime
omnium esse?—cur, nisi quia stultus et insipiens?

CAPITULUM IV
Quomodo insipiens dixit in corde quod cogitari non potest.

Verum quomodo dixit in corde quod cogitare non potuit, aut quomodo
cogitare non potuit quod dixit in corde, cum idem sit dicere in corde et
5 cogitare? Quod si vere—immo quia vere—et cogitavit quia dixit in
corde, et non dixit in corde quia cogitare non potuit, non uno tantum
modo dicitur aliquid in corde vel cogitatur. Aliter enim cogitatur res
cum vox eam significans cogitatur, aliter cum id ipsum quod res est
intelligitur. Illo itaque modo potest cogitari deus non esse, isto vero
10 minime. Nullus quippe intelligens id quod deus est, potest cogitare quia
deus non est, licet haec verba dicat in corde aut sine ulla aut cum aliqua
extranea significatione. Deus enim est id quo maius cogitari non potest.
Quod qui bene intelligit, utique intelligit id ipsum sic esse ut nec cogitatione queat non esse. Qui ergo intelligit sic esse deum, nequit eum non
15 esse cogitare.

Gratias tibi, bone domine, gratias tibi, quia quod prius credidi te
donante, iam sic intelligo te illuminante ut si te esse nolim credere, non
possim non intelligere.

CAPITULUM V
Quod deus sit quidquid melius est esse quam non esse;
et solus existens per se omnia alia faciat de nihilo.

Quid igitur es, domine deus, quo nil maius valet cogitari? Sed quid es
5 nisi id quod summum omnium solum existens per seipsum, omnia alia
fecit de nihilo? Quidquid enim hoc non est, minus est quam cogitari
possit. Sed hoc de te cogitari non potest. Quod ergo bonum deest

Fool say in his heart that God does not exist?[30]—why |indeed| except because |he is| foolish and a fool!

CHAPTER FOUR

How the Fool said in his heart that which cannot be thought.

Yet, since to speak in one's heart and to think are the same thing, how did |the Fool| say in his heart that which he was unable to think, or how was he unable to think that which he did say in his heart? Now, if he truly |i.e., really|—rather, since he truly—both thought |what he did| because he said |it| in his heart and did not say |it| in his heart because he was unable to think |it|, then it is not the case that something is said in the heart, or is thought, in only one way. For in one way a thing is thought when the word signifying it is thought, and in another way |it is thought| when that which the thing is is understood. Thus, in the first way but not at all in the second, God can be thought not to exist. Indeed, no one who understands that which God is can think that God does not exist, even though he says these words |viz., "God does not exist"| in his heart either without any signification or with some strange signification. For God is that than which a greater cannot be thought. Anyone who rightly understands this,[31] surely understands that that |than which a greater cannot be thought| exists in such way that it cannot even conceivably not exist. Therefore, anyone who understands that God is such |a being| cannot think that He does not exist.

Thanks to You, good Lord, thanks to You—because what at first I believed through Your giving, now by Your enlightening I understand to such an extent that |even| if I did not want to believe that You exist, I could not fail to understand |that You exist|.[32]

CHAPTER FIVE

God is whatever it is better to be than
not to be. Alone existing through Himself,
He makes all other things from nothing.

What, then, are You, O Lord God, than whom nothing greater can be thought? What indeed are You except that which—as highest of all things, alone existing through Himself—made all other things from nothing? For whatever is not this is less great than can be thought. But this[33] cannot be thought of You. Therefore, what good is lacking to the

summo bono, per quod est omne bonum? Tu es itaque iustus, verax,
beatus, et quidquid melius est esse quam non esse. Melius namque est
10 esse iustum quam non-iustum, beatum quam non-beatum.

CAPITULUM VI

Quomodo sit sensibilis, cum non sit corpus.

Verum cum melius sit esse sensibilem, omnipotentem, misericordem,
impassibilem quam non esse: quomodo es sensibilis si non es corpus, aut
5 omnipotens si omnia non potes, aut misericors simul et impassibilis?
Nam si sola corporea sunt sensibilia, quoniam sensus circa corpus et in
corpore sunt: quomodo es sensibilis, cum non sis corpus sed summus
spiritus, qui corpore melior est? Sed si sentire non nisi cognoscere aut
non nisi ad cognoscendum est—qui enim sentit cognoscit secundum sen-
10 suum proprietatem, ut per visum colores, per gustum sapores—non
inconvenienter dicitur aliquomodo sentire, quidquid aliquomodo cognoscit. Ergo, domine, quamvis non sis corpus, vere tamen eo modo summe
sensibilis es quo summe omnia cognoscis, non quo animal corporeo
sensu cognoscit.

CAPITULUM VII

Quomodo sit omnipotens, cum multa non possit.

Sed et omnipotens quomodo es, si omnia non potes? Aut si non potes
corrumpi nec mentiri nec facere verum esse falsum, ut quod factum est
5 non esse factum, et plura similiter: quomodo potes omnia? An haec
posse, non est potentia sed impotentia? Nam qui haec potest, quod sibi
non expedit et quod non debet potest. Quae quanto magis potest, tanto
magis adversitas et perversitas possunt in illum, et ipse minus contra illas.
Qui ergo sic potest, non potentia potest, sed impotentia. Non enim ideo

VI, 3 misericordem: misericordiem *B*
VI, 12 domine: *supra lin. B*

Supreme Good, through whom every good exists? Consequently, You are just, truthful, blessed, and whatever it is better to be than not to be.[34] For it is better to be just than not-just, blessed than not-blessed.

CHAPTER SIX

How God is able to perceive
even though He is not something corporeal.

Now, since to be able to perceive and to be omnipotent, merciful, and impassible is better than not to be |any of these|, how are You able to perceive if You are not something corporeal, or how are You omnipotent if You cannot do all things, or how are You both merciful and impassible? For if only corporeal things are able to perceive (inasmuch as the senses have to do with a body and are in a body), how are You able to perceive, since You are not something corporeal but are Supreme Spirit, which is better than what is corporeal? But if perceiving is only knowing or only for the sake of knowing (for anyone who perceives knows in accordance with the characteristic capabilities of the respective senses— e.g., colors |are known| through sight, flavors through taste), then whatever in some way knows is not unsuitably said in some way to perceive. Therefore, O Lord, even though You are not something corporeal, truly You are supremely able to perceive in the sense that You know supremely all things—not |in the sense that You know| in the way that an animal does, by means of bodily senses.

CHAPTER SEVEN

How He is omnipotent even though He cannot do many things.

But how are You also omnipotent if You cannot do all things? Or how can You do all things if You are not able to be corrupted or to tell a lie or to make what is true be false—for example, |to make| what has already happened not to have happened—and, likewise, many |other| things?[35] Or is the "ability" to do these things not power but lack of power?[36] For anyone who is able to do these things is able to do what is disadvantageous to himself and what he ought not to do. And the more he is able to do these things, the more powerful are adversity and perversity over him and the less powerful he is against them. Therefore, anyone who in this way is able, is able not by a power but by a lack of power. For it is not the case that he is said to be able because he himself is able;

10 dicitur posse quia ipse possit, sed quia sua impotentia facit aliud in se
posse—sive aliquo alio genere loquendi, sicut multa improprie dicuntur
(ut cum ponimus "esse" pro "non-esse," et "facere" pro eo quod est
"non-facere," aut pro "nihil facere.") Nam saepe dicimus ei qui rem
aliquam esse negat "sic est quemadmodum dicis esse," cum magis prop-
15 rie videatur dici "sic non est quemadmodum dicis non esse." Item dicimus: "iste sedet sicut ille facit" aut "iste quiescit sicut ille facit," cum
sedere sit quiddam non facere et quiescere sit nihil facere. Sic itaque cum
quis dicitur habere potentiam faciendi aut patiendi quod sibi non expedit
aut quod non debet: impotentia intelligitur per potentiam, quia quo plus
20 habet hanc potentiam, eo adversitas et perversitas in illum sunt potenti-
ores, et ille contra eas impotentior. Ergo, domine deus, inde verius es
omnipotens quia nihil potes per impotentiam, et nihil potest contra te.

CAPITULUM VIII

Quomodo sit misericors et impassibilis.

Sed et misericors simul et impassibilis quomodo es? Nam si es impassibilis, non compateris; si non compateris, non est tibi miserum cor ex com-
5 passione miseri, quod est esse misericordem. At si non es misericors,
unde miseris est tanta consolatio? Quomodo ergo es et non es misericors,
domine, nisi quia es misericors secundum nos et non es secundum te? Es
quippe secundum nostrum sensum, et non es secundum tuum. Etenim
cum tu respicis nos miseros: nos sentimus misericordis effectum; tu non
10 sentis affectum. Et misericors es igitur quia miseros salvas et peccatoribus
tuis parcis; et misericors non es, quia nulla miseriae compassione afficeris.

VII, 21 Ergo: *ex* Ego *corr.* (ᴦ *supra lin.*) *B²*

rather, |he is said to be able| because his own lack of power causes something else to be powerful over him—or |for some other reason coinciding| with some other way of speaking (even as we say many things improperly—for example, when we substitute "to be" for "not to be" and substitute "to do" for "not to do" or for "to do nothing").[37] For we often say to someone who denies that something is the case, "It's as you say |it| is," although we would say more properly, "It's not, as you say it's not."[38] Likewise, we say, "This man is sitting even as that man is |also| doing" or "This man is resting even as that man is |also| doing"— although sitting is not doing anything and resting is doing nothing. So, then, when someone is said to have the power to do or to experience what is not advantageous to himself or what he ought not |to do or to experience|, by "power" a powerlessness is understood. For the more he has the |alleged| ability, the more powerful are adversity and perversity over him and the more powerless he is against them. Therefore, O Lord God, You are more truly omnipotent because You are not at all powerful through powerlessness and because nothing is powerful over You.

CHAPTER EIGHT
How He is merciful and impassible.

But how are you both merciful and impassible? For if You are impassible You have no compassion. And if You do not have compassion, You do not have a heart sorrowful out of compassion for the wretched—the very thing which being merciful is. And if You are not merciful, from where is there such great consolation for the wretched? How, then, are You and are You not merciful, O Lord, except because You are merciful from our point of view but are not merciful in Yourself? Indeed, You are |merciful| according to our experience but are not |merciful| according to Your experience. For when You behold us in our wretched condition, we experience the effect of Your mercy; but You do not experience any emotion. And so, You are merciful because You save |us| wretched |creatures| and spare |us| who have sinned against You; and You are not merciful, because You do not experience compassion for wretchedness.

Quomodo totus iustus et summe iustus parcat malis;
et quod iuste misereatur malis.

Verum malis quomodo parcis, si es totus iustus et summe iustus? Quo-
5 modo enim totus et summe iustus facit aliquid non iustum? Aut quae
iustitia est merenti mortem aeternam dare vitam sempiternam? Unde
ergo, bone deus, bone bonis et malis, unde tibi salvare malos, si hoc non
est iustum et tu non facis aliquid non iustum? An quia bonitas tua est
incomprehensibilis, latet hoc in luce inaccessibili quam inhabitas? Vere in
10 altissimo et secretissimo bonitatis tuae latet fons, unde manat fluvius
misericordiae tuae. Nam cum totus et summe iustus sis, tamen idcirco
etiam malis benignus es: quia totus summe bonus es. Minus namque
bonus esses, si nulli malo esses benignus. Melior est enim qui et bonis et
malis bonus est, quam qui bonis tantum est bonus. Et melior est qui
15 malis et puniendo et parcendo est bonus, quam qui puniendo tantum.
Ideo ergo misericors es quia totus et summe bonus es. Et cum forsitan
videatur cur bonis bona et malis mala retribuas, illud certe penitus est
mirandum: cur tu totus iustus et nullo egens malis et reis tuis bona tri-
buas. O altitudo bonitatis tuae, deus! Et videtur unde sis misericors, et
20 non pervidetur. Cernitur unde flumen manat, et non perspicitur fons
unde nascatur. Nam et de plenitudine bonitatis est quia peccatoribus tuis
pius es, et in altitudine bonitatis latet qua ratione hoc es. Etenim licet
bonis bona et malis mala ex bonitate retribuas, ratio tamen iustitiae hoc
postulare videtur. Cum vero malis bona tribuis: et scitur quia summe
25 bonus hoc facere voluit, et mirum est cur summe iustus hoc velle potuit.

CHAPTER NINE
How He who is completely and supremely just spares those who are evil. He is justly merciful to them.

But how is it that You spare those who are evil if You are completely and supremely just?[39] For how is it that He who is completely and supremely just does something which is not just? Or what justice is there in giving eternal life to one deserving eternal death? Why, then, good God—good to those who are good and to those who are evil—why do You save those who are evil, if |to do| this is not just and if You do not do anything that is not just? Inasmuch as Your goodness is incomprehensible, is this |reason| hidden in the inaccessible light in which You dwell?[40] Truly, in the deepest and inmost seat of Your goodness is hidden a fount from which the stream of Your mercy flows. For although You are completely and supremely just, nevertheless because You are completely and supremely good You are also beneficent to those who are evil. For You would be less good if You were beneficent to none of those who are evil. For someone who is good both to those who are good and to those who are evil is better than someone who is good only to those who are good. And someone who is good by virtue of both punishing and sparing those who are evil is better than someone who |is good| by virtue merely of punishing |them|. Therefore, You are merciful because You are completely and supremely good. Now, although we do perhaps discern why You reward with good things those who are good and with evil things those who are evil, surely we are completely baffled as to why You, who are completely just and in need of no one else, give good things to those who are evil and guilty in Your sight. O God, the depth of Your goodness! We see why You are merciful, and yet we do not fully see why. We see from where the stream |of Your mercy| flows, and yet we do not see the Fount itself from which it flows. For that You are gracious to those who sin against You comes from the abundance of Your goodness; and in the depth of Your goodness lies hidden the reason why You are this.[41] For although out of goodness You reward with good things those who are good and with evil things those who are evil, the principle of justice seems to require this. But when You give good things to those who are evil, we know that He who is supremely good willed to do this, but we wonder why He who is supremely just was able to will this.

O misericordia, de quam opulenta dulcedine et dulci opulentia nobis profluis! O immensitas bonitatis dei, quo affectu amanda es peccatoribus! Justos enim salvas iustitia comitante, istos vero liberas iustitia damnante; illos meritis adiuvantibus, istos meritis repugnantibus; illos bona

30 quae dedisti cognoscendo, istos mala quae odisti ignoscendo. O immensa bonitas, quae sic omnem intellectum excedis, veniat super me misericordia illa quae de tanta opulentia tui procedit! Influat in me quae profluit de te! Parce per clementiam; ne ulciscaris per iustitiam! Nam etsi difficile sit intelligere quomodo misericordia tua non absit a tua iustitia, neces-

35 sarium tamen est credere quia nequaquam adversatur iustitiae quod exundat ex bonitate, quae nulla est sine iustitia—immo vere concordat iustitiae. Nempe si misericors es quia es summe bonus, et summe bonus non es nisi quia es summe iustus, vere idcirco es misericors: quia summe iustus es. Adiuva me, iuste et misericors deus, cuius lucem quaero; ad-

40 iuva me ut intelligam quod dico. Vere ergo ideo misericors es quia iustus.

Ergone misericordia tua nascitur ex iustitia tua? Ergone parcis malis ex iustitia? Si sic est, domine, si sic est, doce me quomodo est. An quia iustum est te sic esse bonum ut nequeas intelligi melior, et sic potenter operari ut non possis cogitari potentius? Quid enim hoc iustius? Hoc

45 utique non fieret, si esses bonus tantum retribuendo et non parcendo, et si faceres de non bonis tantum bonos, et non etiam de malis. Hoc itaque modo iustum est ut parcas malis et ut facias bonos de malis. Denique quod non iuste fit, non debet fieri; et quod non debet fieri, iniuste fit. Si ergo non iuste malis misereris, non debes misereri; et si non debes mis-

50 ereri, iniuste misereris. Quod si nefas est dicere, fas est credere te iuste misereri malis.

O mercy, from what rich sweetness and sweet richness You flow forth unto us! O immensity of divine goodness, with what affection sinners ought to love You! For You save those-who-are-just, since justice accompanies |them|; but You free those-who-are-evil, even though justice condemns |them|. Those who are just |You save| through the aid of their merits; those who are evil |You free| in spite of their demerits. |You save| the just by taking account of the good things, which You have given them; |You free| those-who-are-evil by overlooking the evil things, which You hate. O immense goodness, which so exceeds all understanding, let there come upon me that mercy which proceeds from Your so great richness! Let there flow into me |the mercy| which flows out of You! Spare |me| out of mercy; do not punish |me| out of justice! For although it is difficult to understand how Your mercy is compatible with Your justice, it is necessary to believe that what flows forth from goodness is not at all opposed to justice. (Without justice, goodness is not goodness—indeed, |goodness| is truly concordant with justice.) Assuredly, if you are merciful because You are supremely good, and if You are supremely good only because You are supremely just, then truly You are merciful because You are supremely just. Help me, O just and merciful God, whose light I seek; help me to understand what I am saying. Truly, then, You are merciful because You are just.

Is Your mercy, then, begotten from Your justice? Do You, then, spare evil ones out of justice? If so, O Lord, if so, then teach me how so. Is it because it is just for You to be so good that You cannot be understood to be any better and |because it is just for You| to work so powerfully that You cannot be thought |to work| more powerfully? For what is more just than this?[42] But surely this would not be the case if You were good only by way of retributing and not |also| by way of sparing—and if You were to make good men only from those who are not good instead of also from those who are evil. And so, in this way, it is just that You spare those who are evil and that You make good men from evil ones. Finally, that which is not done justly ought not to be done; and what ought not to be done is done unjustly. Therefore, if You were not justly merciful to those who are evil, it would be the case that You ought not to be merciful |to them|; and if You ought not to be merciful, then You are unjustly merciful. Now, if it is blasphemous to say this,[43] then it is right to believe that You are justly merciful to those who are evil.

Quomodo iuste puniat et iuste parcat malis.

Sed et iustum est ut malos punias. Quid namque iustius quam ut boni
bona et mali mala recipiant? Quomodo ergo et iustum est ut malos
5 punias, et iustum est ut malis parcas? An alio modo iuste punis malos, et
alio modo iuste parcis malis? Cum enim punis malos, iustum est quia
illorum meritis convenit; cum vero parcis malis, iustum est, non quia illorum meritis sed quia bonitati tuae condecens est. Nam parcendo malis
ita iustus es secundum te et non secundum nos, sicut misericors es
10 secundum nos et non secundum te. Quoniam salvando nos quos iuste
perderes: sicut misericors es non quia tu sentias affectum, sed quia nos
sentimus effectum, ita iustus es non quia nobis reddas debitum, sed quia
facis quod decet te summe bonum. Sic itaque sine repugnantia iuste
punis et iuste parcis.

Quomodo "universae viae domini misericordia et veritas,"
et tamen "iustus dominus in omnibus viis suis."

Sed numquid etiam non est iustum secundum te, domine, ut malos
5 punias? Iustum quippe est te sic esse iustum ut iustior nequeas cogitari.
Quod nequaquam esses, si tantum bonis bona et non malis mala red-
deres. Iustior enim est qui et bonis et malis, quam qui bonis tantum,
merita retribuit. Iustum igitur est secundum te, iuste et benigne deus, et
cum punis et cum parcis. Vere igitur "universae viae domini misericordia
10 et veritas," et tamen "iustus dominus in omnibus viis suis." Et utique sine
repugnantia—quia quos vis punire, non est iustum salvari, et quibus vis
parcere, non est iustum damnari. Nam id solum iustum est quod vis, et
non iustum quod non vis. Sic ergo nascitur de iustitia tua misericordia

CHAPTER TEN

How He justly punishes and justly spares those who are evil.

Yet, it is also just that You punish those who are evil. For what is more just than for those who are good to receive good things and for those who are evil to receive bad things? But, then, how is it just for You to punish those who are evil and likewise just for You to spare them? Do You justly punish them in one respect and justly spare them in another? For when You punish those who are evil, it is just |for You to do so| because |punishment| besuits their merits. But when You spare them, it is just |for You to do so|, not because |sparing them| besuits their merits but because it befits Your goodness. For in sparing them, You are *just* in Yourself but are not just from our viewpoint, even as You are merciful from our viewpoint but are not merciful in Yourself. For in saving us whom You could justly damn, You are *just* not because You requite us as we deserve but because You do what befits You as supremely good, even as You are merciful not because You experience any emotion but because we experience the effect |of Your mercy|. So, then, without inconsistency, You both punish justly and spare justly.

CHAPTER ELEVEN

How "all the ways of the Lord are mercy and truth,"
and yet, "the Lord is just in all His ways."

But, O Lord, is it not also just, in accordance with Yourself, for You to punish those who are evil? To be sure, it is just that You be so just that You cannot be thought to be more just. But You would not at all be this[44] if You rewarded only those who are good with good things but not those who are evil with bad things. For someone who rewards according to their merits both those who are good and those who are evil is more just than someone who rewards only those who are good. Thus, O just and beneficent God, in accordance with Yourself it is just both when You punish and when You spare. Truly, then, "all the ways of the Lord are mercy and truth," and yet, "the Lord is just in all His ways."[45] And, assuredly, |these two statements hold true| without inconsistency, because it is not just that those whom You will to punish should be saved nor just that those whom You will to spare should be condemned. For only what You will is just, and only what You do not will is not just. So, then, Your mercy is begotten from Your justice, because it is just for You to be good

tua, quia iustum est te sic esse bonum ut et parcendo sis bonus. Et hoc
15 est forsitan cur summe iustus potest velle bona malis. Sed si utcumque
capi potest cur malos potes velle salvare: illud certe nulla ratione comprehendi potest cur de similibus malis hos magis salves quam illos per
summam bonitatem, et illos magis damnes quam istos per summam
iustitiam.
20   Sic ergo vere es sensibilis, omnipotens, misericors, et impassibilis,
quemadmodum vivens, sapiens, bonus, beatus, aeternus, et quidquid
melius est esse quam non esse.

CAPITULUM XII

Quod deus sit ipsa vita qua vivit, et sic de similibus.

Sed certe quidquid es, non per aliud es quam per teipsum. Tu es igitur
ipsa vita qua vivis, et sapientia qua sapis, et bonitas ipsa qua bonis et
5 malis bonus es, et ita de similibus.

CAPITULUM XIII

Quomodo solus sit incircumscriptus et aeternus, cum
alii spiritus sint incircumscripti et aeterni.

Sed omne quod clauditur aliquatenus loco aut tempore, minus est quam
5 quod nulla lex loci aut temporis coërcet. Quoniam ergo maius te nihil
est, nullus locus aut tempus te cohibet, sed ubique et semper es. Quod
quia de te solo dici potest, tu solus incircumscriptus es et aeternus.
Quomodo igitur dicuntur et alii spiritus incircumscripti et aeterni? Et
quidem solus es aeternus, quia solus omnium sicut non desinis, sic non
10 incipis esse. Sed solus quomodo es incircumscriptus? An creatus spiritus
ad te collatus, est circumscriptus, ad corpus vero incircumscriptus?
Nempe omnino circumscriptum est quod cum alicubi totum est, non
potest simul esse alibi—quod de solis corporeis cernitur. Incircumscriptum vero quod simul est ubique totum—quod de te solo intelligitur.

to such an extent that You are good even in sparing. And perhaps this is why He who is supremely just can will good things for those who are evil. But if we can somehow grasp why You can will to save those who are evil, surely we cannot at all comprehend why from among those who are similarly evil You save some and not others because of Your supreme goodness, and condemn some and not others because of Your supreme justice.

So, then, truly You are able to perceive and are omnipotent, merciful, and impassible—as well as living, wise, good, blessed, eternal, and whatever it is better to be than not to be.[46]

CHAPTER TWELVE
God is the life by which He lives,
and similarly for similar |attributes|.

But, surely, whatever You are You are through no other than through Yourself. Therefore, You are the life by which You live, the wisdom by which You are wise, the goodness by which You are good both to those who are good and to those who are evil, and similarly for similar |attributes|.[47]

CHAPTER THIRTEEN
How He alone is unlimited and eternal, although
other spirits are |also| unlimited and eternal.

Now, anything which is at all confined by place or by time is less great than that which is not at all subject to the law of place or of time. Therefore, since it is not the case that anything is greater than You, no place or time restricts You, but You exist everywhere and always. Because this can be said of You alone, You alone are unlimited and eternal. How, then, are other spirits, as well, said to be unlimited and eternal? To be sure, You alone are eternal because You alone of all things do not begin to exist, even as You do not cease to exist. Yet, how are You alone unlimited? Is a created spirit, although unlimited in comparison with something corporeal, limited in comparison with You? Assuredly, that which while existing somewhere as a whole is not able at the same time to exist elsewhere is limited in every respect—something which is seen to be the case with corporeal objects only. And what exists at once everywhere as a whole is unlimited—something which is under-

[handwritten marginal note: God is absolutely simple, so that the divine attributes are not accidents but rather the very essence of God (see Monolog. 16-17)]

15 Circumscriptum autem simul et incircumscriptum est quod cum alicubi sit totum, potest simul esse totum alibi, non tamen ubique—quod de creatis spiritibus cognoscitur. Si enim non esset anima tota in singulis membris sui corporis, non sentiret tota in singulis. Tu ergo, domine, singulariter es incircumscriptus et aeternus, et tamen et alii spiritus sunt

20 incircumscripti et aeterni.

CAPITULUM XIV

Quomodo et cur videtur et non videtur deus a quaerentibus eum.

An invenisti, anima mea, quod quaerebas? Quaerebas deum, et invenisti eum esse quiddam summum omnium, quo nihil melius cogitari potest; et

5 hoc esse ipsam vitam, lucem, sapientiam, bonitatem, aeternam beatitudinem, et beatam aeternitatem; et hoc esse ubique et semper. Nam si non invenisti deum tuum: quomodo est ille hoc quod invenisti et quod illum tam certa veritate et vera certitudine intellexisti? Si vero invenisti: quid est quod non sentis quod invenisti? Cur non te sentit, domine deus,

10 anima mea, si invenit te? An non invenit, quem invenit esse lucem et veritatem? Quomodo namque intellexit hoc, nisi videndo lucem et veritatem? Aut potuit omnino aliquid intelligere de te, nisi per lucem tuam et veritatem tuam? Si ergo vidit lucem et veritatem, vidit te. Si non vidit te, non vidit lucem nec veritatem. An et veritas et lux est quod vidit, et

15 tamen nondum te vidit, quia vidit te aliquatenus, sed non vidit te sicuti es?

Domine deus meus, formator et reformator meus, dic desideranti animae meae, quid aliud es quam quod vidit, ut pure videat quod desiderat. Intendit se ut plus videat, et nihil videt ultra hoc quod vidit nisi

20 tenebras—immo non videt tenebras, quae nullae sunt in te, se videt se non plus posse videre propter tenebras suas. Cur hoc, domine, cur hoc? Tenebratur oculus eius infirmitate sua, aut reverberatur fulgore tuo? Sed

stood to be the case with You alone. But that which while existing somewhere as a whole is able at the same time to exist as a whole elsewhere, but not everywhere, is both limited and unlimited—something which is known to be the case with created spirits. For example, if the soul were not present as a whole in each of the members of its body, the soul as a whole would not experience feeling in each of them. Therefore, O Lord, You are uniquely unlimited and eternal; and yet, other spirits are also unlimited and eternal.

CHAPTER FOURTEEN

How and why God is both seen and
not seen by those who seek Him.

My soul, have you found that which You were seeking? You were seeking God, and you have found that He is something highest of all—than which nothing better can be thought. |And you have found that| this |being| is life itself, light, wisdom, goodness, eternal blessedness, and blessed eternity, and that this |being| exists everywhere and always. Now, if you have not found your God, then how is He this |being| which you have found and which with such certain truth and true certainty you have understood Him to be? On the other hand, if you have found |Him|, then why is it that you do not experience what you have found? O Lord God, why does my soul not experience You if it has found You? Has it not found Him whom it has found to be light and truth? For how has it understood this[48] except by seeing light and truth? Was it able to understand anything at all about You except through Your light and Your truth?[49] Therefore, if |my soul| saw light and truth, it saw You. If it did not see You, it did not see light and truth. Or |is it rather the case that| light and truth are what it saw but |that| it has not yet seen You because it saw You to some extent but did not see You as You are?[50]

O Lord my God, my Creator and Renewer, tell my yearning soul what else You are other than what it has seen, so that it may see clearly what it longs |to see. My soul| strains to see more; but beyond what it has already seen it sees only darkness. Or better, it does not see darkness, which is not present in You;[51] rather, it sees that it can see no farther because of its own darkness. Why is this, O Lord? Why is this? Is the eye of the soul darkened as a result of its own weakness, or is it dazzled by Your brilliance? Surely, the soul's eye is both darkened within itself

certe et tenebratur in se et reverberatur a te. Utique et obscuratur sua brevitate et obruitur tua immensitate. Vere et contrahitur angustia sua et
25 vincitur amplitudine tua. Quanta namque est lux illa, de qua micat omne verum quod rationali menti lucet! Quam ampla est illa veritas, in qua est omne quod verum est, et extra quam non nisi nihil et falsum est! Quam immensa est, quae uno intuitu videt quaecumque facta sunt, et a quo et per quem et quomodo de nihilo facta sunt! Quid puritatis, quid simplici-
30 tatis, quid certitudinis et splendoris ibi est! Certe plus quam a creatura valeat intelligi.

CAPITULUM XV
Quod maior sit quam cogitari possit.

Ergo, domine, non solum es quo maius cogitari nequit, sed es quiddam maius quam cogitari possit. Quoniam namque valet cogitari esse aliquid
5 huiusmodi: si tu non es hoc ipsum, potest cogitari aliquid maius te—quod fieri nequit.

CAPITULUM XVI
Quod haec sit lux inaccessibilis quam inhabitat.

Vere, domine, haec est lux inaccessibilis, in qua habitas. Vere enim non est aliud quod hanc penetret, ut ibi te pervideat. Vere ideo hanc non
5 video quia nimia mihi est; et tamen quidquid video, per illam video—sicut infirmus oculus quod videt per lucem solis videt, quam in ipso sole nequit aspicere. Non potest intellectus meus ad illam. Nimis fulget; non capit illam; nec suffert oculus animae meae diu intendere in illam. Reverberatur fulgore, vincitur amplitudine, obruitur immensitate, con-
10 funditur capacitate. O summa et inaccessibilis lux, o tota et beata veritas, quam longe es a me, qui tam prope tibi sum! Quam remota es a conspectu meo, qui sic praesens sum conspectui tuo! Ubique es tota praesens,

XVI, 12 Ubique: *ex* Ubi *corr.* (que *supra lin.*) *B*

and dazzled by You. Surely, it is darkened because of its own shortness of vision and is overwhelmed by Your immensity; truly, it is restricted because of its own narrowness and is overcome by Your vastness. For how great that Light is from which shines everything true that illumines the rational mind! How vast that Truth is in which resides everything that is true and outside of which there is only nothing and what is false! How immense |that Truth| is which beholds in one spectrum all created things and beholds by whom, through whom, and in what manner |all things| were created from nothing! What purity, what simplicity, what assurance and splendor are present there. Surely, |these| surpass what can be understood by any creature.

CHAPTER FIFTEEN
He is greater than can be thought.

Therefore, O Lord, not only are You that than which a greater cannot be thought, but You are also something greater than can be thought.[52] For since there can be thought to exist something of this kind,[53] if You were not this |being| then something greater than You could be thought—|a consequence| which is impossible.

CHAPTER SIXTEEN
This is the inaccessible light in which He dwells.

Truly, O Lord, this is the inaccessible light in which You dwell.[54] For, truly, there is not anything else which can penetrate this |light|, so that it sees You therein. Truly, the reason I cannot stand to look at this |light| is that it is too resplendent for me. Nevertheless, whatever I see I see by means of this |light|—even as a frail eye sees what it does by means of sunlight, which it cannot stand to look at in the sun itself. My understanding is not able to comprehend this light, which shines forth too brilliantly. |My understanding| does not grasp it; and the eye of my soul cannot bear to gaze at length upon it. |My soul's eye| is dazzled by its splendor, overcome by its vastness, overwhelmed by its immensity, confounded by its capacity. O supreme and inaccessible Light, O complete and blessed Truth, how distant You are from me, who am so near for You! How far removed You are from my sight, though I am so present to Yours! You are everywhere present as a whole; and yet, I do not see

et non te video. In te moveor et in te sum, et ad te non possum accedere. Intra me et circa me es, et non te sentio.

CAPITULUM XVII

Quod in deo sit harmonia, odor, sapor, lenitas,
pulchritudo, suo ineffabili modo.

Adhuc lates, domine, animam meam in luce et beatitudine tua, et idcirco
5 versatur illa adhuc in tenebris et miseria sua. Circumspicit enim, et non videt pulchritudinem tuam. Auscultat, et non audit harmoniam tuam. Olfacit, et non percipit odorem tuum. Gustat, et non cognoscit saporem tuum. Palpat, et non sentit lenitatem tuam. Habes enim haec, domine deus, in te tuo ineffabili modo, qui ea dedisti rebus a te creatis suo
10 sensibili modo; sed obriguerunt, sed obstupuerunt, sed obstructi sunt sensus animae meae vetusto languore peccati.

CAPITULUM XVIII

Quod in deo nec in aeternitate eius,
quae ipse est, nullae sint partes.

Et iterum ecce turbatio, ecce iterum obviat maeror et luctus quaerenti
5 gaudium et laetitiam! Sperabat iam anima mea satietatem, et ecce iterum obruitur egestate! Affectabam iam comedere, et ecce magis esurire! Conabar assurgere ad lucem dei, et recidi in tenebras meas—immo non modo cedidi in eas, sed sentio me involutum in eis. Ante cecidi quam conciperet me mater mea. Certe in illis conceptus sum, et cum earum
10 obvolutione natus sum. Olim certe in illo omnes cecidimus in quo omnes peccavimus. In illo omnes perdidimus qui facile tenebat et male sibi et nobis perdidit, quod cum volumus quaerere nescimus, cum quaerimus non invenimus, cum invenimus non est quod quaerimus. Adiuva me tu propter bonitatem tuam, domine. "Quaesivi vultum tuum; vultum
15 tuum, domine, requiram; ne avertas faciem tuam a me." Releva me de me ad te. Munda, sana, acue, illumina oculum mentis meae, ut intueatur te. Recolligat vires suas anima mea, et toto intellectu iterum intendat in te, domine.

Quid es, domine, quid es, quid te intelliget cor meum? Certe vita es,

XVII, 6 harmoniam: armoniam *B*

You. In You I move, and in You I exist;[55] and yet, I cannot approach You. You are within me and round about me; and yet, I do not experience You.

CHAPTER SEVENTEEN

Harmony, fragrance, succulence, softness, and beauty
are present in God in their own ineffable manner.

Amidst Your blessedness and light, O Lord, You are still hidden from my soul. Therefore, my soul still dwells in darkness and in its own unhappiness. For it looks in all directions but does not see Your beauty. It listens but does not hear Your harmony. It fills its nostrils but does not smell Your fragrance. It tastes but does not savor Your succulence. It feels but does not detect Your softness. For in Your ineffable manner, O Lord God, You have these |features| within You; and You have bestowed them, in their own perceptible manner, upon the things created by You. But the senses of my soul have been stiffened and deadened and impaired by the oldtime infirmity of sin.

CHAPTER EIGHTEEN

There are no parts in God or in the eternity which He is.

And, behold, once again confusion![56] Behold, once again sorrow and grief beset me as I seek joy and gladness.[57] My soul hoped for fulness; and, lo, once again it is overwhelmed with need. I desired to eat; and, lo, the more I hunger! I tried to mount upward to the divine light, but I lapsed downward into my own darkness. Indeed, not only did I fall into darkness but I feel enshrouded by it. I fell before my mother conceived me.[58] Surely, I was conceived in darkness and born surrounded by it. Surely, once long ago we all fell in him[59] in whom we all sinned. In him (who easily possessed but evilly lost for himself and for us) we all lost that which when we desire we do not know how to seek, when we seek we do not find, when we find is not what we are seeking. Help me, O Lord, because of Your goodness.[60] "I have sought Your countenance; Your countenance, O Lord, will I seek. Do not turn Your face from me."[61] Raise me out of myself and unto You. Cleanse, heal, focus, illumine[62] the eye of my mind so that it may behold You.[63] Let my soul muster its strength and with all its understanding strive once more unto You, O Lord. What are You, O Lord? What are You? What shall my heart understand

20 sapientia es, veritas es, bonitas es, beatitudo es, aeternitas es, et omne verum bonum es. Multa sunt haec; non potest angustus intellectus meus tot uno simul intuitu videre, ut omnibus simul delectetur. Quomodo ergo, domine, es omnia haec? An sunt partes tui, aut potius unumquodque horum est totum quod es? Nam quidquid partibus est iunctum,
25 non est omnino unum, sed quodam modo plura et diversum a seipso, et vel actu vel intellectu dissolvi potest—quae aliena sunt a te, quo nihil melius cogitari potest. Nullae igitur partes sunt in te, domine, nec es plura, sed sic es unum quiddam et idem tibi ipsi ut in nullo tibi ipsi sis dissimilis—immo tu es ipsa unitas, nullo intellectu divisibilis. Ergo vita et
30 sapientia et reliqua non sunt partes tui, sed omnia sunt unum, et unumquodque horum est totum quod es et quod sunt reliqua omnia. Quoniam ergo nec tu habes partes nec tua aeternitas quae tu es: nusquam et numquam est pars tua aut aeternitatis tuae, sed ubique totus es, et aeternitas tua tota est semper.

CAPITULUM XIX
Quod non sit in loco aut tempore, sed omnia sint in illo.

Sed si per aeternitatem tuam fuisti et es et eris, et fuisse non est futurum esse, et esse non est fuisse vel futurum esse: quomodo aeternitas tua tota
5 est semper? An de aeternitate tua nihil praeterit, ut iam non sit; nec aliquid futurum est, quasi nondum sit? Non ergo fuisti heri aut eris cras, sed heri et hodie et cras es—immo nec heri nec hodie nec cras es, sed simpliciter es, extra omne tempus. Nam nihil aliud est heri et hodie et cras quam in tempore; tu autem, licet nihil sit sine te, non es tamen in
10 loco aut tempore, sed omnia sunt in te. Nihil enim te continet, sed tu contines omnia.

You to be? Surely, You are life, wisdom, truth, goodness, blessedness, eternity—You are every true good. These are many things; and my limited understanding cannot in a single view behold so many at one time in order to delight in all together. How is it, then, O Lord, that You are all these things? Are they Your parts, or, instead, is each one of them the whole of what You are? For whatever is composed of parts is not absolutely one but is in a way many and is different from itself and can be divided actually or conceivably (*intellectu*). But these |consequences| are foreign to You, than whom nothing better can be thought. Hence, there are no parts in You, O Lord. Nor are You more than one thing. Rather, You are something so one and the same with Yourself that in no respect are You dissimilar to Yourself. Indeed, You are Oneness itself, divisible in no respect (*nullo intellectu*). Therefore, life and wisdom and the other |characteristics| are not parts of You but are all one thing; and each one of them is the whole of what You are and the whole of what all the others are. Thus, since neither You nor the eternity which You are has any parts, nowhere and never is there a part of You or of Your eternity; rather, You exist everywhere as a whole, and Your eternity exists always as a whole.

CHAPTER NINETEEN
He is not in place or in time; but all things are in Him.

But if through Your eternity You were, You are, and You will be, and if (1) being past is not being future and (2) being present is not being past or being future, how is it that Your eternity exists always as a whole? Or does none of Your eternity pass away, so that it no longer is? And is none of it going to be—as if it not yet were? Then, in no case *were* You yesterday or *will* You *be* tomorrow; instead, yesterday, today, and tomorrow You *are*. Or better, You do not exist yesterday or today or tomorrow, but You simply *are*—|existing| beyond all time. For yesterday, today, and tomorrow are nothing other than |distinctions| in time. Now, although without You nothing would exist, You are not in place or in time, but all things are in You. For You are not contained by anything, but, rather, You contain all |other| things.[64]

CAPITULUM XX
Quod sit ante et ultra omnia etiam aeterna.

Tu ergo imples et complecteris omnia; tu es ante et ultra omnia. Et quidem ante omnia es, quia antequam fierent tu es. Ultra omnia vero 5 quomodo es? Qualiter enim es ultra ea quae finem non habebunt? An quia illa sine te nullatenus esse possunt, tu autem nullo modo minus es, etiam si illa redeunt in nihilum? Sic enim quodam modo es ultra illa. An etiam quia illa cogitari possunt habere finem, tu vero nequaquam? Nam sic illa quidem habent finem quodam modo, tu vero nullo modo. Et 10 certe quod nullo modo habet finem, ultra illud est quod aliquomodo finitur. An hoc quoque modo transis omnia etiam aeterna: quia tua et illorum aeternitas tota tibi praesens est, cum illa nondum habeant de sua aeternitate quod venturum est, sicut iam non habent quod praeteritum est? Sic quippe semper es ultra illa, cum semper tibi sis praesens seu cum 15 illud semper sit tibi praesens ad quod illa nondum pervenerunt.

CAPITULUM XXI
An hoc sit saeculum saeculi sive saecula saeculorum.

An ergo hoc est saeculum saeculi sive saecula saeculorum? Sicut enim saeculum temporum continet omnia temporalia, sic tua aeternitas con- 5 tinet etiam ipsa saecula temporum. Quae saeculum quidem est propter indivisibilem unitatem, saecula vero propter interminabilem immensitatem. Et quamvis ita sis magnus, domine, ut omnia sint te plena et sint in te: sic tamen es sine omni spatio ut nec medium nec dimidium nec ulla pars sit in te.

CAPITULUM XXII
Quod solus sit quod est et qui est.

Tu solus ergo, domine, es quod es, et tu es qui es. Nam quod aliud est in toto et aliud in partibus, et in quo aliquid est mutabile, non omnino est

---

XX, 3 complecteris: *habent ET* contemplecteris *B*
XX, 11 modo: *supra lin. B²*
XX, 12 tibi: *ex ? corr. B*
XX, 14 tibi: ibi *BET* (sis ibi *ad* ibi sis *transponit B*) *ad* tibi *correxi (cf. Proslogion XX 12)*

CHAPTER TWENTY

He is before and beyond all things—even eternal things.

Therefore, You fill and encompass all things; You are before and beyond all things. Indeed, You are before all things because before they were made You already are.[65] But how is it that You are beyond all things? For how are You beyond those things which will have no end? Is it because they cannot at all exist without You, whereas You would not at all be less great even if they returned to nothing?[66] For in this way You are beyond them in a certain respect. Is it also because they can be thought to have an end, whereas You |can| not at all |be thought to have an end|? For, indeed, they do in this respect have a kind of end, whereas You |do| not in any respect |have an end|. Now, surely what in no respect has an end is beyond that which in some respect has an end. Do You also surpass all things—even eternal things—in that both Your eternity and theirs is present to You as a whole, whereas they do not yet have that |part| of their eternity which is yet to come, even as they no longer have that |part| which is already past? Indeed, then, You are always beyond them because You are always |wholly| present to Yourself and because there is always present to You that |part of their eternity| to which they have not yet come.

CHAPTER TWENTY-ONE

Whether this |eternity| is one aeon or more than one.

Is, then, this |eternity of Yours| one aeon or more than one?[67] For just as the aeon of times contains all things temporal, so Your eternity contains even the aeons of times. Indeed, Your eternity is one aeon on account of its indivisible oneness, but it is more than one aeon on account of its endless immensity. Moreover, although You are so great, O Lord, that all things are filled with Your presence and exist in You, nevertheless You are so free from all spatial determination that in You there is neither center nor half nor any part.[68]

CHAPTER TWENTY-TWO

He alone is what He is and who He is.

Therefore, O Lord, You alone are what You are, and You are who You are. For anything having parts distinct from its whole, and anything in which there is something mutable, is not altogether what it is. And what (1)

5 quod est. Et quod incepit a non-esse et potest cogitari non esse, et nisi per aliud subsistat redit in non-esse, et quod habet fuisse quod iam non est, et futurum esse quod nondum est: id non est proprie et absolute. Tu vero es quod es, quia quidquid aliquando aut aliquomodo es, hoc totus et semper es.

10 Et tu es qui proprie et simpliciter es, quia nec habes fuisse aut futurum esse, sed tantum praesens esse, nec potes cogitari aliquando non esse. Et vita es et lux et sapientia et beatitudo et aeternitas et multa huiusmodi bona, et tamen non es nisi unum et summum bonum, tu tibi omnino sufficiens, nullo indigens, quo omnia indigent ut sint et ut bene sint.

CAPITULUM XXIII

Quod hoc bonum sit pariter pater et filius
et spiritus sanctus; et hoc sit unum necessarium,
quod est omne et totum et solum bonum.

5 Hoc bonum es tu, deus pater; hoc est verbum tuum, id est filius tuus. Etenim non potest aliud quam quod es, aut aliquid maius vel minus te, esse in verbo quo te ipsum dicis, quoniam verbum tuum sic est verum quomodo tu verax; et idcirco est ipsa veritas, sicut tu, non alia quam tu; et sic es tu simplex ut de te non possit nasci aliud quam quod tu es. Hoc 10 ipsum est amor unus et communis tibi et filio tuo, id est sanctus spiritus ab utroque procedens. Nam idem amor non est impar tibi aut filio tuo, quia tantum amas te et illum, et ille te et seipsum, quantus es tu et ille; nec est aliud a te et ab illo quod dispar non est tibi et illi; nec de summa simplicitate potest procedere aliud quam quod est de quo procedit. Quod 15 autem est singulus quisque, hoc est tota trinitas simul, pater et filius et spiritus sanctus—quoniam singulus quisque non est aliud quam summe simplex unitas et summe una simplicitas, quae nec multiplicari nec aliud et aliud esse potest.

"Porro unum est necessarium." Porro hoc est illud unum necessarium

XXII, 14 et: *supra lin. B²*

began to exist from not-being, (2) can be thought not to exist, (3) returns to not-being unless it exists through something else, (4) has a past which it no longer is, and (5) has a future which it not yet is—this does not exist in the proper and unqualified sense |of "existing"|.[69] But You are what You are, because whatever You once or in any respect are, this You are always and as a whole.

And in a proper and unqualified sense You are who You are,[70] because You have neither a past nor a future but only a present, and because You cannot be thought ever not to exist. And You are life and light and wisdom and blessedness and eternity and many such good things. Nevertheless, You are only one supreme good, altogether sufficient unto Yourself, needing no one |else| but needed by all |other| things in order to exist and to fare well.

CHAPTER TWENTY-THREE

The Father, the Son, and the Holy Spirit are equally
this |supreme| good. It is the one necessary |Being|,
which is every good, complete good, and the only good.

You, God the Father, are this |supreme| good; and Your Word, i.e., Your Son, is this |supreme good|.[71] For in the Word by which You speak of Yourself there cannot be anything other than what You are or anything greater or lesser than You. For Your Word is as true as You are truthful; and so, just as are You, it is Truth itself—not |a truth that is| other than You. You are so simple |in nature| that from You cannot be begotten anything other than what You are. The one Love common to You and to Your Son, viz., the Holy Spirit who proceeds from You both, is |also| this |same supreme good|.[72] For this Love is not unequal to You or to Your Son; for You love Yourself and Your Son, and He loves Himself and You, in proportion to Your greatness and His. And what is not unequal to You and to Him is not something other than You and Him; nor can there proceed from Supreme Simplicity anything which is other than what the one from whom it proceeds is. But that which each of them (considered distinctly) is, this the Trinity—Father, Son, and Holy Spirit—is as a whole and all together. For each, considered distinctly, is nothing other than a supremely simple oneness and a supremely singular simplicity which cannot be made multiple and cannot be different things.

Now, one thing is necessary,[73] viz., the one necessary |Being| in which

20 in quo est omne bonum—immo quod est omne et unum et totum et solum bonum.

CAPITULUM XXIV

Coniectatio quale et quantum sit hoc bonum.

Excita nunc, anima mea, et erige totum intellectum tuum, et cogita quantum potes, quale et quantum sit illud bonum. Si enim singula bona
5 delectabilia sunt, cogita intente quam delectabile sit illud bonum quod continet iucunditatem omnium bonorum; et non qualem in rebus creatis sumus experti, sed tanto differentem quanto differt creator a creatura. Si enim bona est vita creata: quam bona est vita creatrix? Si iucunda est salus facta: quam iucunda est salus quae facit omnem salutem? Si ama-
10 bilis est sapientia in cognitione rerum conditarum: quam amabilis est sapientia quae omnia condidit ex nihilo? Denique si multae et magnae delectationes sunt in rebus delectabilibus: qualis et quanta delectatio est in illo qui fecit ipsa delectabilia?

CAPITULUM XXV

Quae et quanta bona sint fruentibus eo.

O qui hoc bono fruetur: quid illi erit, et quid illi non erit! Certe quidquid volet erit, et quod nolet non erit. Ibi quippe erunt bona corporis et ani-
5 mae, qualia "nec oculus vidit nec auris audivit nec cor hominis" cogi-tavit. Cur ergo per multa vagaris, homuncio, quaerendo bona animae tuae et corporis tui? Ama unum bonum, in quo sunt omnia bona, et sufficit. Desidera simplex bonum, quod est omne bonum, et satis est. Quid enim amas, caro mea, quid desideras, anima mea? Ibi est, ibi est
10 quidquid amatis, quidquid desideratis. Si delectat pulchritudo: "fulgebunt iusti sicut sol." Si velocitas aut fortitudo, aut libertas corporis cui nihil obsistere possit: "erunt similes angelis dei," quia "seminatur corpus ani-male, et surget corpus spirituale," potestate utique non natura. Si longa et salubris vita: ibi est sana aeternitas et aeterna sanitas, quia "iusti in

---

XXIV, 4 illud bonum: bonum illud *ad* illud bonum *transponit B*
XXV, 11 sicut: *om. B habent ET*

there is every good—yea, which is every good,[74] one good, complete good, and the only good.

CHAPTER TWENTY-FOUR
A conjecture about what kind of good this is and about how great it is.

And now, my soul, arouse and elevate your whole understanding; ponder as best you can what kind of good this is and how great it is. For if the individual good things are enjoyable, reflect attentively upon how enjoyable is that Good which contains the joyfulness of all good things. |This is| not the kind |of joyfulness| that we have experienced in created things but rather is as different |therefrom| as the Creator is different from the creature. For if created life is good, how good is that Life which creates! If created security (*salus*) is enjoyable, how enjoyable is the Salvation (*salus*) which creates all security! If wisdom in regard to the knowledge of created things is lovable, how lovable is the Wisdom which created all things from nothing! In short, if there are many great joys in enjoyable things, how rich and how great is the joy |to be found| in Him who made these enjoyable things!

CHAPTER TWENTY-FIVE
The kinds and the quantity of goods for those who enjoy this |Good|.

O what he shall have who will enjoy this Good, and what he shall not have! Surely, he shall have what he shall want and shall not have what he shall not want.[75] Indeed, he shall there possess the goods of the body and of the soul—|goods| of such kind as the eye has not seen nor the ear heard nor the human heart conceived.[76] O insignificant man, why then do you go from one good to another in quest of what is good for your soul and good for your body? Love the one Good in which are all goods, and it shall suffice |you|. Desire the simple Good which itself is every good, and it shall be enough |for you|. For what do you love, O my flesh? What do you desire, O my soul? It is there; all that both of you love is there, all that you desire. If *beauty* delights |you|: the just shall shine forth as the sun.[77] If |you take delight in| the *swiftness, strength,* or *freedom of a body* which nothing can resist: |the just| shall be like the angels of God,[78] because their bodies are sown as fleshly but will arise as spiritual[79]—|bodies spiritual|, of course, in power not in nature. If a *long* and *sound life* |delights you|: a sound eternity and an eternal soundness

15 perpetuum vivent" et "salus iustorum a domino." Si satietas: satiabuntur "cum apparuerit gloria" dei. Si ebrietas: "inebriabuntur ab ubertate domus" dei. Si melodia: ibi angelorum chori concinunt sine fine deo. Si quaelibet non immunda sed munda voluptas: "torrente voluptatis suae potabit eos" deus. Si sapientia: ipsa dei sapientia ostendet eis seipsam. Si
20 amicitia: diligent deum plus quam seipsos, et invicem tamquam seipsos, et deus illos plus quam illi seipsos, quia illi illum et se et invicem per illum, et ille se et illos per seipsum. Si concordia: omnibus illis erit una voluntas, quia nulla illis erit nisi sola dei voluntas. Si potestas: omnipotentes erunt suae voluntatis ut deus suae. Nam sicut poterit deus quod
25 volet per seipsum, ita poterunt illi quod volent per illum—quia sicut illi non aliud volent quam quod ille, ita ille volet quidquid illi volent; et quod ille volet non poterit non esse. Si honor et divitiae: deus suos servos bonos et fideles supra multa constituet—immo filii dei et dii vocabuntur et erunt. Et ubi erit filius eius, ibi erunt et illi, "heredes quidem dei, co-
30 heredes autem Christi." Si vera securitas: certe ita certi erunt numquam et nullatenus ista vel potius istud bonum sibi defuturum, sicut certi erunt se non sua sponte illud amissuros, nec dilectorem deum illud dilectoribus suis invitis ablaturum, nec aliquid deo potentius invitos deum et illos separaturum.
35   Gaudium vero quale aut quantum est, ubi tale ac tantum bonum est? Cor humanum, cor indigens, cor expertum aerumnas—immo obrutum aerumnis: quantum gauderes, si his omnibus abundares? Interroga intima tua, si capere possint gaudium suum de tanta beatitudine sua. Sed certe si quis alius, quem omnino sicut teipsum diligeres, eandem beatitudinem
40 haberet, duplicaretur gaudium tuum, quia non minus gauderes pro eo quam pro teipso. Si vero duo vel tres vel multo plures idipsum haberent,

XXV, 21 et[3]: *supra lin. B[2]*
XXV, 38 possint: *ex* possunt *(?) corr. B*

is there, because the just shall live forever[80] and the salvation of the just comes from the Lord.[81] If |you delight in| *fulness*: |the just| shall be filled when the glory of God is manifested.[82] If *intoxication*: they shall be intoxicated from the abundance of the house of God.[83] If *melody*: there choirs of angels sing to God without end. If any *pleasure* whatsoever that is not impure: God shall grant to them to drink from the torrent of His pleasure.[84] If *wisdom*: the wisdom of God shall manifest itself unto them.[85] If *friendship*: they shall love God more than themselves and shall love one another as themselves;[86] and God |shall love| them more than they |love| themselves. For through Him they |shall love| Him and themselves and one another; but He |loves| Himself and them through Himself. If |you delight in| *unison*: they shall all have one will, because they shall have no will except the will of God. If *power*: they shall be all-powerful in will, even as God is all-powerful in will. For just as God is able to do through Himself that which He wills, so they shall be able to do through Him that which they shall will. For just as they shall will nothing other than what He |shall will|, so He shall will whatever they shall will. And what He shall will cannot fail to occur. If *honor* and *riches* |delight you|: God shall set His good and faithful servants over many things;[87] indeed, they shall be, as well as be called, sons of God[88] and gods.[89] And where His Son shall be, there they too shall be;[90] indeed, |they are| heirs of God and joint-heirs with Christ.[91] If true *security*: surely, they shall be certain that they shall never in any way lack these many goods—or, rather, this |one| Good—even as they shall be certain (1) that they shall not lose it of their own free wills, (2) that God, who loves them, shall not rend it away from them against their wills while they are loving Him, and (3) that nothing more powerful than God shall separate them from God against their wills.[92]

But where a good of such quality and of such magnitude is present, how rich and how intense is the |corresponding| joy! O human heart, heart beset with need, heart versed in tribulations—yea, overwhelmed with tribulations—how much you would rejoice were you to abound in all these |goods|! Ask your inmost self whether it can contain its own joy over its own so great happiness. Now, surely, if someone else whom you loved in every respect as you do yourself were also to have the same |kind of| happiness, then your own joy would be doubled; for you would rejoice for him no less than for yourself. And if two or three or many more |persons| were to have the same |kind of joy|, you would rejoice for

tantundem pro singulis quantum pro teipso gauderes, si singulos sicut teipsum amares. Ergo in illa perfecta caritate innumerabilium beatorum angelorum et hominum, ubi nullus minus diliget alium quam seipsum, 45 non aliter gaudebit quisque pro singulis aliis quam pro seipso. Si ergo cor hominis de tanto suo bono vix capiet gaudium suum: quomodo capax erit tot et tantorum gaudiorum?

    Et utique quoniam quantum quisque diligit aliquem, tantum de bono eius gaudet: sicut in illa perfecta felicitate unusquisque plus amabit sine 50 comparatione deum quam se et omnes alios secum, ita plus gaudebit absque existimatione de felicitate dei quam de sua et omnium aliorum secum. Sed si deum sic diligent toto corde, tota mente, tota anima, ut tamen totum cor, tota mens, tota anima non sufficiat dignitati dilectionis: profecto sic gaudebunt toto corde, tota mente, tota anima ut totum cor, 55 tota mens, tota anima non sufficiat plenitudini gaudii.

CAPITULUM XXVI

An hoc sit gaudium plenum quod promittit dominus.

Deus meus et dominus meus, spes mea et gaudium cordis mei, dic animae meae, si hoc est gaudium de quo nobis dicis per filium tuum: "petite et 5 accipietis, ut gaudium vestrum sit plenum." Inveni namque gaudium quoddam plenum, et plus quam plenum. Pleno quippe corde, plena mente, plena anima, pleno toto homine gaudio illo: adhuc supra modum supererit gaudium. Non ergo totum illud gaudium intrabit in gaudentes, sed toti gaudentes intrabunt in gaudium. Dic, domine, dic servo tuo intus 10 in corde suo, si hoc est gaudium in quod intrabunt servi tui, qui intrabunt in gaudium domini sui. Sed gaudium illud certe quo gaudebunt electi tui, "nec oculus vidit, nec auris audivit, nec in cor hominis ascendit." Nondum ergo dixi aut cogitavi, domine, quantum gaudebunt illi beati tui. Utique tantum gaudebunt, quantum amabunt; tantum amabunt, quantum cognos- 15 cent. Quantum te cognoscent, domine, tunc, et quantum te amabunt?

each of them as much as for yourself—assuming that you loved each as you do yourself. Therefore, in the case of that perfect love on the part of countless blessed angels and men, where no one |of them| will love the other less than himself, each |of them| will rejoice for each of the others no differently than for himself. If, then, the heart of man shall scarcely |be able to| contain its own joy over its own so great good, how shall it be able to contain so many |other| very great joys?

Surely, each person rejoices in another's good |fortune| to the extent that he loves this other. Therefore, in that perfect happiness, just as each |person| will love God incomparably more than himself and all those who are with himself, so |each| will rejoice inestimably more over the blessedness of God than over either his own blessedness or that of all the others who are with himself. But if |each of the just| shall love God— with all his heart, all his mind, and all his soul,[93] but in such way that his whole heart, whole mind, and whole soul will not suffice |to fill up the measure of God's| worthiness to be loved—surely, with all his heart, all his mind, and all his soul |each| shall so rejoice that his whole heart, whole mind, and whole soul will not be able to contain the fulness of |that| joy.

CHAPTER TWENTY-SIX
Whether this is the full joy which the Lord promises.

My Lord and my God, my hope and my heart's joy, tell my soul whether this is the joy about which You speak to us through Your Son, |who said|: ask and you shall receive, so that your joy may be full.[94] For I have found an abundant joy—even a superabundant joy. Indeed, when the heart, the mind, the soul—when the whole man is filled with that joy, there will still remain joy without limit. Therefore, the whole of that joy will not enter into those who are rejoicing; instead, all those who are rejoicing will enter into Your joy. Speak, O Lord, and tell Your servant in his heart whether this is the joy into which Your servants will enter when they will enter into the joy of their Lord.[95] Now, surely, no eye has seen, no ear has heard—nor has there entered into the heart of man— that joy with which Your elect ones will rejoice.[96] Therefore, I have not yet said or thought, O Lord, how much Your blessed ones will rejoice. Surely, they will rejoice in the degree that they will love. And they will love in the degree that they will know. How much will they know You

Certe "nec oculus vidit, nec auris audivit, nec in cor hominis ascendit" in hac vita, quantum te cognoscent et amabunt in illa vita.

Oro, deus, cognoscam te, amem te, ut gaudeam de te. Et si non possum in hac vita ad plenum, vel proficiam in dies usque dum veniat illud ad

20 plenum. Proficiat hic in me notitia tui, et ibi fiat plena; crescat amor tuus, et ibi sit plenus: ut hic gaudium meum sit in spe magnum, et ibi sit in re plenum. Domine, per filium tuum iubes—immo consulis—petere; et promittis accipere, ut gaudium nostrum plenum sit. Peto, domine, quod consulis per admirabilem consiliarium nostrum; accipiam quod promittis

25 per veritatem tuam, ut gaudium meum plenum sit. Deus verax, peto; accipiam, ut gaudium meum plenum sit. Meditetur interim inde mens mea; loquatur inde lingua mea. Amet illud cor meum; sermocinetur os meum. Esuriat illud anima mea; sitiat caro mea; desideret tota substantia mea: donec intrem in gaudium domini mei, qui est trinus et unus deus,

30 benedictus in saecula. Amen.

XXVI 30 Amen: Explicit proslogion (s *supra lin.*) liber anselmi cantuariensis archiepiscopi *add. B*

in that day, O Lord? How much will they love You? Surely, in this life no eye has seen, no ear has heard, nor has there entered into the heart of man how much they will know and love You in the next life.

O God, I pray, let me know and love You, so that I may rejoice in You. And if I cannot in this life |know, love, and rejoice in You| fully, at least let me advance day by day until the point of fulness comes. Let knowledge of You progress in me here and be made full |in me| there. Let love for You grow |in me here| and be |made| full |in me| there, so that here my joy may be great with expectancy and there may be full in realization. O Lord, You command—or, rather, You counsel—|us| to ask through Your Son; and You promise |that we shall| receive, so that our joy may be full.[97] O Lord, I ask for what You counsel through our marvelous Counselor;[98] may I receive what You promise through Your Truth, so that my joy may be full. O God of Truth, I ask; may I receive, so that my joy may be full. Until then, may my mind meditate upon |what You have promised|; may my tongue speak of it. May my heart love it; may my mouth proclaim it. May my soul hunger for it; may my flesh thirst for |it|;[99] may my whole substance desire |it| until such time as I enter into the joy of my Lord,[100] the trine and one God, blessed forever.[101] Amen.

GAUNILO PRO INSIPIENTE

ON BEHALF OF THE FOOL

GAUNILO PRO INSIPIENTE

QUID AD HAEC RESPONDEAT QUIDAM PRO INSIPIENTE

[1.] Dubitanti utrum sit vel neganti quod sit aliqua talis natura qua nihil maius cogitari possit, cum esse illam hinc dicitur primo probari quod ipse negans vel ambigens de illa, iam habeat eam in intellectu cum audiens illam dici, id quod dicitur intelligit; deinde quia quod intelligit, necesse est
5 ut non in solo intellectu sed etiam in re sit, et hoc ita probatur quia maius est esse et in re quam in solo intellectu, et si illud in solo est intellectu, maius illo erit quidquid etiam in re fuerit, ac sic maius omnibus minus erit aliquo et non erit maius omnibus, quod utique repugnat; et ideo necesse est ut maius omnibus, quod esse iam probatum est in intellectu, non in
10 solo intellectu sed et in re sit, quoniam aliter maius omnibus esse non poterit: respondere forsan potest:

[2.] Quod hoc iam esse dicitur in intellectu meo, non ob aliud nisi quia id quod dicitur intelligo: nonne et quaecumque falsa ac nullo prorsus modo in seipsis existentia in intellectu habere similiter dici possem, cum ea dicente aliquo, quaecumque ille diceret, ego intelligerem? Nisi forte tale
5 illud constat esse ut non eo modo quo etiam falsa quaeque vel dubia, haberi possit in cogitatione, et ideo non dicor illud auditum cogitare vel in cogitatione habere, sed intelligere et in intellectu habere, quia scilicet non

---

GAUNILO PRO INSIPIENTE: *supplevi*   *Titulus* Quid . . . insipiente: *sic habet B*
1 1 *Numeros tractatus supplevi*
1 6 et[1]: *supra lin. B[2]*
1 10 et: *supra lin. B*

ON BEHALF OF THE FOOL

What Someone,[1] on Behalf of the Fool,[2]
Replies to These |Arguments|.

[1.][3] To one who doubts whether there exists or denies that there exists
some such nature than which nothing greater can be thought, the claim
is made that the existence of this nature is proved from two considera-
tions: first, from the fact that the very one who doubts or denies |the
existence of| this |nature| already has this |nature| in his understanding
when, upon hearing it spoken of, he understands what is said; and,
secondly, from the fact that, necessarily, what he understands exists not
only in his understanding but also in reality. This |second consideration|
is |allegedly| established by the following reasoning:

> To exist also in reality is greater than to exist solely in the understanding. Now, if
> this thing existed solely in the understanding, then whatever[4] existed also in reality
> would be greater than it. Thus, the greater than all |others|[5] would be less great
> than some |other| and would not be greater than all |others|—something which,
> surely, is contradictory. Therefore, it is necessary that the greater than all |others|,
> having already been proved to exist in the understanding, exist not only in the
> understanding but also in reality. For otherwise it could not be greater than all
> |others|.

When |these claims are made, the doubter or denier, i.e., the Fool,| can
perhaps make the replies |which follow|.

[2.][6] Regarding the fact that this thing is said to exist in my under-
standing simply because I understand what is said, |I ask|: could I not
similarly be said to have in my understanding—because if someone were
to speak of them I would understand whatever he said—all manner of
false |i.e., unreal| things that in no way exist in themselves?[7] But suppose
it to be evident that this thing |than which nothing greater can be
thought| is such that it cannot exist in thought in the same way as even
all manner of false and doubtfully real things do. And |suppose that|,
accordingly, I am not said to think this thing of which I have heard (or
to have it in thought) but |am said| to understand it (and to have it in the
understanding) since I could not think it except by understanding (i.e.,

265

possim hoc aliter cogitare, nisi intelligendo, id est scientia comprehendendo, re ipsa illud existere. Sed si hoc est, primo quidem non hic erit iam
10 aliud idemque tempore praecedens habere rem in intellectu, et aliud idque tempore sequens intelligere rem esse—ut fit de pictura, quae prius est in animo pictoris, deinde in opere. Deinde vix umquam poterit esse credibile, cum dictum et auditum fuerit istud, non eo modo posse cogitari non esse quo etiam potest non esse deus. Nam si non potest: cur contra negantem
15 aut dubitantem quod sit aliqua talis natura, tota ista disputatio est assumpta? Postremo quod tale sit illud ut non possit nisi mox cogitatum, indubitabilis existentiae suae certo percipi intellectu: indubio aliquo probandum mihi est argumento, non autem isto quod iam sit hoc in intellectu meo cum auditum intelligo, in quo similiter esse posse quaecumque alia
20 incerta vel etiam falsa ab aliquo cuius verba intelligerem dicta adhuc puto—et insuper magis, si illa deceptus ut saepe fit crederem, qui istud nondum credo.

[3.] Unde nec illud exemplum de pictore picturam quam facturus est iam in intellectu habente, satis potest huic argumento congruere. Illa enim pictura antequam fiat in ipsa pictoris arte habetur, et tale quippiam in arte artificis alicuius nihil est aliud quam pars quaedam intelligentiae ipsius—
5 quia et sicut sanctus Augustinus ait: "cum faber arcam facturus in opere, prius habet illam in arte; arca quae fit in opere non est vita; arca quae est in arte vita est, quia vivit anima artificis, in qua sunt ista omnia antequam proferantur." Ut quid enim in vivente artificis anima vita sunt ista, nisi quia nil sunt aliud quam scientia vel intelligentia animae ipsius? At vero
10 quidquid extra illa quae ad ipsam mentis noscuntur pertinere naturam aut auditum aut excogitatum intellectu percipitur verum: aliud sine dubio est verum illud, aliud intellectus ipse quo capitur. Quocirca etiam si verum sit

by comprehending with cognitive certainty) that it exists in reality.[8] But if this were so, then (to begin with) there would no longer be a difference here between first having the thing in the understanding and subsequently understanding the thing to exist—as happens in the case of a painting, which first is in the painter's mind and then later is an actual product. Secondly, it could scarcely at all be plausible that when this thing is spoken of and heard of, it could not be thought not to exist in the way that even God can |be thought| not to exist. For if |this thing| cannot |be thought not to exist|, why was your entire disputation enjoined against one who doubts or denies that there is any such nature |as this|? Lastly, the claim "This |being| is such that as soon as it is thought of, it cannot but be apprehended with sure understanding of its indubitable existence" would have to be proved to me by means of an indubitable consideration, not by means of the |consideration| that this thing is already in my understanding when I understand what I have heard. |For| I still maintain that in my understanding there could likewise be whatever other dubiously real and even false things are spoken of by someone whose words I have understood. And it would be all the more true |that they are in my understanding| if I, who do not yet believe that this thing |exists|, were mistakenly to believe that those things |exist|, as often happens.

[3.] Hence, even the example about the painter's already having in his understanding a picture which he is going to paint cannot satisfactorily cohere with your line of reasoning. For before that painting is made it exists in the painter's art. And such a thing in the art of a painter is nothing other than a part of the painter's understanding. For as St. Augustine says:

> When a craftsman is about to make a chest, he first has it in his art. The chest which is produced is not alive; but the chest which is in the art is alive because the soul of the craftsman is alive, and in it exist all these |artefacts| before they are produced.[9]

For why are these |artefacts| alive in the living soul of the craftsman except because they are nothing other than his soul's certain knowledge and its understanding? But except for things which are known to pertain to the very nature of the mind, whatever true |i.e., real| thing, when heard of or thought of, is apprehended by the understanding: without doubt that true thing is other than the understanding by which it is appre-

esse aliquid quo maius quidquam nequeat cogitari, non tamen hoc auditum et intellectum tale est qualis nondum facta pictura in intellectu
15 pictoris.

[4.] Huc accedit illud quod praetaxatum est superius: quia scilicet illud
omnibus quae cogitari possint maius, quod nihil aliud posse esse dicitur
quam ipse deus, tam ego secundum rem vel ex specie mihi vel ex genere
notam, cogitare auditum vel in intellectu habere non possum, quam nec
5 ipsum deum, quem utique ob hoc ipsum etiam non esse cogitare possum.
Neque enim aut rem ipsam novi aut ex alia possum conicere simili, quan-
doquidem et tu talem asseris illam ut esse non possit simile quidquam.
Nam si de homine aliquo mihi prorsus ignoto, quem etiam esse nescirem,
dici tamen aliquid audirem: per illam specialem generalemve notitiam qua
10 quid sit homo vel homines novi, de illo quoque secundum rem ipsam quae
est homo cogitare possem. Et tamen fieri posset ut mentiente illo qui
diceret, ipse quem cogitarem homo non esset—cum tamen ego de illo
secundum veram nihilominus rem, non quae esset ille homo, sed quae est
homo quilibet, cogitarem. Nec sic igitur ut haberem falsum istud in cogita-
15 tione vel in intellectu, habere possum illud cum audio dici deus aut
aliquid omnibus maius, cum quando illud secundum rem veram mihi-
que notam cogitare possem, istud omnino nequeam nisi tantum secundum
vocem, secundum quam solam aut vix aut numquam potest ullum cogitari
verum. Siquidem cum ita cogitatur, non tam vox ipsa (quae res est utique
20 vera), hoc est litterarum sonus vel syllabarum, quam vocis auditae significatio cogitetur—sed non ita ut ab illo qui novit quid ea soleat voce
significari, a quo scilicet cogitatur secundum rem vel in sola cogitatione

---

4 20 litterarum: literarum *ad* litterarum *corr.* (t *supra lin.*) B

hended. Therefore, even if it were true that there exists something than which a greater cannot be thought, nevertheless when it was heard of and understood it would not be like an as yet unproduced painting in the understanding of a painter.

[4.] To this may be added a point previously alluded to: viz., that upon hearing of that |which is| greater than all |others| that can be thought (which is said to be able to be nothing other than God Himself), I cannot think of this thing (or have it in the understanding) by reference to any object known to me through species or genus—just as |in this way I| also |can| not |think of| God Himself (whom, surely, for this very reason, I can also think not to exist). For neither am I acquainted with this thing itself nor am I able to make inferences |about it| on the basis of some other similar thing; for even you maintain that it is such that there cannot be anything else similar |to it|.[10] Now, suppose that I were to hear something being said about a man totally a stranger to me—|a man| whom I was not even sure existed. Still, by means of the specific or generic knowledge by which I know what a man is (or what men are), I would be able to think of him as well, by reference to the very thing that a man is. However, it could happen that the one who told |me about this stranger| was lying and that the man whom I thought of does not exist. Nonetheless, I would still have thought of him by reference to the true |i.e., real| thing which *any* man is (though not which *that* man is). But when I hear someone speaking of God or of something greater than all |others|, I cannot have this thing |in my thought and understanding| in the way that I might have that false thing |i.e., that unreal man| in my thought and understanding. For although I can think of that |nonexistent man| by reference to a true |i.e., a real| thing known to me, I cannot at all |think of| this |supreme| thing except only with respect to the word. And with respect only to a word a true thing can scarcely or not at all be thought of.[11] For, indeed, when one thinks in this way |i.e., with respect to a mere word|, he thinks not so much the word itself (i.e., not so much the sound of the letters or of the syllables), which assuredly is a true thing, as he does the signification of the word that is heard. Yet, |the signification is| not |thought| in the manner of one who knows what is usually signified by this word—i.e., one who thinks in accordance with the true thing, even if |it exists| in thought alone. Rather, |the signification is thought| in the manner of one who does not know that |which is usually

veram, verum ut ab eo qui illud non novit et solummodo cogitat secundum animi motum illius auditu vocis effectum significationemque percep-
25 tae vocis conantem effingere sibi. Quod mirum est, si umquam rei veritate potuerit. Ita ergo nec prorsus aliter adhuc in intellectu meo constat illud haberi, cum audio intelligoque dicentem esse aliquid maius omnibus quae valeant cogitari.

Haec de eo: quod summa illa natura iam esse dicitur in intellectu meo.

[5.] Quod autem et in re necessario esse inde mihi probatur quia nisi fuerit, quidquid est in re maius illa erit, ac per hoc non erit illud maius omnibus quod utique iam esse probatum est in intellectu: ad hoc respondeo: Si esse dicendum est in intellectu, quod secundum veritatem cuius-
5 quam rei nequit saltem cogitari: et hoc in meo sic esse non denego. Sed quia per hoc esse quoque in re non potest ullatenus obtinere: illud ei esse adhuc penitus non concedo, quousque mihi argumento probetur indubio. Quod qui esse dicit hoc quod maius omnibus, aliter non erit omnibus maius: non satis attendit cui loquatur. Ego enim nondum dico—immo
10 etiam nego vel dubito—ulla re vera esse maius illud; nec aliud ei esse concedo quam illud, si dicendum est "esse," cum secundum vocem tantum auditam rem prorsus ignotam sibi conatur animus effingere. Quomodo igitur inde mihi probatur maius illud rei veritate subsistere quia constet illud maius omnibus esse, cum id ego eo usque negem adhuc
15 dubitemve constare ut ne in intellectu quidem vel cogitatione mea eo saltem modo maius ipsum esse dicam quo dubia etiam multa sunt et incerta? Prius enim certum mihi necesse est fiat re vera esse alicubi maius ipsum; et tum demum ex eo quod maius est omnibus, in seipso quoque subsistere non erit ambiguum.

signified by the word| but who thinks only (1) according to the movement-of-mind that is brought about by hearing this word and (2) in the fashion of one trying to represent to himself the signification of the word he has heard. (But it would be surprising if he could ever |in this manner discern| the true nature of the thing.) Therefore, it is still evident that in this way, and not at all in any other way, this thing is in my understanding when I hear and understand someone who says that there is something greater than all |others| that can be thought.

All of this |is my reply| with regard to the claim that this supreme nature already is in my understanding.

[5.] But that, necessarily, |this being| exists also in reality is proved to me from the following |consideration|: unless it existed |in reality|, whatever does exist in reality would be greater than it; and, accordingly, that which (assuredly) was proved to exist already in the understanding would not be greater than all |others|.

To this |reasoning| I reply: If that which cannot even be thought in accordance with the true nature of anything must |nonetheless| be said to be in the understanding, then I do not deny that in this |improper| sense it is in my |understanding|. But since from this |concession| its existence also in reality cannot at all be inferred, I still will not at all concede to it that existence |in reality| until |that existence| is proved to me by an indubitable line of reasoning. Now, anyone who says, "That which is greater than all |others| exists, |for| otherwise it would not be greater than all |others|" does not pay enough attention to whom he is speaking. For I do not yet admit—indeed, I even doubt and deny—that that |which is| greater |than all others| exists at all in reality. I do not concede to it any other existence than that |existence| (if it is to be called existence) present when the mind tries to represent to itself a thing completely unknown, |trying to do so| in accordance with a word which it has merely heard. How, then, from the |alleged| fact that it is, patently, greater than all |others| does one prove to me that that |which is| greater |than all others| exists in reality? For I still so doubt and deny it to exist that I claim that this greater |than all others| is not even in my thought and understanding even in the way that numerous doubtfully real and uncertainly real things are. For I must first be made certain that this greater |than all others| exists somewhere in reality; only then will there be no doubt that *because* it is greater than all |others| it exists also in itself |i.e., in reality|.[12]

[6.] Exempli gratia: Aiunt quidam alicubi oceani esse insulam, quam ex difficultate vel potius impossibilitate inveniendi quod non est, cognominant aliqui "perditam," quamque fabulantur multo amplius quam de fortunatis insulis fertur, divitiarum deliciarumque omnium inaestima-
5 bili ubertate pollere, nulloque possessore aut habitatore universis aliis quas incolunt homines terris possidendorum redundantia usquequaque praestare. Hoc ita esse dicat mihi quispiam, et ego facile dictum, in quo nihil est difficultatis, intelligam. At si tunc velut consequenter adiungat ac dicat "Non potes ultra dubitare insulam illam terris omnibus praestantiorem
10 vere esse alicubi in re quam et in intellectu tuo non ambigis esse. Et quia praestantius est non in intellectu solo sed etiam esse in re, ideo sic eam necesse est esse, quia nisi fuerit, quaecumque alia in re est terra, praestantior illa erit, ac sic ipsa iam a te praestantior intellecta praestantior non erit"—si inquam per haec ille mihi velit astruere de insula illa quod vere
15 sit ambigendum ultra non esse: aut iocari illum credam aut nescio quem stultiorem debeam reputare, utrum me si ei concedam, an illum si se putet aliqua certitudine insulae illius essentiam astruxisse, nisi prius ipsam praestantiam eius solummodo sicut rem vere atque indubie existentem nec ullatenus sicut falsum aut incertum aliquid in intellectu meo
20 esse docuerit.

[7.] Haec interim ad obiecta insipiens ille responderit. Cui cum deinceps asseritur tale esse maius illud ut nec sola cogitatione valeat non esse, et hoc rursus non aliunde probatur quam eo ipso quod aliter non erit omnibus maius: idem ipsum possit referre responsum et dicere: Quando
5 enim ego rei veritate esse tale aliquid (hoc est, maius omnibus) dixi, ut ex hoc mihi debeat probari in tantum etiam re ipsa id esse ut nec possit cogitari non esse?

Quapropter certissimo primitus aliquo probandum est argumento ali-

6 10 et¹: *supra lin. B*

[6.] For example, some people say that there is an island somewhere in the ocean. Some call it Lost Island because of the difficulty—or, rather, the impossibility—of finding what does not exist. They say that it abounds with inestimable plenitude of all riches and all delights—much more so than is reported of the Isles of the Blessed. Having no owner or inhabitant |it is said| to excel completely—because of the superabundant goods for the taking—all other lands in which men dwell. Now, should someone tell me that this is the case, I would easily understand what he said, wherein there is nothing difficult. But suppose he were then to add, as if it followed logically: "You can no more doubt that this island which is more excellent than all |other| lands truly exists somewhere in reality than you |can| doubt that |it| is in your understanding. And since |for it| to exist not only in the understanding but also in reality is more excellent |than for it to exist in the understanding alone|, then, necessarily, it exists in reality. For if it did not exist |in reality|, then whatever other land did exist in reality would be more excellent than it, and thus this |island|, which has already been understood by you to be more excellent |than all other lands|, would not be more excellent |than all others|." [13] If through these |considerations| he wanted to prove to me regarding this island that it ought no longer to be doubted truly to exist, then either I would think he were jesting or I would not know whom I ought to regard as the more foolish—either myself, were I to assent thereto, or him, were he to suppose that he had proved with any degree of certainty the existence of this island. For he would first have to prove that this island's excellence is in my understanding only as |is the excellence of| a thing which truly and certainly exists and not at all as |is the excellence of| a thing which is false or doubtfully real.

[7.] These replies the Fool might make to the |arguments| presented at the outset. And when he is next told that that |which is| greater |than all others| is such that not even conceivably is it able not to exist, and this |step|, in turn, is proved from no other consideration than that otherwise |this being| would not be greater than all |others|, he can point to this same reply and ask: "When, indeed, did I admit that some such thing— viz., one |which is| greater than all |others|—exists in reality, so that from this |admission| there could be proved to me that it exists so greatly also in reality that it cannot even be thought not to exist?"

Therefore, first of all one must prove by a most certain line of reason-

quam superiorem (hoc est, maiorem ac meliorem) omnium quae sunt
10 esse naturam, ut ex hoc alia iam possimus omnia comprobare, quibus
necesse est illud quod maius ac melius est omnibus non carere. Cum
autem dicitur quod summa res ista non esse nequeat cogitari: melius
fortasse diceretur quod non esse aut etiam posse non esse, non possit
intelligi. Nam secundum proprietatem verbi istius falsa nequeunt intelligi,
15 quae possunt utique eo modo cogitari, quo deum non esse insipiens
cogitavit. Et me quoque esse certissime scio, sed et posse non esse nihilominus scio. Summum vero illud quod est, scilicet deus, et esse et non
esse non posse indubitanter intelligo. Cogitare autem me non esse quamdiu esse certissime scio, nescio utrum possim. Sed si possum, cur non et
20 quidquid aliud eadem certitudine scio? Si autem non possum, non erit
iam istud proprium deo.

[8.] Cetera libelli illius tam veraciter et tam praeclare sunt magnifice-
que disserta, tanta denique referta utilitate et pii ac sancti affectus intimo
quodam odore fragrantia, ut nullo modo propter illa quae in initiis recte
quidem sensa, sed minus firmiter argumentata sunt, ista sint contem-
5 nenda; sed illa potius argumentanda robustius, ac sic omnia cum ingenti
veneratione et laude suscipienda.

---

7 17 et²: *supra lin. B*
8 5 argumentanda: argumentanda (n² *supra lin.*) *B*

ing that there exists a nature which is higher (i.e., greater and better) than all |other| existing things, so that on the basis of this |proof| we can go on to derive all the other |characteristics| which that which is greater and better than all |others| must not fail to have. But when one says that this Supreme Thing *cannot be thought* not to exist,[14] he might better say that it *cannot be understood* not to exist or even to be able not to exist. For in accordance with the proper meaning of this verb |viz., "to understand"|, false things |i.e., unreal things| cannot be understood; but, surely, they can be thought—in the way in which the Fool thought that God does not exist.[15] Now, I know most certainly that I too exist; yet, I also know no less certainly that |I| am able not to exist. Moreover, I understand indubitably that that |being| which is supreme, viz., God, exists and cannot fail to exist. Still, I do not know whether, during the time when I know most certainly that I exist, I can think that I do not exist. But if I can, why |can I| not also |think not to exist| whatever else I know with the same certainty |as I know my own existence|? On the other hand, if I cannot |think that I do not exist|, then this |property of not being able to be thought not to exist| will no longer be a unique characteristic of God.

[8.] The other parts of that treatise are argued so truthfully, so brilliantly, |so| impressively, and, indeed, abound with such great usefulness and with such great fragrance (because of an innermost scent of devout and holy affection) that they are not at all to be despised on account of the things which in the beginning parts are rightly sensed but less cogently argued. Instead, the initial parts are to be more cogently argued—and, thus, all parts to be received with very great respect and praise.

AD GAUNILONEM
RESPONSIO ANSELMI

REPLY TO GAUNILO

AD GAUNILONEM RESPONSIO ANSELMI

QUID AD HAEC RESPONDEAT EDITOR IPSIUS LIBELLI

[I.] Quoniam non me reprehendit in his dictis ille insipiens contra quem sum locutus in meo opusculo, sed quidam non insipiens et catholicus pro insipiente, sufficere mihi potest respondere catholico.

Dicis quidem—quicumque es qui dicis haec posse dicere insipientem—
5 quia non est in intellectu aliquid quo maius cogitari non possit aliter quam quod secundum veritatem cuiusquam rei nequit saltem cogitari, et quia non magis consequitur hoc quod dico *quo maius cogitari non possit* ex eo quia est in intellectu esse et in re, quam perditam insulam certissime existere ex eo quia cum describitur verbis, audiens eam non ambigit
10 in intellectu suo esse. Ego vero dico: Si quo maius cogitari non potest non intelligitur vel cogitatur nec est in intellectu vel cogitatione: profecto deus aut non est quo maius cogitari non possit, aut non intelligitur vel cogitatur et non est in intellectu vel cogitatione. Quod quam falsum sit, fide et conscientia tua pro firmissimo utor argumento. Ergo quo maius
15 cogitari non potest vere intelligitur et cogitatur, et est in intellectu et cogitatione. Quare aut vera non sunt quibus contra conaris probare, aut ex eis non consequitur quod te consequenter opinaris concludere.

Quod autem putas ex eo quia intelligitur aliquid quo maius cogitari nequit, non consequi illud esse in intellectu, nec si est in intellectu ideo
20 esse in re: certe ego dico: si vel cogitari potest esse, necesse est illud esse. Nam quo maius cogitari nequit non potest cogitari esse nisi sine initio. Quidquid autem potest cogitari esse et non est, per initium potest cogitari

AD . . . ANSELMI: *supplevi*   *Titulus* Quid . . . libelli: *sic habet B*
1 1 *Numeros tractatus supplevi*
1 5 non²: *supra lin. B*
1 13 quam: quoniam *BT*   quam *E*
1 14 et: *supra lin. B²*

REPLY TO GAUNILO

What the Author of That Treatise
Replies to These |Objections|.

[1.]¹ Since |the one who| criticizes me, in these statements |of his, is| not
that Fool against whom I spoke in my work but a certain nonfoolish
Catholic on behalf of the Fool, it can suffice for me to reply to the
Catholic.

Now, you argue (whoever you are² who claims that the Fool can
make these |objections|) as follows:

> Something than which a greater cannot be thought is in the understanding in no
> other way than |as something| which cannot even be thought in accordance with
> the true nature of anything. Moreover, from the fact that it (viz., what I am calling
> *that than which a greater cannot be thought*) is in the understanding there does not
> follow that it exists also in reality—any more than there follows that Lost Island
> most certainly exists, from the fact that when it is described in words the one who
> is listening does not doubt that it is in his understanding.

But I contend that if that than which a greater cannot be thought is not
understood or thought and is not in the understanding or in thought,
then, surely, either (1) God is not that than which a greater cannot be
thought or (2) He is not understood or thought and is not in the understanding or in thought. But I make use of your faith and conscience as a
very cogent consideration |in support of| how false these |inferences|
are.³ Therefore, that than which a greater cannot be thought is indeed
understood and thought, and is in your understanding and in your
thought. Hence, either |those premises| are not true by which you try to
prove the opposite or from them there does not follow what you suppose
you infer logically.

From the fact that something than which a greater cannot be thought
is understood there does not follow, you think, that it is in the under-
standing. Or if it is in the understanding, there does not follow, |you
think,| that it exists in reality. But with confidence I assert that if it can
be even thought to exist, it is necessary that it exist. For that than which
a greater cannot be thought can be thought to exist only without a
beginning. Now, whatever can be thought to exist but does not exist can

279

esse. Non ergo quo maius cogitari nequit cogitari potest esse et non est. Si ergo cogitari potest esse, ex necessitate est.

25   Amplius. Si utique vel cogitari potest, necesse est illud esse. Nullus enim negans aut dubitans esse aliquid quo maius cogitari non possit, negat vel dubitat quia si esset, nec actu nec intellectu posset non esse. Aliter namque non esset quo maius cogitari non posset. Sed quidquid cogitari potest et non est: si esset, posset vel actu vel intellectu non esse.

30 Quare si vel cogitari potest, non potest non esse, quo maius cogitari nequit.

Sed ponamus non esse si vel cogitari valet. At quidquid cogitari potest et non est: si esset, non esset quo maius cogitari non possit. Si ergo esset quo maius cogitari non possit, non esset quo maius cogitari non possit—

35 quod nimis est absurdum. Falsum est igitur non esse aliquid quo maius cogitari non possit si vel cogitari potest. Multo itaque magis si intelligi et in intellectu esse potest.

Plus aliquid dicam. Procul dubio quidquid alicubi aut aliquando non est: etiam si est alicubi aut aliquando, potest tamen cogitari numquam et

40 nusquam esse, sicut non est alicubi aut aliquando. Nam quod heri non fuit et hodie est: sicut heri non fuisse intelligitur, ita numquam esse subintelligi potest. Et quod hic non est et alibi est: sicut non est hic, ita potest cogitari nusquam esse. Similiter cuius partes singulae non sunt, ubi aut quando sunt aliae partes, eius omnes partes et ideo ipsum totum possunt

45 cogitari numquam aut nusquam esse. Nam et si dicatur tempus semper esse et mundus ubique, non tamen illud totum semper aut iste totus est

be thought to exist through a beginning. Thus, it is not the case that that than which a greater cannot be thought can be thought to exist and yet does not exist. Therefore, if it can be thought to exist, |there follows|, of necessity, |that| it exists.

Furthermore: if indeed it can be even thought, it is necessary that it exist. For no one who doubts or denies that there exists something than which a greater cannot be thought doubts or denies that if it were to exist it would neither actually nor conceivably (*nec actu nec intellectu*) be able not to exist. For otherwise |i.e., if it existed but in either respect were able not to exist| it would not be that than which a greater cannot be thought. Now, as for whatever can be thought but does not exist: if it were to exist, it would actually and conceivably (*vel actu vel intellectu*) be able not to exist. Therefore, if that than which a greater cannot be thought can be even thought, it is not able not to exist.

But let us suppose that |it| does not exist even though it can be thought. Now, whatever can be thought and yet does not exist would not, if it were to exist, be that than which a greater cannot be thought. Hence, if that than which a greater cannot be thought, |assumed for the sake of the argument not to exist,| were to exist, it would not be that than which a greater cannot be thought—|a consequence| which is utterly absurd. Therefore, it is false |to suppose| that something than which a greater cannot be thought does not exist even though it can be thought. Consequently, |it is| all the more |false to suppose that it does not exist| if it can be understood and can be in the understanding.

I will add a further point. As regards whatever does not exist at some given place or at some given time: without doubt, even if it does exist elsewhere or at another time, it can be thought never and nowhere to exist—even as it does not exist at that given place or at that given time. For with regard to something which did not exist yesterday but does exist today: even as it is understood not to have existed yesterday, so it can be consistently supposed never to exist. And with regard to something which is not in this place but is in that place: even as it is not in this place, so it can be thought nowhere to exist. Likewise, if it is not the case that each of a thing's parts exist where or when its other parts exist, then all of its parts—and thus the thing as a whole—can be thought never or nowhere to exist. For even were we to say that time exists always and that the world exists everywhere, nevertheless it is not the case that time exists always as a whole or that the world exists every-

ubique. Et sicut singulae partes temporis non sunt quando aliae sunt, ita possunt numquam esse cogitari. Et singulae mundi partes, sicut non sunt ubi aliae sunt, ita subintelligi possunt nusquam esse. Sed et quod partibus
50 coniunctum est, cogitatione dissolvi et non esse potest. Quare quidquid alicubi aut aliquando totum non est: etiam si est, potest cogitari non esse. At quo maius nequit cogitari: si est, non potest cogitari non esse. Alioquin si est, non est quo maius cogitari non possit—quod non convenit. Nullatenus ergo alicubi aut aliquando totum non est, sed semper et ubique
55 totum est.

Putasne aliquatenus posse cogitari vel intelligi, aut esse in cogitatione vel intellectu, de quo haec intelliguntur? Si enim non potest, non de eo possunt haec intelligi. Quod si dicis non intelligi et non esse in intellectu quod non penitus intelligitur: dic quia qui non potest intueri purissimam
60 lucem solis, non videt lucem diei, quae non est nisi lux solis. Certe vel hactenus intelligitur et est in intellectu quo maius cogitari nequit ut haec de eo intelligantur.

[2.] Dixi itaque, in argumentatione quam reprehendis, quia cum insipiens audit proferri "quo maius cogitari non potest," intelligit quod audit. Utique qui non intelligit si nota lingua dicitur, aut nullum aut nimis obrutum habet intellectum. Deinde dixi quia si intelligitur, est in intel-
5 lectu. An est in nullo intellectu, quod necessario in rei veritate esse monstratum est? Sed dices quia et si est in intellectu, non tamen consequetur quia intelligitur. Vide quia consequitur esse in intellectu, ex eo quia intelligitur. Sicut enim quod cogitatur, cogitatione cogitatur, et quod cogitatione cogitatur, sicut cogitatur sic est in cogitatione: ita quod intelligitur

---

1 60 videt: *ex* vidit *corr. B²*
2 6 consequetur: *ex* consequenter *(?) corr. B*   consequitur *E*   consequenter *T*

where as a whole. Now, even as it is not the case that each of the parts of time exist when the others do, so |the parts of time| can be thought never to exist. And even as it is not the case that each of the parts of the world exist where the other |parts| do, so |the parts of the world| can be consistently supposed nowhere to exist. Now, even that which is a unified composite is able to be divided in thought and is able not to exist. Therefore, with regard to whatever at some place or time does not exist as a whole: even if this thing does exist, it can be thought not to exist. But with regard to that than which a greater cannot be thought: if it exists, it cannot be thought not to exist. For otherwise,[4] if it existed it would not be that than which a greater cannot be thought—|a consequence| which is inconsistent. Therefore, it does not at all fail to exist as a whole at any time or at any place but exists as a whole always and everywhere.

Don't you think that that thing about which these |statements| are understood can to some extent be thought and understood, and to some extent can be in thought and in the understanding? For if it cannot |be thought or understood|, then the foregoing |statements| cannot be understood about it. But if you say that what is not fully understood is *not* understood and is *not* in the understanding, then say |as well| that someone who cannot stand to gaze upon the most brilliant light of the sun does not see daylight, which is nothing other than the sun's light.[5] Surely, that than which a greater cannot be thought is understood and is in the understanding at least to the extent that the foregoing |statements| are understood about it.

[2.] And so, in the argument which you criticize I said that when the Fool hears the utterance "that than which a greater cannot be thought," he understands what he hears. (Surely, if it is spoken in a language one knows, then one who does not understand |what he hears| has little or no intelligence |*intellectus*|.) Next, I said that if it is understood, |what is understood| is in the understanding. (Or would what |I claim| to have been necessarily inferred to exist in reality not at all[6] be in the understanding?) But you will say that even if it is in the understanding, there would not follow |therefrom| that it is understood. Notice, |though|, that from the fact of its being understood, there does follow that |it| is in the understanding. For what is thought is thought by thinking; and with regard to what is thought by thinking: even as it is thought, so it is in |our| think-

10 intellectu intelligitur, et quod intellectu intelligitur, sicut intelligitur ita est in intellectu. Quid hoc planius?

Postea dixi quia si est vel in solo intellectu, potest cogitari esse et in re—quod maius est. Si ergo in solo est intellectu: idipsum, scilicet quo maius non potest cogitari, est quo maius cogitari potest. Rogo quid con-
15 sequentius? An enim si est vel in solo intellectu, non potest cogitari esse et in re? Aut si potest, nonne qui hoc cogitat, aliquid cogitat maius eo, si est in solo intellectu? Quid igitur consequentius quam si quo maius cogitari nequit est in solo intellectu, idem esse quo maius cogitari possit? Sed utique quo maius cogitari potest, in nullo intellectu est quo maius cogi-
20 tari non possit. An ergo non consequitur quo maius cogitari nequit, si est in ullo intellectu, non esse in solo intellectu? Si enim est in solo intellectu, est quo maius cogitari potest—quod non convenit.

[3.] Sed tale est, inquis, ac si aliquis insulam oceani omnes terras sua fertilitate vincentem, quae difficultate—immo impossibilitate—inveniendi quod non est, "perdita" nominatur, dicat idcirco non posse dubitari vere esse in re, quia verbis descriptam facile quis intelligit. Fidens loquor quia
5 si quis invenerit mihi aut re ipsa aut sola cogitatione existens praeter quo maius cogitari non possit, cui aptare valeat conexionem huius meae argumentationis: inveniam et dabo illi perditam insulam amplius non perdendam.

Palam autem iam videtur quo non valet cogitari maius non posse cogi-
10 tari non esse, quod tam certa ratione veritatis existit. Aliter enim nullatenus existeret. Denique si quis dicit se cogitare illud non esse, dico quia cum

ing. Similarly, what is understood is understood by the understanding; and with regard to what is understood by the understanding: even as it is understood, so it is in the understanding. What is more obvious than this?

Next, I went on to maintain that if |that than which a greater cannot be thought| were only in the understanding, it could be thought to exist also in reality—something which is greater |than existing only in the understanding|. Therefore, if it were only in the understanding, then that than which a greater cannot be thought would be that than which a greater *can* be thought. What, I ask, follows more logically? For if it were only in the understanding, could it not be thought to exist also in reality? And if it can be |thus thought|, would not anyone who thinks this |i.e., thinks it to exist also in reality| think something greater than it—if it were only in the understanding? Therefore, what follows more logically than |this conclusion, viz.|: if that than which a greater *cannot* be thought were only in the understanding, it would be that than which a greater *can* be thought? But, surely, that than which a greater cannot be thought is in no respect[7] that than which a greater can be thought. Does it not follow, therefore, that if that than which a greater cannot be thought is at all[8] in the understanding, then it is not in the understanding alone? For if it were only in the understanding, it would be that than which a greater *can* be thought—|a consequence| which is inconsistent.

[3.] But according to you |my reasoning| is analogous to someone's claiming that an island in the ocean (|an island| which because of its abundance excels all |other| lands and which because of the difficulty—or, rather, the impossibility—of finding what does not exist is called Lost Island) cannot be doubted truly to exist in reality since one readily understands when it is described in words. With confidence I reply: if besides that than which a greater cannot be thought anyone finds for me |anything else| (whether existing in reality or only in thought) to which he can apply the logic of my argument, then I will find and will make him a present of that lost island—no longer to be lost.

However, it now seems clear that that than which a greater cannot be thought is not able to be thought not to exist, seeing that it exists on such a sure basis of truth. For otherwise |i.e., if it could be *thought* not to exist|, it would not at all exist.[9] Indeed, if someone says that he thinks

hoc cogitat, aut cogitat aliquid quo maius cogitari non possit, aut non cogitat. Si non cogitat, non cogitat non esse quod non cogitat. Si vero cogitat, utique cogitat aliquid quod nec cogitari possit non esse. Si enim
15 posset cogitari non esse, cogitari posset habere principium et finem. Sed hoc non potest. Qui ergo illud cogitat, aliquid cogitat quod nec cogitari non esse possit. Hoc vero qui cogitat, non cogitat idipsum non esse. Alioquin cogitat quod cogitari non potest. Non igitur potest cogitari non esse quo maius nequit cogitari.

[4.] Quod autem dicis, quia cum dicitur quod summa res ista non esse nequeat cogitari, melius fortasse diceretur quod non esse aut etiam posse non esse non possit intelligi: potius dicendum fuit non posse cogitari. Si enim dixissem rem ipsam non posse intelligi non esse, fortasse tu ipse,
5 qui dicis quia secundum proprietatem verbi istius falsa nequeunt intelligi, obiceres nihil quod est posse intelligi non esse. Falsum est enim non esse quod est. Quare non esse proprium deo non posse intelligi non esse. Quod si aliquid eorum quae certissime sunt potest intelligi non esse, similiter et alia certa non esse posse intelligi. Sed hoc utique non potest
10 obici de cogitatione, si bene consideretur. Nam et si nulla quae sunt possint intelligi non esse, omnia tamen possunt cogitari non esse, praeter id quod summe est. Illa quippe omnia et sola possunt cogitari non esse, quae initium aut finem aut partium habent coniunctionem, et, sicut iam dixi, quidquid alicubi aut aliquando totum non est. Illud vero solum non
15 potest cogitari non esse, in quo nec initium nec finem nec partium coniunctionem, et quod non nisi semper et ubique totum ulla invenit cogitatio.

Scito igitur quia potes cogitare te non esse, quamdiu esse certissime

that this thing does not exist, I reply that when he thinks this, either he is or he is not thinking of something than which a greater cannot be thought. If he is not thinking of |it|, then he is not thinking that |it| (i.e., what he is not thinking of) does not exist. And if he is thinking of |it|, then, surely, he is thinking of something which cannot even be thought not to exist. For if it could be thought not to exist, it could be thought to have a beginning and an end. But this |consequence| is impossible. Therefore, anyone who thinks of this thing thinks of something which cannot even be thought not to exist. Now, anyone who thinks of this |viz., what cannot even be thought not to exist| does not think that it does not exist. Otherwise, he would be thinking what cannot be thought. Therefore, it is not the case that that than which a greater cannot be thought can be thought not to exist.

[4.] As for your claim that when we say that this Supreme Thing *cannot be thought* not to exist we would perhaps do better to say that it *cannot be understood* not to exist or even to be able not to exist, |I answer|: it was necessary to say "cannot be thought." For had I said that this thing cannot be understood not to exist, then perhaps you yourself—who say that false |i.e., unreal| things cannot be "understood," in the proper sense of the word—might have objected that nothing which exists can be understood not to exist. For it is false that what exists does not exist; thus, it would not be a unique characteristic of God not to be able to be understood not to exist. On the other hand, if any of the things which most assuredly exist *can* be understood not to exist, then likewise other certainly existing things |e.g., God| can also be understood not to exist. But, assuredly, these objections cannot be made with regard to *thinking*, if the matter is rightly considered. For even if no existing things could be *understood* not to exist, still they could all be *thought* not to exist—with the exception of that which exists supremely. Indeed, all and only things which have a beginning or an end or are composed of parts—and whatever (as I have already said) at any place or time does not exist as a whole—can be thought not to exist. But only that in which thought does not at all find a beginning or an end or a combination of parts, and only that which thought finds existing only as a whole always and everywhere, cannot be thought not to exist.

Be aware, then, that you can think that you do not exist even while knowing most certainly that |you| do exist. (I am surprised that you

scis—quod te miror dixisse nescire. Multa namque cogitamus non esse
20 quae scimus esse, et multa esse quae non esse scimus—non existimando,
sed fingendo ita esse ut cogitamus. Et quidem possumus cogitare aliquid
non esse, quamdiu scimus esse, quia simul et illud possumus et istud
scimus. Et non possumus cogitare non esse, quamdiu scimus esse, quia
non possumus cogitare esse simul et non esse. Si quis igitur sic distinguat
25 huius prolationis has duas sententias, intelliget nihil, quamdiu esse scitur,
posse cogitari non esse, et quidquid est praeter id quo maius cogitari
nequit, etiam cum scitur esse, posse non esse cogitari. Sic igitur et proprium est deo non posse cogitari non esse, et tamen multa non possunt
cogitari, quamdiu sunt, non esse. Quomodo tamen dicatur cogitari deus
30 non esse, in ipso libello puto sufficienter esse dictum.

[5.] Qualia vero sint et alia quae mihi obicis pro insipiente, facile est
deprehendere vel parum sapienti, et ideo id ostendere supersedendum
existimaveram. Sed quoniam audio quibusdam ea legentibus aliquid contra me valere videri, paucis de illis commemorabo.

5   Primum, quod saepe repetis me dicere quia quod est maius omnibus
est in intellectu; si est in intellectu, est et in re; aliter enim omnibus maius
non esset omnibus maius: nusquam in omnibus dictis meis invenitur
talis probatio. Non enim idem valet quod dicitur "maius omnibus" et
"quo maius cogitari nequit" ad probandum quia est in re quod dicitur. Si
10 quis enim dicat quo maius cogitari non possit non esse aliquid in re aut
posse non esse aut vel non esse posse cogitari, facile refelli potest. Nam
quod non est, potest non esse; et quod non esse potest, cogitari potest
non esse. Quidquid autem cogitari potest non esse: si est, non est quo

expressed uncertainty about this point.) For many things which we know to exist we think not to exist, and many things which we know not to exist |we think| to exist—not by judging, but by imagining, |them| to be as we think |they are|. Indeed, |both of the following statements are true:| (1) We can think that something does not exist even while knowing that |it| does exist; for we can |think, i.e., imagine| the one state and at the same time know the other. And (2) we cannot think that |something| does not exist while knowing that |it| does exist; for we cannot think |it| to exist and at the same time think |it| not to exist. Hence, if someone distinguishes in this manner these two senses of this expression |"to think"|, he will discern (*intelliget*) that (2) a thing cannot be thought not to exist while known to exist and also that (1) whatever there is (except that than which a greater cannot be thought) can be thought not to exist even while it is known to exist. So, then, |in one sense| it is a unique characteristic of God not to be able to be thought not to exist; and nevertheless |in another sense| many |other| things, while existing, are not able to be thought not to exist. But about the way in which God is said to be thought not to exist, I deem that enough has been stated in the treatise itself |i.e., in the *Proslogion*|.[10]

[5.] It is easy even for someone of very little intelligence to detect what is wrong with the other objections which you raise against me on behalf of the Fool; and so, I thought I ought to forego showing this. But because I hear that they do seem to some readers to avail somewhat against me, I will deal with them briefly.

For one thing, you say repeatedly that I argue as follows: "That which is greater than all |others| is in the understanding. And if it is in the understanding, it exists also in reality; for otherwise |i.e., if it did not exist in reality, that which is| greater than all |others| would not be greater than all |others|." But nowhere in all of my statements is there found such a line of reasoning. For the expression "|that which is| greater than all |others|" and the expression "that than which a greater cannot be thought" are not equally effective in proving that what is spoken of exists in reality. For if someone claims that that than which a greater cannot be thought (1) is not something really existent or (2) is able not to exist or, at least, (3) is able to be thought not to exist, he can easily be refuted. For what does not exist is able not to exist; and what is able not to exist is able to be thought not to exist. But regarding whatever *can* be

maius cogitari non possit. Quod si non est: utique si esset, non esset quo
15 maius non possit cogitari. Sed dici non potest quia quo maius non possit
cogitari si est, non est quo maius cogitari non possit, aut si esset, non
esset quo non possit cogitari maius. Patet ergo quia nec non est nec
potest non esse aut cogitari non esse. Aliter enim si est, non est quod
dicitur; et si esset, non esset. Hoc autem non tam facile probari posse
20 videtur de eo quod maius dicitur omnibus. Non enim ita patet quia quod
non esse cogitari potest, non est maius omnibus quae sunt, sicut quia non
est quo maius cogitari non possit; nec sic est indubitabile quia si est
aliquid maius omnibus, non est aliud quam quo maius non possit cogitari, aut si esset, non esset similiter aliud, quomodo certum est de eo
25 quod dicitur quo maius cogitari nequit. Quid enim si quis dicat esse
aliquid maius omnibus quae sunt, et idipsum tamen posse cogitari non
esse, et aliquid maius eo etiam si non sit, posse tamen cogitari? An hic
sic aperte inferri potest "non est ergo maius omnibus quae sunt" sicut ibi
apertissime diceretur "ergo non est quo maius cogitari nequit"? Illud
30 namque alio indiget argumento quam hoc quod dicitur omnibus maius;
in isto vero non est opus alio quam hoc ipso quod sonat quo maius
cogitari non possit. Ergo si non similiter potest probari de eo quod maius
omnibus dicitur, quod de se per seipsum probat quo maius nequit cogitari: iniuste me reprehendisti dixisse quod non dixi, cum tantum differat
35 ab eo quod dixi. Si vero vel post aliud argumentum potest, nec sic me

5 17 quo: quod *B* quo *ET* (**5** 16-17 esset . . . maius: non esset non esset quo maius
cogitari non possit *E*)
5 28 inferri: inferri (r¹ *supra lin.*) *B²*

thought not to exist: if it does exist, it is not that than which a greater cannot be thought; and if it does not exist, then (assuredly) if it were to exist, it would not be that than which a greater cannot be thought. But regarding that than which a greater *cannot* be thought: we cannot say that if it exists it is not that than which a greater cannot be thought, or that if it were to exist it would not be that than which a greater cannot be thought. Therefore, it is evident that |that than which a greater cannot be thought| neither (1) fails to exist nor (2) is able not to exist nor (3) is able to be thought not to exist. For otherwise |i.e., were it able not to exist or able to be thought not to exist|, if it exists it is not what it is said to be; and if it were to exist it would not be |what it is said to be|. But this |consequence| seems not to be able to be so easily derived regarding what is said to be greater than all |others|. For it is not obvious that that which can be thought not to exist is not |that which is| greater than all |other| existing things, as |it is obvious| that it is not that than which a greater cannot be thought. And it is not certain that if there is something greater than all |others| it is identical with that than which a greater cannot be thought (or that if it were to exist it would likewise be identical with |that than which a greater cannot be thought|), as |this inference| is certain about what is called that than which a greater cannot be thought. For what if someone were to say that there exists something which is greater than all |other| existing things and, yet, that this thing can be thought not to exist and that something greater than it—even if |this greater being| does not exist—can be thought? Could the inference "Therefore, it is not greater than all |other| existing things" obviously be drawn in that case—just as the inference "Therefore, it is not that than which a greater cannot be thought" could very obviously be drawn in my case? Your |inference| requires a consideration other than the consideration that |that thing| is said to be greater than all |others|; but with regard to my |inference| there is no need of any other |consideration| than that |this thing| is spoken of as that than which a greater cannot be thought. Therefore, if with regard to what is said to be |that which is| greater than all |others| the proof cannot proceed in like fashion as through itself "that than which a greater cannot be thought" proves about itself, then you unjustly criticized me for having said what I did not say, since |your rendering| differs so greatly from what I said. On the other hand, if according to another consideration it can |be proved that what is greater than all others exists|, you ought not thus to have criticized me for having said

debuisti reprehendere dixisse quod probari potest. Utrum autem possit, facile perpendit qui hoc posse quo maius cogitari nequit cognoscit. Nullatenus enim potest intelligi quo maius cogitari non possit nisi id quod solum omnibus est maius. Sicut ergo quo maius cogitari nequit intelli-
40 gitur et est in intellectu et ideo esse in rei veritate asseritur: sic quod maius dicitur omnibus, intelligi et esse in intellectu et idcirco re ipsa esse ex necessitate concluditur. Vides ergo quam recte me comparasti stulto illi, qui hoc solo quod descripta intelligeretur, perditam insulam esse vellet asserere?

[6.] Quod autem obicis quaelibet falsa vel dubia similiter posse intelligi et esse in intellectu, quemadmodum illud quod dicebam: miror quid hic sensisti contra me dubium probare volentem, cui primum hoc sat erat: ut quolibet modo illud intelligi et esse in intellectu ostenderem,
5 quatenus consequenter consideraretur utrum esset in solo intellectu, velut falsa, an et in re, ut vera. Nam si falsa et dubia hoc modo intelliguntur et sunt in intellectu quia cum dicuntur, audiens intelligit quid dicens significet, nihil prohibet quod dixi intelligi et esse in intellectu.

Quomodo autem sibi conveniant quod dicis?: quia falsa dicente aliquo
10 quaecumque ille diceret intelligeres, et quia illud quod non eo modo quo etiam falsa habetur in cogitatione, non diceris auditum cogitare aut in cogitatione habere, sed intelligere et in intellectu habere, quia scilicet non possis hoc aliter cogitare nisi intelligendo, id est scientia comprehendendo re ipsa illud existere. Quomodo inquam conveniant et falsa intel-
15 ligi et intelligere esse scientia comprehendere existere aliquid? Nil ad me; tu videris. Quodsi et falsa aliquomodo intelliguntur, et non omnis sed

something which can be proved. Now, whether it can |be proved| is easily apprehended by one who recognizes that that than which a greater cannot be thought is able |to be| this |i.e., to be that which is greater than all others|. For that than which a greater cannot be thought can only be understood to be that which alone is greater than all |others|. Therefore, just as that than which a greater cannot be thought is understood and is in the understanding and hence is affirmed to exist in reality, so what is said to be greater than all |others| is inferred to be understood and to be in the understanding and, hence, necessarily, to exist in reality. Do you see, then, the respect in which you did rightly compare me with that fool who wanted to assert the existence of Lost Island from the mere fact that its description was understood?

[6.] Now, you |also| object that all manner of false |i.e., unreal| and doubtfully real things can be understood and can be in the understanding in a way similar to the thing I was speaking of. I am surprised that here you have found fault with me—I who aimed to prove |the existence of| what |was assumed to be| doubtfully real, and for whom it was sufficient at the outset to show that this thing was somehow understood and was somehow in the understanding, so that subsequently there could be considered whether it exists in the understanding alone, as do false things, or whether it exists also in reality, as do true things. For if false things and uncertainly real things are understood and are in the understanding in the sense that when they are spoken of the hearer understands what the speaker is signifying, then nothing prevents what I have spoken of from being understood and being in the understanding.

But how are the statements which you make consistent? |On the one hand you say| that if someone spoke of false things you would understand whatever he said. And |on the other hand| with regard to that which is present in thought but not in the manner in which false things also are, you say not that you think it or have it in thought (when you hear of it) but rather that you understand it and have it in the understanding; for |you say that| you can think it only by understanding |it|—i.e., |only| by comprehending with cognitive certainty that it exists in reality.[11] How, I ask, are |these two statements| consistent?—viz., (1) that false things are understood and (2) that to understand is to comprehend, with cognitive certainty, that a thing exists. |This contradiction| is not my concern; you attend to it.[12] Yet, if false things *are* in some manner under-

cuiusdam intellectus est haec definitio: non debui reprehendi quia dixi quo maius cogitari non possit intelligi et in intellectu esse, etiam antequam certum esset re ipsa illud existere.

[7.] Deinde quod dicis vix umquam posse esse credibile, cum dictum et auditum fuerit istud, non eo modo posse cogitari non esse quo etiam potest cogitari non esse deus: respondeant pro me qui vel parvam scientiam disputandi argumentandique attigerunt. An enim rationabile est ut
5 idcirco neget aliquis quod intelligit?: quia esse dicitur id quod ideo negat quia non intelligit. Aut si aliquando negatur quod aliquatenus intelligitur, et idem est illi quod nullatenus intelligitur: nonne facilius probatur quod dubium est de illo quod in aliquo quam de eo quod in nullo est intellectu? Quare nec credibile potest esse idcirco quemlibet negare quo
10 maius cogitari nequit, quod auditum aliquatenus intelligit: quia negat deum, cuius sensum nullo modo cogitat. Aut si et illud quia non omnino intelligitur negatur: nonne tamen facilius id quod aliquomodo quam id quod nullo modo intelligitur probatur? Non ergo irrationabiliter contra insipientem ad probandum deum esse attuli "quo maius cogitari non
15 possit," cum illud nullo modo, istud aliquomodo intelligeret.

[8.] Quod vero tam studiose probas quo maius cogitari nequit non tale esse qualis nondum facta pictura in intellectu pictoris: sine causa fit. Non enim ad hoc protuli picturam praecogitatam, ut tale illud de quo agebatur vellem asserere, sed tantum ut aliquid esse in intellectu, quod esse
5 non intelligeretur, possem ostendere.

Item quod dicis quo maius cogitari nequit secundum rem vel ex genere tibi vel ex specie notam te cogitare auditum vel in intellectu

stood, and if your definition is |a definition| of a special |mode of| under-standing rather than of every |mode of| understanding, then I ought not to have been criticized for having said that that than which a greater cannot be thought is understood and is in the understanding, |and for having said this| even before it was certain that this thing exists in reality.

[7.] Next, it can scarcely at all be plausible, you say, that when this thing is spoken of or heard of, it cannot be thought not to exist in the way that even God |you say| can be thought not to exist. Let those who have attained even a little knowledge of disputation and argumentation reply on my behalf. For is it reasonable for someone to deny what he understands |and to do so| because it is said to be |identical with| that which he denies because he does not understand? Or if ever someone denies that which to some extent he understands, and if it is identical with that which he does not at all understand, is not what is in question more easily proved about that which in some respect he understands than about that which he does not at all[13] understand? Therefore, |on the one hand| it cannot even be plausible for someone to deny that than which a greater cannot be thought (which, when he hears of, he under-stands to some extent) because he denies God (in no way thinking the signification of the word "God")[14] On the other hand, if he denies God because he does not at all[15] understand .|the signification of the word "God"|, then is it not easier to prove that which in some way is under-stood than that which is not at all understood? Therefore, in order to prove that God exists I, not unreasonably, adduced against the Fool |the description| "that than which a greater cannot be thought." For he might not at all understand the |signification of the word "God,"| but he would to some extent understand the |description|.

[8.] Now, you go to so much trouble to prove that that than which a greater cannot be thought is not analogous to an as yet unproduced painting in the understanding of a painter. But there was no reason for you to do so. For I introduced the |example of a| preenvisioned painting not because I wanted to assert that the thing I was discussing |is| analo-gous |thereto| but only so that I could show that in the understanding there is something which is not understood |i.e., judged| to exist |in reality|.

Moreover, you maintain that upon hearing of that than which a greater cannot be thought you cannot think it (or have it in the under-

habere non posse, quoniam nec ipsam rem nosti nec eam ex alia simili potes conicere: palam est rem aliter sese habere. Quoniam namque omne
10 minus bonum in tantum est simile maiori bono inquantum est bonum, patet cuilibet rationabili menti quia, de bonis minoribus ad maiora conscendendo, ex iis quibus aliquid maius cogitari potest multum possumus conicere illud quo nihil potest maius cogitari. Quis enim verbi gratia vel hoc cogitare non potest, etiam si non credat in re esse quod cogitat?:
15 scilicet si bonum est aliquid quod initium et finem habet, multo melius esse bonum quod licet incipiat non tamen desinit; et sicut istud illo melius est, ita isto esse melius illud quod nec finem habet nec initium, etiam si semper de praeterito per praesens transeat ad futurum; et sive sit in re aliquid huiusmodi sive non sit, valde tamen eo melius esse id quod
20 nullo modo indiget vel cogitur mutari vel moveri. An hoc cogitari non potest, aut aliquid hoc maius cogitari potest? Aut non est hoc ex iis quibus maius cogitari valet, conicere id quo maius cogitari nequit? Est igitur unde possit conici quo maius cogitari nequeat. Sic itaque facile refelli potest insipiens, qui sacram auctoritatem non recipit, si negat quo
25 maius cogitari non valet ex aliis rebus conici posse. At si quis catholicus hoc neget, meminerit quia "invisibilia dei a creatura mundi, per ea quae facta sunt, intellecta, conspiciuntur—sempiterna quoque eius virtus et divinitas."

[9.] Sed et si verum esset non posse cogitari vel intelligi illud quo maius nequit cogitari, non tamen falsum esset "quo maius cogitari nequit" cogitari posse et intelligi. Sicut enim nil prohibet dici "ineffabile," licet illud dici non possit quod ineffabile dicitur; et quemadmodum

standing) by reference to any object known to you through species or genus. For |you claim that| you are neither acquainted with this thing itself nor able to make inferences about it on the basis of some other similar thing. Yet, the facts of the matter are clearly otherwise. For every lesser good is, insofar as it is a good, similar to a greater good. Therefore, to any rational mind it is clear that by ascending from lesser goods to greater goods, we can—on the basis of those things than which something greater can be thought—make many inferences about that than which nothing greater can be thought. Is there anyone, for example— even if he does not believe really to exist that of which he is thinking— who is unable to think at least the following?: that if something which has a beginning and an end is a good, then a good which although it begins does not cease is a much better |good|. And just as this |second good which has a beginning but no end| is a better |good| than that |first good|, so also that |good| which has neither a beginning nor an end is a better |good| than this |second good. This third good is better than the second| even if |the third| is always moving from the past through the present toward the future. Yet, that |good| which in no way needs to be, or is compelled to be, changed or moved is far better (whether or not there exists in reality some such thing) than this |third good, which does change|. Can this |unchanging good| not be thought? Can anything greater than it be thought? Is not this |procedure the same as| making inferences—on the basis of those things than which a greater can be thought—about that than which a greater cannot be thought? Therefore, there is a way to make inferences about that than which a greater cannot be thought. In this way, then, the Fool, who does not accept sacred authority |i.e., Scripture|, can easily be refuted if he denies that on the basis of other things inferences can be made about that than which a greater cannot be thought. But if a Catholic makes this denial, let him remember that "the invisible things of God (including His eternal power and divinity), being understood through those things that have been made, are clearly seen from the mundane creation."[16]

[9.] Yet, even if it were true that that than which a greater cannot be thought could not be thought or understood, nonetheless it would not be false that "that than which a greater cannot be thought" can be thought and understood. Nothing prevents our saying |the word| "unsayable," even though that which is called unsayable cannot be said. Moreover, we

5 cogitari potest *non-cogitabile*, quamvis illud cogitari non possit cui convenit *non-cogitabile* dici: ita cum dicitur "quo nil maius valet cogitari," procul dubio quod auditur cogitari et intelligi potest, etiam si res illa cogitari non valeat aut intelligi, qua maius cogitari nequit. Nam et si quisquam est tam insipiens ut dicat non esse aliquid quo maius non possit
10 cogitari: non tamen ita erit impudens ut dicat se non posse intelligere aut cogitare quid dicat. Aut si quis talis invenitur, non modo sermo eius est respuendus, sed et ipse conspuendus. Quisquis igitur negat aliquid esse quo maius nequeat cogitari: utique intelligit et cogitat negationem quam facit. Quam negationem intelligere aut cogitare non potest sine partibus
15 eius. Pars autem eius est "quo maius cogitari non potest." Quicumque igitur hoc negat, intelligit et cogitat "quo maius cogitari nequit." Palam autem est quia similiter potest cogitari et intelligi "quod non potest non esse." Maius vero cogitat, qui hoc cogitat, quam qui cogitat quod possit non esse. Dum ergo cogitatur "quo maius non possit cogitari": si cogi-
20 tatur quod possit non esse, non cogitatur "quo non possit cogitari maius." Sed nequit idem simul cogitari et non cogitari. Quare qui cogitat "quo maius non possit cogitari" non cogitat quod possit, sed quod non possit, non esse. Quapropter necesse est esse quod cogitat, quia quidquid non esse potest, non est quod cogitat.

[10.] Puto quia monstravi me, non infirma sed satis necessaria argumentatione, probasse in praefato libello re ipsa existere aliquid quo maius cogitari non possit, nec eam alicuius obiectionis infirmari firmitate. Tantam enim vim huius prolationis in se continet significatio ut hoc
5 ipsum quod dicitur, ex necessitate eo ipso quod intelligitur vel cogitatur, et revera probetur existere, et id ipsum esse quidquid de divina substantia oportet credere. Credimus namque de divina substantia quidquid abso-

---

9 10 se: *ex* si *corr. B*
9 14 non: *supra lin. B*

can think |the concept| *unthinkable*, even though that which it besuits to be called unthinkable cannot be thought. By the same token, when "that than which nothing greater can be thought" is uttered, without doubt what is heard can be thought and understood, even if that thing than which a greater cannot be thought could not be thought or understood. For even if anyone were so foolish as to say that something than which a greater cannot be thought does not exist, nevertheless he would not be so shameless as to say that he cannot think or understand what he is saying. Or if some such |impudent person| is found, not only is his word to be rejected but he himself is to be despised. Therefore, with regard to whoever denies the existence of something than which a greater cannot be thought: surely, he thinks and understands the denial he is making. And he cannot think or understand this denial without |thinking or understanding| its parts—one of which is "that than which a greater cannot be thought." Therefore, whoever denies this |viz., that this being exists| thinks and understands |the signification of| "that than which a greater cannot be thought." But it is evident that, likewise, "that which is not able not to exist" can be thought and understood. Now, someone who thinks this thinks of something greater than does someone who thinks of that which is able not to exist. Therefore, while "that than which a greater cannot be thought" is being thought: if that which is able not to exist is being thought of, then "that than which a greater cannot be thought" is not being thought. Now, since the same thing cannot at the same time be both thought and not thought, someone who thinks "that than which a greater cannot be thought" does not think of that which is able not to exist but rather thinks of that which is not able not to exist. Hence, it is necessarily the case that there exists that of which he thinks—because whatever is able not to exist is not that of which he is thinking.

[10.] I have now showed, I believe, that in the aforementioned treatise |viz., the *Proslogion*| I proved—not by inconclusive reasoning but by very compelling reasoning—that something than which a greater cannot be thought exists in reality. And |I have showed| that this |reasoning| was not weakened by any strong objection. For the signification of this utterance |viz., "that than which a greater cannot be thought"| contains so much force that what is spoken of is, by the very fact that it is understood or thought, necessarily proved to exist in reality and to be whatever ought to be believed about the Divine Substance. For we believe

lute cogitari potest melius esse quam non esse. Verbi gratia, melius est
esse aeternum quam non-aeternum, bonum quam non-bonum—immo
10 bonitatem ipsam quam non-ipsam-bonitatem. Nihil autem huiusmodi
non esse potest, quo maius aliquid cogitari non potest. Necesse igitur est
quo maius cogitari non potest, esse quidquid de divina essentia credi
oportet.

Gratias ago benignitati tuae et in reprehensione et in laude mei opus-
5 culi. Cum enim ea quae tibi digna susceptione videntur, tanta laude extu-
listi: satis apparet quia quae tibi infirma visa sunt, benevolentia non
malevolentia reprehendisti.

about the Divine Substance whatever can in every respect be thought of as better |for something| to be than not to be.[17] For example, it is better to be eternal than not to be eternal, better to be good than not to be good—or, rather, to be goodness itself than not to be goodness itself. But that than which something greater cannot be thought cannot fail to be anything of this kind. Therefore, it is necessarily the case that that than which a greater cannot be thought is whatever ought to be believed about the Divine Being.

I am grateful for your kindness both in criticizing and in praising my treatise. For since you praised so lavishly those things which seem to you worthy of acceptance, it is quite evident that you criticized out of good will rather than out of malevolence the things which seemed to you untenable.

NOTES

BIBLIOGRAPHY

INDEX OF PERSONS

NOTES

1. Gabriel Gerberon, in his edition of Anselm's works (Paris, 1675), was the first editor to identify the author of *On Behalf of the Fool*. Gerberon's edition was reprinted under the editorship of J.-P. Migne, with slight emendations (*Patrologia Latina*, Vols. 158 & 159, Paris, 1853 & 1854). Migne retains Gerberon's manuscript information and variant readings. From this information we learn that Gaunilo, monk of Marmoutier, was the author of *Pro Insipiente*. Gerberon cites two French mss., one of which is Latin Ms. C 54 from the abbey at Jumièges, France (in the vicinity of Rouen). This twelfth-century ms. is now Lat. Ms. 539 of the Bibliothèque Municipale of Rouen. At the end of Anselm's *Reply* we find: "*Explicit responsio Anselmi ad Gaunilonem, Majoris monasterii monachum.*" See *PL* 158:18, as well as the variant readings at 158:242n and 158:248n.

2. Previous English translations of the *Monologion (M)*, the *Proslogion (P)*, *On Behalf of the Fool (BF)*, and *Reply to Gaunilo (R)* are the following: (1) Max J. Charles-worth. *St. Anselm's Proslogion*. Oxford: Clarendon Press, 1965 (*P; BF; R*). (2) Sidney N. Deane. *St. Anselm: Basic Writings*. La Salle, Illinois: Open Court, 1962 [1st ed., *St. Anselm: Proslogium; Monologium; an Appendix in Behalf of the Fool by Gaunilon; and Cur Deus Homo*. Chicago: Open Court, 1903. The translation of the *Cur Deus Homo* was made by James G. Vose and was first published in 1854-1855]. (3) Eugene R. Fairweather. *A Scholastic Miscellany: Anselm to Occam*. Philadelphia: Westminster Press, 1956 (*P*; excerpt from *R*). (4) John H. Hick and Arthur C. McGill. *The Many-faced Argument: Recent Studies of the Ontological Argument for the Existence of God*. New York: Macmillan, 1967 (excerpt from *P; BF; R*; translations are by McGill). (5) Jasper Hopkins. *Anselm of Canterbury: Volume One*. New York: Mellen Press, 1974; 2nd ed. 1975 (*M; P; BF; R*). (6) J. S. Maginnis. "Translations from Anselm," *Bibliotheca Sacra*, 8 (July 1851), 529-553 (*P*). (7) J. S. Maginnis. "Proofs of the Existence of God. A Reply to Anselm and Anselm's Rejoinder," *Bibliotheca Sacra*, 8 (October 1851), 669-715 (*BF;R*). (8) William E. Mann. "Anselm," pp. 261-279 in *Classics of Western Philosophy*. Edited by Steven M. Cahn. Indianapolis: Hackett, 1977 (*P*). (9) Anton C. Pegis. *The Wisdom of Catholicism*. New York: Random House, 1949 (*P*). (10) Benedicta Ward. *The Prayers and Meditations of Saint Anselm*. Baltimore: Penguin Books, 1973 (*P*). (11) C.C.J. Webb. *The Devotions of Saint Anselm*. London: Methuen, 1903 (*P*). (12) John F. Wippel and Allen B. Wolter. *Medieval Philosophy: From St. Augustine to Nicholas of Cusa*. New York: Free Press, 1969 (excerpt from *P; OB; R*).

3. "*Bei der Übersetzung liess ich mich von dem Bewusstsein leiten, dass jede Unge-nauigkeit und 'Freiheit' bei einem Werke, in dem jedes Wort genau erwogen ist, zum Nachteil des Gedankens ausschlagen muss.*" See p. 7 of F. S. Schmitt's German transla-tion of the *Proslogion* (Stuttgart-Bad Cannstatt: F. Frommann Verlag, 1962).

4. Gregory Schufreider, *An Introduction to Anselm's Argument* (Philadelphia: Temple University Press, 1978), p. 94.

5. *Ibid.*, p. 94.

6. Gillian Evans, *Anselm and Talking about God* (New York: Oxford University Press, 1978), p. 1.

7. Marcia Colish, *The Mirror of Language: A Study in the Medieval Theory of Knowledge* (Lincoln, Nebraska: University of Nebraska Press, revised edition, 1983). See my critique on pp. 325-340 of my *Nicholas of Cusa's Dialectical Mysticism*.

8. Benedicta Ward, writing in *Speculum*, 49 (October 1974), pp. 742-743.

9. I have seen such a published translation of an excerpt from Anselm's work. Courtesy prevents my documenting it here.

10. *Anselm of Canterbury: Volume One* (New York: Mellen Press, 1974; 2nd ed. 1975). This volume also contains my translation of Anselm's *Meditation on Human Redemption*—a translation I deem to be still of value.

11. "On Understanding and Preunderstanding St. Anselm," *The New Scholasticism*, 52 (Spring 1978), 243-260. "On an Alleged Definitive Interpretation of *Proslogion* 2-4: A Discussion of G. Schufreider's *An Introduction to Anselm's Argument*," *The Southern Journal of Philosophy*, 19 (1981), 129-139.

12. *A Companion to the Study of St. Anselm* (Minneapolis: University of Minnesota Press, 1972) and *Anselm of Canterbury: Volume Four: Hermeneutical and Textual Problems in the Complete Treatises of St. Anselm* (New York: Mellen Press, 1976).

NOTES TO THE INTRODUCTION

1. Canberra, Australia: Australian National University Press, 1976. Note the critique made by Peter Geach in *Philosophy*, 52 (1977), 234-236.

The present discussion is adapted from *The New Scholasticism*, 52 (Spring 1978), 243-260. It takes account of Campbell's article "On Preunderstanding St. Anselm," *ibid.*, 54 (Spring 1980), 189-193, where he defends his book.

2. See pp. 10 and 205. Campbell refers to the argumentation in *P* 2-4 as "the Argument."

3. For clarity, Campbell always hyphenates the phrase "something-than-which-nothing-greater-can-be-thought," and its variants. I feel that the expression is clear without the hyphenation; and so, I shall use hyphenation only when directly quoting from his text.

4. Campbell makes use of F. S. Schmitt's edition of the Latin text of *P* and the *Debate with Gaunilo*. Accordingly, for the sake of fairness to Campbell in the present discussion, I allude to Schmitt's text and punctuation, though I also give references to my own edition.

5. A fuller discussion of this passage is presented in Section II of the present Introduction.

6. But Campbell's translation gives the impression that Anselm *is* making a point about *manner*.

7. In the name of literalism Campbell often presents us with translations which are either in clumsy or in unclear English (or both). Consider, for example, the translation: "He should first show that its very excellence is precisely as a genuinely and undeniably real thing and not as a false or uncertain something in my understanding" (p. 184). The reader will have no trouble finding other such examples.

8. Campbell, p. 150. See also pp. 11 and 174.

9. What Anselm calls *true existence* varies with the context. In *M* 31 he refers to the Divine Word as true Existence (*veritas essentiae*). This point is an extension of his assertion, in *M* 28, that *in comparison with* the Supreme Spirit other things do not exist. (This point is associated with *P* 22, not with *P* 2 and 3.) By contrast, Anselm in *M* 36 specifies a sense in which there do exist objects other than the Supreme Being. They exist less truly than does the Supreme Being but more truly than do their "likenesses" in our knowledge. In this context, objects (are said to) exist-in-some-degree-of-truth in our percepts and concepts of them. However, in *P* 2 and 3 Anselm contrasts existing in the understanding with existing also in reality. In *this* context, he is prepared to say that *in comparison with* what exists outside the understanding, what exists merely in the understanding does not (truly) exist [just as in comparison with God what is other than God does not (truly) exist]. Thus, he switches from the expression "*esse in re*" (*P* 2) to "*esse vere*" (*P* 3), and then simply to "*esse*" (last sentence of *P* 4).

10. It is time for all scholars to dispense altogether with Stolz's hobby-horse interpretation of Anselm's argument.

11. One reason some people are led to believe that Anselm's major argument terminates no later than *P* 4 is that many mss., in appending to *P* the *Debate with Gaunilo*, repeat *P* 2-4 in this appendix. Bodley 271 is one such ms. However, Eadmer tells us, in his *Vita Anselmi*, of Anselm's request to append both the attack on behalf of the Fool and his own rejoinder thereto. Eadmer does not mention any request by Anselm to repeat any part of *P* immediately before *On Behalf of the Fool*. And not all mss.—e.g., not Lambeth Palace (London) 356—contain any such repetition. The obvious rationale for excerpting only Chaps. 2-4 is that Gaunilo criticized only these chapters.

12. In one respect Anselm is following the same procedure in *P* as in *M*: viz., to prove that there exists a Being which is the highest of all beings and has such and such attributes, and to identify this Being with God. In *M* proper (i.e., exclusive of the preface) he introduces the word "God" only at the very end of the very last chapter. By contrast, in *P*—because of its genre as an address to God—he introduces the word "God" throughout. Yet, the fact that he addresses God should not be allowed to obscure a further fact: viz., that his procedure is to prove truths regarding something than which nothing greater can be thought and then to conclude that these truths are truths about God, who is something than which nothing greater can be thought. (This strategy is made clear in *Reply to Gaunilo* 10, where Anselm says: "*Necesse . . . est quo maius cogitari non potest esse quidquid de divina essentia credi oportet.*") For God is that than which a greater cannot be thought, since that than which a greater cannot be thought can be shown to be the unique thing which has created all else from nothing and which possesses all the other (traditionally agreed-upon) divine attributes.

Although in *P* Anselm as early as Chap. 2 identifies God with something than which nothing greater can be thought, his *argument* is always presumed to be two-stepped: *x* is true of something than which nothing greater can be thought; so *x* is true of God, who is that than which nothing greater can be thought. Sometimes, however, he conflates these two steps. Accordingly, although in *Reply* 10 he states that *something than which a greater cannot be thought* is whatever can be thought to be better than not to be it, in *P* 5 he immediately says of *God* "You are . . . whatever it is better to be than not to

be"—without passing through the intervening step.

13. Gaunilo, let us note incidentally, claims that God *can* be thought not to exist. And Anselm, in reply, rejects this claim—as he had already in *P* 4—on the basis of his own claim that God is something than which a greater cannot be thought. Now, if the reason that God alone cannot be thought not to exist is that He alone is something than which a greater cannot be thought, then the reason that He alone is something than which a greater cannot be thought, cannot (without circularity be said to) be that He alone cannot be thought not to exist.

14. Cf. *M* 3-4. N. B.: In *M* 1-8 Anselm thought it important to try to prove that there is only one Creator. Thus, it would be strange if in *P* he did not make a similar attempt but, instead, chose to introduce the doctrine only as an article of faith. I take the prayer at the end of *P* 4 to indicate that Anselm now *understands* that God exists— granted that God is that than which a greater cannot be thought.

15. With respect to conclusions *a* and *b* I follow the labelling and the order found on p. 190 of Campbell's paper "On Preunderstanding Anselm." In that paper Campbell labels as "*a*" that which in his book (p. 129) he calls "*b*," and he labels as "*b*" that which in his book he calls "*a*". I also follow the paper in reading *b* as "God is *that* than which a greater cannot be thought" rather than reading it, according to the book (pp. 129 and 133), as "God is *something* than which a greater cannot be thought" (my italics).

The foregoing two conclusions, *a* and *b*, are said by Campbell also to be derivable from the alternative premise in Stage Three, viz., the premise that I have hitherto been discussing: "if any mind could think of something better than You, the creature would rise above the Creator and would sit in judgment over the Creator—something which is utterly absurd." Conclusion *b* is immediately derivable from this premise; and conclusion *a* is said by Campbell to be derivable therefrom in conjunction with Stages One and Two and an extra premise such as "of any two things one can be thought to be greater than the other." This way of deriving the two conclusions constitutes what Campbell calls the *first* leg of Stage Three.

16. Cf. n. 13 above. Campbell might want to reconstruct the argument of *P* 3; but that is a different thing from interpreting it. I find contorted and contrived Campbell's attempted interpretation of the second half of *P* 3 (= Campbell's Stage Three, as set out in Chap. 6 of his book).

17. Campbell presumes that Anselm was too astute not to be invoking the distinction between a definite and an indefinite description in *P* 2-4. This presumption serves as another reason for Campbell's conviction that by the end of *P* 3 Anselm had established (to his own satisfaction) that God is the one and only thing than which a greater cannot be thought. For unless Anselm is taken to have proved this, *P* 4 will have to be viewed as containing an inconsistent use of the definite description. For, as Campbell realizes, the description in *P* 4 cannot be (in disguise) merely "a *singular* proposition which asserts of some arbitrary individual that *it* satisfies all that the original premise stated to be true of something" (p. 33)—i.e., merely an indefinite description.

On my view, Anselm does not until *P* 5 establish that there is only one thing than which a greater cannot be thought. And he does not systematically differentiate his use of "*id quo maius . . .* " from his use of "*aliquid quo maius . . .* " This is why, later in the text, he often writes simply "*quo maius. . . .* " And it is also the reason for his not

challenging Gaunilo's disjunction *"deus aut aliquid omnibus maius"* in *On Behalf of the Fool* 4. If Anselm had been insisting upon a distinction between *"id quo maius . . ."* and *"aliquid quo maius . . . ,"* then (it is reasonable to believe that) he would have corrected Gaunilo's indiscriminate use of these in *On Behalf of the Fool* 4, just as he "corrected" his use of *"maius omnibus."*

18. It is noteworthy that in one early (i.e., 12th-century) ms version of *P* we find (in the section which corresponds to *P* 2): *"Similiter insipiens homo convincitur esse vel in intellectu aliquod quo nichil maius cogitari potest,* scilicet deum, *quia cum audit hoc dici, intelligit aliquomodo . . . ."* This passage is from Hereford Cathedral Library (England) Ms. O.I.vi. Dr. Gillian R. Evans discovered that it contains a different version of some parts of the fuller *Proslogion*. See her article "The Hereford *Proslogion*," *Anselm Studies,* 1 (1983), 253-273. The foregoing transcription, however, is mine (from fol. 81ᵛ). Punctuation and roman emphasis are editorializations by me.

19. Accordingly, the assumption is not regarded as an absolute presupposition.

20. There are a number of minor weaknesses. For instance, Campbell completely ignores Jules Vuillemin's article "Id quo nihil maius cogitari potest. Über die innere Möglichkeit eines rationalen Gottesbegriffs," *Archiv für Geschichte der Philosophie,* 53 (1971), 279-299, and his book *Le Dieu d'Anselme et les apparences de la raison* (Paris: Les Éditions Montaigne, 1971). He seems to presume that only within the Anglo Saxon tradition are there philosophers who deal with the *Proslogion* argument analytically. In this respect his book is parochial. Then too, the index is inadequate; and various points in the text itself need to be cross-referenced. Or again, he attributes to medieval thought the (self-contradictory) view that the heavenly bodies are nonmaterial (p. 109).

21. There is some truth in the point about Brentano and the point about Wittgenstein. But Campbell tends to overstate it.

22. See J. Hopkins, "Anselm's Debate with Gaunilo," pp. 97-117 of *Anselm of Canterbury: Volume Four* (New York: Mellen Press, 1976).

23. See *M* 62, 10, and 33.

24. Toward the beginning of *De Concordia* III, 6 Anselm implies that the meaning of a word forms something in the mind. (*"Vox . . . sine sensu nihil constituit in corde."*) In the *Philosophical Fragments* he states that the name "man" signifies the (mental) concept *man;* see p. 21 of my translation in *Anselm of Canterbury: Volume Two* (New York: Mellen Press, 1976).

25. Or in Campbell's exact words: "it can be thought that there exists something which . . . " (p. 94).

26. And what about *"An ergo non est aliqua talis natura . . . ?"* in *P* 2—a passage which Campbell himself renders as: "But is there any such nature . . . ?" Surely, "is there?" here means "does there exist?" Note how Anselm interchanges *"existere ex nihilo"* with *"esse ex nihilo"* in *M* 6:43-45 (=*S* I, 19:30-32). And in *M* 16:23-24 (=*S* I, 30:23) he uses *"existit iustitia"* in place of *"est iustitia"* (cf. *M* 16:21-22 = *S* I, 30:21). Anselm's terminology is so flexible that he is not even averse to saying *"posse inveniri"* for *"posse existere"* (*De Grammatico* 12. *S* I, 156: 29-30. In line 29, also note the use of *"est"* to mean "there is.").

27. I presume that Campbell understands the word "else" here. Otherwise he would not have supposed that *his* feeling-for-the-argument is different from that of those

who adhere to the alternative translation.

28. There is a second alternative translation, which Campbell denounces merci-
lessly: viz., Charlesworth's translation of this passage as "Something can be thought to
exist that cannot be thought not to exist." Campbell insists on calling the logical form of
this sentence *conjunctive* (pp. 91-94). However, my sense of Charlesworth's sentence is to
take it as tantamount to "There can be thought to exist something that cannot be thought
not to exist."

29. Other examples of Campbell's imprecisions in interpreting the writings of St.
Anselm occur in his article "Anselm's Background Metaphysics," *Scottish Journal of
Theology*, 33 (August 1980), 317-343. See my critique thereof in my book *Nicholas of
Cusa's Dialectical Mysticism*, pp. 319-325.

30. Philadelphia: Temple University Press, 1978. Schufreider makes use of F. S.
Schmitt's Latin text as it is reprinted in Max Charlesworth's *St. Anselm's Proslogion*
(Oxford: Clarendon Press, 1965). Accordingly, for the sake of fairness to Schufreider in
the present discussion, I allude to Schmitt's text and punctuation, though I also give
references to my own edition.

My discussion in this section is a revised version of what was originally published in
The Southern Journal of Philosophy, 19 (1981), 129-139. The new version takes
account of Schufreider's defense of his book in his article "Reunderstanding Anselm's
Argument," *The New Scholasticism* (Summer 1983), 384-409. I accept Schufreider's
conclusion about the correct translation of "*ratio*" in *M* 10—accept it not because of the
reason he gives (although I regard his reference to *M* 33 as important) but because of
parallels in *De Veritate* 11. I also accept his protest that his interpretation of the second
sentence of *P* 3 is not "conjunctive." And I give him the benefit of the doubt regarding
his intent in originally making the patently false statement (p. 32): "It is of the utmost
importance to realize that when we speak of something that can be thought not to exist,
we are speaking of something that exists. For, in a sense the claim that something *can* be
thought not to exist retains a significant force only if we are thinking about something
that exists." Schufreider supposes to be trivial the claim that something which does not
exist can be thought not to exist. But the claim is not necessarily trivial. Someone might
well contend that God does not exist but that He cannot be thought of as not existing if
He is thought of as that than which a greater cannot be thought. As for the rest, I deem
my original criticisms to hold good; and I therefore repeat them here. The reader will
have to judge their validity for himself. I wish him well in working his way through the
various inconsistencies of exposition in Schufreider's book.

In "Reunderstanding Anselm's Argument" Schufreider makes matters worse for himself. (See n. 35 below.) Astonishingly, he does not avail himself of the opportunity to
retract his brash claim to have offered a definitive account of Anselm's argument. Even
Richard Campbell, who, as we have seen, intimates that he himself has understood *P* 2-4
better than anyone else between Aquinas and Charlesworth, does not arrogate to himself
the self-congratulatory rubric "definitive account."

31. Schufreider seeks to identify Anselm's argument, not to assess its soundness.
Hence, when he uses the word "show," he is usually doing so only from what he takes to
be Anselm's point of view.

32. In his book Schufreider shows no awareness of the passage in *M* 36; nor does

he mention the passage in *Reply 5*.

33. Parts of Schufreider's further exposition are inconsistent with what he states here. *Nil ad me; is viderit.*

34. My italics, for emphasis.

35. In "Reunderstanding Anselm's Argument" Schufreider compounds his errors by making an additional false inference, this time with reference to *M* 31: "Just as '*summa essentia*' is what '*summe est*,' it would not be stretching the point to insist that in accord with this passage, '*veram essentiam*' is what '*vere est*' " (p. 393). But, contrary to Schufreider's judgment: in *M* 31 *vera essentia* is not what *vere est* but what *verissime est*. For in *M* 31 Anselm uses "*vera essentia*" in the sense of "*simplex absolutaque essentia*"; and this latter expression indicates *quod verissime est*, not merely *quod vere est*. It is not surprising, then, that as early as *M* 20:10 (=*S* I, 35:14-15) Anselm links "*summe est*" with "*verissime est*" when he alludes to the Supreme Being (*summa essentia*) as *quod verissime et summe est*. Nor is it surprising that, later, viz., in *M* 34, Anselm implicitly links "*veritas existendi*" with "*verissime est*" when he declares: "For in themselves |created things| are a mutable being, created according to immutable Reason. But in this Spirit they are the primary Being and the primary true Existence; and the more created things |in themselves| are in any way like this true Existence, the more truly and excellently they exist." That is, they exist more or less truly in relation to the Supreme Spirit, which, as *veritas existendi*, exists most truly. Of course, because the Supreme Spirit exists most truly, He also exists truly. And Anselm speaks of Him in this latter way not only in the title of *P* 2 but also at *M* 21:68-69 (=*S* I, 38:10): "*Praesens . . . quomodo non habet, si vere est?*" ("If |this Being| truly *is*, how would it fail to have a present?") Anything which truly exists has a present, as does also the Supreme Being; but only that which also exists most truly, viz., the Supreme Being, has a timeless present. Cf. *P* 13.

36. This last point is seen clearly by Richard La Croix in his *Proslogion II and III: A Third Interpretation of Anselm's Argument* (Leiden: E. J. Brill, 1972). *Reply to Gaunilo* 7 makes clear that Anselm identifies, with God, that than which a greater cannot be thought. Cf. *Reply* 10:4-7 (=*S* I, 138:30 - 139:3).

37. My translation.

38. The spoken or the written word may be used to signify a man qua risible being or qua featherless biped, for example—i.e., other than qua what he is essentially. See the segment (of the present Introduction) that falls between the points marked by notes 84 and 85.

39. Note Anselm's expression "*rationis . . . contemplatio*" in *De Veritate* 11 (*S* I, 191:11-12). Yet, even in this passage Anselm does not use "*rationis contemplatio*" to mean anything like *a radically purified rational vision of the matter itself*—a vision in which *existing creatures are annulled and are made to fade from reason's sight*. In fact, nowhere at all—whether in *P* or any other treatise or meditation—does Anselm use either "*ratio*" or "*intellectus*" in this sense. To be sure, in *De Conceptu Virginali* 13 (*S* II, 155:15-16) Anselm writes: "*Si diligenter puro rationis intuitu sapientem dei speculamur iustitiam . . .* " (my roman emphasis). But from the continuation of the sentence we easily recognize that no mystical contemplation is meant: " *. . . nimis absurdum intelligitur, ut per illud semen quod non creata natura, non voluntas creaturae, non ulli data potestas producit aut seminat, sed solius dei propria voluntas ad procreandum hominem nova*

virtute, mundum a peccato, de virgine segregat: alieni peccati seu debiti sive poenae ad eundem hominem necessitas ulla pertranseat, etiam si non assumatur in personam dei, sed ut purus homo fiat."

40. Cf. *Reply to Gaunilo* 7 (especially *Reply* 7:11-13 = *S* I, 137:1-3). Also note, *ibid.*, 1:56-62 (=*S* I, 132:3-9).

41. In the *Reply* Anselm speaks of his points as having been obvious and of his proof as having been conclusive.

42. Especially noteworthy are the errors found in the Latin passages on pp. 7, 18, 33, and 53. Equally noteworthy is the omission from the Latin text on p. 73. Note 5 on p. 99 misprints the first list of manuscripts; and the same note should refer the reader to Schmitt page 64*, rather than to 64. The faulty punctuation on virtually every page of the English exposition impedes comprehension. The references to the *Reply to Gaunilo* should include the particular section of the treatise being cited, as well as the page numbers in Charlesworth's translation.

N.B.: I am not stating that (nor have I any interest in whether) *all* these many errors, omissions, and defective referencings are Schufreider's fault rather than his editor's (though some of them surely are his). Regardless of who bears responsibility for them, they are nonetheless symptomatic of the lack of direct contact. It is ironic that in the very sentence of his article (p. 409n) which protests my alleged ascription to him of all these errors, there occurs the grammatical mistake called "run-on sentence": "For while I assume responsibility for the philosophical content of the work, the printing process by means of which it was produced did not allow me to see any proofs, thus all proof-reading as well as editorial work was done by the publisher." (Here Schufreider refuses to take responsibility for a single grammatical error in the typescript copy he submitted to the editors!)

43. A further crucial misreading occurs *à propos* of "*sicut*" (p. 88) in the phrase "*quia es sicut credimus*" from *P* 2. Or again, "*rerum forma*," excerpted from *M* 10, is misunderstood on p. 77, where it is not recognized to be an expression referring to the Word of God, whom Anselm never claims to be *participated* in by created things.

44. E.g., I have left aside a discussion of the following points: (1) that Anselm is not recognized by Schufreider to have misconstrued Gaunilo's use of "*intelligere*"; (2) that Anselm is not recognized to have misunderstood Gaunilo's use of "*maius omnibus*"; (3) that Anselm is mistakenly declared to have had a "propensity for developing technical terminology"; (4) that Anselm is asserted never to have been loose in his language; (5) that A. Stolz is not sufficiently credited for holding and developing the view that the title of *P* 2 fits more harmoniously with the contents of *P* 3; (6) that Schufreider regards it as *unfortunate* that F. S. Schmitt's critical edition of *Anselmi Opera Omnia* has eliminated from the Anselmian corpus a meditation known to be inauthentic [viz., Meditation I in *Patrologia Latina* 158:712 (miscited by Schufreider)].

See Chap. 4 ("Anselm's Debate with Gaunilo") of my *Anselm of Canterbury: Volume Four: Hermeneutical and Textual Problems in the Complete Treatises of St. Anselm* (New York: Mellen Press, 1976) for a discussion of some of the foregoing points—a discussion which does not, however, deal with Schufreider.

45. This article is to be published in Vol. 16, Nos. 3-4 of *The Thoreau Quarterly*, whose actual appearance (as distinguished from its publication date) will be during the

summer of 1986—a time that postdates the deadline for my own manuscript. I am immensely grateful to the editors and the staff of *The Thoreau Quarterly*—especially John M. Dolan, Sandra Menssen, and Pat Kaluza—for making available to me a copy of the final corrected proofs of Professor Anscombe's article and for permitting me to quote from these proofs. Although, under the circumstances, I am able to furnish for the citations only the typescript page numbers, I am certain that readers will have little trouble in locating the cited passages in the published form of Anscombe's relatively brief article.

46. Typescript p. 9.

47. I here deliberately leave this Latin sentence unpunctuated in order not to beg any questions. This Latin sentence is a prime instance of how an editor's interpretation of a text is oftentimes inherent in his very punctuation decisions.

48. Typescript pp. 11-12.

49. I myself prefer to render it as a contrary-to-fact conditional statement: "For if it were only in the understanding, it could be thought to exist also in reality—something which is greater |than existing only in the understanding|." Anselm avoids the subjunctive in order to keep his Latin style simple. As in *M*, so in *P* he aims at unembellished style and uncomplicated disputation. (See *M*, prologue, lines 8-9.) Yet, the logic of his argument is best expressed in English by use of the subjunctive. Cf. n. 87 below.

50. Typescript pp. 8-9.

51. In the present edition I have omitted this repetition of *P* 2-4, which is found in Latin Ms. Bodley 271 immediately before Gaunilo's *On Behalf of the Fool*. Except for minor differences of punctuation, this repeated segment is exactly the same as the earlier segment. See "*Sumptum ex eodem libello*" (*S* I, 123-124).

52. Typescript p. 8.

53. Perhaps in comparison with Gaunilo, Anselm does appear to some readers to have written beautiful Latin. Certainly, he does say some beautiful things—as, for example, in *P* 1. But all things considered—including the prefaces to *M* and *P*—there are good grounds for qualifying the claim "Anselm wrote beautiful Latin."

54. Typescript p. 12.

55. Typescript p. 8.

56. See my rendering in the translation part of the present work. Note also *Reply to Gaunilo* 5:17-19: "Therefore, it is evident that |that than which a greater cannot be thought| neither (1) fails to exist nor (2) is able not to exist nor (3) is able to be thought not to exist. For otherwise |i.e., were it able not to exist or able to be thought not to exist|, if it exists it is not what it is said to be; and if it were to exist it would not be |what it is said to be|."

57. The last sentence means something like: "For if it were only in the understanding, could it not be thought to exist also in reality?"

58. Anscombe does not mention any of the other manuscript-traditions with regard to the sentence in question. For example, a number of mss., including Latin Ms. Paris 2700, at the *Bibliothèque Nationale*, have "*Quidquid enim*", or an orthographic variant thereof, in place of "*Si enim*". In particular, the sentence in Paris 2700 reads: "*Quicquid enim solo intellectu est potest cogitari et in re esse quod maius est.*" And this sentence does not admit of Anscombe's translation of "*quod maius est.*" Instead, it coheres with

understanding *"quod"* as "which," in the sentence *"Si enim vel in solo intellectu est potest cogitari esse et in re quod maius est."* Although in Paris 2700 the section of the manuscript that contains *P* was copied during the 13th century, it is remotely cognate with Vaticanus Latinus 532, which Schmitt judges to have been copied during the first half of the twelfth century and probably to have come from Bec. Schmitt supposes the text in 532 to be a version of *P* that reflects a recension which is earlier than is Bodley 271. None of these considerations show that Anscombe's reading is wrong. But once the wrongness of her reading has been demonstrated on other textual grounds, as was just done in the main exposition, then these present considerations may acceptably be viewed as corroborating evidence (whether or not Vaticanus Latinus 532 stems from a *prior recensio*).

59. *P* 3:13-15 reads: *"Solus igitur verissime omnium, et ideo maxime omnium, habes esse—quia quidquid aliud est, non sic vere, et idcirco minus, habet esse."*

60. N.B. *M* 2:7-9.

61. *M* 31. Cf. *M* 34.

62. I am not here ascribing to Anscombe this reason for repudiating the traditional interpretation of *P* 2.

63. Richard Campbell, *From Belief to Understanding: A Study of Anselm's Proslogion Argument on the Existence of God* (Canberra: Australian National University Press, 1976).

64. Richard La Croix, *Proslogion II and III: A Third Interpretation of Anselm's Argument* (Leiden: E. J. Brill, 1972), pp. 14-16 and p. 36.

65. Campbell, *ibid.*, pp. 27-28. Anscombe calls Anselm's formula a *definition* on typescript p. 1: "Descartes defines God as supremely perfect being. Anselm, as: that than which nothing greater can be conceived."

66. I am referring to such minor improvements as the following: (1) indicating that in Bodley 271, Chap. 8 of *M* begins with *"Nam"*, not with *"Sed"*; (2) reading *"significat"* instead of *"significant"* at *M* 38:13 [see Schmitt's corrections in Frommann Verlag's Tome I of the *Opera Omnia Anselmi*]; (3) supplying *"sim"* at *P* 1:69; (4) recording, at *P* 6:3, the variant *"misericordiem"*; (5) improving upon Schmitt's punctuation, which, incidentally, in his transcription of the chapter-titles at the beginning of *P* differs from the punctuation in his transcription of the same chapter-titles as they are reproduced in the body of *P*.

67. Schmitt's text was originally published in 1938 in Seckau, Austria. It was republished in 1946 by Thomas Nelson & Sons, Edinburgh, Scotland, as the first of six volumes, which, collectively, constitute the *Opera Omnia Anselmi*. In 1968 these six volumes, in turn, were reprinted as two tomes by Friedrich Frommann Verlag, Stuttgart-Bad Cannstatt, West Germany. This last edition contains an introduction, by Schmitt, that draws together his major articles on Anselm. A list of *addenda* to, and *corrigenda* for, the Latin texts is also appended to each of the Frommann tomes. Tome I contains Nelson's Vols. I-II; and Tome II contains Nelson's Vols. III-VI. References to Schmitt's edition may therefore continue to be in terms of six volumes.

68. Since the first two folia of *M* are missing in Bodley 271, the present text follows Rawlinson A.392, also at Oxford University, with regard to this segment. Where parts of some words in Rawlinson A.392 have either flaked away or are for other reasons illegi-

ble, the present text has recourse to Edinburgh 104.

69. Even Schmitt's edition is not as critical as it should be. For it does not systematically record all the variants in the mss. deemed by Schmitt himself to be significant. Indeed, its recording of variants appears, at times, to be arbitrary. *S* I, 24:28 lists the trivial variant reading "*res ipse*" for "*res ipsae*", but it does not mention, vis-à-vis Bodley 271, the variant "*propriae*" for "*proprie*" [in *M* 56:5 (=*S* I, 67:25)]. And many of the variants in Edinburgh 104, and elsewhere, are ignored by Schmitt. For example, at *P* 2:16 (=*S* I, 101:15) there is no mention of the fact that instead of "*quo*", Ms. Paris 2700 has "*quod*". Moreover, some of the variant readings from Paris 2700 are cited by Schmitt in his section "*Priores recensiones*"; but other of the variant readings from this same ms. are placed with the variant readings which are not from *Priores recensiones*. (This practice, extended to the other prior recensions as well, is needlessly confusing. See, e.g., *S* I, 101n. N.B.: In spite of the fact that Schmitt dates as 13th century the portion of Paris 2700 that contains *P*, he regards this portion as stemming from a prior recension.) Elsewhere, Schmitt indicates that he knows of "very good" mss. of which he does not make use; but he does not name these for us. [See p. 213* of "Prolegomena seu Ratio Editionis," in Tome I of Frommann Verlag's edition of *Opera Omnia Anselmi*.] He claims only to have compared enough mss. to guarantee the assured accuracy of his printed texts. All in all, I would judge Schmitt's texts to provide us with a *semi-critical* edition. But there is no doubt that his discussion of the chronology of Anselm's works is masterly.

Other mss. of *M* and *P*—i.e., other than those used by Schmitt—are abundant. The following are some of the listings which I came across in catalogues at the Hill Monastic Library, St. John's University, Collegeville, Minnesota. Regarding the list which follows, I vouch for the accuracy only of those entries that have an asterisk. These are the entries that I was able to check against microfilms—no microfilms being available for the remaining entries. *MONOLOGION*: (1) *Graz, Austria, University Library, Lat. Ms. 739, fol. 15^r - 42^r (XIV^2 c.). (2) *Lincoln, England, Cathedral Library, Lat. Ms. 84, fol. 82^r -101^r (14th c.). (3) London, British Museum, Royal Mss., Lat. Ms. 5.C.IV, fol. 33^v ff. (early 14th c.). (4) *Ibid.*, Lat. Ms. 7.B.IX, fol. 105^r ff. (13th c.). (5) *London, Lambeth Palace Library, Lat. Ms. 356, fol. 210^r - 244^v (12th - 13th c.). (6) *Munich, Bavarian Staatsbibliothek, Lat. Ms. 26612, fol. 165^v - 188^r (ca. 1429-1431; as of 1982 the folios were not consistently numbered). (7) Oxford, England, Bodleian Library, Lat. Ms. 428 (XIII^1 c.; incomplete). (8) *Ibid.*, Lat. Ms. Laudian Miscellaneus 264, fol. 44^r ff. (14th c.). (9) Paris, Bibliothèque de L'Arsenal, Lat. Ms. 324, fol. 126^r - 140^v (14th c.). (10) *Ibid.*, Lat. Ms. 984, fol. 107^v - 132^v (12th c.). (11) Paris, Bibliothèque Nationale, Lat. Ms. 1694, fol. 213^v ff. (15th c.; incomplete). (12) *Ibid.*, Lat. Ms. 1769, fol. 181^v ff. (end of 14th c.). (13) *Ibid.*, Lat. Ms. 2155, fol. 55^r ff. (13th - 14th c.). (14) *Ibid.*, Lat. Ms. 2375, fol. 154^r - 174^r (14th c.). (15) *Ibid.*, Lat. Ms. 2475, fol. 30^v ff. (13th c.). (16) *Ibid.*, Lat. Ms. 2570, fol. 80^r ff. (13th c.). (17) *Ibid.*, Lat. Ms. 2884, fol. 53^v - 64^v (13th c.). (18) Prague, State Library of the Czechoslovak Republic, Lat. Ms. IV.D.8 (13th - 14th c.). (19) *Ibid.*, Lat. Ms. IV.H.4, fol. 52^r - 81^r (15th c.). (20) Perth, Australia, State Reference Library of Western Australia, Lat. Ms. 232, fol. 172^r - 188^v (13th c.). (21) Worcester, England, Cathedral Library, Lat. Ms. F 41 (15th c.). (22) *Ibid.*, Lat. Ms. F 132, fol. 119^v - 138^v (late 14th c.). *PROSLOGION*: (1) *Admont, Austria, Monastic Library, Lat. Ms. 631, fol.

56^r - 66^v (12th c.). (2) Avignon, France, Bibliothèque Municipale, Lat. Ms. 248, fol. 29^v - 41^v (XV^2 c.). (3) Chalon-sur-Saône, France, Bibliothèque Municipale, Lat. Ms. 6, fol. 174^r ff. (13th -14th c.). (4) Chartres, France, Cathedral Library, Lat. Ms. 242, fol. 192^r - 196^v (13th-14th c.). (5) Dijon, France, Bibliothèque Municipale, Lat. Ms. 182, fol. 76^v - 85^v (12th c.). (6) Florence, Biblioteca Medicea Laurenziana, Lat. Ms. S. Marco 661, fol. 38^v - 43^v (1429). (7) *Graz, Austria, University Library, Lat. Ms. 607, fol. 113^r - 118^v (ca. 1400). (8) *Ibid.*, Lat. Ms. 737, fol. 114^v - 120^v (12th c.). (9) *Ibid.*, Lat. Ms. 739, fol. 43^r - 51^r (XIV^2 c.). (10) Grenoble, France, Bibliothèque Municipale, Lat. Ms. 177, fol. 74^r ff. (15th c.). (11) *Hereford, England, Cathedral Library, Lat. Ms. O.I.vi, fol. 81^r (last line) - 83^v (12th c.; excerpt). (12) *Lincoln, England, Cathedral Library, Lat. Ms. 84, fol. 63^v - 68^v (14th c.). (13) London, British Museum, Royal Mss., Lat. Ms. 5.C.IV, fol. 47^v ff. (early 14th c.). (14) *Ibid.*, Lat. Ms. 7.B.IX, fol. 131^v ff. (13th c.). (15) *London, Lambeth Palace Library, Lat. Ms. 356, fol. 244^v - 255^v (12th - 13th c.). (16) Milan, Biblioteca Nazionale, Lat. Ms. Braid. AD.IX.44, fol. 114^r - 119^v (14th c.). (17) *Munich, Bavarian Staatsbibliothek, Lat. Ms. 21516, fol. 37^v - 42^v (12th - 13th c.). (18) *Ibid.*, Lat. Ms. 23461, fol. 30^r - 32^v (15th c.; folios misnumbered as of 1982). (19) *Ibid.*, Lat. Ms. 23649, fol. 95^v - 99^v (15th c.). (20) Naples, Italy, Biblioteca Nazionale, Fondo Principale, Lat. Ms. 194.VI.F.34, fol. 4^r - 40^v (15th c.). (21) *Ibid.*, Lat. Ms. 354.VII.G.15, fol. 194^r - 200^r (15th c.). (22) Oxford, England, Bodleian Library, Lat. Ms. 383, fol. 164^r ff. (XV^1 c.) (23) *Ibid.*, Lat. Ms. 436, fol. 131^r ff. (15th c.). (24) *Ibid.*, Lat. Ms. 867, fol. 224^v ff. (15th c.; incomplete). (25) *Ibid.*, Lat. Ms. Hamilton 21, fol. 246^r ff. (15th c.). (26) *Ibid.*, Lat. Ms. Laudian Miscellaneus 264, fol. 58^r ff. (14th c.). (27) Paris, Bibliothèque de L'Arsenal, Lat. Ms. 984, fol. 132^v - 139^v (12th c.). (28) Paris, Bibliothèque Nationale, Latin Ms. 564, fol. 123^v ff. (12th c.). (29) *Ibid.*, Lat. Ms. 1694, fol. 229^v ff. (15th c.). (30) *Ibid.*, Lat. Ms. 1769, fol. 197^v - 200^v (end of 14th c.). (31) *Ibid.*, Lat. Ms. 2155, fol. 68^v ff. (13th - 14th c.). (32) *Ibid.*, Lat. Ms. 2375, fol. 149^v ff. (14th c.). (33) *Ibid.*, Lat. Ms. 2377, fol. 69^v ff. (14th c.). (34) *Ibid.*, Lat. Ms. 2475, fol. 62^r ff. (13th c.; excerpt). (35) *Ibid.*, Lat. Ms. 2476, fol. 94^v ff. (14th c.). (36) *Ibid.*, Lat. Ms. 2568, fol. 21^r ff. (XIII^2 - XIV c.; meditational excerpt). (37) *Ibid.*, Lat. Ms. 2570, fol. 58^r - 61^v and 102^r - 105^v (13th c.). (38) *Ibid.*, Lat. Ms. 2692, fol. 154^v ff. (15th c.; excerpt). (39) *Ibid.*, Lat. Ms. 2883, fol. 2^r - 10^r (12th c.). (40) *Ibid.*, Lat. Ms. 2884, fol. 27^r - 30^v (13th c.). (41) Perth, Australia, State Reference Library of Western Australia, Lat. Ms. 232, fol. 167^r - 171^v (13th c.). (42) Prague, State Library of the Czechoslovak Republic, Lat. Ms. IV.D.8 (13th - 14th c.). (43) *Ibid.*, Lat. Ms. IV.H.4, fol. 81^r - 89^v (15th c.). (44) *Ibid.*, Lat. Ms. X.H.17, fol. 64^v - 69^v (15th c.). (45) Rome, Biblioteca Angelica, Lat. Ms. 1485 (V.2.22), fol. 154^v - 156^r (13th c.). (46) Rome, Biblioteca Casanatense, Lat. Ms. 804, fol. 136^v - 145^r (14th c.). (47) Rome, Biblioteca Vallicelliana, Lat. Ms. C.100, fol. 105^v - 114^r (14th c.). (48) *Salzburg, St. Peter Archabbey, Lat. Ms. a.I.18, fol. 1^r - 18^v (14th - 15th c.). (49) *Ibid.*, Lat. Ms. a.III.18, fol. 173^r - 177^v (1431; meditational excerpt). (50) *Ibid.*, Lat. Ms. a.VII.27, fol. 59^r - 62^r (1432; meditational excerpt). (51) San Daniele del Friuli, Italy, Biblioteca Communale Guarneriana, Lat. Ms. 39, fol. 203^r - 216^v (15th c.). (52) Trier, Germany, Stadtbibliothek, Lat. Ms. 200, fol. 21^r - 27^r (14th c.). (53) Vatican City, Biblioteca Apostolica, Lat. Ms. 456, fol. 35^r - 36^v (15th c.; excerpt). (54) *Ibid.*, Lat. Ms. 467, fol. 85^r - 93^v (15th c.). (55) *Ibid.*, Lat. Ms. 1041, fol. 349^v ff. (15th c.; meditational excerpt). (56) *Ibid.*, Lat. Ms. 4257, fol. 9^r ff. (15th c.). (57) *Ibid.*, Lat. Ms. 4578, fol. 18^v -

21ʳ (15th c.). (58) *Ibid.*, Lat. Ms. Chig. A.IV.93, fol. 81ʳ - 93ʳ (15th c.). (59) *Ibid.*, Lat. Ms. Chig. A.VI.181, fol. 41ʳ - 51ʳ (14th c.). (60) *Ibid.*, Lat. Ms. Palat. 191, fol. 215ᵛ - 220ᵛ (15th c.; excerpt?). (61) *Ibid.*, Lat. Ms. Palat. 226, fol. 181ʳ - 195ᵛ (15th c.). (62) Wolfenbüttel, Germany, Herzog-August-Bibliothek, Lat. Ms. 50.6.Aug.4ᵗᵒ, fol. 55ʳ - 61ʳ (14th c.). (63) *Ibid.*, Lat. Ms. 78.Aug.fol., fol. 186ᵛ - 192ᵛ (15th c.). (64) Worcester, England, Cathedral Library, Lat. Ms. F 41 (15th c.). (65) *Ibid.*, Lat. Ms. F 132, fol. 47ʳ - 51ᵛ (late 14th c.).

70. N.B. pp. 231* - 234* of F. S. Schmitt's "Prolegomena seu Ratio Editionis" in Tome I of Frommann Verlag's edition of *Opera Omnia Anselmi*.

71. E.g., see *M* 3:21-22.

72. Peter Geach also insists on the "of". See p. 234 of his review of Campbell in *Philosophy*, 52 (April 1977).

73. Even the verb "to conceive" sometimes takes the preposition "of", as does "conceiving" in the sentence marked by this note. Presumably, someone might contend that "*aliquid quo maius . . .* " should be translated as "something than which nothing greater can be conceived of." But I find it idiomatic to drop the "of" following the passive voice both of "to conceive" and of "to think." E.g., one might say idiomatically: "Unicorns are among the things that can be thought, among the things that can be conceived."

74. See especially my translation of *Reply to Gaunilo* 9:19-21. Note also the translation of "*cogitat*" in *Reply* 3:11-19.

75. Cf. *M* 10:7-9.

76. Cf. *Reply to Gaunilo* 1:24-25: "*Si ergo cogitari potest esse, ex necessitate est. Amplius. Si utique vel cogitari potest, necesse est illud esse.*" Since, in the first sentence, I render "*Si . . . cogitari potest esse*" as "If . . . it can be thought to exist," I prefer to render "*Si . . . vel cogitari potest,*" in the second sentence, as "If . . . it can be even thought . . . . "

77. Cf. *On Behalf of the Fool* 4:19-25 with *Reply to Gaunilo* 7:11. Note also *M* 10:9-21; *M* 65:32-33; and *Philosophical Fragments* 42:22 ff. (i.e., the section on "*aliquid*").

78. See Chap. 6 ("What Is a Translation?") of my *Hermeneutical and Textual Problems in the Complete Treatises of St. Anselm* (New York: Mellen Press, 1976).

79. I have no objection to someone's calling a translation an interpretation, provided he make clear that interpretation qua translation is importantly different from interpretation in the more extended sense.

80. G. Schufreider, "Reunderstanding Anselm's Argument," p. 385n.

81. *De Conceptu Virginali* 29 (*S* II, 173:6-7).

82. Cf. the interchangeable use of "*significet*" and "*designet*" at *M* 38:22-23 and the interchanging of "*expressa*" and "*designata*" at *M* 65:29-30.

83. Cf. the interchangeable use of "*esset per se*" and "*per se subsistat*" at *M* 44:16-17

84. Cf. *M* 15:22, where Anselm speaks of the Supreme Being as *maior et melior* than whatever is not what it itself is. Note also *M* 4:5-6, where "*praestantior*" is interchanged with "*melior*" in speaking of created things.

85. Admittedly, Anselm's language does foster misapprehension in those cases

where it is *preunderstood* by a reader as "technical."

86. By comparison, it would be equally ungrammatical to presume to translate every subjunctive sentence of Anselm's into a corresponding subjunctive sentence in English.

87. Interestingly, Hereford Cathedral Library Lat. Ms. O.I.vi, fol. 81ᵛ does employ the subjunctive in *P* 2. To cite an example: "*Et certe id quo maius cogitari nequit, non potest esse in |solo| intellectu. Si enim vel in solo intellectu esset, posset cogitari esse et in re, quod maius est*" (my transcription; punctuation editorialized by me; "*solo*" supplied qua word inadvertently omitted by the copyist).

88. Anselm Stolz, " 'Vere esse' im Proslogion des hl. Anselm," *Scholastik*, 9 (1934), 400-409.

89. Kurt Flasch, "Der philosophische Ansatz des Anselm von Canterbury im Monologion und sein Verhältnis zum augustinischen Neuplatonismus," pp. 1-43 in *Analecta Anselmiana*. Edited by F. S. Schmitt (Frankfurt/Main: Minerva Verlag, 1970). See pp. 21-25. Flasch is right, however, in his judgment that *M* 3:13-14 shows that Anselm accepts the doctrine of participation qua participation-in-substance (and not just qua participation-in-quality). But the fact remains that Anselm—in claiming in *M* 1-4 that all good things are good through some one thing, which is good through itself—is not teaching that all good things participate in God (who is the Supreme Good).

90. I cannot agree with Richard Campbell's many adulatory allusions—such as "a thinker as scrupulously careful as we have found Anselm to be" (p. 139), "one with as acute a mind as he undoubtedly had" (p. 5), "a careful writer like Anselm" (p. 95), "his keen logical sense" (p. 102). No doubt, Anselm had an acute mind—indeed, a certain genius. But he is neither the logician nor the careful writer that Campbell makes him out to be. See Campbell's *From Belief to Understanding: A Study of Anselm's Proslogion Argument on the Existence of God, op. cit.*

91. See also *M* 4:12-14 and *M* 14:10-11.

92. An equally acceptable translation would be "Therefore, if it can be thought to exist: of necessity, it exists."

93. Cf. the references in notes 3-8 of the Preface.

94. See my discussion of *M* in *Anselm of Canterbury: Volume Four: Hermeneutical and Textual Problems in the Complete Treatises of St. Anselm, op. cit.*

NOTES TO THE TRANSLATIONS

MONOLOGION: Preface and Text

1. Anselm uses "*essentia*" sometimes in place of "*esse*" and "*existentia*" and sometimes in place of "*natura*" and "*substantia*." With respect to the former use, cf. *S* I, 189:24 with 188:29 (*De Veritate* 9); cf. *S* I, 276:3 with 276:7 (*De Casu Diaboli* 28); cf. *S* I, 235:3-5 with 235:7 (*De Casu Diaboli* 1); note also *M* 6:60-65, as well as *S* I, 261:7-8 (*De Casu Diaboli* 16). With respect to the latter use, see *M* 3:33-35 and *M* 4:21-22 and 37; cf. *S* I, 245:22-24 (*De Casu Diaboli* 8) with the last half of *De Casu Diaboli* 1. We must remember that "*essentia*" replaces Augustine's word "*natura*," which sometimes means "natural existent."

In *M* 4:19 Anselm uses "*essentia*" for *what* a thing is.

Unlike the German word *"Wesen"* the English word "essence" cannot easily serve all of the above purposes. In general, the most accurate English translation of Anselm's *"essentia"* is "being." And at the beginning of *De Casu Diaboli* 8 Anselm explains that there are many beings (*essentiae*) besides the ones which are properly called substances. Other relevant references in *M* are 44:38-40 and 21:39. Note *PF* 42:30; 42:32-33; 43:14-15, where Anselm interchanges *"non existit in rerum natura,"* *"est absque omni essentia,"* and *"habet nec ullam existentiam."* Note Gaunilo's use of *"essentia"* for "existence" in *On Behalf of the Fool* 6:17. And, finally, see Augustine's *Catholic and Manichean Ways of Life* 2.2.2 (*PL* 32:1346) and *DT* 5.2.3 (*CCSL* 50, p. 207).

2. Cf. *DT* 1.4.7. In *M* 79 Anselm's reference to God as three substances may have disturbed some of his readers, since this terminology had become alien to the Latin Church, which insisted that God is one substance. Anselm's concern that the preface be transcribed with the work itself may indicate as well that some readers were puzzled by his dialectic in Chapters 20-24, not understanding the technique of "disputing with oneself."

3. Regarding the antecedent of *"illo"* (in *"illo prosequente"* at *M* 1:16) cf. *M* 29:5.

4. Anselm deduces consequences not mentioned in Scripture, which is considered to be authoritative. Cf. Anselm, *De Concordia* III, 6 (*S* II, 271:28 - 272:7).

5. Cf. Augustine's reasoning in *DT* 8.3.4-5 (*CCSL* 50, pp. 271-274).

6. That is, it is good through one thing, not through two things.

7. Throughout *M* Anselm's argument draws upon this distinction between *esse per se* and *esse per aliud*.

8. This meaning of "greatness" applies to Anselm's description of God (in *P* 2) as "that than which a greater cannot be thought." Note *P* 14:4 and *P* 18:26-27.

9. Anselm is arguing, then, that there cannot be more than one being which, strictly speaking, exists *per se*. In *M* 44 he distinguishes between existing *per se* and existing *de alio* and maintains that these are compatible modes of existing. The Son of God exists *through* Himself while existing *from* the Father, because the Son has from the Father the fact of existing through Himself. Yet, in the present chapter Anselm is not drawing upon the *per se/de alio* distinction. According to the present argument a thing can exist *per se* in some respect without existing *per se* in every respect. As *summa essentia* and *summum esse*, God alone exists absolutely *per se*, for He shares His nature with no other.

10. *"Essentia,"* *"substantia,"* *"natura"* are here (but not everywhere) used interchangeably. N.B. *M* 26 and 79. See n. 1 above.

11. Cf. Augustine, *City of God* 12.1 (*CCSL* 48, p. 356).

12. What exists *per se* is the highest being of all. And, conversely, the highest being of all exists *per se*.

13. See n. 1 above.

14. Anselm takes this division of causes from Cicero's *Topics*. Anselm did not know Boethius's discussion of Cicero's division of causes. See F. S. Schmitt, "Anselm und der (Neu-)Platonismus," *Analecta Anselmiana* I (Frankfurt: Minerva Press, 1969), p. 44.

15. Literally: "Hence, no thing even conceivably preceded—through which thing this |Nature| existed from nothing."

16. Anselm makes no distinction—either here or elsewhere—between existing and

subsisting. In most places *"subsistere"* can be translated as "to exist."

17. Fredegisus († 834) had maintained that the nothingness from which God created the world was other than absolutely nothing (*PL* 105:752).

18. Note also *M* 34:10-12. Anselm adapts the doctrine of exemplarism from Augustine. See *Eighty-Three Different Questions* 46.2 (*CCSL* 44A, p. 71); *On the Gospel of John* 1.17 (*PL* 35:1387); *Literal Commentary on Genesis* 5.14.31 (*PL* 34:332). Anselm modifies this doctrine in an important way. See the discussion on pp. 77-78 of Vol. IV of my *Anselm of Canterbury*.

19. Concerning the example of the craftsman see *P* 2 and *On Behalf of the Fool* 3. On the distinction between thinking words and thinking things, see *P* 4 and *On Behalf of the Fool* 4.

20. Note *DT* 8.6.9 (*CCSL* 50, pp. 281-282), where Augustine calls mental images *words*. Cf. *M* 32, n. 64 below.

21. Cf. Anselm, *Cur Deus Homo* II, 11 (*S* II, 109:8-11): "I think that mortality pertains not to sinless human nature but to corrupt human nature. Indeed, if man had never sinned and if his immortality had been immutably confirmed, he would have been no less a real man; and when mortals will rise in incorruptibility, they will be, no less, real men."

See also *Cur Deus Homo* I, 9 (*S* II, 61:25-28); I, 22 (*S* II, 90:20-23); II, 2 (*S* II, 98:10-11); II, 3. Note Boethius, *On Aristotle's Categories* (*PL* 64:163); *On Cicero's Topics* (*PL* 64:1096). Cf. Augustine, *DT* 7.4.7 (*CCSL* 50, p. 255); *DT* 15.7.11 (*CCSL* 50A, p. 474); *On Order* 2.11.31 (*CCSL* 29, p. 124).

22. Cf. Augustine, *DT* 14.7.10 (*CCSL* 50A, p. 434); *DT* 15.10.19 (*CCSL* 50A, p. 485).

23. Cf. Augustine *DT* 11.8.14 (*CCSL* 50, p. 351).

24. Cf. Augustine's *Ep.* 7.3.6 (*PL* 33:70).

25. Rom. 11:36. When in *M* 14 Anselm states that the Supreme Being exists through all things (*est per omnia*), he means that it is present in all things—not that it derives its existence from all things.

26. Note Augustine's distinction between predicating *secundum substantiam, secundum accidens,* and *secundum relativum: DT* 5.3.4 to 5.5.6 (*CCSL* 50, pp. 208-211). See also *DT* 5.8.9 (*CCSL* 50, pp. 215-216); *DT* 15.5.8 (*CCSL* 50A, p. 470); *On the Gospel of John* 39.3-4 (*PL* 35:1683).

27. For a discussion of *M* 15 see Nelson Pike, "The Justification of the Doctrine of Timelessness: Anselm," in his *God and Timelessness* (London: Routledge and Kegan Paul, 1970), pp. 130-166.

28. Augustine in *DT* 5.1.2 (*CCSL* 50, p. 207) speaks of understanding God (if we are able, and as best we are able) to be "good without quality, great without quantity, Creator without need, ruling from no position, containing all things without *having*, present as a whole everywhere but without place, everlasting without time, making mutable things without Himself changing, and Himself suffering nothing."

29. *DT* 6.7.8 (*CCSL* 50, p. 237).

30. Cf. Augustine, *City of God* 11.10. (*CCSL* 48, pp. 330-331).

31. Chap. 16.

32. That Anselm here ascribes will to the Supreme Being accords with his reason-

ing in the last (English) paragraph of *M* 15.

33. Chap. 16.

34. This argument is repeated in *DV* 1.

35. Anselm is contrasting (1) treating nothing as a kind of being and (2) making a negation of the form "There is no x such that x taught me to fly."

36. Chap. 14.

37. Chap. 18.

38. Anselm begins a dialectical section which concludes with two contradictory statements. Chapters 22-24 attempt to resolve the contradiction.

39. Chap. 16.

40. Chap. 17.

41. Chap. 20.

42. Chaps. 18 and 20 respectively.

43. Cf. Augustine, *Confessions* 5.2.2 (*CCSL* 27, p. 57).

44. Cf. Augustine, *Expositions of the Psalms* 7.19 (*CCSL* 38, p. 49).

45. See Chap. 14.

46. *Intellectus*: the intellect, the understanding. See *P* 2, n. 26 below.

47. See Chap. 18.

48. From Boethius, *Consolation of Philosophy* 5.6 (*PL* 63:858).

49. Chap. 22.

50. Chap. 17.

51. Cf. Augustine, *DT* 5.16.17 (*CCSL* 50, pp. 225-226).

52. This Spirit is a particular, not a universal.

53. Chaps. 17 and 25.

54. Note Augustine, *Expositions of the Psalms* 134.4 (*CCSL* 40, p. 1940).

55. Chaps. 10-12.

56. Chaps. 3, 7, and 13.

57. Chap. 27.

58. See Chap 27, n. 52.

59. Chap. 12.

60. Note Augustine, *Confessions* 11.7.9 (*CCSL* 27, pp. 198-199).

61. See Chap. 10, n. 20.

62. Note Augustine, *Eighty-Three Different Questions* 51.2 (*CCSL* 44A, pp. 79-80).

63. On Anselm's view, all thoughts (these he also calls words) that are thoughts of objects are *images* of these objects. They mentally depict these objects. But though the English expression "my thought of x" makes sense, the expression "my word of x" does not. To preserve the sense of "of" which Anselm has in mind, it seems best to translate "*verbum eorum* . . . " as "Word |or Image| of those things . . . . " N.B. *M* 38:24-28; *M* 46:11-15; *M* 63:29-30 and 35-36.

64. It is important to notice that Anselm is not discussing words in the usual sense. He is talking about words "by which an object is *thus* mentally spoken"—i.e., about thoughts which "depict" what they are thoughts of. Hence, what he means by "every word is a word of some thing" is: every mental image is the image of some thing. And when he declares, "There can be no word of that which neither did exist, does exist, nor

will exist," he is not suggesting the absurd theory that our language can have no words for nonexistent things such as unicorns. Rather, he is stating that an image is not rightly said to be the *image* of some thing unless that thing at some time exists. See *M* 11, especially the English sentence marked by n. 24. Cf. *M* 48:13-15; *M* 63:8-10. Note the second sentence of *M* 31. N.B.: Anselm uses "image" and "word" equivocally. E.g., he calls both thoughts and memory-images *words*, as well as calling them both *images* (Cf. *M* 33, 62, and 10).

65. This reasoning is rejected by Anselm.

66. Like Augustine, Anselm uses *"memini"* and *"reminisci"* in a broader sense than the English word "remembering." The Latin verbs encompass *being mindful of, being aware of, being conscious of.* Cf. Eccl. 12:1: "Remember your Creator in the days of your youth."

67. . . . i.e., just as also the Word by which the Creator speaks created things is what the Creator is.

68. As the second member of the Trinity, the Word of God is (1) the Image or Likeness of God the Father (Col. 1:15; Heb. 1:3; *M* 33) and also (2) the eternally begotten Son of God the Father (John 3:16; Heb. 1:5; *M* 42). Corresponding to these two identifications are two different uses of the genitive in the phrase "Word of God" (*"verbum dei"*). This difference can best be seen in English by using two different prepositions. (1) The Word is similar *to* God the Father; (2) the Word is *from* God the Father. In the context above, Anselm is employing "Word of this Spirit" in the first sense: the Word is similar to God the Father (so similar as to be consubstantial with Him) and is the Image of God the Father.

In other passages Anselm switches to the second use of the genitive—even using the phrase *"suum verbum"* (e.g., *M* 31:14-15; the title of *M* 34; *M* 33:37-38 and 44-45).

69. The Latin word *"caracter"* is the equivalent of *"figura."*

70. Cf. Augustine, *On the Gospel of John* 1.17 (*PL* 35:1387), and Gaunilo, *On Behalf of the Fool* 3.

71. Cf. Chap. 9 above.

72. Cf. John 1:3-4.

73. Cf. Col. 1:16.

74. Note Augustine, *DT* 13.2.5 (*CCSL* 50A, p.386). See also *M* 43.

75. Chap. 29.

76. "Spirit" is in Latin a masculine noun (*spiritus*); "truth" and "wisdom" are feminine nouns (*veritas, sapientia*).

77. I.e., properties of the Supreme Spirit and its offspring.

78. This same idea is expressed in Chap. 38.

79. Cf. John 5:26.

80. Chaps. 27 and 39.

81. Chap. 38.

82. See Chap. 32, n. 66 above.

83. See Augustine, *DT* 10.1.2 through 10.2.4 (*CCSL* 50:312-316).

84. Anselm subscribes to the *filioque* doctrine. N.B. his treatise *De Processione Spiritus Sancti.* Augustine, too, refers to the Father as Memory, the Son as Understanding, and their Spirit as Will, or Love (*DT* 15.7.12).

85. Cf. Anselm, *De Processione Spiritus Sancti* 1 (*S* II, 183:22-29).

86. *"Spiritus"* means both *spirit* and *breath*. Hence, the one who proceeds from the Father and from the Son can plausibly be called spirit *because* He is breathed out, as it were. Anselm distinguishes the Spirit of the Father and of the Son (the Holy Spirit) from the Supreme Spirit (God).

87. I.e., the fact that no one of the three is greater than the other two, that no one of them can exist apart from the others or outside the others.

88. Chap. 59.

89. Literally: "How *there* there is only one of one."

90. Chap. 38.

91. Chap. 29.

92. Chaps. 33 and 42.

93. *Loc. cit.*

94. Cf. *Cur Deus Homo* I, 25 (*S* II, 96:2-3).

95. Isa. 53:8.

96. Chap. 26.

97. Cf. *PF* (e.g., 34:16 ff.).

98. Anselm subscribes to the doctrine of "analogy of being." Cf. Chaps. 31, 66, and 67.

99. I Cor. 13:12.

100. Chap. 31.

101. Chap. 31.

102. Cf. I Cor. 13:12.

103. I.e., can be conscious of itself. See n. 66 above.

104. Cf. Augustine, *City of God* 22.30. (*CCSL* 48, p. 863).

105. I Cor. 13:12.

106. *De Concordia* III, 9.

107. Cf. the next to last paragraph in the *Monologion* preface.

108. Matt. 22:37.

109. The Latin idiom is difficult to capture in English. I have used the following renderings: *tendere in (illam)* - to strive unto; *tendere ad (illam)* - to strive for; *credere in (illam)* - to believe in; *credere ad (illam)* - to believe on.

110. Jas. 2:20 and 26.

111. Gal. 5:6.

112. Cf. Boethius, *The Person and the Two Natures* 3 (*PL* 64:1343).

113. Chap. 26.

114. Chap. 13.

PROSLOGION: Preface and Text

1. *M* was completed during the second half of 1076. *P* was probably written about 1077-1078. The controversy with Gaunilo occurred in the next year or so. See F. S. Schmitt, "Zur Chronologie der Werke des hl. Anselm von Canterbury," *Revue Bénédictine* 44 (1932), 322-350.

2. Note also Anselm's Epistle 109 (S III, 242).

3. † 1106.

4. Cf. Matt. 6:6; Isa. 26:20.

5. Ps. 26:8 (27:8).

6. I Tim. 6:16.

7. Ps. 50:13 (51:11).

8. Ps. 77:25 (78:25).

9. Ps. 126:2 (127:2).

10. Ps. 121:9 (122:9).

11. Jer. 14:19.

12. Ps. 114:3 (116:3).

13. Ps. 37:9 (38:8).

14. Ps. 6:4; 12:1 (6:3; 13:1).

15. Ps. 12:4 (13:3).

16. Ps. 79:4 and 8 (80:3 and 7).

17. Ps. 78:9 (79:9).

18. Job 3:24.

19. Ps. 37:5 (38:4).

20. Ps. 68:16 (69:15).

21. See *M* 67:13-14; *M* 32 n. 66.

22. Cf. Isa. 7:9. Anselm takes this reading from Augustine, who follows an Old Latin translation of the Septuagint. See *DT* 15.2.2 (*CCSL* 50A, p. 461). As *Christian Doctrine* 2.12.17 (*PL* 34:43) attests, Augustine was not unaware of the alternative translation: "Unless you believe, you will not continue" (*Nisi credideritis, non permanebitis*).

23. Cf. Heb. 11:6.

24. Ps. 13:1; 52:1 (14:1; 53:1).

25. By "greater" Anselm means "better," "more perfect," "more excellent." Note *M* 2:7-9; *P* 14:3-4; *P* 18:26-27.

26. Obviously "to have in the understanding" is idiomatic for Anselm in the way that "to have in mind" is idiomatic for us. Anselm uses *"intellectus"* to indicate, variously, (1) an act of understanding, (2) intelligence (*Reply to Gaunilo* 2:3-4), (3) a capability, or power, of the soul (*Reply to Gaunilo* 2:9-11 and *M* 23:10-11), (4) a meaning or a respect (*Reply to Gaunilo* 2:19 and *M* 19:27).

What is understood (for an act of understanding) is understood by the understanding (a capability of the soul) and is therefore in the understanding (a manner of speaking). Because reflective thinking is an operation of the rational soul, understanding (which is a mode of thinking) is also an operation of the soul.

27. Cf. *M* 10 and *On Behalf of the Fool* 3.

28. *P* 2 has come to be called Anselm's ontological argument. This label is not Anselm's but derives from the period of Kant (though it is not original with Kant). In the *Critique of Pure Reason* Kant attacks the "ontological" arguments of Gottfried Wilhelm von Leibniz and Christian Wolff, whose formulations are different from Anselm's. Also, Anselm does not speak of God as *ens realissimum* but refers to Him as *summa essentia* (*M* 16), *summum esse* (*M* 19), *aliquid quo nihil maius cogitari potest* (*P* 2).

29. Anselm, like Augustine, subscribes to a theory of degrees of reality (note *M* 28, 31, and 34). God is more real, exists more, than do created things.

30. Ps. 13:1; 52:1 (14:1; 53:1).

31. I.e., rightly understands what is signified by "that than which a greater cannot be thought."

32. This paragraph is the conclusion for Chaps. 2-4 and not merely for Chap. 4. In *Cur Deus Homo* I, 1 (S II, 48:19-24) Boso indicates that he would continue to believe even if he could not understand. Anselm does not call upon Boso to suspend his belief but to suspend appeal to his belief in order to prove by rational necessity (*rationes necessariae*) that the Son of God became incarnate. Anselm's "rationalism" is therefore a methodological rationalism, as Schmitt indicates ["Die wissenschaftliche Methode in Anselms 'Cur Deus homo'," *Spicilegium Beccense* (Paris 1959), 349-370]. The same methodology obtains in *M* and *P*.

33. I.e., it cannot be thought of You that You are less great than can be thought.

34. See *M* 15 and *Reply to Gaunilo* 10 for a statement of this same principle.

35. Peter Damian (1007-1072) had raised the question about whether God could make what has happened not to have happened. See *De Divina Omnipotentia* (*PL* 145:618-620).

36. Note *PF* 24:16; *De Veritate* 8; *De Casu Diaboli* 12; *Cur Deus Homo* II, 17.

37. Note *PF* 26:23ff.

38. Note *PF* 43:20-23.

39. "*Iustus*" and "*iustitia*" mean *just* and *justice* in the sense of *righteous* and *righteousness*.

40. I Tim. 6:16.

41. " . . . why You are this"—i.e., why You are gracious to sinners.

42. " . . . more just than this"—i.e., more just than Your being so good and Your working so powerfully that . . . etc.

43. " . . . to say this"—i.e., to say that You are unjustly merciful to those who are evil.

44. Viz., the greatest conceivable justice.

45. Ps. 24:10; 144:17 (25:10; 145:17).

46. See *M* 15 and *Reply to Gaunilo* 10.

47. Cf. *M* 16.

48. " . . . has understood this"—i.e., has understood that You are light and truth.

49. Ps. 42:3 (43.3).

50. Cf. I John 3:2.

51. Cf. I John 1:5.

52. See *M* 65.

53. " . . . something of this kind"—i.e., something which is greater than can be thought.

54. I Tim. 6:16.

55. Acts 17:28.

56. Jer. 14:19.

57. Cf. Ps. 50:10 (51:8).

58. Ps. 50:7 (51:5).

59. Rom. 5:12.

60. Cf. Ps. 24:7 (25:7).

61. Ps. 26:9 (27:9).

62. Ps. 12:4 (13:3).
63. Cf. S. of Sol. 6:13.
64. Cf. *M* 22.
65. Ps. 89:2 (90:2). Cf. *M* 19.
66. Cf. *M* 15.
67. Scripture uses the phrases "*in saeculum saeculi*" (singular) and "*in saecula saeculorum*" (plural) to express eternity, or what is forever and ever, "world without end." Cf. Ps. 111:9 (112:9) with I Pet. 4:11, for example. In *P* 21 Anselm questions whether or not there are numerically different eternities in God. The issue is explored more fully in *De Incarnatione Verbi* 15 and *De Processione* 16. Note Augustine, *City of God* 12.20 (*CCSL* 48, p. 376).
68. Note *M* 14 and 23.
69. See n. 29 above.
70. Ex. 3:14.
71. Cf. *M* 42, where the Word is identified as the Son.
72. Cf. *M* 49-50.
73. Luke 10:42. Note Augustine, *Sermon* 103.3.4 (*PL* 38:614-615); *Sermon* 255.6.6 (*PL* 38:1189).
74. Cf. *P* 18, where God is called every true good. Note also *P* 22. Cf. Augustine, *City of God* 22.30 (*CCSL* 48, pp. 862-863).
75. Cf. Augustine, *Catholic and Manichean Ways of Life* 1.3.4 (*PL* 32:1312): "In my opinion, we cannot call happy (1) him who does not have what he loves, whatever it be, nor (2) him who has what he loves, if [what he loves] is harmful, nor (3) him who does not love what he has, even if [what he has] be the best."
76. I Cor. 2:9.
77. Matt. 13:43.
78. Matt. 22:30.
79. I Cor. 15:44.
80. Wisd. 5:15.
81. Ps. 36:39 (37:39).
82. Ps. 16:15 (17:15).
83. Ps. 35:9 (36:8).
84. *Loc. cit.*
85. Cf. John 14:21.
86. Cf. Matt. 22:37-39.
87. Cf. Matt. 25:21 and 23.
88. Matt. 5:9.
89. Cf. John 10:32.
90. John 14:3.
91. Rom. 8:17.
92. Rom. 8:38-39.
93. Matt. 22:37.
94. John 16:24.
95. Matt. 25:21.
96. I Cor. 2:9.

97. John 16:24.
98. Isa. 9:6.
99. Cf. Ps. 62:2 (63:1).
100. Matt. 25:21.
101. Rom. 1:25.

ON BEHALF OF THE FOOL

1. Early mss. do not contain Gaunilo's name. See S I, 125n.
2. Ps. 13:1; 52:1 (14:1; 53:1).
3. Most of the early mss. do not contain these divisions. See S I, 125 n.
4. Gaunilo here misstates Anselm's argument. Anselm does not argue that if that than which a greater cannot be thought does not exist, then *any* existing being is greater than it. He argues that if it did not exist, it could be thought to exist, and thus could be thought to be greater than it is—a contradiction.

5. Gaunilo switches from the description "a nature than which nothing greater can be thought" to the description "the greater than all |others|" (*maius omnibus*). Probably he intended "*maius omnibus*" as an abbreviation of "*illud maius omnibus quae cogitari possunt*": "that |which is| greater than all |others| that can be thought." (See the beginning and the end of Section 4. Note also 3:13.) But Anselm reads "*maius omnibus*" as a shorthand for "*maius omnibus quae sunt*": "that which is greater than all |other| existing beings" *Reply to Gaunilo* 5:19-21); he therefore remonstrates with Gaunilo over confusing the expression "*quo maius nequit cogitari*" with the expression "*maius omnibus.*" And, indeed, Gaunilo does once use the description '*maior natura omnium quae sunt*' (7:9-10). But here he is not employing it as a substitute for Anselm's formula (as he *does* use "*maius omnibus quae cogitari possunt*" substitutionally). Rather, he is calling upon Anselm to abandon his *Proslogion* 2 argument, regarded as fallacious, in favor of a sound argument to show that there really exists a being greater than all others, viz., God. See "Anselm's Debate with Gaunilo," Chap. 4 of my *Anselm of Canterbury: Volume Four: Hermeneutical and Textual Problems in the Complete Treatises of St. Anselm.*

Both Gaunilo and Anselm understand the word "*aliis*" as supplied in the phrase "*maius omnibus |aliis|.*" Gaunilo once omits "*aliis*" when talking about an island greater than all *others*, though he obviously intends for the reader to supply this word (cf. *On Behalf of the Fool* 6:5). Anselm himself, like all medieval writers, does not always explicitly add "*aliud*" to contexts where it obviously belongs (e.g., *M* 64:11).

6. Sections 2-4 deal mainly with the question of how that than which a greater cannot be thought is in the understanding. Sections 5-6 attack the claim that this nature exists also in reality. The first half of Section 7 responds to *P* 3; and the second half speaks for Gaunilo himself (not for the Fool) in recommending that *P* 3 describe God as "not able to be *understood* not to exist."

7. " . . . in no way exist in themselves"—i.e., in no way exist actually.

8. Gaunilo is not here proposing to substitute "understand" for "think" in Anselm's argument. Rather, he is surmising that Anselm might intend this move.

Just as *Reply to Gaunilo* 4 speaks to *On Behalf of the Fool* 7, so Anselm's Section 6 takes issue with Gaunilo's Section 2. But Anselm misunderstands Gaunilo's dialectic and therefore charges Section 2 with a blatant inconsistency. See "Anselm's Debate with

Gaunilo," cited in n. 5 above.

9. *On the Gospel of John* 1.17 (*PL* 35:1387). See *M* 9 and 34.

10. In fact, however Anselm subscribes to the doctrine of "analogy of being." See *M* 31 and *M* 65-67.

11. See *M* 10 and *P* 4.

12. That is, Gaunilo thinks that Anselm's argument begs the question of God's existence. Yet, even if Anselm does beg the question, Gaunilo does not really discern the *reductio ad impossibile* structure of the argument. Note William Rowe's "The Ontological Argument and Question-Begging," *International Journal for Philosophy of Religion*, 7 (1976), 425-432.

13. Cf. the last paragraph of n. 5 above.

14. Having finished with the Fool's response, Gaunilo now speaks for himself. Thus, he can say: "I understand indubitably that that |being| which is supreme, viz., God, exists and cannot fail to exist."

15. That is, the Fool thinks a proposition which both Anselm and Gaunilo regard as a falsehood, viz., that God does not exist. But, maintains Gaunilo, the Fool cannot *understand* this falsehood because, strictly speaking, only truths can be understood.

REPLY TO GAUNILO

1. Most early mss. do not contain the subsequent divisions into sections. (See S I, 130n.) At the beginning of Section 5 Anselm indicates that his reply deals first with Gaunilo's more important objections and later with those so obviously wrong as not really to need refuting. Thus, Anselm's response does not follow the order of Gaunilo's criticisms.

2. Anselm does not seem to know the name or the identity of the defender of the Fool. Nor does Eadmer (*Vita Anselmi*) mention Gaunilo by name or location. See *On Behalf of the Fool*, n. 1.

3. That is, Anselm replies to the Christian rather than to the Fool by taking for granted both that God is correctly described as that than which a greater cannot be thought and that Gaunilo understands this description. Still, in Section 8 Anselm does reply also to the Fool by explaining how that than which a greater cannot be thought can in some respects be conceived by reference to created things.

4. I.e., if it could be thought not to exist . . . .

5. Cf. *M* 65.

6. *In nullo intellectu* (*Reply to Gaunilo* 2.5). Comparison of *Reply to Gaunilo* 7:6-9 with 7:12-13 makes clear the nuances of this phrase.

N.B. the phrases "*nec actu nec intellectu potest non esse*," "*potest vel actu vel intellectu non esse*," "*vel actu vel intellectu dissolvi potest*," and "*nec cogitatione potest non esse*." (See *Reply to Gaunilo* 1:27; 1:29; *P* 18:26; *P* 4:13-14 respectively.) In the English translation of these expressions no difference between *intellectu* and *cogitatione* is called for. Both words are accurately translated as "conceivably." Note also *M* 6:35; *M* 6:46 and 49.

7. See n. 6 above.

8. *In ullo intellectu.* Cf. n. 6 above.

9. The reason is that for that than which a greater cannot be thought to be thought

not to exist involves, claims Anselm, an inconsistency.

    10. *P* 4.

    11. Cf. *On Behalf of the Fool* 2:7-9. Anselm repeats Gaunilo's phrase "*non |posse| hoc aliter cogitare, nisi intelligendo id est scientia comprehendendo re ipsa illud existere.*" But Anselm's continuation shows that he understands this phrase differently from Gaunilo (and thus I have translated it differently in the two cases). For Anselm interprets Gaunilo to be defining "*intelligere*" as "*scientia comprehendere re ipsa illud existere.*" But what Gaunilo did was to construe "*intelligere*" as "*scientia comprehendere*"; thus, he identified *intelligere re ipsa illud existere* with *scientia comprehendere re ipsa illud existere*. Gaunilo's meaning would stand out better with the use of parentheses: *non |posse| hoc aliter cogitare, nisi intelligendo (id est scientia comprehendendo) re ipsa illud existere*.

    12. Cf. Matt. 27:4.

    13. See n. 6 above.

    14. Literally: " . . . because he denies *God*, whose signification [*sensus*] he in no way thinks."

    15. See n. 6 above.

    16. Rom. 1:20.

    17. See *P* 5 and *M* 15 for a statement of this same principle.

BIBLIOGRAPHY

[Anselm of Canterbury]. *St. Anselm's Treatise on Free Will* (15th-century English translation). Introduced by Gregory S. Cox. Mount Durand, St. Peter Port, Guernsey, C.I., via Britain: Toucan Press, 1977.

_____. *Opere Filosofiche*. Translated by Sofia Vanni Rovighi. Bari: Editori Laterza, 1969 [Italian translation of *Monologion, Proslogion, Debate with Gaunilo, De Grammatico, De Veritate, De Libero Arbitrii, De Casu Diaboli, De Concordia*].

Bäck, Allan. "Existential Import in Anselm's Ontological Argument," *Franciscan Studies*, 41 (1981), 97-109.

Barnette, R. L. "Anselm and the Fool," *International Journal for Philosophy of Religion*, 6 (Winter 1975), 201-218.

Barral, Mary R. "Truth and Justice in the Mind of Anselm," *SB II*, pp. 571-582.

Basham, R. Robert. "The 'Second Version' of Anselm's Ontological Argument," *Canadian Journal of Philosophy*, 6 (December 1976), 665-683.

Berlinger, Rudolf. "Das höchste Sein. Strukturmomente der Metaphysik des Anselm von Canterbury," pp. 43-53 in Wilhelm Arnold and Hermann Zeltner, editors, *Tradition und Kritik* (Festschrift for Rudolf Zocher). Stuttgart: F. Frommann, 1967.

Bianco, Alberto. "S. Anselmo tra cultura monastica e scolastica," *Rivista Rosminiana di Filosofia e di Cultura* [Milan], 74 (1980), 132-147.

Bonansea, Bernardino M. "Duns Scotus and St. Anselm's Ontological Argument," pp. 128-141 in John K. Ryan, editor, *Studies in Philosophy and the History of Philosophy*, Vol. 4. Washington, D.C.: Catholic University Press, 1969.

_____. "The Ontological Argument: Proponents and Opponents," pp. 135-192 in John K. Ryan, editor, *Studies in Philosophy and the History of Philosophy*, Vol. 6. Washington, D.C.: Catholic University Press, 1973.

Brecher, Bob. "Aquinas on Anselm," *Philosophical Studies* [Ireland], 23 (1975), 63-66.

Brechtken, Josef. "Das Unum Argumentum des Anselm von Canterbury. Seine Idee und Geschichte und seine Bedeutung für die Gottesfrage von heute," *Freiburger Zeitschrift für Philosophie und Theologie* [Fribourg, Switzerland], 22 (1975), 171-203.

Briancesco, Eduardo. "¿Cómo interpretar la moral de San Anselmo?" *Revista Latinoamericana de Filosofía*, 4 (July 1978), 119-140.

_____. "Justicia y verdad en San Anselmo: el capítulo 12 del 'De Veritate,' " *Patristica et Mediaevalia* 2 (1981), 5-20.

_____. "Le portrait du Christ dans le *Cur deus homo*: Herméneutique et démythologisation," *SB II*, pp. 631-646.

Bultot, Robert. *Le XIe Siècle: Jean de Fécamp, Hermann Contract, Roger de Caen, Anselme de Canterbury* [Vol. 4 of *La doctrine du mépris du monde, en Occident, de S. Ambroise à Innocent III*]. Paris: Béatrice-Nauwelaerts, 1964.

_____. "La dignité de l'homme selon saint Anselme de Cantorbéry," pp. 549-568 in Gabriel-Ursin Lange *et al.*, *La Normandie bénédictine au temps de Guillaume le Conquérant (XIe siècle)*. Lille: Facultés Catholiques de Lille, 1967.

331

Burlikowski, Bronislaw. *Anzelma z Aosty: próba racjonalizacji wiary.* Warsaw: Państwowe Wydawnictwo Naukowe, 1971.

Campbell, Richard. "Anselm's Theological Method," *Scottish Journal of Theology,* 32 (December 1979), 541-562.

————. "On Preunderstanding St. Anselm," *The New Scholasticism,* 54 (Spring 1980), 189-193.

————. "Anselm's Background Metaphysics," *Scottish Journal of Theology,* 33 (August 1980), 317-343.

————. "The Systematic Character of Anselm's Thought," *SB II,* pp. 549-560.

Cantin, André. "Saint Anselme au départ de l'aventure européenne de la raison," *SB II,* pp. 611-621.

Cattin, Yves. *"Proslogion* et *De veritate*: 'Ratio, fides, veritas,' " *SB II,* pp. 595-610.

Cenacchi, Giuseppe. *Il pensiero filosofico di Anselmo d'Aosta.* Padova: Cedam, 1974.

Chatillon, Jean. "Saint Anselme et l'Ecriture," *SB II,* pp. 431-442.

Chibnall, Marjorie. "From Bec to Canterbury: Anselm and Monastic Privilege," *Anselm Studies,* 1 (1983), 23-44.

Chubb, Jehangir N. "Commitment and Justification: A New Look at the Ontological Argument," *International Philosophical Quarterly,* 13 (September 1973), 335-346.

————. "The Modal Argument," pp. 139-161 in his *Faith Possesses Understanding: A Suggestion for a New Direction in Rational Theology.* New Delhi: Concept Publishing Co., 1983.

Colish, Marcia L. "Eleventh-Century Grammar in the Thought of St. Anselm," pp. 785-795 in *Arts libéraux et philosophie au Moyen Age.* Paris: J. Vrin, 1969.

————. "St Anselm's Philosophy of Language," *Anselm Studies,* 1 (1983), 113-123.

————. "Anselm: The Definition of the Word," pp. 55-109 in her book *The Mirror of Language: A Study in the Medieval Theory of Knowledge.* Lincoln, Nebraska: University of Nebraska Press, 1983 [revised edition; first edition published by Yale University Press, 1968].

Collinge, William. "Monastic Life as a Context for Religious Understanding in St. Anselm," *American Benedictine Review,* 35 (December 1984), 378-388.

Corbin, Michel. "Nécessité et liberté. Sens et structure de l'argument du *Cur Deus Homo* d'Anselme de Cantorbéry," pp. 599-632 in Charles Kannengiesser and Yves Marchasson, editors, *Humanisme et foi chrétienne* (Mélanges scientifiques du centenaire de l'Institut Catholique de Paris). Paris: Beauchesne, 1976.

————. "L'événement de Vérité: Lecture du *de Veritate* d'Anselme de Cantorbéry," Chap. 2 (=pp. 59-107) in his *L'Inouï de Dieu: Six études christologiques.* Paris: Desclée De Brouwer, 1980.

————. "De L'impossible en Dieu. Lecture du 8ᵉ chapitre du dialoque de saint Anselme sur la liberté," *Revue des sciences philosophiques et théologiques,* 66 (October 1982), 523-550.

————. "Cela dont plus grand ne puisse être pensé," *Anselm Studies,* 1 (1983), 59-83.

————. "Se tenir dans la vérité: Lecture du chapitre 12 du dialogue de saint Anselme sur la Vérité," *SB II,* pp. 649-666.

Corti, E. C. "Verdad y Libertad: Lectura del 'De Veritate' de Anselmo de Canterbury," *Stromata,* 39 (July-December 1983), 351-363.

Dalferth, Ingolf U. "Fides quaerens intellectum. Theologie als Kunst der Argumentation in Anselms Proslogion," *Zeitschrift für Theologie und Kirche*, 81 (January 1984), 54-105.

Dal Pra, Mario. " 'Cogitatio vocum' e 'cogitatio rerum' nel pensiero di Anselmo," *Rivista critica di storia della filosofia*, 9 (July-August 1954), 309-343.

————. "Gaunilone e il problema logico del linguaggio," *Rivista critica di storia della filosofia*, 9 (September-October 1954), 456-484.

————. *Logica e realtà: Momenti di pensiero medievale*. Rome: Laterza, 1974.

Daniels, Donald E. "Anselm's Admonition," *Studies in Medieval Culture* [series title], 10 (1977), 69-74.

Davis, Stephen T. "Anselm and Gaunilo on the 'Lost Island,' " *Southern Journal of Philosophy*, 13 (Winter 1975), 435-448.

————. "Does the Ontological Argument Beg the Question?" *International Journal for Philosophy of Religion*, 7 (1976), 433-442.

————. "Anselm and Question-Begging: A Reply to William Rowe," *International Journal for Philosophy of Religion*, 7 (1976), 148-157.

————. "Loptson on Anselm and Rowe," *International Journal for Philosophy of Religion*, 13 (1982), 219-224.

Dazeley, Howard L. and Wolfgang L. Gombocz. "Interpreting Anselm as Logician," *Synthese*, 40 (1979), 71-96.

Devine, Philip E. " 'Exists' and St. Anselm's Argument," *Grazer philosophische Studien*, 3 (1977), 59-70.

Diamond, Cora. "Riddles and Anselm's Riddle," *Proceedings of the Aristotelian Society, Supplementary Volume* 51 (1977), 143-168.

Dou, Alberto. "Formalización del argumento anselmiano," *Pensamiento*, 23 (July-September 1967), 263-272.

Duclow, Donald F. "Anselm's Proslogion and Nicholas of Cusa's Wall of Paradise," *Downside Review*, 100 (January 1982), 22-30.

Duncan, Roger. "Analogy and the Ontological Argument," *The New Scholasticism*, 54 (Winter 1980), 25-33.

Enders, Heinz W. "Die 'quinque viae' des Thomas Aquinas und das Argument aus Anselms Proslogion. Eine bezeichnungstheoretische Analyse," *Wissenschaft und Weisheit*, 40 (1977), 158-188.

Englebretsen, George. "Anselm's Second Argument," *Sophia* [Australia], 23 (April 1984), 34-37.

Evans, Gillian R. "*Inopes verborum sunt Latini*: Technical Language and Technical Terms in the Writings of St. Anselm and some Commentators of the Mid-twelfth Century," *Archives d'histoire doctrinale et littéraire du Moyen Age*, 53 (1976), 113-134.

————. "St. Anselm and Teaching," *History of Education*, 5 (1976), 89-101.

————. "The Use of Technical Terms of Mathematics in the Writings of Anselm," *Studia Monastica* [Barcelona], 18 (1976), 67-75.

————. "*Argumentum* and *Argumentatio*: The Development of a Technical Terminology up to c. 1150," *Classical Folia*, 30 (1976), 81-93.

————. "St. Anselm's Analogies," *Vivarium*, 14 (November 1976), 81-93.

————. "St. Anselm's Images of Trinity," *Journal of Theological Studies*, 27 (April 1976), 46-57.

————. "St. Anselm's Theory of Vision and His Observations of Optical Phenomena," *Communication and Cognition* [Ghent], 10 (1977), 51-59.

————. "Anselm of Canterbury and Anselm of Havelberg: The Controversy with the Greeks," *Analecta Praemonstratensia*, 53 (1977), 158-175.

————. "The *Cur Deus Homo*: The Nature of St. Anselm's Appeal to Reason," *Studia Theologica*, 31 (1977), 33-50.

————. "St. Anselm's Technical Terms of Rhetoric," *Latomus*, 36 (January-March 1977), 171-179.

————. "Interior homo": Two Great Monastic Scholars on the Soul: St. Anselm and Ailred of Rievaulx," *Studia Monastica* [Barcelona], 19 (1977), 57-73.

————. "St. Anselm and Knowing God," *Journal of Theological Studies*, 28 (October 1977), 430-444.

————. "St Anselm's Definitions," *Archivum Latinitatis Medii Aevi*, 41 (1977-78), 91-100.

————. "St. Anselm and St. Bruno of Segni: the Common Ground," *Journal of Ecclesiastical History*, 29 (April 1978), 129-144.

————. "Why the Fall of Satan?" *Recherches de Théologie ancienne et médiévale*, 45 (1978), 130-146.

————. "Past, Present and Future in the Theology of the Late Eleventh and Early Twelfth Century," *Studia Theologica*, 32 (1978), 133-149.

————. *Anselm and Talking about God.* Oxford: Oxford University Press, 1978.

————. "St. Anselm's Technical Terms of Grammar," *Latomus*, 38 (April-June 1979), 413-421.

————. *Anselm and a New Generation.* New York: Oxford University Press, 1980.

————. "A Theology of Change in the Writings of St. Anselm and His Contemporaries," *Recherches de Théologie ancienne et médiévale*, 47 (January-December 1980), 53-76.

————. "Abbreviating Anselm," *Recherches de Théologie ancienne et médiévale*, 48 (January-December 1981), 78-108.

————. "The Hereford *Proslogion*," *Anselm Studies*, 1 (1983), 253-273.

————, editor. *A Concordance to the Works of St. Anselm.* Millwood, N. Y.: Kraus International Publications, 1984 (4 vols.).

Farinelli, Luigi. "S. Anselmo e l'argomento ontologico," *Filosofia e Vita*, 2 (January-March 1961), 41-53.

Forest, Aimé. "Remarques sur l'argument du 'Proslogion', " pp. 147-172 in *Scritti in onore di Carlo Giacon*. Padua: Editrice Antenore, 1972.

Fournée, Jean. "Du *De conceptu virginali* de saint Anselme au *De conceptione sanctae Mariae* de son disciple Eadmer," *SB II*, pp. 711-721.

Friedman, Joel I. "Necessity and the Ontological Argument," *Erkenntnis*, 15 (November 1980), 301-331.

Fröhlich, Walter. "Die Entstehung der Briefsammlung Anselms von Canterbury," *Historisches Jahrbuch* (1980), 457-466.

————. "The Genesis of the Collections of St. Anselm's Letters," *American Benedictine*

Review, 35 (September 1984), 249-266 [English version, with inconsequential differences, of his immediately foregoing German article].

Garrido, M. "San Anselmo y el argumento de analogía en el misterio de la Trinidad," *Verdad y Vida*, 13 (July-September 1955), 349-361.

Geyer, Hans-Georg. "Gedanken über den ontologischen Gottesbeweis," pp. 101-127 in Eberhard Busch *et al.*, editors, *Parrhesia*. Zurich: EVZ-Verlag, 1966.

Gilbert, Paul. " 'Id est summum omnium quae sunt' (S. Anselme, 'Monologion', chap. i-iv)," *Revue philosophique de Louvain*, 82 (May 1984), 199-223.

Gogacz, Mieczyslaw. "Les termes 'notion' et 'existence' permettent-ils d'entendre la preuve ontologique de saint Anselme conformément au contenu du 'Proslogion'?" *Mediaevalia Philosophica Polonorum*, 10 (1961), 25-32.

Gombocz, Wolfgang L. *Über E! Zur Semantik des Existenzprädikates und des ontologischen Argumentes für Gottes Existenz von Anselm von Canterbury*. Vienna: Verband der wissenschaftlichen Gesellschaften Österreichs, 1974.

————. "Zu neueren Beiträgen zur Interpretation von Anselms Proslogion," *Salzburger Jahrbuch für Philosophie*, 20 (1975), 131-135.

————. "Logik und Existenz im Mittelalter," *Philosophische Rundschau*, 24 (1977), 255-267.

————. "St. Anselm's Two Devils but One God," *Ratio*, 20 (December 1978), 142-146.

————. "Anselm von Canterbury. Ein Forschungsbericht über die Anselm-Renaissance seit 1960," *Philosophisches Jahrbuch*, 87 (1980), 109-134.

————. "Anselm über Sinn und Bedeutung," *Anselm Studies*, 1 (1983), 125-141.

————. " 'Facere esse veritatem,' " *SB II*, pp. 561-569.

Goodwin, George L. *The Ontological Argument of Charles Hartshorne*. Missoula, Montana: Scholars Press, 1978.

————. "The Ontological Argument in Neoclassical Context: Reply to Friedman," *Erkenntnis*, 20 (September 1983), 219-232.

Gray, Christopher B. "Freedom and Necessity in St. Anselm's *Cur Deus Homo*," *Franciscan Studies*, 36 (1976), 177-191.

Gregory, Donald R. "On Behalf of the Second-Rate Philosopher: A Defense of the Gaunilo Strategy Against the Ontological Argument," *History of Philosophy Quarterly*, 1 (January 1984), 49-60.

Greshake, Gisbert. "Erlösung und Freiheit. Zur Neuinterpretation der Erlösungslehre Anselms von Canterbury," *Theologische Quartalschrift*, 153 (1973), 323-345.

Grim, Patrick. "Plantinga, Hartshorne, and the Ontological Argument," *Sophia* [Australia], 20 (July 1981), 12-16.

————. "In Behalf of 'In Behalf of the Fool,' " *International Journal for Philosophy of Religion*, 13 (1982), 33-42.

Guardini, Romano. "Anselm von Canterbury und das Wesen der Theologie," pp. 33-65 in his *Auf dem Wege. Versuche*. Mainz: Matthias-Grünewald, 1923.

Hannah, John D. "Anselm on the Doctrine of Atonement," *Bibliotheca Sacra*, 135 (October-December 1978), 333-344.

Hartshorne, Charles. "John Hick on Logical and Ontological Necessity," *Religious Studies*, 13 (June 1977), 155-165.

————. "Anselm and Aristotle's First Law of Modality," *Anselm Studies*, 1 (1983), 51-58.

————. "What Did Anselm Discover?" Chap. 8 of his *Insights and Oversights of Great Thinkers: An Evaluation of Western Philosophy*. Albany: State University of New York Press, 1983.

Hasker, William. "Is There a Second Ontological Argument?" *International Journal for Philosophy of Religion*, 13 (1982), 93-101.

Haubst, Rudolf. *Vom Sinn der Menschwerdung: "Cur Deus homo."* Munich: Hueber, 1969.

Heinzmann, Richard. "Anselm von Canterbury (1033/1034-1109)," pp. 165-180 and 406-408 in Heinrich Fries and Georg Kretschmar, editors, *Klassiker der Theologie*, Vol. I. Munich: C. H. Beck, 1981.

Hendley, Brian. "Anselm's *Proslogion* Argument," pp. 838-846 in Jan P. Beckmann *et al., Sprache und Erkenntnis im Mittelalter*, Vol. II. Berlin: W. de Gruyter, 1981.

Henry, Desmond P. *Commentary on De Grammatico: The Historical-Logical Dimensions of a Dialogue of St. Anselm's*. Boston: Reidel, 1974.

————. "Two Medieval Critics of Traditional Grammar," *Historiographia Linguistica*, 7 (1980), 85-107.

————. "Anselmian Categorial and Canonical Language," *SB II*, pp. 537-548.

Heron, Alasdir. "Anselm and the *Filioque*: A Responsio pro Graecis," *Anselm Studies*, 1 (1983), 159-164.

Herrera, Robert A. "The *Proslogion* Argument Viewed from the Perspective of *De casu diaboli*," *SB II*, pp. 623-629.

Heyer, George S. "Anselm Concerning the Human Role in Salvation," pp. 163-172 in W. Eugene Marsh, editor, *Texts and Testaments: Critical Essays on the Bible and Early Church Fathers*. San Antonio: Trinity University Press, 1980.

Hick, John. "The Ontological Argument: First Form" and "The Ontological Argument: Second Form," pp. 68-83 (=Chap. 5) and pp. 84-100 (=Chap. 6) of his *Arguments for the Existence of God*. New York: Herder and Herder, 1971.

Holt, Dennis C. "Timelessness and the Metaphysics of Temporal Existence," *American Philosophical Quarterly*, 18 (April 1981), 149-156.

Hopkins, Jasper. "On Understanding and Preunderstanding St. Anselm," *The New Scholasticism*, 52 (Spring 1978), 243-260.

————. "On an Alleged Definitive Interpretation of *Proslogion* 2-4: A Discussion of G. Schufreider's *An Introduction to Anselm's Argument*," *Southern Journal of Philosophy*, 19 (Spring 1981), 129-139.

————. "Anselm and Talking about God" [a review article], *The New Scholasticism*, 55 (Summer 1981), 387-396.

————. "Anselm of Canterbury," pp. 311-315 in Vol. I of the *Dictionary of the Middle Ages*. Edited by Joseph R. Strayer. New York: Charles Scribner's Sons, 1982.

————. "Anselm on Freedom and the Will: A Discussion of G. Stanley Kane's Interpretation of Anselm," *Philosophy Research Archives*, 9 (1983), 471-493.

————. [Discussion on Anselm], pp. 315-340 in his *Nicholas of Cusa's Dialectical Mysticism: Text, Translation, and Interpretive Study of De Visione Dei*. Minneapolis: Banning Press, 1985.

Huftier, Maurice. "Libre arbitre, liberté et péché chez saint Anselm," pp. 505-548 in

Gabriel-Ursin Lange *et al., La Normandie bénédictine au temps de Guillaume le Conquérant (XI* *siècle)*. Lille: Facultés Catholiques de Lille, 1967.

Javelet, Robert. "L'argument dit 'ontologique' et la *speculatio*," *SB II*, pp. 501-510.

Johnson, Harold J. "The Ontological Argument and the Languages of 'Being'," pp. 724-737 in Jan P. Beckmann *et al.*, editors, *Sprache und Erkenntnis im Mittelalter*. Vol. II. Berlin: W. de Gruyter, 1981.

Jones, Richard H. "The Religious Irrelevance of the Ontological Argument," *Union Seminary Quarterly Review*, 37 (Fall/Winter 1981-1982), 143-157.

Kane, G. Stanley. "Elements of Ethical Theory in the Thought of St. Anselm," *Studies in Medieval Culture* [series title], 12 (1978), 61-71.

————. *Anselm's Doctrine of Freedom and the Will*. New York: The Edwin Mellen Press, 1981.

Kane, R. "The Modal Ontological Argument," *Mind*, 93 (July 1984), 336-350.

Keilbach, Wilhelm. "Der *Proslogion*-Beweis im Lichte philosophischer Gotteserkenntnis und mystischer Gotterfahrung," pp. 1113-1117 in *Arts libéraux et philosophie au Moyen Age*. Paris: J. Vrin, 1969.

Kenney, Terrence R. "Faith and Reason in Anselm" *Covenant Quarterly*, 38 (May 1980), 9-27.

Kienzler, Klaus. *Glauben und Denken bei Anselm von Canterbury*. Vienna: Herder, 1981.

King, Peter. "Anselm's Intentional Argument," *History of Philosophy Quarterly*, 1 (April 1984), 147-165.

King-Farlow, John. " 'Nothing Greater Can Be Conceived' (Zeno, Anselm and Tillich)," *Sophia* [Australia], 21 (April 1982), 19-23.

Külling, Heinz. *Wahrheit als Richtigkeit. Eine Untersuchung zur Schrift 'De veritate' von Anselm von Canterbury*. New York: Peter Lang, 1984.

Labande, Edmond-René. "Guibert de Nogent, disciple et témoin d'Anselme au Bec," *SB II*, pp. 229-236.

Lakebrink, Bernhard. "Anselm von Canterbury und der Hegelsche Gottesbeweis," pp. 182-201 in his *Studien zur Metaphysik Hegels*. Freiburg: Rombach, 1969. [Reprinted from *Parusia. Studien zur Philosophie Platons und zur Problemgeschichte des Platonismus*, 1965.]

Lang, Helen. "Anselm's Use of Scripture and His Theory of Signs," *SB II*, pp. 443-456.

Lazzarini, Renato. "L'argomento ontologico e opzione intenzionale definitiva," pp. 173-188 in *Scritti in onore di Carlo Giacon*. Padua: Editrice Antenore, 1972.

Lewis, Charles. "Phillips, Barth, and the Concept of God," *International Journal for Philosophy of Religion*, 8 (1977), 151-168.

Loptson, Peter J. "Anselm, Meinong, and the Ontological Argument," *International Journal for Philosophy of Religion*, 11 (Fall 1980), 185-194.

————. "Anselm and Rowe: A Reply to Davis," *International Journal for Philosophy of Religion*, 15 (1984), 67-71.

Losoncy, Thomas A. "Anselm's Response to Gaunilo's Dilemma—An Insight Into the Notion of 'Being' Operative in the *Proslogion*," *The New Scholasticism*, 56 (Spring 1982), 207-216.

————. "Will in St. Anselm: An Examination of His Biblical and Augustinian Origins," *SB II*, pp. 701-710.

de Lubac, Henri. " 'Seigneur, je cherche ton visage'. Sur le chapitre XIV^c du Proslogion de saint Anselme," *Archives de philosophie,* 39 (April-June 1976), 201-225; 39 (July-September 1976), 407-426.

————. *Recherches dans la foi. Trois études sur Origène, saint Anselme et la philosophie chrétienne.* Paris: Beauchesne, 1979.

Luscombe, D. E. "St Anselm and Abelard," *Anselm Studies,* 1 (1983), 207-229.

Maccagnolo, Enzo. "La continuità di 'Monologion' e 'Proslogion,' " pp. 345-367 in E. Agazzi, editor, *Studi di filosofia in onore di Gustavo Bontadini,* Vol. I (Pubblicazioni della Università Cattolica). Milan: Vita e Pensiero, 1975.

Madec, Goulven. "Y-a-t-il une herméneutique anselmienne?" *SB II,* pp. 491-500.

Malcolm, John. "A No-Nonsense Approach to St. Anselm," *Franciscan Studies,* 41 (1981), 336-345.

Mann, William E. "The Perfect Island," *Mind,* 85 (July 1976), 417-421.

————. "Divine Simplicity," *Religious Studies,* 18 (December 1982), 451-471.

Martinich, Aloysius P. "Scotus and Anselm on the Existence of God," *Franciscan Studies,* 37 (1977), 139-152.

————. "*Credo ut intelligam,*" *Studies in Medieval Culture* [series title], 12 (1978), 55-59.

Mason, Perry. "The Devil and St. Anselm," *International Journal for Philosophy of Religion,* 9 (1978), 1-15.

Maydole, Robert E. "A Modal Model for Proving the Existence of God," *American Philosophical Quarterly,* 17 (April 1980), 135-142.

McGrath, Patrick J. "Where Does the Ontological Argument Go Wrong?" *Philosophical Studies* [Ireland], 30 (spring 1984), 144-164.

Miethe, T. L. "The Ontological Argument: A Research Bibliography," *Modern Schoolman,* 54 (January 1977), 148-166.

Möhler, Johann A. *The Life of St. Anselm, Archbishop of Canterbury: A Contribution to a Knowledge of the Moral, Ecclesiastical, and Literary Life of the Eleventh and Twelfth Centuries.* London: T. Jones, 1842. [Translated from German by Henry Rymer.]

Moreau, Joseph. "Logique et dialectique dans l'argument du 'Proslogion'," pp. 718-723 in Jan P. Beckmann *et al.,* editors, *Sprache und Erkenntnis im Mittelalter,* Vol. II. Berlin: W. de Gruyter, 1981.

Morreall, John. "The Aseity of God in St. Anselm," *Studia Theologica: Scandinavian Journal of Theology,* 36 (1982), 37-46.

————. "The Aseity of God in St. Anselm," *Sophia* [Australia], 23 (October 1984), 35-44.

Morris, Thomas V. "The God of Abraham, Isaac, and Anselm," *Faith and Philosophy,* 1 (April 1984), 177-187.

Müller, Max. *Anselm von Canterbury. Das Verhältnis seiner Spekulationen zum theologischen Begriffe des Übernatürlichen.* Munich, 1914 [Ph.D. dissertation, Ludwig-Maximilians-Universität].

Oakes, Robert A. "The Second Ontological Argument and Existence-*Simpliciter,*" *International Journal for Philosophy of Religion,* 6 (Fall 1975), 180-184.

————. "A Prolegomenon to Future Exploration of the Ontological Argument," *Per-*

sonalist, 58 (October 1977), 344-351.

O'Gorman, F. P. "Yet Another Look at the Ontological Argument," *Philosophical Studies* [Ireland], 23 (1975), 49-62.

Øhrstrøm, Peter. "Anselm, Ockham and Leibniz on Divine Foreknowledge and Human Freedom," *Erkenntnis* [Dordrecht], 21 (July 1984), 209-222.

Olsen, Glenn W. "Hans Urs von Balthasar and the Rehabilitation of St. Anselm's Doctrine of the Atonement," *Scottish Journal of Theology*, 34 (February 1981), 49-61.

Ottaviano, Carmelo. "Le basi psicologiche dell'argomento ontologico in un importante brano dei 'Dicta Anselmi'," *Sophia* [Italy], 38 (1970), 68-79.

Payot, Roger. "L'argument ontologique et le fondement de la métaphysique," *Archives de philosophie*, 39 (April-June 1976), 227-268; (July-September 1976), 427-444; (October-December 1976), 629-645.

Pelikan, Jaroslav. "A First-Generation Anselmian, Guibert of Nogent," pp. 71-82 in F. Forrester Church and Timothy George, editors, *Continuity and Discontinuity in Church History*. Leiden: E. J. Brill, 1979.

Plantinga, Alvin. "Aquinas on Anselm," pp. 122-139 in Clifton Orlebeke and Lewis Smedes, editors, *God and the Good: Essays in Honor of Henry Strob*. Grand Rapids, Michigan: W. B. Eerdman's, 1975.

———. "The Ontological Argument," pp. 85-112 in his *God, Freedom, and Evil*. Grand Rapids, Michigan: W. B. Eerdmans, 1977 edition.

Poletti, Vincenzo. *Anselmo d'Aosta, filosofo mistico*. Faenza: Lega, 1975.

Poppi, Antonino. "La struttura elenctica dell'argomento anselmiano," *Verifiche*, 10 (1981), 195-203.

Pottinger, Garrell. "A Formal Analysis of the Ontological Argument," *American Philosophical Quarterly*, 20 (January 1983), 37-46.

Pouchet, Jean-Robert. "Le Proslogion de saint Anselme et l'esprit de saint Bonaventure," pp. 103-124 in Anton C. Pegis *et al.*, *S. Bonaventura. 1274-1974*, Vol. II. Rome: Collegio S. Bonaventura, 1973.

———. "Saint Anselme lecteur de saint Jean," *SB II*, pp. 457-468.

Pranger, M. Burcht. *Consequente Theologie: Een studie over het denken van Anselmus van Canterbury*. Assen: Van Gorcum, 1975.

———. "*Studium Sacrae Scripturae*: Comparaison entre les méthodes dialectiques et méditatives dans les oeuvres systématiques et dans la première méditation d'Anselme," *SB II*, pp. 469-490.

Preuss, Peter. "Ontological Vertigo," *International Journal for Philosophy of Religion*, 11 (Summer 1980), 93-110.

Rabinowicz, Wlodzimierz. "An Alleged New Refutation of St. Anselm's Argument," *Ratio*, 20 (December 1978), 149-150.

Read, Stephen. "Reflections on Anselm and Gaunilo," *International Philosophical Quarterly*, 21 (December 1981), 437-438.

Riché, Pierre. "La vie scolaire et la pédagogie au Bec au temps de Lanfranc et de saint Anselme," *SB II*, pp. 213-227.

Richman, Robert J. "The Devil and Dr. Waldman," *Philosophical Studies*, 11 (October 1960), 78-80.

———. "A Serious Look at the Ontological Argument," *Ratio*, 18 (June 1976), 85-89.

Robles Carcedo, Lureano. "¿El método anselmiano, inspirado en las Confesiones?" *Augustinus*, 14 (1969), 177-184.

Rohatyn, Dennis. "Anselm's Inconceivability Argument," *Sophia* [Australia], 21 (October 1982), 57-63.

Rossi, Osvaldo. "Un aspetto dell'indagine anselmiana intorno alla realtà di Dio," *Studia Patavina: Rivista di Scienze Religiose*, 30 (September - December 1983), 525-535.

Rousseau, Edward L. "St. Anselm and St. Thomas: A Reconsideration," *The New Scholasticism*, 54 (Winter 1980), 1-24.

Rowe, William. "The Ontological Argument and Question-Begging," *International Journal for Philosophy of Religion*, 7 (1976), 425-432. [Condensed from "The Ontological Argument," pp. 8-17 in Joel Feinberg, editor, *Reason and Responsibility*. Encino, California: Dickenson Publishing Co., 3rd edition 1975.]

_____. "Comments on Professor Davis' 'Does the Ontological Argument Beg the Question?' " *International Journal for Philosophy of Religion*, 7 (1976), 443-447.

Russell, Bruce. "The Ontological Argument," *Sophia* [Australia], 24 (April 1985), 38-47.

Schedler, George. "Anselm and Aquinas on the Fall of Satan: A Case Study of Retributive Punishment," *Proceedings of the American Catholic Philosophical Association*, 56 (1982), 61-69.

Schufreider, Gregory. "The Identity of Anselm's Argument," *Modern Schoolman*, 54 (May 1977), 345-361.

_____. *An Introduction to Anselm's Argument*. Philadelphia: Temple University Press, 1978.

_____. "What Is It for God To Exist?" *The New Scholasticism*, 55 (Winter 1981), 77-94.

_____. "Reunderstanding Anselm's Argument," *The New Scholasticism*, 57 (Summer 1983), 384-409.

Sen, Sushanta. "The Ontological Argument Revisted," *Indian Philosophical Quarterly*, 10 (January 1983), 219-242.

Serene, Eileen F. "Anselm's Modal Conceptions," pp. 117-162 in Simo Knuuttila, editor, *Reforging the Great Chain of Being*. Dordrecht, Holland: D. Reidel, 1981.

_____. "Anselmian Agency in the *Lambeth Fragments*: A Medieval Perspective on the Theory of Action," *Anselm Studies*, 1 (1983), 143-156.

Simonis, Walter. *Trinität und Vernunft. Untersuchungen zur Möglichkeit einer rationalen Trinitätslehre bei Anselm, Abaelard, den Viktorinern, A. Günther und J. Frohschammer*. Frankfurt am Main: J. Knecht, 1972.

Sontag, Frederick. "Anselm and the Concept of God," *Scottish Journal of Theology*, 35 (1982), 213-218.

Southern, Richard W. "Anselm at Canterbury," *Anselm Studies*, 1 (1983), 7-22.

Spade, Paul Vincent. "Anselm and Ambiguity," *International Journal for Philosophy of Religion*, 7 (1976), 433-445.

Springer, Johannes L. *Argumentum ontologicum: proeve eener existentieele interpretatie van het speculatieve Godsbewijs in het Proslogion van S. Anselmus, Aartsbisschop van Canterbury*. Van Gorcum, 1946.

Streveler, Paul A. "Gregory of Rimini and the Black Monk on Sense and Reference: An Example of Fourteenth-Century Philosophical Analysis," *Vivarium*, 18 (May 1980),

67-78. [Mentions *Proslogion* 15.]

————. "Anselm on Future Contingencies: A Critical Analysis of the Argument of the *De concordia*," *Anselm Studies*, 1 (1983), 165-173.

Thamm, Georg. "Zum Proslogionbeweis des hl. Anselm," *Theologie und Glaube*, 65 (1975), 289-292.

Tichý, Pavel. "Existence and God," *Journal of Philosophy*, 76 (August 1979), 403-420.

Torrance, Thomas F. "The Place of Word and Truth in Theological Inquiry according to St. Anselm," pp. 133-160 in Pedro Čapkun-Delić *et al.*, *Studia mediaevalia et mariologica*. Rome: Antonianum, 1971.

Ullmann, Wolfgang. "Zur Auseinandersetzung Anselms von Canterbury mit der trinitätstheologischen Terminologie Augustins," *Philologus*, 123 (1979), 75-79.

Ulrich, Ferdinand. "Cur non video praesentem? Zur Implikation der 'griechischen' und 'lateinischen' Denkform bei Anselm und Scotus Erigena," *Freiburger Zeitschrift für Philosophie und Theologie* [Fribourg, Switzerland], 22 (1975), 70-170.

Vanderjagt, A. J. "Knowledge of God in Ghazālī and Anselm," pp. 852-861 in Jan P. Beckmann *et al.*, editors, *Sprache und Erkenntnis im Mittelalter*, Vol. II. Berlin: W. de Gruyter, 1981.

Vanni Rovighi, Sofia. " 'Ratio' in S. Anselmo d'Aosta," *Studia Anselmiana*, 63 (1974), 65-79. [Reprinted in her *Studi di filosofia medioevale*. Milan: Vita e Pensiero, 1978.]

————. "Libertà e libero arbitrio in sant'Anselmo d'Aosta," pp. 45-60 in her *Studi di filosofia medieovale*, Vol I. Milan: Vita e Pensiero, 1978.

Vaughn, Sally N. "Anselm of Canterbury, Reluctant Archbishop?" *Albion*, 6 (1974), 240-250.

————. "St Anselm of Canterbury: The Philosopher-saint as Politician," *Journal of Medieval History*, 1 (October 1975), 279-305.

Vignaux, Paul. "Saint Anselme, Barth et au delà," pp. 83-95 in Henri Marrou *et al.*, *Dieu connu en Jésus Christ* (Vol. I of the series *Les quatre fleuves. Cahiers de recherche et de réflexion religieuses*). Paris: Seuil, 1973.

————. "Nécessité des raisons dans le Monologion," *Revue des sciences philosophiques et théologiques*, 64 (January 1980), 3-25.

Villecco, Adalberto. "El tomismo y el supuesto a priori anselmiano," pp. 481-485 in Karl Rahner *et al.*, *Dio e l'economia della salvezza*. Naples: Edizioni Domenice Itali ane, 1976.

Viola, Coloman. "Foi et vérité chez saint Anselme," *SB II*, pp. 583-593.

Visvader, John. "Anselm's Fool," *Studies in Religion / Sciences Religieuses*, 9 (1980), 441-449.

Vitali, Theodore R. "The Ontological Argument: Model for Neoclassical Metaphysics," *Modern Schoolman*, 57 (January 1980), 121-135.

Wainwright, William J. "On an Alleged Incoherence in Anselm's Argument: A Reply to Robert Richman," *Ratio*, 20 (December 1978), 147-148.

————. "The Ontological Argument, Question-Begging, and Professor Rowe," *International Journal for Philosophy of Religion*, 9 (1978), 254-257.

Walton, Douglas N. "St. Anselm and the Logical Syntax of Agency," *Franciscan Studies*, 36 (1976), 298-312.

————. "Logical Form and Agency," *Philosophical Studies*, 29 (February 1976), 75-89.

————. "The Circle in the Ontological Argument," *International Journal for Philosophy of Religion*, 9 (1978), 193-218.

————. "On the Logical Form of Some Commonplace Action Expressions," *Grazer philosophische Studien*, 10 (1980), 141-148.

Watson, Gordon. "Karl Barth and St Anselm's Theological Programme," *Scottish Journal of Theology*, 30 (1977), 31-45.

Weinberg, Julius R. "The Argument of Anselm and Some Medieval Critics," pp. 3-14 in his *Ockham, Descartes, and Hume: Self-Knowledge, Substance, and Causality*. Madison: University of Wisconsin Press, 1977. [Posthumous papers; readied for press by W. J. Courtenay, W. H. Hay, and K. E. Yandell.]

————. "Gregory of Rimini's Critique of Anselm," pp. 15-21 in his *Ockham, Descartes, and Hume: Self-Knowledge, Substance, and Causality*. Madison: University of Wisconsin Press, 1977.[Posthumous papers; readied for press by W. J. Courtenay, W. H. Hay, and K. E. Yandell.]

Wells, Norman J. "The Language of Possibility—Another Reading of Anselm," pp. 847-851 in Jan P. Beckmann *et al., Sprache und Erkenntnis im Mittelalter*, Vol. II. Berlin: W. de Gruyter, 1981.

Werner, Hans-Joachim. "Anselm von Canterburys Dialogue 'De veritate' und das Problem der Begründung praktischer Sätze," *Salzburger Jahrbuch für Philosophie*, 20 (1975), 119-130.

Wiese, Hans-Ulrich. "Die Lehre Anselms von Canterbury über den Tod Jesu in der Schrift 'Cur deus homo'," *Wissenschaft und Weisheit*, 41 (1978), 149-179 and 42 (1979), 34-55.

INDEX OF PERSONS